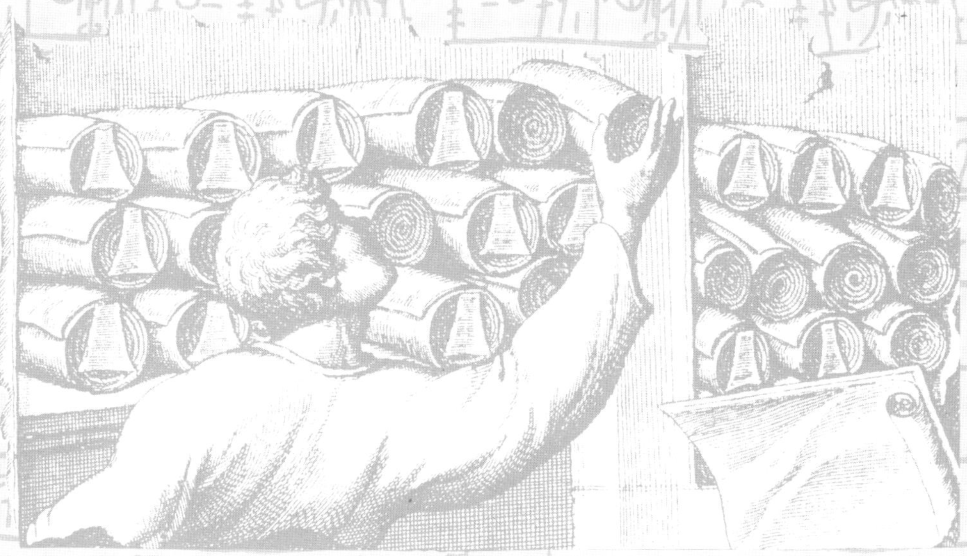

THE HISTORY OF THE LIBRARY IN
WESTERN CIVILIZATION

I: *From Minos to Cleopatra*
The Greek World from the Minoans' Archival Libraries to the Universal Library of the Ptolemies

This is the first in a series of five volumes.
Forthcoming volumes will cover the:

II: *The Roman World. From Cicero to Hadrian*

From the first Bilingual Collections to the Monumental Libraries of the Empire.

III: *The Byzantine World*
From Constantine the Great to Cardinal Bessarion

The Influence of the Church on the Spread of Learning and the Foundation of University Libraries.

IV: *The Medieval World in the West*
From Cassiodorus to Furnival

The Influence of the Church on the Spread of Learning and the Foundation of University Libraries.

V: *The Renaissance. From Petrarch to Michelangelo*

The Role of the Revival of ancient Literature and the Spread of Printing in the Foundation of Humanistic Libraries.

The entire series will be published in English (in a period of three years time approximatly) in a co-publication with OAK KNOLL PRESS and HES & DE GRAAF Publishers BV.

Dust jacket: *Representation of a cult ceremony on a gold signet ring. Early part of the Late Minoan period (1600-1550 B.C.). Iraklion, Archaeological Museum.*
Votive stele dating from the time of Cleopatra VII (51 B.C.[?]). Paris, Musée du Louvre.

Front cover: *Imaginary reconstruction of the Museum in Alexandria, from the title page of M. Meibonius,* Diogenes Laertius, *Amsterdam 1698.*

Endpapers: *Engraving of a lost Roman relief from Neumagen, on the Moselle.*

THE HISTORY OF THE LIBRARY IN WESTERN CIVILIZATION

From Minos to Cleopatra

CAUTION: PP. 145-160 ARE MISBOUND:
THEY ARE BOUND BETWEEN PP 128 & 129

First English Edition, 2004

Published by **Oak Knoll Press**
310 Delaware Street, New Castle, Delaware, USA
Web:http://www.oakknoll.com
and
HES & DE GRAAF Publishers BV
Tuurdijk 16, 3997 MS 't Goy-Houten, The Netherlands
Web:http://www.hesdegraaf.com
and
Kotinos Publications, Aravantinou 10, Athens, Greece
e-mail: kotinos@libraries.gr

ISBN: 1-58456-114-9 (USA)
ISBN: 90-6194-239-X (EUROPE)

Title: The History of the Library in Western Civilization -
From Minos to Cleopatra
Author: Konstantinos Sp. Staikos
Translated from the original greek manuscript: Timothy Cullen
Editor: K. Sp. Staikos
Typographer: Petros Balidis, Athens, Greece
Photographic Editor: Socrates Mavrommatis
Publishing Director: J. Lewis von Hoelle

Library of Congress Cataloging-in-Publication Data

Staikos, K.
[Historia tes vivliothekes ston Dytiko politismo. Apo ton Minoa sten Kleopatra. English]
The history of the library in Western civilization. From Minos to Cleopatra /
Konstantinos Sp. Staikos.
p. cm.
Includes bibliographical references and index.
ISBN 1-58456-114-9; ISBN 90-6194-239-X
1. Libraries – Greece – History – To 400. 2. Books – Greece – History – To 400. 3. Greek – language – Alphabet. 4. Greek language – Writing. 5. Written communication – Greece – History. 6. Greece – Civilization – To 146 B.C. 7. Civilization, Aegean. I. Title.

Z722.S73 2004
027.038-dc22

2003058221

This work was printed in Athens, Greece on XXX #
archival, acid-free paper meeting the requirements of the American Standard for Permanence of Paper for Printed Library Materials.

THE HISTORY OF THE LIBRARY IN WESTERN CIVILIZATION

FROM MINOS TO CLEOPATRA

The Greek World from the Minoans' Archival Libraries to the Universal Library of the Ptolemies

I

KONSTANTINOS SP. STAIKOS

Translated by
TIMOTHY CULLEN

OAK KNOLL PRESS
HES & DE GRAAF Publishers BV
KOTINOS
2004

Acknowledgements

While writing this first volume of *The History of the Library in Western Civilization*, I have been fortunate enough to receive support and encouragement from many friends and acquaintances, to whom I am deeply indebted for their help in making the text as accurate as possible.

First and foremost, I owe a great debt of gratitude to my friend Yannis Sakellarakis, who read the whole text and gave me excellent advice on the structure of the book and the appropriate style of writing. Since he is not merely a Cretan to his fingertips but has accumulated a priceless store of knowledge about the Minoan and Mycenaean civilizations in many years of excavating, mostly at Archanes, I was able to write the first chapter knowing that I was on safe ground. It was through him, too, that I was put in touch with Dr. Diamantis Panagiotopoulos of Heidelberg University, whose apposite comments, based on the views currently prevailing among archaeologists, did much to improve the final version of the text. I am most grateful to him for his kindness in sparing me his time so willingly.

My sincere thanks are due to Vassilis Karasmanis for his advice concerning the chapter on the Classical period, and to Anna Panayotarea, who read the chapter on the Minoan era with a critical eye and gave me much useful advice. I should also like to thank my friend Linos Benakis for his help with the translation into Modern Greek of passages in Ancient Greek that were beyond me, and my friend Evi Touloupa for the same reason. I am grateful to Alexandra Rozokoki for her help with bibliographical references, and to Itanos Books for providing me with valuable material for the illustrations. Last but not least, my colleague and friend Stella Tsamou, not content with editing the text and reading the proofs, has been the 'guardian angel' of this book – a trusty companion indeed, with a true love of learning

Je n'ai pas plus fait mon livre,
que mon livre m'a fait.

Montaigne

Preface

In this book, the first volume of The History of the Library in Western Civilization, to which I have given the allusive and somewhat flowery title From Minos to Cleopatra: The Greek World from the Minoans' Archival Libraries to the Universal Library of the Ptolemies, I have attempted to trace and recount the methods used by the Minoans, the Mycenaeans and the Greeks generally, from the Early Bronze Age to the end of the Hellenistic period, for storing, classifying and arranging the products of their written tradition, whether those products be clay tablets bearing records of everyday farm life or papyrus rolls immortalizing the great achievements of the Classical period in poetry and philosophy and the entire tradition of scholarship down to the time of the Neoplatonists and the commentators on Aristotle. These records and works of literature or scholarship, written on or in all sorts of books – clay tablets, diptychs and polyptychs, potsherds, parchment, papyrus sheets and rolls – were stored in public and private archives variously referred to as *demosia grammata*, *chreophylakion*, *grammateion*, *grammatophylakion*, *syngraphophylakion* and *bibliothekai*.

Both in Minoan Crete and in the Mycenaean world it seems that there may have been a certain mystique surrounding the scribes – the élite who possessed knowledge and the secret of reading and writing. Not only are their names never mentioned, but they are not even used by artists as models in the magnificent, colourful frescoes or the lavish vase-paintings of the Minoan civilization. These scribes, who devised the pictographic and Linear A and B scripts, and the 'prototypographer' who impressed the Phaistos Disc were destined to preserve their anonymity and to keep their secrets so closely guarded that their pictographic and Linear A scripts remain largely undeciphered to this day. And although the Cretans and Mycenaeans had well-developed commercial and diplomatic relations with the countries of the Near East, especially Egypt, it would seem that the prestige attached to scribes in those countries, on account of their mastery of the secrets of reading and writing, was not a feature of Minoan society. So perhaps the best way to pay tribute to the scribes of the land of the Keftiu (as the Egyptians called the Cretans) is by quoting a passage from an Egyptian poem which indicates the high repute in which scribes were held in Egypt, as being the sole repositories of knowledge and wisdom:

> *The all-wise scribes in the age that shall come after the gods, those whose prophecies come true. Their names shall be preserved forever.... They shall live on in the books they have written and in their teachings.*

At some time in the Mycenaean period, between about 1100 B.C. (when the art of writing was forgotten) and the middle of the eighth century B.C. (when the Greek alphabet was invented), Homer ensured that future generations would be well provided with subjects for recitation by singing of the calamities visited by the gods upon the human race; but in all his verses he never once refers to any community of scribes or their working environment. His solitary allusion to writing presents a satanic picture of the role and symbolism of the power of the written word: Bellerophon, the hero who slew the Chimaera, was sent to the king of Lycia bearing a message consisting of 'signs with a deadly meaning' – actually his own death sentence. However, the oral tradition created by Homer, in which mortals and gods fight superhuman battles on the plain beneath the beetling walls of Troy and heroes contend with the forces of nature, was to beget two great epics – the *Iliad* and the *Odyssey* – that fostered an awareness of the need to establish fixed written texts of oral epics and, as a natural consequence, to found public libraries.

While Homer's 'heirs', the guild of itinerant rhapsodists called the Homeridae, continued to celebrate the exploits of the Achaeans and Trojans in song, around the beginning of the sixth century a competition was instituted as part of the Panathenaea festival in which rhapsodists had to recite Homer in accordance with a fixed text. This innovation, attributed to Solon, paved the way for the founding of the first Athenian public library by Pisistratus. However, Xenophanes of Colophon took issue with the moral basis of epic poetry, castigating the poets for their anthropomorphic depiction of the gods and urging the Greeks to acknowledge the 'eternal sphere' as the one true god. The strife provoked by this pious itinerant rhapsodist, who was himself a poet, split Greek society down the middle; and Plato, who rejected outright the whole idea of the gods and goddesses quarrelling and fighting each other, actually banished Homer from his ideal state on those very grounds.

In the time of the itinerant rhapsodists a new philosophical movement came into being in southern Italy. It involved mystic rites (of which Orpheus was regarded as the patron) to do with life and death, and by the middle of the sixth century B.C. the words of these rites had been put in writing in a fixed form. The famous gold plates (*deltoi*) inscribed with the words of burial rites, the Pythagorean oral tradition and the writings of 'natural philosophers' were eventually gathered together into a corpus of sacred texts that were widely read in Athens. Heraclitus deposited a copy of his book *On Nature* in the Temple of Artemis at Ephesus; Pherecydes, who is said to have acquired most of his knowledge from 'the secret books of the Phoenicians', bequeathed his books to Thales of Miletus; and Plato used some of the money given to him by Dionysius I of Syracuse to buy the 'unwritten doctrines' of Pythagoras edited by Philolaus.

The reading habit that started developing in the early sixth century, chiefly among Athenian intellectuals, did not carry all before it: at first there were many who rejected the usefulness of building up a library of scholarly books and strenuously opposed the whole idea. It is said that Pythagoras wrote nothing himself because he had more faith in the power of oral teaching. But whereas he simply mistrusted the written word and left it at that, Plato went further, frequently enumerating the reasons for his opposition to books. In his dialogue *Timaeus* he asserts: 'But the father and maker of all this universe is past finding out; and even if we found him, to tell of him to all men would be impossible.' And in *Phaedrus* he recounts an Egyptian myth, according to which the use of writing 'will create forgetfulness in the learners' souls, because they will not use their memories; they will trust to the external written characters and not remember of themselves.' The written word, he says, is like a picture, which appears to be alive but can give no answer to a question, and has only a deceitful likeness of a living creature. But Plato's opposition to books, which probably sprang from the attitude of Socrates himself, could not avert what David E. Bynum calls 'the commotion of a terrific warrior's approach, first heard by high trees', in other words the sophists' conquest of the Athenian intellectual scene.

'Le monde est fait pour aboutir à un beau livre.' This now hackneyed epigram by Mallarmé would have been entirely appropriate in fifth-century Athens, to which (from the middle of the century) sophists flocked from every corner of the Greek world, bringing with them a radically different approach to education and scholarship. What they set out to do, by giving instruction in the art of clever speaking (*deinon poiein legein*), was to extol their own qualities and their knowledge to such an extent that they would be able to promise an answer to every question, and in this books were their best allies. While Socrates dismissed Anaxagoras's book on 'the Mind' (*On Nature*) with the mocking remark that his books could not be worth much if they could be bought in the Agora for one drachma apiece, Plato singled out what he called 'The Mind of the School' in his Academy. By this he meant his most brilliant pupil, Aristotle, whose public reading of philosophical treatises was tantamount to their publication.

Aristotle's working methods, his firm belief in the importance of setting down philosophers' opinions in writing and his conviction that the only way to promote the development of a scientific approach to scholarship was through books finally silenced the voices of the anti-book faction. He himself amassed a fine collection of books and set his students at the Lyceum to compile written records and descriptions of natural phenomena and human existence and behaviour; and between them they produced a very substantial corpus of work. The fate of Aristotle's own books after his death reads more like fiction than fact: they were bequeathed to Theophrastus, subsequently came into the possession of Neleus and about two hundred years later were bought by a bumptious bibliophile who took it upon himself to make textual emendations in some of the manuscripts, which were in imperfect condition. They were then carried off to Rome by Sulla, as spoils of war, after his conquest of Athens. There, in the villas of the Roman aristocracy, Cicero had his first opportunity to read the authentic manuscripts of Aristotle's teaching books, and he was constantly expressing his admiration for Aristotle to his friend Atticus. While immersing himself in the flow of the philosopher's thoughts, he wrote his philosophical essay *Hortensius* (now lost), which St. Augustine acknowledged to have been responsible for his conversion: 'Now it was this book which quite definitely changed my whole attitude and turned my prayers toward thee, O Lord, and gave me new hope and new desires. Suddenly every vain hope became worthless to me, and with an incredible warmth of heart I yearned for an immortality of wisdom and began now to arise that I might return to thee' (Augustine, *Confessions*, III.4.7).

The famous copy of the *Iliad* that Aristotle edited for Alexander the Great, known as the 'casket edition', can be seen as a symbol of the Macedonian conqueror's love of the written tradition and of his belief in the power of books to disseminate knowledge. It was his project of having the secular and sacred writings of the oriental civilizations translated into Greek that suggested the ambitious idea of creating a comprehensive library containing not only every work of Greek scholarship and literature but also the occult and mystical writings of the East, from the Avesta (the sacred texts attributed to Zoroaster) to the legends and historical narratives relating to the early Chaldaean kings. As he advanced on his victorious march, Alexander sent material to Aristotle for his planned magnum opus on the constitutions of 158 cities and he combed through the libraries of the Middle East with their hundreds of thousands of tablets inscribed in the cuneiform script, such as Assurbanipal's library at Nineveh and the famed royal library at Babylon (which he made the capital of his empire). It must have been Alexander, therefore, who sowed in Ptolemy I's mind the first seeds of the idea of founding a Universal Library.

The idea of creating a Universal Library is absolutely in keeping with what we know of Alexander's character and aspirations, as expressed in his speech at Opis. However, the great libraries of the East, containing books written in unknown languages and scripts and typifying an outlook (particularly characteristic of Babylonia, Judaea and Egypt) in which mysticism and often symbolism featured largely, must have made it clear that the hope of seeing the project through to completion was hardly more than a utopian dream. In spite of that, and even though the lucidity and anthropocentrism of philosophical thought in Classical Greece was opposed to that oriental way of thinking, many attempts were made to propagate the cultural traditions of the eastern peoples in Greek, the lingua franca of the period. The greatest such endeavour was the translation of the Septuagint, one side-effect of which was the spread of Judaism to such an extent that a body of Jewish literature in Greek came into existence. Although the influence of this cultural interaction on the multiracial society of Alexander's fragmented empire cannot be fully evaluated, it is clearly apparent in the interpretations given to many sacred writings.

The cabbalists, for example, interpreted the famous sentence from the first chapter of the Book of Genesis – 'And God said, let there be light: and there was light' – as meaning that the magical power of God's command springs from the very letters of which it is composed. And the *Book of Creation* (*Sefer Yetzirah*), written in the sixth century A.D., reveals that the almighty God of the Israelites created the universe with the help of the cardinal numbers from one to ten and the twenty-two letters of the alphabet. The postulation of numbers as instruments of creation calls to mind Pythagoras's theories (and those of Iamblichus many centuries later); but ascribing a role in the creation of the universe to the letters of the alphabet suggests an attempt to emphasize the doctrinal authority of the scriptures and to forestall any possibility of their being challenged.

It is against this background, which prevailed from the period of Ptolemy Soter and his successor Ptolemy Philadelphus until the time of Cleopatra, that we have to consider the web of factual evidence interwoven with fancy and legend concerning the Universal Library and its status as an eternal symbol of the worldwide cultural heritage. The Ptolemies, with their virtually limitless wealth, power and influence, embarked on the daunting project of obtaining for their

Library copies of every work ever written, thus activating a market for books that covered the whole of the known world. The all-embracing scope of their project is reminiscent of Cervantes and his voracity for reading matter: Cervantes would read everything down to 'scraps of paper picked up from the street', and similarly the Ptolemies were quite happy to buy every forged, plagiarized or corrupt text that was offered to them. They even decreed that every book carried on board every ship putting in to the busy port of Alexandria was to be handed over to the authorities: copies of these books were made, and the copies (not the originals) were then returned to the owners.

'To us, a book – every book, any book, written in any language – is sacred.' This could well have been the motto of the Ptolemies' Universal Library, judging by the magnitude of their book-collecting drive and the evidence available to us today. Gathered together in their Library were hundreds of thousands of papyrus rolls and books of every form embodying the cultural traditions of all the peoples of the known world, from the wooden 'books' of the Buddhists to the large clay tablets and votive stelae of the Babylonians and Chaldaeans.

Legends abounded concerning this unprecedented 'world library' with its army of eminent men of letters and humble clerks, its literary scholars pent in a golden cage in the palace grounds on pain of imprisonment if they should try to escape without official permission. Legend has it that the Library was burnt down either through Julius Caesar's negligence or because of the dogmatism of Caliph Omar, who believed that he was obeying the injunctions of his own sacred text, the Koran; but the historical evidence suggests that neither of these stories is true. What concerns us here, however, is not so much to investigate the eventual fate of the Universal Library as to assert that Alexander the Great's idea of creating monumental libraries – an initiative that was brought to fruition through the efforts of the Ptolemies and many other Hellenistic monarchs, notably Eumenes II Epiphanes and Seleucus I Nicator – gave a new dimension to the role of books in transmitting and disseminating the world's cultural heritage. The eventual outcome of Alexander's initiative was a far-flung 'universal library' comprising a vast quantity of disparate written material representing the pyramidal fabric of knowledge, whose warp, the Athenian Classical tradition, is interwoven with a cuneiform oriental weft. Thus was created a 'religion' of the book, a magical book, the only thing left to commemorate our world. Or rather, to be more precise, that book is the world.

Konstantinos Sp. Staikos

CONTENTS

I

THE MINOAN AND MYCENAEAN CIVILIZATIONS

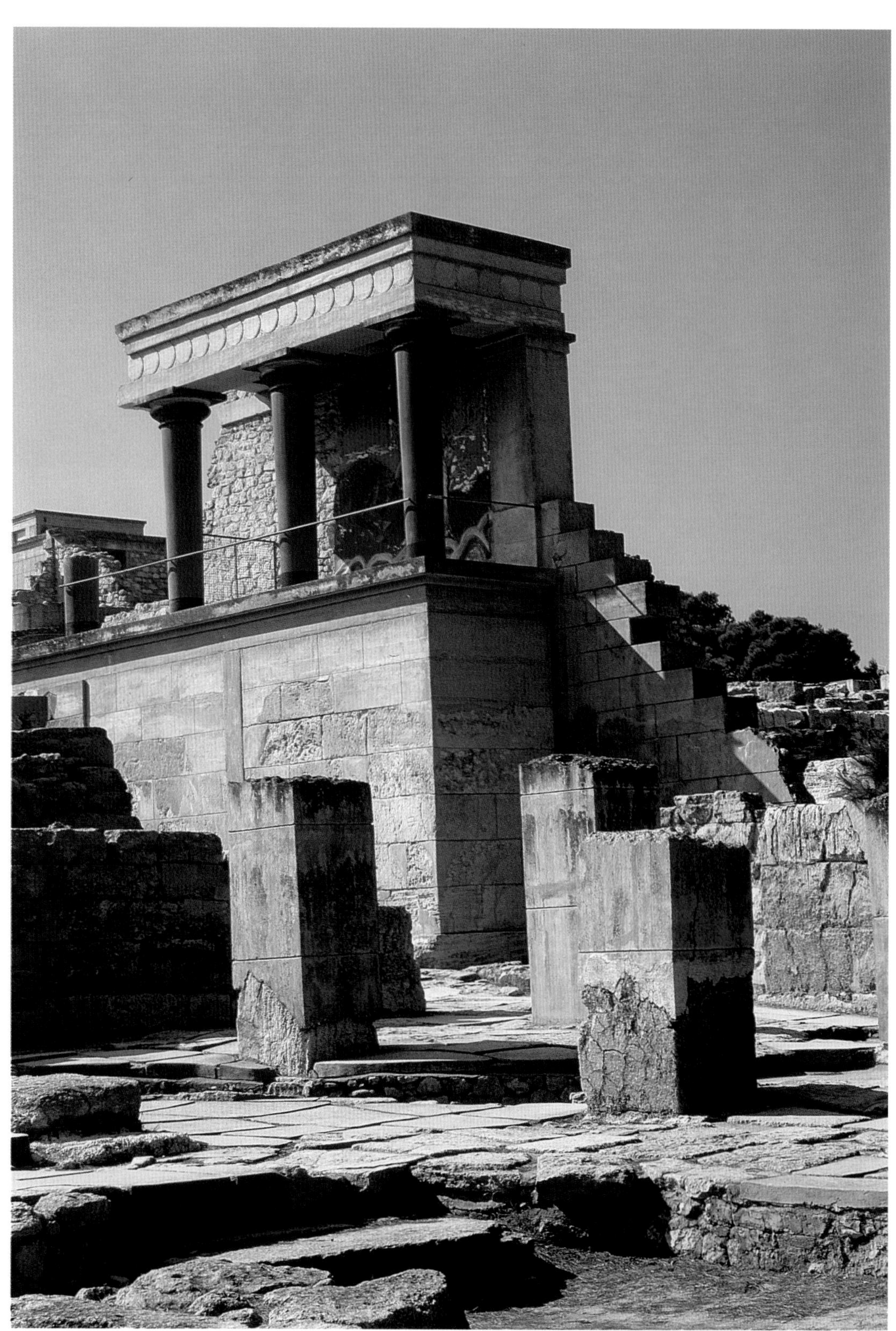

THE MINOAN AND MYCENAEAN CIVILIZATIONS

Scripts and archives in the Bronze Age (ca. 3000 - 1100 B.C.)

The history of the development of special areas for storing archival material or literary works – what we would now call archives (or record offices or muniment rooms) or libraries – is, in the early stages of any civilization, closely bound up with the local linguistic idiom and the nature of the material on which the archives were written. Consequently any account of the social imperatives that led to the storage and classification of written material (in other words the formation of 'libraries') in the traditional Greek world has to start with a discussion of Greek linguistic peculiarities and the materials on which the first phonetic scripts were written, as well as the purposes these 'books' were intended to serve.

Hundreds of years before the Greek alphabet came into being, Greek scribes were already using sharpened reeds and other forms of stylus and beginning to develop a spelling system for their oral language, working from two older scripts of the Minoans: the pictographic and the script known as Linear A. So the syllabic Linear B which evolved from those two, the Greek-language Cypriot syllabary and the Greek alphabet represent the unbroken continuity of the Greek language: from the Mycenaean period, many centuries before the time of Homer, to the present day.[1]

Nevertheless, as far as the keeping of written records in public, royal and private collections is concerned, Bronze Age finds from Crete, Cyprus, the Peloponnese and Central Greece, in contrast to those from the Mesopotamian civilizations, offer no evidence to support the existence of organizational practices or planning traditions as such in the archives, but only of comparatively small stores of tablets with records of transactions of fairly short-term interest; at best, it is possible to identify the handwriting of individual scribes. In the Near East, on the other hand – for example at Sippar, where more than 60,000 tablets have been found, or in the state archives and palace of Ebla –

1. The north entrance of the palace of Knossos, with restoration done by Sir Arthur Evans.

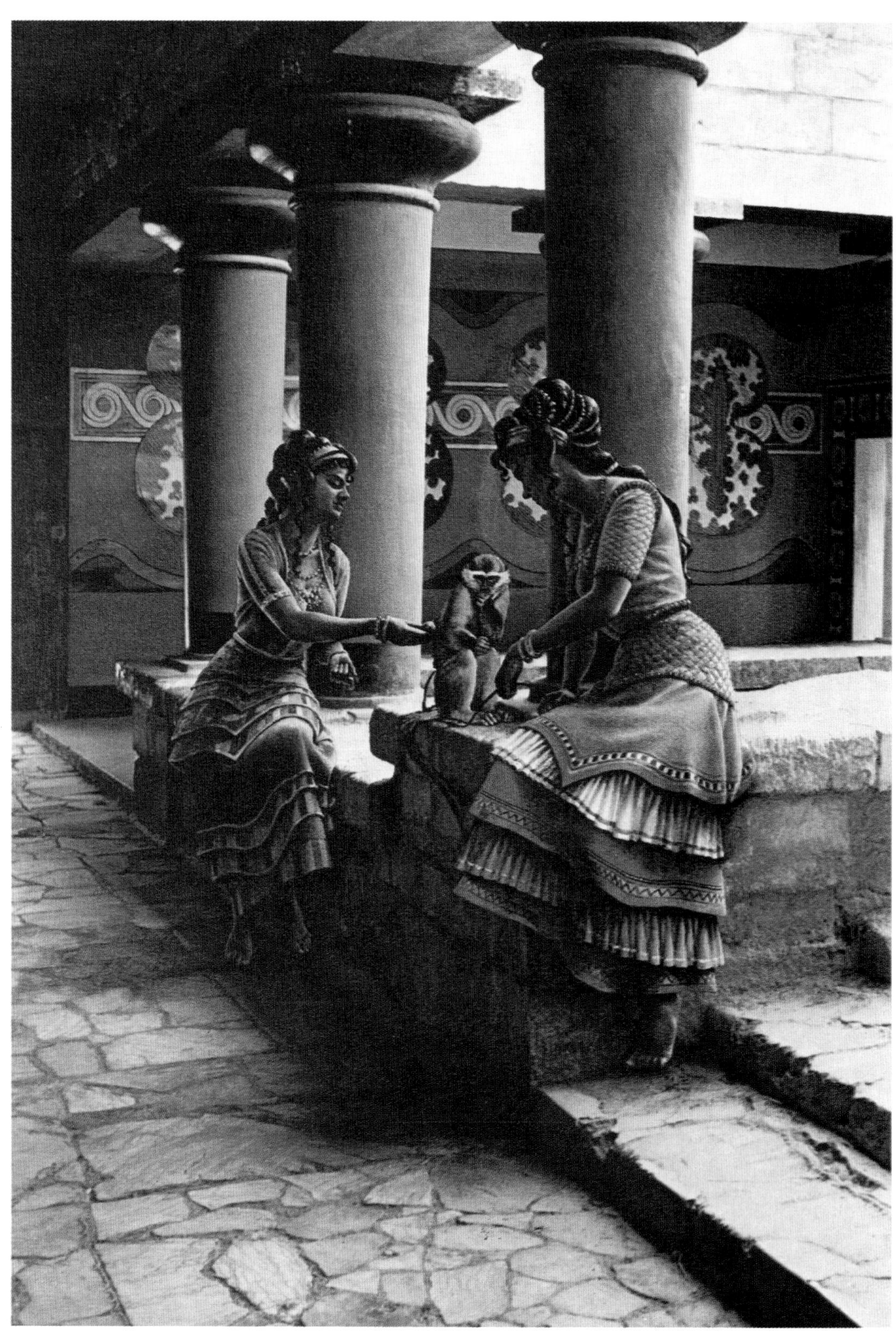

the surviving tablets provide enough evidence for us to be able to work out the systems of librarianship in use and even the method of filing.

Historical background. Since the late nineteenth century, and more systematically since the beginning of the twentieth, excavations have revealed the existence in Crete during the Bronze Age (3000–*ca.* 1100 B.C.) of a highly-developed civilization that had a decisive cultural influence on mainland Greece and the Aegean islands.[2] Sir Arthur Evans and his colleagues and successors, as well as distinguished scholars from the French and Italian Schools of Archaeology and Greek archaeologists too, of course, have uncovered huge palaces at Knossos,[3] Phaistos, Malia, Zakros, Archanes and many other places. For this civilization that developed in Crete in the Bronze Age, Evans coined the name 'Minoan' in memory of the Greek mythological tradition that the king who ruled at Knossos in the heroic age was called Minos.

Minoan-Mycenaean relations

The palace buildings at Knossos were constructed in the Middle Minoan IB (MM IB) period, around 2000 B.C., and those at Phaistos and Malia are of approximately the same date.[4] From then on the Minoans could have contented themselves with their home environment, the magnificent buildings and artistic treasures of palace life, but in fact they proved to be a race of very adventurous travellers, establishing commercial and perhaps other relations with Egypt and the maritime peoples of Asia Minor. First they founded a settlement on Melos, then official trade agencies and warehouses in Egypt and later on Rhodes, at Miletus and perhaps in Cyprus. Round about 1800, towards the end of MM IIA-B, they made contact with the inhabitants of mainland Greece; thereafter, out of the interaction between the Minoans and the Helladic peoples, there evolved a new civilization in Greece that is now called Mycenaean.[5]

Around 1550 B.C. Mycenae, the centre of a population that developed so strongly, both politically and culturally, that in the fullness of time it became the nucleus of Classical Greece, was the biggest and most powerful city in the Peloponnese.[6] Contact between the Mycenaeans and Crete became steadily closer from about that time, but by then catastrophe had struck the northern part of Crete: the first palaces had been destroyed by earthquake and fire in late

2. Two Minoan ladies of the royal court, in their distinctive costume, sitting in the central court of the palace of Knossos, ca. 1500 B.C. Painting by Michael A. Hampshire.

TABLE

A. EVANS	N. PLATON	'Old Dating'	'New Dating'
Final Neolithic		3300 B.C.	3300 B.C.
Early Minoan I (EM I)	Prepalatial Period	3000 B.C.	3000 B.C.
Early Minoan II (EM II)		2700 B.C.	2700 B.C.
Early Minoan III (EM III)		2300 B.C.	2300 B.C.
Middle Minoan IA (MM 1A)		2100 B.C.	2100 B.C.
Middle Minoan IB (MM IB)	Protopalatial (Old Palace) Period	1900 B.C.	2000 B.C.
Middle Minoan IIA-B (MM IIA-B)		1800 B.C.	1900 B.C.
Middle Minoan IIIA-B (MM IIIA-B)	Neopalatial (New Palace) Period	1700 B.C.	1800 B.C.
Late Minoan IA (LM IA)		1600 B.C.	1700 B.C.
Late Minoan IB (LM IB)		1500 B.C.	1600 B.C.
Late Minoan II (LM II)		1450 B.C.	1500 B.C.
Late Minoan IIIA1 (LM IIIA1)		1420 B.C.	1450 B.C.
Late Minoan IIIA2 (LM IIIA2)	Postpalatial (3rd Palace) Period	1370 B.C.	1400 B.C.
Late Minoan IIIB (LM IIIB)		1300 B.C.	1300 B.C.
Late Minoan IIIC (LM IIIC)		1200 B.C.	1200 B.C.
Sub-Minoan		1100 B.C.	1100 B.C.

MM III-LM IA (*ca.* 1750) and then, towards the end of LM IB (*ca.* 1550), the rebuilt palaces and other buildings, villages and towns were again destroyed by the tsunami that followed the eruption of the Thera volcano, and again ravaged by the resulting fires.[7] This led to the gradual evacuation of many Cretan cities, including Tylissos, Nirou Hani, Amnissos, Gournia, Mochlos, Phaistos and Malia, and eventually – but much later (*ca.* 1375 or *ca.* 1200 B.C.) – of Knossos itself; and it signalled the beginning of the end of the Minoan civilization. The Mycenaeans were frequent visitors to Crete, often on what might almost be called predatory raids, and in about 1425 they actually captured Knossos, the capital of the kingdom. From then on the Mycenaeans became thoroughly 'Minoanized' in their culture, among other things through their adoption of the Minoan script which developed into Linear B, the first Greek script. Having clipped the wings of Crete, the Mycenaeans spread rapidly across the eastern Mediterranean basin in the fourteenth and thirteenth centuries, founding workshops and trade agencies in Troy, Sicily, Miletus, Rhodes, Lycia, Cilicia and Cyprus. In fact there were probably Mycenaean communities at Ugarit and perhaps in the ports of the Nile delta as well. These were the first meeting-points between East and West: between the Mycenaeans on the one hand and the Semitic and Egyptian civilizations on the other.[8]

Around 1200 B.C. the Mycenaean civilization collapsed, perhaps destroyed by a severe climatic change which altered the natural environment.[9] This would naturally have provoked popular unrest, reaching its climax with mobs setting fire to the acropolises not only at Mycenae but at other important cities too, including Pylos, Tiryns and Thebes (but not Athens or Iolcus [Volos]).

The Greeks then forgot their syllabic script, which had been valuable as a tool for administration and commerce – and in other fields as well – under the Minoan and Mycenaean civilizations. Round about 1100 B.C. the demographic composition of mainland Greece underwent a significant change and Mycenaean possessions in the eastern Mediterranean were abandoned, to be taken over by Semitic Canaanites from the region corresponding to Lebanon.[10]

The pictographic and linear scripts of the Minoans and Mycenaeans

Scripts in use in the Bronze Age. Writing was introduced into the Aegean region by the Minoans, who took and held the initiative in spreading the new skill in the Mediterranean coastlands (where the Greeks kept expanding their presence until the Classical period) by developing and improving the original script, and in the course of time they passed it on to the Cypriots and Mycenaeans. Whether the Minoan script in its original form was borrowed from elsewhere is a question that has yet to be answered. An even more important question is whether the Minoans and Mycenaeans used not only clay tablets but other kinds of 'books' (such as papyrus rolls or parchment) as well, for literary or historical works, long-term administrative and commercial documents, correspondence or mythological stories, given that almost all the written material preserved from the Minoan and Mycenaean civilizations consists of commercial, economic and administrative records. It is only in inscriptions on some of the Minoan ritual objects known as 'offering tables', and in a few other isolated cases, that we find any exceptions to that rule.

The various scripts used in the Aegean civilizations were in use at the following times:[11]

Pictographic (hieroglyphic): 2500-1800 B.C.
Linear A: 1900-1450 B.C.
Phaistos Disc: *ca.* 1700 B.C.
Linear B: 1400-1200 B.C.
Cypriot syllabary: 1050-320 B.C.

Minoan scripts. The earliest scripts devised by the people of Crete were over a thousand years behind the cuneiform writing of the Sumerians (towards the end of the fourth millennium, *ca.* 3200 B.C.) and the hieroglyphics of the Egyptians (*ca.* 3250 B.C.). Recent excavations in the necropolis of Abydus have brought to light a monumental tomb (V-J) containing objects (bone tablets, pottery) bearing pictographic inscriptions, which have been dated to about 150 years before the reign of the so-called Proto-Pharaoh known as 'Scorpion'.[12] Although cuneiform and hieroglyphics evolved concurrently and the Mesopotamian peo-

The earliest script of the Predynastic era

3. Part of the mace head of King 'Scorpion', showing the Proto-Pharaoh with his retinue at a ritual ceremony.

4. Table of the 135 pictograms or hieroglyphs initially identified by Evans, showing how they evolved from relief images to linear symbols.

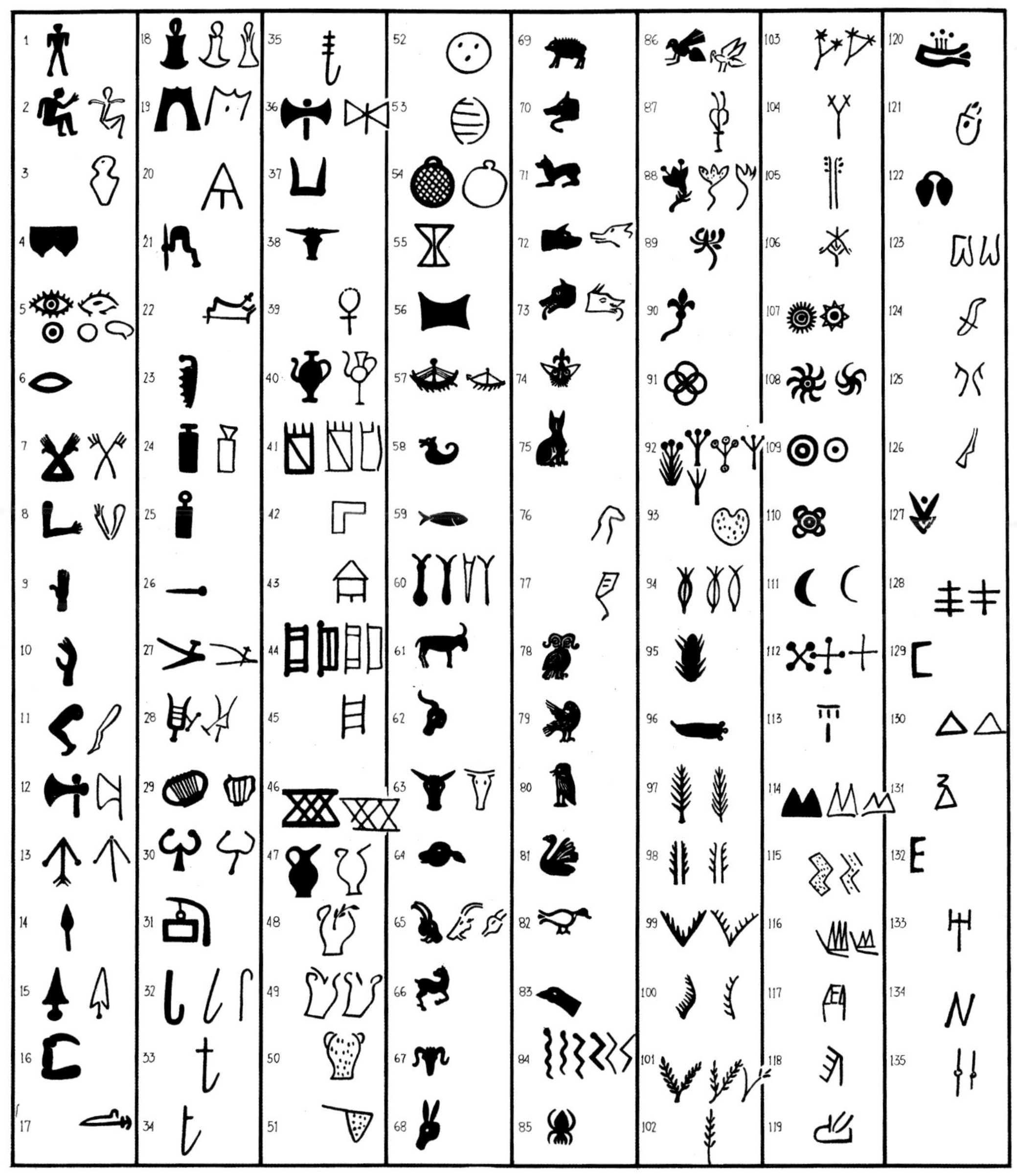
1
2
3
4
5
6
7
8
9
10
11
12
13
14
15
16
17
18
19
20
21
22
23
24
25
26
27
28
29
30
31
32
33
34
35
36
37
38
39
40
41
42
43
44
45
46
47
48
49
50
51
52
53
54
55
56
57
58
59
60
61
62
63
64
65
66
67
68
69
70
71
72
73
74
75
76
77
78
79
80
81
82
83
84
85
86
87
88
89
90
91
92
93
94
95
96
97
98
99
100
101
102
103
104
105
106
107
108
109
110
111
112
113
114
115
116
117
118
119
120
121
122
123
124
125
126
127
128
129
130
131
132
133
134
135

ples had frequent cultural contacts with the Egyptians, these two different writing systems became set in their separate moulds and were used with almost doctrinaire consistency in different kinds of 'books': clay tablets for cuneiform and papyrus rolls for hieroglyphics.[13]

The first inhabitants of Crete may well have come across one of these scripts before they finalized their own. Be that as it may, the Minoans initially adopted both systems, namely the pictographic (hieroglyphic) and phonetic scripts, and they probably used both of the ancient world's commonest types of book: clay tablets and papyrus or parchment rolls.

The dawn of writing in the Aegean civilizations

The pictographic (hieroglyphic) script. From about 2500 B.C., soon after the foundation of the first palaces in Crete, seal-stones are found bearing combinations of symbols that hint at a system of writing. The symbols are ideograms, each one representing a person or thing. As it evolved, this script became phonetic, with a symbol for every sound used in the formation of words. This script, sometimes called hieroglyphic after the corresponding Egyptian writing system, has yet to be deciphered, and it is not known what language it represented. The period when it was mainly used in Crete was towards the end of Middle Minoan IB, that is around 2000 B.C.; thereafter it was used sporadically until about 1800, and it was occasionally used before that time in inscriptions of ritual texts.[14]

Considerable variety is found in the form of the symbols, some of which are ideograms and others not. There are some taken from the animal kingdom, representing cats or lions' heads or ox-heads; others depict parts of the human body or full-length human figures; and a good many represent tools, utensils and everyday objects such as ploughs, lyres, ships and the double axe. Interspersed with the pictographic characters are various auxiliary symbols: small bars, straight lines and (especially) crosses, which probably show the direction in which the writing is to be read or serve as punctuation marks of some kind but definitely have no phonetic value.

So far, more than 135 pictograms of this script have been identified, as well as more than ninety syllabograms which had phonetic values, in other words they stood for the first syllable of the object they represented. These ideograms were easy to decipher, partly because they are often accompanied by numerical symbols. The pictographic script is found on about 331 inscriptions, seal-stones, seal impressions, inscribed plates, medallions, small clay bars, tablets and other articles.[15]

The earliest specimens of this script were found at Fourni and Archanes and are probably to be dated to the end of the Early Minoan I (EM I) period. Most of the ideograms were developed during EM I: examples have been found at thirty-two sites in Crete and in just two other places, Cythera and Samothrace. The most important finds come from the palace at Knossos and the archives of the palace at Malia. The cemetery at Fourni, just outside Archanes, yielded seven seals of various shapes bearing pictographic symbols, made of bone and

5. *Bars and tablets inscribed with hieroglyphs and other marks, from the hieroglyphic archives at Knossos. Photo: L. Godart.*

dated to about 2300-2100 B.C., and a unique fourteen-faced seal consisting of three cubes joined together with a handle at one end. On the evidence of the style of drawing, these symbols are dated to the early period of pictograms in Crete and this particular script is known as the 'Archanes script'.[16]

The pictographic script, which was used until the end of the MM IIA-B period (about 1800 B.C.), overlapping at the end with Linear A (1900-1450), came to be used for religious and liturgical texts, and it may be that the Phaistos Disc itself is an example of this script in its most highly developed form. There are many possible explanations for the concurrent use of the two scripts, one being that perhaps each of them was used for a different language or only for writings on certain subjects.

Linear A. Arthur Evans gave the name 'Linear' to this script precisely because its representations of persons, animals and objects were generally linear: stylized rather than naturalistic. Linear A has been only partially deciphered as yet, but it is thought to have been related to the pictographic script and to be a simplified descendant of that earlier Cretan writing system. The parallel use of the two scripts (to a greater or lesser extent) for at least two centuries and the introduction of a simpler linear script, known as Proto-Linear, confirms that the pictographic and Linear A scripts are related.[17]

Writing comes into use in everyday life

The earliest specimens of Linear A were discovered at Phaistos and are dated to MM II (1900-1800). This script was used very widely. Most examples come from Crete, but others have been found in the Aegean coastlands and islands, where the Cretans had colonies or trading posts: on Thera, Melos, Cythera and Samothrace, at Miletus, and elsewhere.[18] Linear A, which gradually supplanted the pictographic script between MM III (1800-) and LM IIIA (1450), remained in use until the destruction of the Minoan palaces in the mid fifteenth century: one of the latest examples is an inscribed LM IIIA1 figurine from Katsambas.

The decipherment of Linear A is still a matter of conjecture. Some scholars maintain that the symbols have phonetic values, like those of Linear B; others that it is related to the scripts used by eastern peoples such as the Hittites or Luwians; and quite possibly it was used for a pre-Hellenic language of the Aegean peoples and is both ideographic and phonetic in character.

Most of the Linear A tablets are accounting records of some kind, and all the Middle Minoan IB tablets from Phaistos fall into this category: they record facts and figures relating to the king's property, such as harvest returns, or about the labourers who worked on the royal estates, the agents who managed the commercial transactions and the officials who administered the taxes. But the finds from Archanes show Linear A being used in many different ways, in inscriptions or as solitary symbols, on a variety of utensils and other objects: sarcophagi, a basket, earthenware storage jars and a silver pin.[19] And although Linear A has not been deciphered, the use of recognizable ideograms, some syllabograms identical to those of Linear B (in a different language) and numerals arranged in accordance with the decimal system makes it plain that these documents referred to persons or were records of numbers and quantities of storage vessels, wheat, olive oil and other commodities.

6. Table of the ninety Linear A symbols and the decimal numeral system of the Neopalatial period.

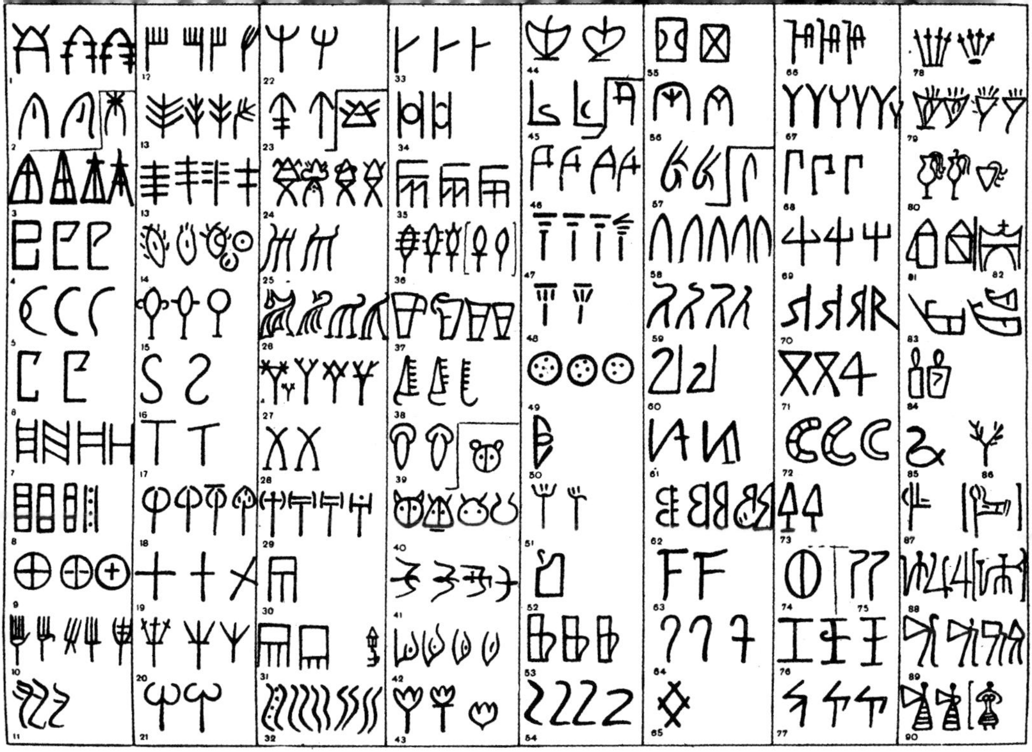

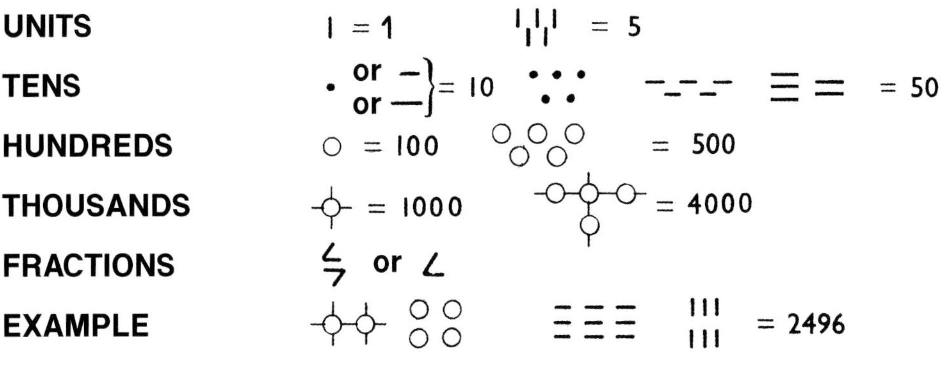

UNITS	I = 1	IIIII = 5
TENS	• or — or — = 10	••••• = 50
HUNDREDS	○ = 100	○○○○○ = 500
THOUSANDS	-○- = 1000	= 4000
FRACTIONS	ϟ or ∠	
EXAMPLE		= 2496

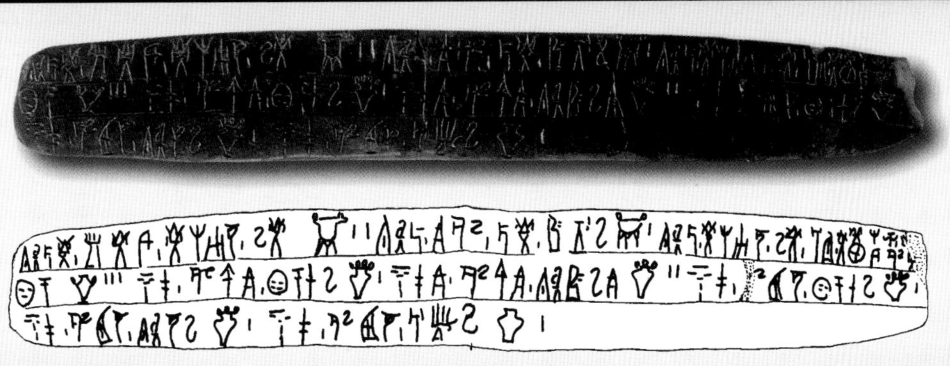

The largest category of Linear A tablets (of which over 1,500 have been found so far) consists of administrative records written on unbaked clay. These are subdivided according to their shape into four main groups: flat tablets, polyhedral sealings, security sealings and discs. Linear A symbols are also found on artefacts of various other materials, of course, including religious objects (ritual goblets, stone spoons and gold axes), and presumably they were also used on other household utensils now lost for ever. Although Linear A scribes in the MM II period confined themselves to keeping accounts, other literate Minoans continued the tradition of the pictographic script, which lived on after MM I, for writing on seals. There is nothing strange about this, nor is it a unique case, for the Hittites (for example) used two scripts concurrently: a cuneiform, inherited from the Babylonian cuneiform, and another script known as Hittite hieroglyphics.

The script common to the Minoan and Mycenaean worlds

Linear B. It was Evans again who coined the name Linear B for this script, recognizing that it was related to Linear A, though later and more highly developed. However, it is possible that Linear B first came into being in mainland Greece and was subsequently imported into Crete. It may be that the stimulus for the invention of Linear B was provided by the cultural contacts between Mycenaeans and Cretans, leading eventually to the gradual conquest of Crete by the Mycenaeans in about 1450, when Linear B replaced Linear A in the archives of the great Cretan palaces.

The earliest examples of Linear B come from a large and important archive of tablets in the palace of Knossos and date from LM II/IIIA1 (*ca.* 1450), the period when the subjugation of the Minoans was completed and the palaces

☜

7. Tablet inscribed with Linear A symbols from Ayia Triada, 15th c. B.C. Iraklion, Archaeological Museum.

8. Tablet inscribed with Linear A symbols from Knossos, ca. 1700 B.C. Iraklion, Archaeological Museum.

9. Tablet inscribed with Linear A symbols from Archanes, ca. 1700 B.C. Iraklion, Archaeological Museum.

10. Tablet inscribed with Linear A symbols from Hania, ca. 1450 B.C., with an inventory of quantities of wine.

11. A 'page' tablet inscribed with Linear B symbols from the palace of Pylos, 13th c. B.C. Athens, National Archaeological Museum.

12. Ivory fourteen-faced claviform seal-stone, ca. 2300-2100 B.C. Iraklion, Archaeological Museum.

13. A 'palm-leaf' tablet inscribed with Linear B symbols from the palace of Knossos, 13th c. B.C., with an inventory of kitchen utensils. Athens, National Archaeological Museum.

14. A 'palm-leaf' tablet inscribed with Linear B symbols, syllabograms and pictograms, 13th c. B.C. Athens, National Archaeological Museum.

15. Line drawing of the syllabograms and pictograms on the above tablet.

16. Portrait of Arthur Evans (1851-1941) with the palace of Knossos in the background. Painting by Sir W.B. Richmond, 1907.

were destroyed.[20] Similar archives of inscribed tablets have been found in other Minoan palaces as well as the most important Mycenaean cities (Mycenae, Tiryns, Thebes[21] and elsewhere). But it was at Pylos that the most significant find of all, an archive of over 1,250 tablets, was unearthed in 1939.[22] Linear B fell into disuse following the downfall of the Mycenaean centres, towards the end of the thirteenth century B.C.

The Linear B symbols are syllabograms that evolved from the symbols of Linear A, which underwent a process of alteration and addition to adapt them for use with the new language, Greek.[23] Ideograms continued to be used, either to represent specific objects or, in combination with numerals, to denote commodities in lists. Eighty-seven syllabograms and many ideograms have been deciphered. The numerical system used in Linear B is decimal, and similar to that of Linear A. Addition and subtraction sums have been recognized on the tablets, as well as groups of compound numbers used for weights and measures. Small marks have been identified as separators, and other marks of a different size are used to emphasize headings or sub-headings or to indicate the subject of the text. The writing on these tablets is regularly spaced, often with horizontal lines between the rows of symbols to make it easier to read.

Linear B tablets come in various shapes, the commonest being the long and thin 'palm-leaf' tablets and the rectangular 'page' tablets, which vary in size according to the scribe's preference. All the known writings in Linear B are accounts, inventories or economic records or are connected with those subjects. The tablets of Series A from Pylos, for instance, list the women, boys and girls employed in the textile workshops, and in some cases the nationalities of the weavers are given, as well as the names of their home towns on the Asia Minor coast or the nearby islands.

Deciphering Linear B. However many years may have passed and however much may have been written about the decipherment of Linear B, it seems to me that any overview of the Minoan-Mycenaean scripts should say something about the brilliant work done by Michael Ventris.

What Ventris did was a truly remarkable achievement because of the complete absence of any written material or linguistic idiom to use as a basis for comparison, for the task he set himself fell into the least promising of the three

17. The plain of Argos and Mycenae. Lithograph after a drawing by Otto von Stackelberg, from «La Grèce. Vues pittoresques et topographiques», Paris [1829]-1834.

standard situations facing a cryptographer wishing to decipher a script: either (a) the language is known, fully or partially, but it is written in an unknown script (as in the case of ancient Persian), or (b) the script is known but the language is not (as in the case of Etruscan), or (c) both the language and the script are unknown. This last was the case with Linear B.

The original Linear B tablets found by Evans could not be deciphered, for various reasons: the absence of a bilingual text, the brevity of the entries in the accounts or lists and the poor state of the tablets (for most were worn, broken and damaged by fire). Then again, many Minoan proper names and place-names were unknown, the language that Linear B represented was also unknown and the symbols possessed no elements that could be used for com-

18. Reconstruction of the southern approach to the palace of Knossos, showing the stepped portico and the characters Minoan columns. Drawing by Thomas Fanourakis.

LINEAR B SYLLABIC GRID

FIGURE 11
WORK NOTE 17
20 FEB 1952

THIRD STATE : REVIEW OF PYLOS EVIDENCE

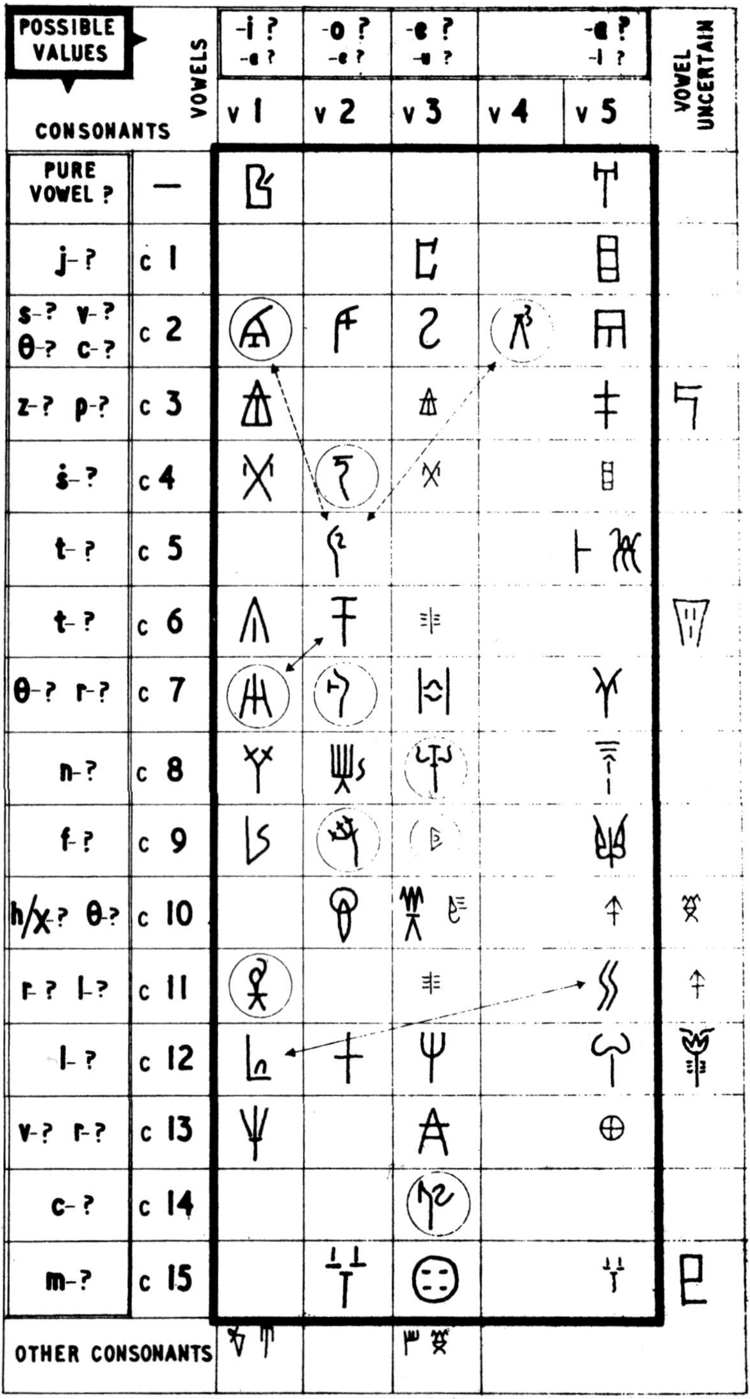

POSSIBLE VALUES / CONSONANTS	VOWELS	-i ? -e ?	-o ? -e ?	-e ? -u ?		-e ? -i ?	VOWEL UNCERTAIN
		v 1	v 2	v 3	v 4	v 5	
PURE VOWEL ?	—						
j- ?	c 1						
s-? v-? θ-? c-?	c 2						
z-? p-?	c 3						
ś- ?	c 4						
t- ?	c 5						
t- ?	c 6						
θ-? r-?	c 7						
n- ?	c 8						
f- ?	c 9						
h/χ-? θ-?	c 10						
r-? l-?	c 11						
l- ?	c 12						
v-? r-?	c 13						
c- ?	c 14						
m- ?	c 15						
OTHER CONSONANTS							

SMALL SIGNS INDICATE UNCERTAIN POSITION. CIRCLED SIGNS HAVE NO OBVIOUS EQUIVALENT IN LINEAR SCRIPT A.

parison with other scripts. However, Evans himself, working on the ideograms found in Linear B, did complete the first stage of the task by classifying the Knossos tablets into groups.[24]

The second stage of the preliminaries towards decipherment was to 'read' the pictorial representations of persons and things by comparing them with contemporary scripts in use in the Near East, which denoted phonetic values, before starting on a systematic tabulation of the other symbols. When it was found that there were about ninety of those symbols, it seemed reasonable to conclude that the script was a syllabary, that is a system of writing in which every phonetic symbol represents a syllable in the relevant language. The first major step towards the method of isolating and evaluating groups of symbols that seemed to indicate rules of grammatical inflection was taken in 1948 by Alice Kober, who found evidence of rules of inflection and drew certain conclusions concerning the phonetic relationships of the symbols themselves.[25] Making good progress with her work, she soon succeeded in compiling what she called a 'provisional phonetic scheme'. Although there was no documentary evidence to confirm this scheme, it set in train a series of conjectures which were eventually proved to be correct and in the meantime provided a valuable tool for progress towards decipherment.

20. Michael Ventris at his drawing-board during the final stage of his decipherment of Linear B, in the middle of 1953.

Once the foundations had been laid by Alice Kober, a young English architect named Michael Ventris, who had been working since 1940 on the decipherment of the Minoan script, undertook to carry on her work.[26] It should be emphasized that in the initial stages he was working with an extremely small amount of material at his disposal: a mere 142 tablets from a relatively large archive discovered by Evans at Knossos.

19. One of the Work Notes drawn up by Michael Ventris for his work on the decipherment of Linear B, with symbols from the Pylos tablets arranged in a grid in the 'third state'. Dated 20 Feb. 1952.

To keep the academic world informed of his activities, from early in 1951 to June 1952 Ventris sent copies of his 'Work Notes on the study of the Minoan language' to other scholars with a professional interest in the subject. In these notes he recorded the progress of his undertaking and the tentative conclusions he drew from it, his primary material having meanwhile been enlarged by the publication of the Pylos tablets in 1951.

In the course of his researches Ventris naturally explored the possibility that the script was based on and related to other linguistic systems and, although he frequently referred to possible connections with the Etruscan language and followed false trails suggested by the Cypriot script, he soon came to the conclusion (already reached by Alice Kober) that the existence of grammatical inflections in Linear B offered the only promising line for a cryptographer to follow. Accordingly, he started putting together the known groups of symbols in which the last symbol, or the last two, showed constant and predictable changes which could reasonably be taken to indicate inflected case endings. The result of this undertaking was the publication on 22nd January 1951 of the first phonetic grid [see fig. 19 (20/2/1952)], in which he placed the Linear B symbols that appeared most frequently, and in this way he was able to identify those that contained the same consonant. In devising this grid, Ventris was attempting to ascribe actual phonetic values to certain symbols that appeared regularly as word endings.

22. Reconstruction of the interior court of Nestor's palace at Pylos. Watercolour by Piet de Jong, 1956.

Working mainly from the Pylos tablets, and developing further the ideas put forward by Alice Kober, Ventris worked out with great accuracy the inflec-

21. Reconstruction of the Throne Room in Nestor's palace at Pylos. Watercolour by Piet de Jong, 1956.

tional characteristics of the language represented by the Linear B symbols. He distinguished between inflected nouns and indeclinable words; assisted by the ideograms, he identified masculine and feminine word endings; and with the help of the 'numerals' he was able to distinguish between singular and plural forms. He also thought that three groups of endings might be verb endings denoting tense, mood or voice. Focusing his attention on certain word endings on the Pylos tablets, he noticed that they looked like the corresponding noun inflections in Greek. So he drew up an improved version of the phonetic grid, incorporating his notes on the Pylos tablets; but, hard though he tried to assign actual phonetic values to the symbols, he eventually decided he was not yet ready to do so.

Following the publication of the drawings and photographs of the Knossos tablets (*Scripta Minoa* II, Oxford 1952), Ventris produced his third grid, in which he provisionally matched a number of phonetic values with the corresponding symbols. By the time he wrote the twentieth and last of his Work Notes he had reached the point at which he asked himself what the result would be if it were accepted that the Linear B texts contained specimens of the Greek language. And even though he still thought there were similarities with the Etruscan script, he noted that sometimes the coincidences with the

Ventris devises his grid

structure of the Greek language really were most remarkable. When he isolated a certain number of groups of nouns from the Knossos and Pylos tablets and observed that an alteration in their final syllable appeared to turn them into adjectives, he realized that they were names of countries (or nationalities) and towns. He then checked a known place-name by checking the phonetic value of each of its syllables against a particular symbol. The place he chose was Amnissos, a Minoan town near Knossos, and he tested his selected group of symbols to see if they matched the phonetic values he had allotted them in his grid: *a-mi-ni-so* = 𐀀 𐀖 𐀛 𐀰 . This word also produced the 'adjectival' forms *a-mi-ni-so-jo* (of Amnissos) and *a-mi-ni-so-de* (to Amnissos).

Next, following the same train of thought, Ventris identified more and more Greek words from their context and established that Greek inflected forms were present. Once he had satisfied himself of the accuracy of his first identifications of Greek words on Linear B tablets, all that remained was to apply the grid to the writing on all the tablets. This he did in collaboration with John Chadwick, a Cambridge classicist. Chadwick made a crucial contribution towards the final resolution of the problem, for he drew up rules of spelling in accordance with what was known about the evolution of the Greek language and was then able to read the tablets, using those rules. Their joint paper on the subject (published in 1953), based on the fourth and last stage of Ventris's phonetic grid, contained translations of a substantial number of the Linear B texts.[27] The story of the decipherment, based on discussions between the two men and on unpublished material in Ventris's papers, was first published by Chadwick in 1958 with the title *The Decipherment of Linear B*.

After Ventris's death in 1956, further progress was made in identifying symbols with the Linear B syllabograms until at last the final phonetic grid was completed. Nevertheless, although most of the Linear B records have been read, there are still a number of words – including some of vital importance for a complete assessment of the texts – that have not been deciphered, either because they bear no relation to known Greek words (which probably means that they went out of use before the historical era) or because they are borrowings from non-Greek languages.[28]

The Phaistos Disc. For nearly a hundred years, the Phaistos Disc has been the subject of innumerable books and papers dealing with the origin of its symbols and their possible identification with other known or unknown scripts of Crete and the Near East. And it presents a challenge that fascinates both specialists and amateurs to this day: the challenge of deciphering its script and interpreting its symbolism.[29]

A unique specimen of an unknown script

Both in its shape and in the matter of the script incised on it, the Phaistos Disc is unique. The Italian archaeologist Luigi Pernier discovered it in 1908 in the palace at Phaistos, the second most important palace in central Crete, which stands on a low hill commanding the lovely Messara plain. It was found in a rectangular room at a depth of about fifty centimetres, lying on the natural rock in a context of earth, ash, charcoal and broken pottery. There was nothing else in the room hinting at its use as an archive room or treasury apart from a single tablet written in Linear A.[30]

A precise date cannot be assigned to the disc because, according to Pernier's excavation reports, it came from a room where the stratigraphy had been disturbed over the centuries. On the evidence of the pottery finds from the same room, the disc could theoretically be dated anywhere between 1700 B.C. and the Hellenistic period. However, the fact that some of the symbols impressed on it were pictograms depicting life in Crete in the second millennium B.C.

23. The two sides of the Phaistos Disc. Photos: L. Godart. ☞

strongly suggests that it was made in a period of the Minoan-Mycenaean civilization, between about 1700 and 1450 B.C.

The disc was made in the same way as most Minoan clay tablets: the clay was kneaded and shaped by hand on a flat surface, without a template, while still soft and moist. The clay it is made of is clean and very fine-grained, of excellent quality, as in the Minoan footed goblets known as 'egg-cups'. However, the Phaistos Disc represents a significant departure from the written tradition of the Minoan tablets inasmuch as, after the characters were imprinted, it was baked in such a way as to acquire – on both sides – the smooth texture characteristic of majolica ware.

24. Line drawing of the incised lines and impressed symbols on the Phaistos Disc. By L. Godart.

The text is impressed in a spiral on both sides of the disc. Most probably the scribe started by incising the outlines of the spiral with a sharp instrument similar to the styli used by the scribes of Linear A and B, working from the outside to the centre, section by section, and as he did so he impressed the symbols in each compartment of the spiral, repeating the process on the other side of the disc. One might call it an early form of printing. At the beginning of the text on each side there is a perpendicular line joining the beginning of the spiral to the outer edge of the disc, with a row of five conspicuous spots on it to show the direction in which the text it is to be read.

The text is 'printed' with a set of forty-five different types or punches in the shape of symbols that are well-drawn and very easily recognizable.[31] If we take it as a working hypothesis that the punches

25. Line drawings of the forty-five different symbols on the Phaistos Disc. By L. Godart.

CHART OF THE SYMBOLS ON THE PHAISTOS DISC

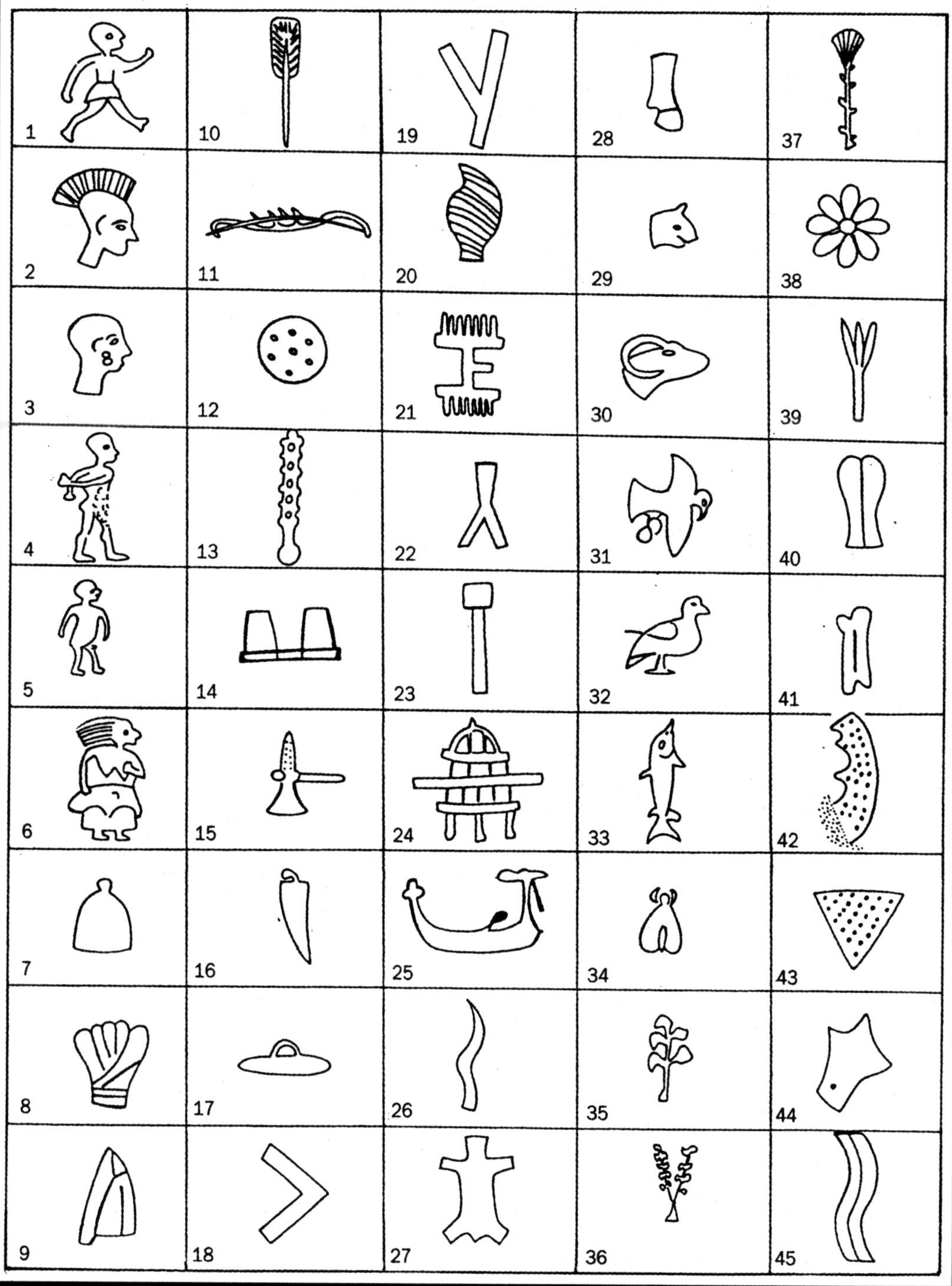

1	10	19	28	37
2	11	20	29	38
3	12	21	30	39
4	13	22	31	40
5	14	23	32	41
6	15	24	33	42
7	16	25	34	43
8	17	26	35	44
9	18	27	36	45

were not made specially for printing the disc and may therefore have been used before, it is reasonable to conclude that they were made of a durable material capable of being used over and over again without loss of clarity. Louis Godart believes they were made of precious metal (probably gold), cast in stone matrices,[32] and were fitted with wooden or bone handles.

The punches are impressed on the disc in the space between the spiral lines, in groups separated by perpendicular lines (see Fig. 25). The impressions depict human figures (male and female), heads with or without a crest, various animals, birds, fishes, plants and flowers, tools and household utensils, a boat, a beehive, weapons and some other objects, as well as symbols of unknown significance.[33]

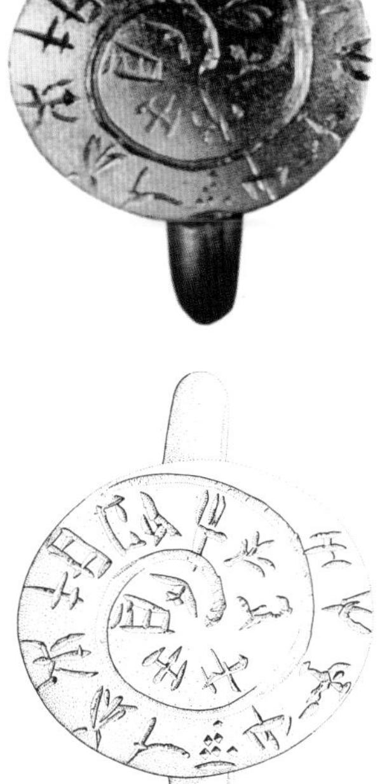

27. *Gold ring with Linear A symbols arranged in a spiral. Found at Knossos (Mavro Spileo). 18th-15th c.* B.C. *Iraklion, Archaeological Museum.*

Once one has determined the direction in which the spirals were drawn and the punches impressed, the next question that arises concerns the direction in which the text is to be read: from the centre to the outer edge, from the outer edge to the centre, or even perhaps *boustrophedon* (i.e. with alternate lines reading from left to right and from right to left, as in the Law Code of Gortyn discovered by Federico Halbherr). Ever since the early stages in the study of the disc, many archaeologists, including Alessandro Della Seta and Godart, have maintained that the inscription runs from right to left, which means that the whole text is to be read from the perimeter to the centre. If this is accepted, it follows that the inscriptions on the two sides of the disc are not separate but run on from one side to the other, side A being the first part and side B the continuation.[34] Until the text is deciphered, the question remains open.

Although many possible suggestions have been put forward for the decipherment of the Phaistos Disc, none of them are based on scientific evidence because there are no data available for comparison with any other script, deciphered or not, from Crete or elsewhere in the Near East.[35] More-

26. *The palace of Phaistos.*

over, nothing is known about the subject matter: whether it is religious or purely literary. What can safely be said is that the script on the disc is totally alien to anything known at present. Another unsolved enigma is the question of its origin: was it imported into Crete, perhaps as a gift, or was it made there? Most archaeologists and epigraphists agree that it was probably made in a Cretan workshop, citing two significant precedents: first, the pictorial symbols on the double axe from Arkalohori,[36] and secondly the Linear A inscription on a gold ring (which, like the Phaistos Disc, is incised in a spiral) found at Mavro Spileo.[37]

28. Bronze double axe with an incised pictographic inscription in three columns, from the Arkalohori cave. Ca. 1600 B.C. *Iraklion, Archaeological Museum.*

Conclusions. Having described the distinctive characteristics of the Phaistos Disc, I have no intention of advancing yet another theory concerning its decipherment. Let us conclude with a summary of certain points that are particularly worth noting and may well repay further study.

First of all, it must be emphasized that the disc was made of clean, pure clay and that, after the text had been impressed on it, it was baked, not by an accident of fate (like the tablets) but presumably to ensure that it would stand up to the passage of time and continuous use. The inference is that it was an object intended for long-term use, the like of which has not been found anywhere else, to the best of my knowledge.

The only explanation I can think of for the choice of a circular shape is that it was dictated by the spiral arrangement of the text. As regards the 'typography', if one may call it that, one is struck by the discrepancy between the amateurish drawing of the dividing lines and the efficient and artistic printing of the symbols, which implies that the printer was using a set of punches with handles.

Analysis of the language of the disc leads to further conclusions. The number of different symbols used on the disc is forty-five: on the basis of the dividing lines forming separate panels in the spiral, the text consists of sixty-one words adding up to a total of 242 characters. Linguistics experts and epigraphists are agreed that these are the symbols of a syllabic script, as there are too few of them for a pictographic script and too many for an alphabet. Of course, there is no guarantee that the text on the disc uses all the symbols available, so the script could theoretically be ideographic; or it could be a hybrid, a mixture of the ideographic and the syllabic.

One last observation worth making about the 'typography' is that the punches, in the form in which they were made, could be inked and used for printing, not only on clay but also on more delicate materials such as papyrus and parchment – and indeed for multiple 'print runs'.

The Cypro-Minoan script and the Cypriot syllabary. In contrast to mainland Greece, the Asia Minor coastlands, the Cyclades, Ceos, Cythera and other places where the Minoan scripts were in use from the beginning of the Middle Minoan IIIA-B period (1800 B.C.), in Cyprus the people developed a linear script of their own.[38] Most probably it was introduced into Cyprus by Minoan merchants before the Mycenaean expansion in the eastern Mediterranean, while its form appears to be derived from Linear A and to date from the sixteenth century B.C.

As early as 1909, Evans studied the inscriptions on Bronze Age clay balls discovered at Enkomi in eastern Cyprus. Noticing the strong resemblance between some of the symbols on the Enkomi pottery and the scripts used by the Minoans, he coined the name 'Cypro-Minoan' for the Cypriot script. Actually, though, the 'Cypro-Minoan' script is closer to Linear A than to Linear B, as the earliest example of its use dates from *ca.* 1500 B.C., a few decades before Linear B came into use in Crete.[39]

29. Line drawings of the symbols incised on the axe of Fig. 28. By Iro Athanasiadou.

Following the Greek colonization of Cyprus – especially the southern part of the island, around Paphos – in the twelfth century B.C.,[40] a new script came into use there. This was probably a blend of Cypro-Minoan and Linear B and is known as the Cypriot syllabary: it remained in use in Cyprus until the time of Alexander the Great (320 B.C.), a period of nearly a thousand years. The phonetic values of the Cypriot syllabary were known to Evans, as the script had been deciphered by George Smith as early as 1781, with the help of a bilingual inscription of the fourth century B.C. (in ancient Greek and the Cypriot script).[41] The structure of the Cypriot syllabary is similar to that of Linear B: every sign represents either a vowel or a combination of a vowel and a consonant.[42] The oldest inscription written in the classical Cypriot

30. 'Bilingual' inscription (in the Greek alphabet and the Cypriot syllabary) of the fifth century B.C.

The origins of writing in Cyprus

syllabary, found on a bronze skewer from Palaipaphos in 1979, consists of five symbols forming the name *Opheltas* or *Opheltes* – a name unknown in Homer – in the genitive. It dates from the eleventh century B.C. and provides the earliest known evidence for the use of the Greek language in Cyprus.[43]

Since Evans's death there have been further finds of inscribed clay balls in Cyprus and some long Late Bronze Age inscriptions have been found at Enkomi, proving that the script was used not only for ordinary archival records[44] but for other purposes as well.

Scribes and their tablets. The scribes of Minoan and Mycenaean tablets are known to us only by their work.[45] Many of the secrets of their calling have remained unsolved to this day, including a number of symbols of the pictographic and Linear A scripts, not to mention the Phaistos Disc. Nor do we know anything about their education, nor about the way in which the language and the art of writing were handed down from generation to generation, nor whether they belonged to an exclusive confraternity, nor whether they had titles, nor whether there was a wider readership for whom they could write if they had literary aspirations. Be all that as it may, there must have been some kind of schooling available, and in the palace there must have been qualified teachers with responsibility for the development of the script and the continuity of the written tradition.[46] The evidence at our disposal suggests that the scribes were probably treated as a privileged class and that writing was a rare accomplishment among the general public, which means that there would not have been any private archives nor libraries of any kind.

Anonymous scribes of the Minoan and Mycenaean civilizations

The excavations at Knossos have proved that there existed a bureaucratically organized labour system for the cultivation of the land and the production and distribution of goods; therefore there must have been 'writing rooms'. Experts who have made a careful study of the tablets have recognized certain groups of scribes with common characteristics, whether in the way their tablets were made or in their 'handwriting' or the shaping of the symbols. It would appear that the scribes – or at least those at the top of the tree – did not make the tablets themselves. Most probably there was a whole team of workers with different responsibilities: there would have been some kneading the clay, others rolling it out and cutting it into tablets and perhaps others shaping them, before the finished product came into the skilled hands of the scribes.[47] Among the scribes themselves, too, there would no doubt have been some kind of hierarchy: the senior ones would presumably have been the teachers and calligraphers, with the younger ones and apprentices writing the easier characters and perhaps doing only the more ephemeral records.

Jean-Pierre Olivier's doctoral dissertation on the subject of the scribes of Knossos identifies the 'handwriting' of sixty-six different scribes and divides them into two groups, the 'principal' (forty-one, numbered from 101 to 141) and the 'secondary' (twenty-five, numbered from 201 to 225); the doctoral dissertation of T. G. Palaima, which deals with the scribes of Pylos, identifies forty-five different handwriting samples; and J. M. Driessen, in his dissertation evaluating the tablets found by Evans in the 'Room of the Chariot Tablets', identifies thirteen scribes and classifies them into ten groups on the basis of their different styles of writing.[48] If one compares the features common to all the Linear B tablets, whether found at Knossos or Phaistos, at Mycenae or Pylos or at other Minoan or Mycenaean palaces, one can easily distinguish the various scribes' different styles by comparing (a) the relative sizes of the different symbols, (b) the differentiation between single symbols and groups of symbols, (c) their artistic form, (d) the manner of incising them, (e) the pattern of the dividing lines on the tablet and the way of forming abbreviations, and (f) the artistic talent shown by the scribe in drawing the ideograms.

With the passage of time, published studies of the countless fragments of tablets in the Athens and Iraklion Archaeological Museums have shown an ever-increasing depth of insight, making it possible for new groups of tablets

31. Scribes in Pharaonic Egypt at work with the tools of their trade. From H. Junker, «Giza».

to be reconstructed; so it seems safe to conclude that we will be able to recognize more and more scribes by their 'handwriting'. However, we have to remember that the extant tablets written in Linear A and Linear B were day-to-day records that would normally have been current for only about twelve months, and so the scribes would not have bothered to use their best calligraphic script. One can only wonder whether these same scribes were the ones who wrote texts on papyrus or parchment.[49]

Lastly, it is worth mentioning that there is not one archaeological find from Crete or anywhere else in the Bronze Age Greek world with a pictorial representation of a scribe at work or of any kind of writing material.

The stylus. The scribe incised the symbols on the clay tablet (while still moist) using a stylus in the form of a sharp-edged, pointed blade that was curved at the end so that he could use the side of the blade as an eraser to correct mistakes. The stylus could be made of a variety of materials: usually bronze or bone, but sometimes reed, in which case the point had to be sharpened regularly. It was used not only for incising the characters but also for setting up the page layout when the tablet was 'page-shaped': often the scribe would draw horizontal lines across it, as on a sheet of ruled paper nowadays, to give himself a clearer picture of his working space.[50]

Preparing the writing tablet. There was no invariable formula for the type or blend of clay to be used in making a writing tablet: even today it is often possible to see that two different qualities have been used in the same tablet, usually a core of relatively coarse clay coated with a finer layer. When the raw material was mixed and ready for use, the scribe or his assistant decided on the dimensions of the tablet and whether it was to be a 'palm-leaf' or a 'page' tablet, according to the length of the text to be written on it. The size and shape may perhaps have served as the scribe's 'trademarks', so to speak: this would explain the differences to be found not only from scribe to scribe but also from palace to palace.

The method of preparing the tablet was as follows. First the clay was

32. Drawing of a stylus from Thebes.

The tablet is washed and sun-dried

kneaded and rolled between the palms of the hands into a cylinder terminating naturally in a conical point. The cylinder was then sometimes threaded with a length of yarn or thin string. Next came the process of 'pagination'. The cone of clay was placed on a flat surface and pressed out into a compact rectangular tablet with one side (the recto) flat and smooth for writing on and the other (the verso) bearing the maker's palm-prints and fingerprints;[51] the verso was often left blank.[52]

The shapes of the tablets vary according to their date and place of manufacture. In the Iraklion Museum there is one (Fh. 346) measuring no more than 3x1 cm., recording the delivery of two portions of oil to a certain *Aigi-*

pa(s)tas, and it seems unlikely that any will be found smaller than this, even allowing for the innumerable fragments that have yet to be fitted together. The biggest tablet found in Crete (As 1516), known as the 'large tablet', with particulars of various working parties, measures 16 x 27 cm. Tablets of similar size have been found at Pylos in considerable numbers. The most numerous are approximately 7 x 15 cm. in size, with a thickness of about 1.5 cm. These are rectangular 'page' tablets with the text separated by horizontal lines.

The writing surface. As already mentioned, the scribe would have known the length of the text before he made the tablet, and he would take that into account when deciding on the shape of the tablet. Next he had to work out the right size of the symbols for the whole text, and then he would draw the horizontal lines. Very often the lines stretched across the full width of the tablet, but sometimes there was a margin down the side in which further particulars were entered.

In both Linear A and Linear B the text reads from left to right. If an entry was too long to fit on one line, it ran on to a second line written above the first. Sometimes the scribe even used the edges of the tablet (at top and bottom, left and right) for brief additional notes. If a list of homogeneous statistics was too long for a single page, it was continued on another tablet or tablets, forming a set that might be described as a sort of booklet. Tablets belonging to the same set can be identified as such by the features they have in common: the 'handwriting' of the scribe, the quality and characteristics of the clay and the marks used to number the tablets for the benefit of readers and archivists. The order in which they were to be read was often indicated by headings, paragraphs or larger characters (capitals, so to speak); otherwise it was left to the archivists to work it out for themselves by following the sequence of the data.

Did books exist in the Minoan-Mycenaean era? If it is accepted that the extant 'documents' of the Minoan-Mycenaean civilization – most of which are crudely-written ephemeral (annual) records of data relating to economic and administrative transactions – cannot possibly be the total output of the Minoan and Mycenaean written tradition, we are left facing a number of questions. In the first place, one would certainly expect the Minoans' and Mycenaeans' trade arrangements with other countries in the Near East – especially Egypt, which was noted for its bureaucracy – to have been enshrined in official intergovernmental agreements on papyrus and parchment.[53] Moreover, a kind of mythology and literature, either epic or novelistic in style, must also have come into being and perhaps circulated in papyrus book form: some examples are the novels and stories current in Egypt from early in the second millennium B.C., including 'The Tale of the Shipwrecked Sailor', 'The Story of the Eloquent Peasant', 'The Contendings of Horus and Set' and the best seller of ancient

33. Stages in the preparation of a 'page' tablet: (a) ruled, and (b) in the process of being inscribed, with the symbols running from left to right.

Literature in the Near East and Egypt

Egyptian literature, 'The Story of Sinuhe'.[54] Besides Egyptian literature, the Minoans and Mycenaeans would surely have known – or at least heard, in poetic form – stories from Phoenician and Canaanite mythology, especially since the majority of those stories were discovered at Ugarit (Ras Shamra), where the Mycenaeans had trading posts from the fourteenth or thirteenth century B.C.

The literature of the ancient Phoenicians, in the Proto-Phoenician language, was represented by epic-style religious poems which are reminiscent of the Homeric epics in many respects, especially the quarrels between the gods and their meddling in human affairs: for example, the epic *The Loves and Wars of Baal and Anath*, sometimes called the *Baaliad* on an analogy with the *Iliad*.[55] In any case, knowing what we do about the Minoans' and Mycenaeans' voyages to unknown places and their contacts with peoples whose ways of life must have seemed very strange to them, one would naturally expect the seafarers' tales of their adventures to be elaborated into moralistic 'novels'. If there is a measure of truth in this working hypothesis, we should also expect to find a class of people with the imagination to write such books, a class of 'official writers', a reading public (however small) and archivists in the palaces to look after the written texts – in other words, a literary world.

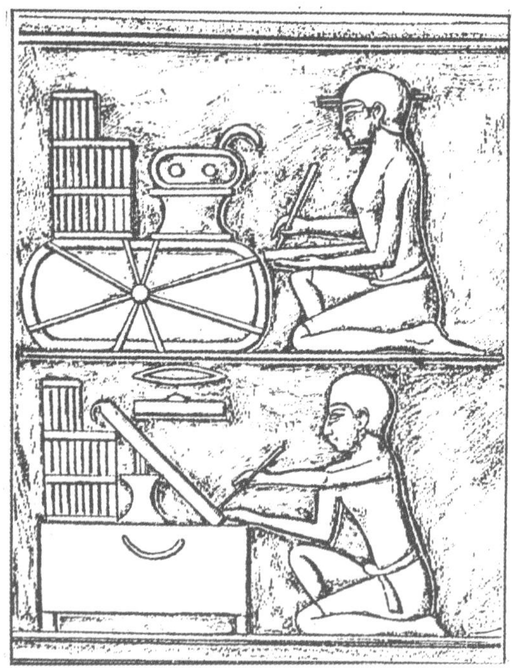

34. Scribes at work in a government office in the period of the Memphite Dynasties. Drawing by Faucher-Gudin, from a wall-painting in the tomb of Khûnas.

Filing systems. Once the tablets had been inscribed and dried, the next step was to file them in the archive room so that they would be easy to locate whenever anyone wanted to read the data recorded on them. It is not possible to say with certainty which room was used for inscribing the tablets, nor whether they were made and inscribed in the same room, as special facilities or the right weather (water supply, sunshine) were needed for the processes of preparing the clay and drying the tablets. It should also be remembered that not every room where tablets have been found was an archive room, because the bureaucratic system used in the palaces required that labels certifying the kind and quality of the produce be attached to all storage containers: in other words, the tablets served as short-term accounting records for the distribution of agricultural produce.[56]

Olivier's book on the scribes of Knossos contains a plan of the palace marking all the rooms in which Linear B tablets have been found.[57] From this it follows that not all the extant tablets were intended to be filed in the archives, because in every storeroom there were tablets on which periodic records were kept of imports and exports. Those tablets that had loops of string or fibre threaded through them were presumably hung on nails in the walls; others were simply stacked in recesses in the walls or in wooden pigeonholes.

There is no evidence that archive rooms conformed to any specific architectural plan in the Minoan-Mycenaean Bronze Age.[58] Moreover, excavations in the large libraries (archival and non-archival) in the Near East – such as the state archives in the palace library at Ebla – have proved that the usual arrangements for filing archives consisted of wooden shelves attached to the walls and supported on wooden posts.[59] Sometimes the shelves held separate 'bookcases' (which were wooden or plaster boxes or wicker baskets), sometimes they were partitioned into pigeonholes where tablets were arranged in much the same way as books are today. In the latter case, depending on the basic principles of the archival system and the shape of the tablets, the tablets sometimes stood vertically like books in a bookcase, with only the edge showing, and sometimes they were stacked lying flat so that the text on the first 'page' was visible, depending on the shape of the tablets.

How the tablets were filed

The excavated remains of Rooms 7 and 8 at Pylos, which held the main archives (each room having a bench along three sides), suggest that there were wooden shelves resting on the bench and affixed to the walls, probably in accordance with the traditional archival practice of the Minoans and Mycenaeans. This would make them similar to the archive rooms of the Near East.

Special mention should be made here of the archives at Knossos, which, according to Driessen, were the oldest in the Mycenaean world and therefore the earliest Greek archives.[60] As the Knossos archives contained early examples of the pictographic script and of Linear A, it may be that they embody the tradition of the Minoan-Mycenaean archival system. The room in question, known as the Room of the Chariot Tablets,[61] is in the west wing of the palace of Knossos. In it were found six hundred tablets written in Linear B as well as numerous fragments of tablets, carved ivories, bronzes and other objects, eighteen sealings and a piece of carved wood. (Incidentally, it is doubtful whether the precious stone *pithoi* probably used in religious ceremonies were stored together with tablets in the same room.) As Evans himself noted, the archives containing the bulk of the tablets were originally situated on the first floor of the west wing in the Thalamos of the Stone Vases, which collapsed in one of the catastrophic fires or earthquakes with the result that the archival material was found together with the objects belonging in the corresponding room on the ground floor.[62]

The material from the Room of the Chariot Tablets does not reveal the scribes' identity, nor does it mention any rank or office they may have held or provide any additional information that might help us to tell them apart.[63] Chadwick believes that the tablets from that room were not real archives but merely writing exercises.[64]

The actual arrangement of these archives is of course a matter of conjecture, based on the evidence of archaeological finds. Nor is it a proven fact that the piece of wood found in the same room was part of a chest for the storage of papyrus or parchment documents, though Evans in his excavation notebooks did mention wooden chests (of which handles, joints and fragments of charred wood were found) as well as small plaster caskets.

The Minoans' earliest official archives

If we accept that other kinds of written material existed in addition to clay tablets, namely papyrus or parchment books, it is a reasonable working hypothesis that they were probably kept in the same rooms as the archives, and some system would naturally have existed for their classification and arrangement. Wicker baskets, with or without lids, and wooden boxes were already in use in Pharaonic Egypt as convenient small 'bookcases' for papyrus rolls, and they were still being used for that purpose in the Late Roman period. However, this filing system worked only for small quantities of books or for temporary records in almost daily use. For bigger collections (certain genres of literature, for example) arranged in alphabetical or some similar order, and also for permanent archival records, there existed another method of classification which presumably consisted of wooden shelves with vertical partitions at intervals of about 40 cm., these spaces being subdivided into rectangular, triangular or lozenge-shaped pigeonholes. This would make it easy for the librarians (and others who had access to the libraries and archives) to put the papyrus rolls back in their original places without disturbing their proper order whenever they needed to take them out from the lower rows of the pyramids formed by the rolls on the shelves.

Sealings. Perhaps it was because there were so many tablets that would sooner or later need to be filed away in the archives that the makers of tablets inserted a length of fibre or string into the centre of the tablet. The free end of the string had to be long enough to be threaded through a clay sealing and firmly knot-

35. Above: Reconstruction of the west wing of the palace of Knossos. Drawn by Thomas Fanourakis. Below: The Throne Room in the palace of Knossos, as reconstructed by Arthur Evans.

ted. Some of these sealings, which were polyhedral lumps of clay, probably served as labels (the *sillyboi* of later antiquity). Some of them summarized the contents of a set of tablets stored in a wooden box or a basket, while others were attached to a single tablet to help the archivist to locate it.[65] Quite possibly such sealings were also used as labels to indicate the contents of papyrus or parchment rolls, especially as no alternative means of labelling had yet been devised for papyrus rolls.[66]

Library systems

The sealings may perhaps have been used for other purposes as well, for example as rough notes to be copied later on to tablets together with other data. This was the case with the fifty-six sealings from Thebes referring to the move-

36. Sealings from the hieroglyphic archives at Knossos, 1750 B.C.

ment of livestock and the transportation of produce from farms and grazing lands to the palace. The Theban sealings, which were found all together, would originally have been hung on nails or stored in a container on a shelf.

Besides sealings, other methods of identifying the contents of tablets were in use. J. L. Melena has concluded that two of the tablets (Nos. 736 and 740) in the Sh series from Pylos, which seem to have been an inventory of military corslets, formed a diptych listing the headings of the other tablets, which were then divided into two groups according to the material of which the corslets were made.[67] Similar practices were adopted in archives in the Near East, especially at Ugarit,[68] long before the Mycenaeans organized their own archives.

37. Mycenaean sealings that were attached to stores of commodities and other objects, either as owners' labels or giving other data. From Nestor's palace at Pylos.

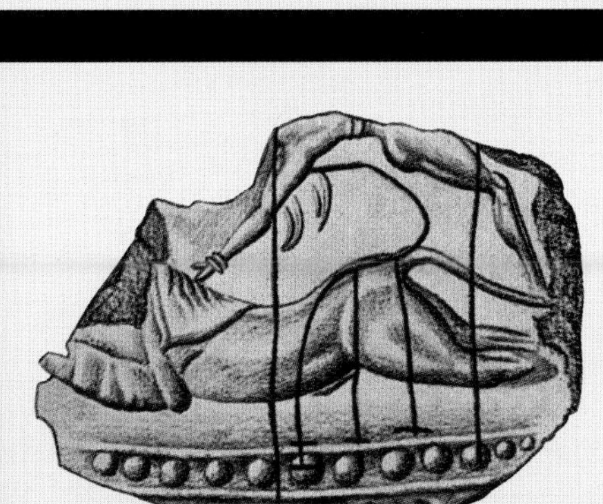

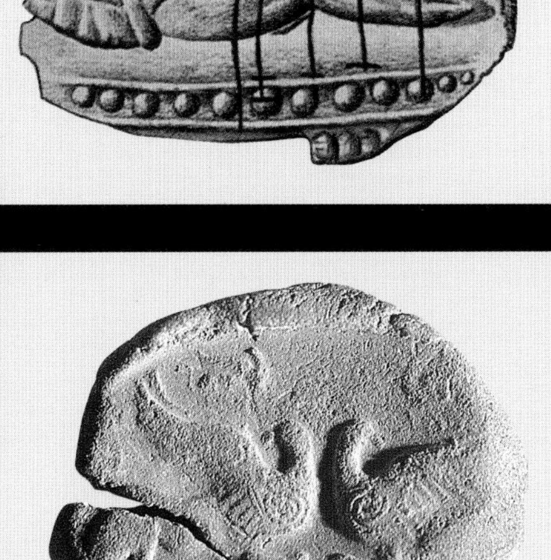

Notes

I

The Minoan and Mycenaean Civilizations

NOTES

1. See R. D. Woodard, *Greek Writing from Knossos to Homer. A Linguistic Interpretation of the Origin of the Greek Alphabet and the Continuity of Ancient Greek Literacy*, New York/Oxford 1997.
2. For an informative overview of the Bronze Age in the Aegean islands and mainland Greece, see S. Marinatos and M. Hirmer, *Crete and Mycenae*, London 1960; M. I. Finley, *Early Greece: The Bronze and Archaic Ages*, London 1970; H. G. Buchholz and V. Karageorghis, *Prehistoric Greece and Cyprus*, tr. F. Garvie, London 1973; P. Warren, *The Aegean Civilizations*, London 1975.
3. Evans's long and close association with Knossos is described in A. Brown, *Arthur Evans and the Palace of Minos*, Oxford 1986.
4. The bibliography on the Minoan civilization is now enormous. See esp.: A. J. Evans, *The Palace of Minos at Knossos*, vols. I-IV, London 1921-1935; J. D. S. Pendlebury, *The Archaeology of Crete*, London 1939; R. W. Hutchinson, *Prehistoric Crete*, Harmondsworth 1962; F. Schachermeyr, *Die minoische Kultur des alten Kreta*, Stuttgart 1964; S. Alexiou, *Μινωικός πολιτισμός. Μέ όδηγό τῶν Άνακτόρων Κνωσοῦ, Φαιστοῦ, Μαλίων*, Iraklion [1969]; M. S. F. Hood, *The Minoans: Crete in the Bronze Age*, London 1971; G. Cadogan, *Palaces of Minoan Crete*, London 1976.
5. On the so-called *Pax Minoica*, its catastrophic collapse and the far-ranging travels of the Minoans, see R. Hägg and N. Marinatos (eds.), *The Minoan Thalassocracy: Myth and Reality. Proceedings of the Third International Symposium of the Swedish Institute in Athens, 31 May - 5 June 1981*, Stockholm 1984; *Acts of the International Archaeological Symposium 'The Relations between Cyprus and Crete, ca. 2000-500 B.C.'*, Nicosia 1979. On the relations between Minoan Crete and Pharaonic Egypt, see the exhibition catalogue entitled *Κρήτη-Αἴγυπτος. Πολιτισμικοί δεσμοί τριῶν χιλιετιῶν*, ed. Alexandra Karetsou and Maria Andreadaki-Vlazaki with N. Papadakis, Iraklion 2000, and the *Proceedings* of the conference on the same theme: Alexandra Karetsou (ed.), *Κρήτη-Αἴγυπτος. Πολιτισμικοί δεσμοί τριῶν χιλιετιῶν*, Athens 2000. See also M. Bietak, 'Connections between Egypt and the Minoan World: New results from Tell el-Dab'a/Avaris' in W. V. Davies and E. Schofield (eds.), *Egypt, the Aegean and the Levant: Interconnections in the Second Millennium B.C.*, London 1995, 19-27; M. Bietak and N. Marinatos, 'Avaris (Tell el-Dab'a) and the Minoan World', in Karetsou, *Κρήτη-Αἴγυπτος...*, 40-44.
6. On the Mycenaean civilization see esp.: G.E. Mylonas, *Mycenae and the Mycenaean Age*, Princeton 1966; E. T. Vermeule, *Greece in the Bronze Age*, Chicago 1972[2]; J. Chadwick, *The Mycenaean World*, Cambridge 1976; J. T. Hooker, *Mycenaean Greece*, London 1977. For an up-to-date overview see Lord W. D. Taylour, *The Mycenaeans* (revised and enlarged edition), London 1983; M. S. Ruipérez and J. L. Melena, *Οί Μυκηναῖοι Ἕλληνες* (= *Los Griegos micénicos*, Madrid 1990, tr. Melina Panayiotidou), Athens 1996.
7. The literature on Thera's destruction by the volcanic eruption and its possible identification with the lost island of Atlantis is very extensive. See, for example: J. V. Luce, *The End of Atlantis*, London 1969

(written for the general reader and copiously illustrated); A. G. Galanopoulos and E. Bacon, *Atlantis: The Truth behind the Legend*, London 1969. See also D. L. Page, *The Santorini Volcano and the Destruction of Minoan Crete*, London 1970; J. Driessen and C. F. Macdonald, *The Troubled Island: Minoan Crete before and after the Santorini Eruption* [*Aegaeum* 17], Liège/Austin 1997.

8. On Mycenaean expansion into Asia Minor and Italy, see F. H. Stubbings, *Mycenaean Pottery from the Levant*, Cambridge 1951; W. D. Taylour, *Mycenaean Pottery in Italy and Adjacent Areas*, Cambridge 1958; F. Schachermeyr, *Ägäis und Orient*, Vienna 1967; *Acts of the International Archaeological Symposium 'The Mycenaeans in the Eastern Mediterranean', Nicosia, 27th March-2nd April, 1972*, Nicosia 1973.
9. But quite possibly the collapse of the Mycenaean civilization was due to internal socio-economic instability brought on by external events, like the upheavals caused by the 'Peoples of the Sea' elsewhere in the Mediterranean. For a general outline see Katie Demakopoulou (ed.), *The Mycenaean World: Five Centuries of Early Greek Culture, 1600-1100 BC*, Athens 1988.
10. The period immediately following 1100 B.C. was the beginning of the Iron Age; the palace at Mycenae had been destroyed by a great fire about a century earlier: see A. M. Snodgrass, *The Dark Age of Greece*, Edinburgh 1971. The fact that no inscriptions have been found in Greece from the four hundred years of the 'dark ages' (approximately 1150-750 B.C.) suggests that the art of writing more or less died out in the post-Mycenaean period, perhaps being remembered by just a few people. See L. R. Palmer, *Descriptive and Comparative Linguistics*, London 1978, 262; M. Andronikos, "*Μυκηναϊκή καί Ἑλληνική γραφή*", in *Μελέτες γιά τήν Ἑλληνική γλώσσα/ Studies in Greek Linguistics*, Thessaloniki 1987, 1-24.
11. These dates are subject to revision in the light of future archaeological research. The dates given for the pictographic script are the approximate terminal dates of the period when it was the script in general use. For a brief general survey of Cretan scripts see Maria P. Tsouli, 'Pre-Alphabetic Scripts in Greece' (with parallel German translation), in *The Greek Script*, Athens 2001, 17-39.
12. In Egypt, the use of symbolic images dates from about 3400 B.C., in the Naqada civilization towards the end of the Predynastic era. The hieroglyphic script made its appearance in the time of the Proto-Pharaoh known as 'Scorpion', who ruled at Abydos *ca.* 3150 B.C. It developed rapidly, making it possible for the rulers to express their political ideology in writing, and was associated with the period of the unification of Upper and Lower Egypt – a troubled time dominated by the personalities of 'Scorpion' and Narmer. See D. Panayiotopoulos, "Ἡ γένεση δύο κωδίκων ἐπικοινωνίας στό παράδειγμα τῆς ἀρχαίας Αἰγύπτου", *Περίαπτο* 1 (1998) 14-28.
13. In Mesopotamia, however, parchment and papyrus were also used as writing materials, especially from the eighth to the second century B.C., that is during the Assyrian and Neo-Babylonian periods and after: see R.P. Dougherty, 'Writing upon Parchment and Papyrus among the Babylonians and Assyrians', *Journal of the American Oriental Society* 42 (1928) 109-135. Besides clay tablets, parchment and papyrus, two other materials that were widely used for writing on were ivory and wood. The wooden

writing-boards were often coated with a thin film of wax, on which the scribes wrote with a stylus. The oldest tablets of this type were discovered in a well in the north-west wing of the palace at Nimrud: see D. J. Wiseman, 'Assyrian Writing-Boards', *Iraq* 17 (1955) 3-13.

14. For general information on the Cretan pictographic (hieroglyphic) script see A. J. Evans, *Scripta Minoa* I, Oxford 1909; F. Chapouthier, *Les écritures minoënnes au palais de Mallia* [*Études Crétoises* 2], Paris 1930. For more detail see E. L. Bennett, Jr., 'Some Minoan Texts in the Iraklion Museum', in *Minoica*, 35-49; S. Alexiou, 'Neue hieroglyphisch Siegel aus Kreta', *Kadmos* 2 (1963) 79-83; E. Grumach and J. Sakellarakis, 'Die neuen Hieroglyphensiegel vom Phourni, Archanes I', *Kadmos* 5 (1966) 109-114; J.-P. Olivier, 'La scrittura geroglifica cretese', *La parola del passato* 31 (1976) 17-23; Id., 'The Possible Methods in Deciphering the Pictographic Cretan Script', in *Problems in Decipherment*, 39-58; also the relevant chapter in R. Treuil, P. Darcque, J.-C. Poursat and G. Touchais, *Les civilisations égéennes du néolithique et de l'âge du bronze*, Paris 1989.
15. See the recent publication by J.-P. Olivier and L. Godart, *Corpus hieroglyphicarum inscriptionum Cretae* [*Études Crétoises* 31], Paris 1996.
16. On the 'hieroglyphic' seals from Archanes (Fourni) see J. and E. Sakellarakis, *Ἀρχάνες, μιά νέα ματιά στή Μινωική Κρήτη*, 2 vols., Athens 1997, 327-330. For more on the fourteen-faced seal and the 'Archanes script' see P. Yule, *Early Cretan Seals: A Study of Chronology* [*Marburger Studien zur Vor- und Frühgeschichte* 4], Mainz 1980, 100, 169-172.
17. On Linear A in general, see W. C. Brice, *Inscriptions in the Minoan Linear Script of Class A*, Oxford 1961; L. Godart and J.-P. Olivier, *Receuil des inscriptions en linéaire A* [*Études Crétoises* 21], I-V, Paris 1976-1985. For a comprehensive index see J. Raison and M. W. M. Pope, *Index transnuméré du linéaire A*, Louvain 1977. On the frequency of each symbol's occurrence see D. W. Packard, *Minoan Linear A*, Berkeley/Los Angeles/London 1974. Recent studies on the subject include: J.-P. Olivier, 'La bague en or de Mauro Spélio et inscription en linéaire A', in Lydie Hadermann-Misguich et al. (eds.), *Rayonnement grec: Hommages à C. Delvoye*, Brussels 1982, 15-26; M. W. M. Pope, *Aegean Writing and Linear A*, Lund 1964 (on the relationship with other scripts); L. Godart, 'La scrittura Lineare A', *La parola del passato* 31 (1976) 30-47; Y. Duhoux, 'Le linéaire A: problèmes de déchiffrement', in *Problems in Decipherment*, 59-120. On the dating of Linear A see F. Vandenabeele, 'La chronologie des documents en Linéaire A', *BCH* 109 (1985) 3-20.
18. On the spread of Linear A outside Crete, see: (on Melos) C.C. Edgar and A.J. Evans, *Excavations at Phylacopi in Melos* [*Hellenic Society suppl. paper* 4], London 1904, 177-185; A. C. Renfrew and W. C. Brice, 'A Linear A Tablet Fragment from Phylacopi in Melos', *Kadmos* 16 (1977) 111-119; (in and around Mycenae) E. Grumach, 'Neue Bügelkannen aus Tiruns', *Kadmos* 1 (1962) 85-86; (on Naxos) N. Kontoleon, 'Zwei Beschriftete Scherben aus Naxos', *Kadmos* 4 (1965) 84-85; (on Ceos) J. L. Caskey, 'Inscriptions and Potters' Marks from Ayia Irini in Keos', *Kadmos* 9 (1970) 107-117; (on Thera) S. Marinatos, *Excavations at Thera*, IV, Athens 1971, 43-45.
19. See A. Lembessi, J.-P. Olivier and L. Godart, "Πινακίδες Γραμμικῆς Α ἐξ Ἀρχανῶν", *AE* (1974) 113-167; J. and E. Sakellarakis, *Ἀρχάνες...*, 330-337.

20. The most recent reappraisal of the tablets and of Evans's finds is by J. Driessen in his book *An Early Destruction in the Mycenaean Palace at Knossos: A New Interpretation of the Excavation Field-Notes of the South-East Area of the West Wing*, Louvain 1990. The corpus of inscriptions from Knossos is in preparation: see J. Chadwick, L. Godart, J. T. Killen, J.-P. Olivier, A. Sacconi and I. A. Sakellarakis, *Corpus of Mycenaean Inscriptions from Knossos*, Cambridge/ Rome, I:1986, II:1990.
21. On the archives at Thebes see Th. Spyropoulos and J. Chadwick, *The Thebes Tablets* II [*Minos* Suppl. 4], Salamanca 1975; Ch. Piteros, J.-P. Olivier and J. L. Melena, 'Les inscriptions en linéaire B des nodules de Thèbes (1982): la fouille, les documents, les possibilités d'interprétation', *BCH* 114/1 (1990) 103-184; V. Aravantinos, 'The Mycenaean Incised Sealings from Thebes: Problems of Contents and Functions', *Aegaeum* 5 (1990) 149-164. A recent publication on the subject is: V. L. Aravantinos, L. Godart and Anna Sacconi, *Thèbes: Fouilles de la Cadmée*, I. *Les tablettes en linéaire B de la odos Pelopidou*, Pisa/Rome 2001.
22. Among the standard works on Pylos and the tablets, sealings and labels found there are: E. L. Bennett, Jr., *The Pylos Tablets*, Princeton 1955; and articles by M. L. Lang, *AJA* (1958-1965). For a transcription of all the known inscriptions see E. L. Bennett, Jr. and J.-P. Olivier, *The Pylos Tablets Transcribed*, 2 vols., Rome 1973-1976; also T. G. Palaima and J. C. Wright, 'Ins and Outs of the Archives at Pylos: Form and Function in a Mycenaean Palace', *AJA* 89 (1985) 251-262.
23. On the evolution of Linear B see S. Marinatos, 'Zur Entzifferung der mykenischen Schrift', *Minos* 4 (1956) 13-16; J. T. Hooker, *The Origin of the Linear B Script* [*Minos* Suppl. 8], Salamanca 1979*; A. Heubeck, 'L'origine della Lineare B', *SMEA* 23 (1982) 195-207; [J. Chadwick, *Linear B and Related Scripts*, London 1987]; J. T. Hooker, *Linear B: An Introduction*, Bristol 1980.
24. See Evans, *The Palace of Minos...*, IV, 666-763.
25. See Alice E. Kober, 'Evidence of Inflection in the "Chariot Tablets" from Knossos', *AJA* 49 (1945) 141-151, 50 (1946) 268-276, 52 (1948) 91-99.
26. The techniques of decipherment are described by J. Chadwick in his paper 'Linear B', in T.A. Sebeok (ed.), *Current Trends in Linguistics*, 11: *Diachronic, Areal and Typological Linguistics*, The Hague/Paris 1973, 537-568; and more recently by E. L. Bennett, Jr., 'Michael Ventris and the Pelasgian Solution', and M. W. M. Pope, 'Ventris Decipherment: First Causes', in *Problems in Decipherment*, 9-24 and 25-38 respectively. See also A. Robinson, *The Man Who Deciphered Linear B: The Story of Michael Ventris*, London 2002. On the progress of decipherment see M. Ventris, *Work Notes on Minoan Language Research and Other Unedited Papers*, ed. A. Sacconi, Rome 1988.
27. The decipherment was announced in a paper by M. Ventris and J. Chadwick entitled 'Evidence for Greek Dialect in the Mycenaean Archives', *JHS* 73 (1953) 84-103. A verbatim transcription of Ventris's work notes was published by Anna Sacconi under the title of *Work Notes on Minoan Language Research and Other Unedited Papers*, Rome 1988.
28. For more about the theoretical principles applied by Ventris in deciphering the script, see: E. Sittig, 'Methodologisches zur Entzifferung der kretischen Silbenschrift Linear B', *Minos* 3 (1954)

10-19; A.P. Treweek, 'An Examination of the Validity of the Ventris Decipherment', *BICS* 4 (1957) 10-26; F. Schachermeyr, *Saeculum* 10 (1959) 66-71; H.D. Ephron, 'Mycenaean Greek: A Lesson in Cryptanalysis', *Minos* 7 (1961) 63-100.

29. Out of the extensive bibliography relating to the many conjectural readings of the disc and theories concerning its place of origin, see esp. A. Della Seta, 'Il disco di Phaistos', *Rendiconti della Reale Accademia dei Lincei* 18 (1909) 297-367: this was the first publication of the disc and contains one of the most original theses ever written on the processes of impressing and reading it. See also Alice E. Kober, 'The Minoan Scripts: Fact and Theory', *AJA* 52 (1948) 82-103; E. Grumach, 'Die Korrecturen des Diskus von Phaistos', *Kadmos* 1 (1962) 16-26; J.-P. Olivier, 'Encore des corrections du disque de Phaistos', in *Antichità Cretesi*, I, Catania 1973, 182-185; Id., 'Le disque de Phaistos', *BCH* 99 (1975) 5-34; L. Godart, *'Ο Δίσκος τῆς Φαιστοῦ. Τό αἴνιγμα μιᾶς γραφῆς τοῦ Αἰγαίου*, Athens 1995.

30. See L. Pernier, 'Il disco di Phaestos con caratteri pittografici', *Ausonia* 3 (1908) 255-302; Id., 'Un singolare monumento della scrittura pittografica cretese', *Rendiconti della Reale Accademia dei Lincei, Classe di Scienze Morali, Storiche e Filologiche* 5 (1908) No. 17, 642-651; Evans, *Scripta Minoa* I, 272-293.

31. See Godart, *'Ο Δίσκος τῆς Φαιστοῦ*, 57-111, which has an exceptionally clear photograph of the disc with separate photographs and drawings of each individual word. Many of the symbols are open to different interpretations as to their exact meaning: for example, it has been suggested that the 'beehive' symbol does not represent a beehive but a Lycian sarcophagus, or alternatively a portable chair.

32. Godart, *'Ο Δίσκος τῆς Φαιστοῦ*, 114.

33. For a detailed table of the symbols and signs, see Godart, *'Ο Δίσκος τῆς Φαιστοῦ*, 90-115. Godart also comments on the similarities to symbols and cultural features then current among other Near Eastern peoples.

34. On the theories concerning the reading of the text from left to right and the scribe's efforts to print the symbols in such a way as to occupy the least possible width, see Della Seta, *op. cit.*

35. In their attempts to identify certain pictograms on the disc with other, similar representations – as in the case of the crested head, which some equate with the pictures of the 'Peoples of the Sea' on the walls of the Temple of Ramses III at Medinet Habu, while others maintain that it represents a Philistine – many archaeologists have suggested that the disc was made elsewhere and imported into Crete: this theory still has many supporters. On the temple at Medinet Habu see H.H. Nelson et al., *Medinet Habu I* and *II* [= *Medinet Habu I: Earlier Historical Records of Ramses III; Medinet Habu II: Later Historical Records of Ramses III*], Chicago 1930-1932.

36. On the script incised on the double axe see S. Marinatos, 'Ausgrabungen und Funde auf Kreta 1934-1935', *AA* (1935) 252-254; N.K. Boufidis, "Κρητομυκηναϊκαί ἐπιγραφαί ἐξ Ἀρκαλοχωρίου", *AE* (1953-54/2) 61-74. Of its origin there is no doubt whatsoever: it was a ritual object made in a Cretan workshop. Some of the symbols in the three-column inscription on the axe are found here and there in texts written in the pictographic script and in Linear A; but the resemblance between some of the symbols on the axe and those used in other Cretan scripts does not prove that the inscription on the axe is written in one

of the scripts used in Minoan Crete. Lastly, the ideograms on the axe are distinctly primitive in design and simply do not bear comparison with the draughtsmanship of the punches used on the Phaistos Disc.

37. The ring was found in 1926 when Evans's foreman, while searching in a field being ploughed near Mavro Spileo, discovered a passage leading to a chamber tomb. On opening the tomb he found this ring, just 13 mm. in diameter, with nineteen Linear A syllabograms carved on it in a spiral. See the paper by Evans's successor, E.J. Forsdyke, 'The Mavro Spelio Cemetery at Knossos', *BSA* 28 (1926-1927) 243-296, tables XVII-XXIII.
38. On writing in Cyprus generally, see J. F. Daniel, 'Prolegomena to the Cypro-Minoan Script', *AJA* 45 (1941) 249-282; Jacqueline V. Karageorghis, 'Quelques observations sur l'origine du syllabaire chypro-minoen', *RA* 2 (1958) 1-19; Ead., 'Histoire de l'écriture chypriote', *ΚΣ* 25 (1961) 43-60.
39. See Evans, *Scripta Minoa* I, 68-73.
40. On the Mycenaean presence in Cyprus see V. Karageorghis, *Οἱ πρῶτοι Ἕλληνες στήν Κύπρο. Ἀρχαιολογικές μαρτυρίες*, tr. D. Kyriakou and K. Touloumis, Athens 1991.
41. On the decipherment of the Cypriot syllabary see E. Doblhofer, *Voices in Stone: The Decipherment of Ancient Scripts and Writings*, tr. M. Savill, London 1973, Ch. VII.
42. On the origin of the Cypriot syllabary see J. Chadwick, 'The Minoan Origin of the Classical Cypriot Script', in *Acts of the International Archaeological Symposium 'The Relations between Cyprus and Crete, ca. 2000-500 B.C.'*, Nicosia 1979, 139-143.
43. See V. Karageorghis, "Οἱ ἀρχαῖοι Ἕλληνες στήν Κύπρο" in Demakopoulou, *The Mycenaean World*, 64-65; T.B. Mitford and O. Masson, 'The Cypriot Syllabary', in *Cambridge Ancient History*, III.3, Cambridge 1982^2, 71-82. On the Greek language in Cyprus generally, see Jacqueline Karageorghis and O. Masson (eds.), *The History of the Greek Language in Cyprus: Proceedings of an International Symposium sponsored by the Pierides Foundation, Larnaca, 8-13 September 1986*, Nicosia 1988.
44. On Cypro-Minoan scripts and research in this field, see T. G. Palaima, 'Cypro-Minoan Scripts: Problems of Historical Context', in *Problems in Decipherment*, 121-187. On the classical Cypriot syllabary see O. Masson, *Les inscriptions chypriotes syllabiques*, Paris 1983.
45. See E.L. Bennett, Jr., 'Anonymous Writers in Mycenaean Palaces', *Archaeology* 13 (1960) 26-32; also the fictitious diary of a scribe's working day by Eftychia Stavrianopoulou, "Μία ἀσυνήθιστη μέρα τοῦ ἀνακτορικοῦ γραφέα Κεραμέα" in A. Haniotis (ed.), *Ἔργα καί Ἡμέρες στήν Κρήτη, Ἀπό τήν Προϊστορία στό Μεσοπόλεμο*, Iraklion 2000, 73-119.
46. See C. Camera, 'Una presunta scuola degli scrivani a Cnosso', *SMEA* 7 (1968) 116-128.
47. T. G. Palaima, 'Evidence for the Identification of a Master Scribe at Pylos', *AJA* 84 (1980) 226.
48. On the various writing styles, classified according to the characteristic features of each individual scribe's handwriting, see J.-P. Olivier, *Les Scribes de Cnossos. Essai de classement des archives d'un palais mycénien*, Rome 1967; T. G. Palaima, *The Scribes of Pylos*, Rome 1988. On the identification of the same scribe working in two different palaces, see J. Driessen's doctoral dissertation, *The Scribes of the Room of the Chariot Tablets at Knossos. Interdisciplinary Approach to the Study of*

a Linear B Deposit [*Minos* Suppl. 15], Salamanca 2000, 230-232.

49. From the evidence presently at our disposal, it seems that there was a basic difference between the scribes of the Minoan-Mycenaean civilization and those of Mesopotamia and Egypt. As far as I am aware, the names of scribes writing in the Cretan scripts are never mentioned, or at least they have not come down to us, whereas in the Mesopotamian civilizations not only did most scribes sign their tablets, from the Fara period (*ca.* 2600 B.C.) onwards, but many of them became famous and were treated with honour and respect even by royalty. In fact there are many cases where a scribe wrote in the colophons of his tablets not only his own name but also the names of his father, his ancestors and the founder of his family or of the 'dynasty' of scribes to which he belonged: see C. B. F. Walker, 'Le cunéiforme', in Larissa Bonfante et al., *La naissance des écritures: Du cunéiforme à l'alphabet* (= *Reading the Past: Ancient Writing from Cuneiform to the Alphabet*, London 1990, tr. Christiane Zivie-Coche), Paris 1994, 27-29. On the scribes of Ugarit, a city with which the Minoans and Mycenaeans traded on a fairly large scale, see A. F. Rainey, 'The Scribe in Ugarit', *Proceedings of the Israel Academy of Sciences and Humanities* 11 (1969) 136-146; J. Krecher, 'Schreiberschulung in Ugarit: Die Tradition von Listen und sumerischen Texten', *UF* 1 (1969) 131-158; W. J. Horwitz, 'The Ugaritic Scribe', *UF* 11 (1979) 389-394.
50. The stylus was the basic implement for writing on tablets in the Minoan-Mycenaean civilization. Louis Godart has conducted experiments to show exactly how Linear B characters were inscribed on a tablet, using a stylus of bone and bronze resembling a lancet with a sharp, curved point. Bone styli 13 cm. in length and 0.5 cm. in diameter were found by Christos Piteros when he excavated the Liangas property in Thebes in 1982.
51. See P. Åström and S. A. Eriksson, *Fingerprints and Archaeology* [*SIMA* 28], Göteborg 1980.
52. On the preparation of tablets, their size and shape and the writing process, see Ruipérez and Melena, *Οἱ Μυκηναῖοι Ἕλληνες*, 50-66. On palm-prints and fingerprints see K-E. Sjöquist and P. Åström, *Pylos: Palmprints and Palmleaves*, Göteborg 1985; and on archivists and kneaders see K-E. Sjöquist and P. Åström, *Knossos: Keepers and Kneaders* [*SIMA Pocketbook* 82], Göteborg 1991.
53. To what extent other writing materials were used in the Creto-Mycenaean world is a matter of conjecture. However, Olivier's notes on the contracts for the sale of 'slaves' (J.-P. Olivier, 'Des extraits de contrats de vente d'esclaves dans les tablettes de Knossos', in *Studies Chadwick*, 497-498) support the hypothesis that other materials besides clay were used for archival records, as does the discovery of a writing board in the Ulu Burun shipwreck. For a general discussion of this topic see R. Payton, 'The Ulu Burun Writing-Board Set', *Anatolian Studies* 91 (1991) 99-106; D. Symington, 'Late Bronze Age Writing Boards and Their Uses: Textual Evidence from Anatolia and Syria', *Anatolian Studies* 91 (1991) 111-123.
54. On looking through Egyptian prose literature and poetry, I have found no reference to any mythological writings or novels of the Keftiu (as the Egyptians called the Cretans), nor to descriptions of Crete by travellers or merchants. References to Crete do exist in Egyptian writings, of course: the Ebers Papyrus

contains a prescription for a laxative made of 'Keftiu beans' and the 'Admonitions of Ipuwer' states that 'the Keftiu come no more'; and a wall-painting at Egyptian Thebes depicts the Keftiu bringing precious gifts to the Pharaoh's court. These references, and others carved on tombs and monuments, date from the Eighteenth and Nineteenth Dynasties (*ca.* 1580-1200 B.C.). On Egyptian literature in general see esp.: G. Maspero, *Les contes populaires de l'Égypte ancienne*, Paris 1882; A. Erman, *Die Literatur des Aegypter*, Leipzig 1923; A.H. Gardiner, *Late Egyptian Stories*, Brussels 1932; S. Schott, *Les chants d'amour de l'Égypte ancienne*, Paris 1956; G. Lefebvre, *Romans et contes égyptiens de l'époque pharaonique*, Paris 1988. On ancient Egyptian love poems see Ch.E. Maravelias, *Τά Ἐρωτικά Ποιήματα τῆς Ἀρχαίας Αἰγύπτου*, Athens 1996.
For an imaginary account of a voyage from Egypt to Crete in 1425 B.C. (in the reign of Thothmes III), see D. Panayiotopoulos, "Ἡ ἀφήγηση τοῦ Μίν. Τό χρονικό μιᾶς αἰγυπτιακῆς ἀποστολῆς στή Μινωική Κρήτη" in Haniotis, *Ἔργα καί ἡμέρες...*, [1]-53.

55. See C.F.A. Schaeffer, *The Cuneiform Text of Ras Schamra–Ugarit*, London 1939; C.H. Gordon, *Ugaritic Literature*, Rome 1940; H.L. Ginsberg, *The Legend of King Keret*, New Haven 1946; Sibylle von Reden, *Ugarit und seine Welt*, Lübbe 1992. Some excerpts from the literature of the Near East are given (in Greek) by D. Tsinikopoulos in his book *Φῶς ἐξ Ἀνατολῆς (Ex Oriente Lux). Λογοτεχνικά κείμενα τῆς ἀρχαίας Ἐγγύς Ἀνατολῆς*, Athens 1996.
56. On the difference between real archives and deposits, see E.C. Harris, *Principles of Archaeological Stratigraphy*, London 1979; and J.K. Stein, 'Deposits for Archaeologists', *Advances in Archaeological Method and Theory* 11 (1987) 337-395. Palaima (*The Scribes of Pylos*, 180) and J.-P. Olivier ('Administrations at Knossos and Pylos. What Differences?' in *Pylos Comes Alive*, 15) use the terms 'specialized and non-specialized bureaux' when referring to the writing workshops.
57. Olivier, *Les Scribes de Cnossos*, 21.
58. See J. Bennet, 'The Structure of the Linear B Administration at Knossos', *AJA* 89 (1985) 231-249; J.-P. Olivier, 'Structure des archives palatiales en Linéaire A et en Linéaire B', in *Système palatial*, 227-235.
59. For general information on the storage arrangements and interior layout of archive rooms and the containers used for keeping inscribed tablets in the Near East, see E. Posner, *Archives in the Ancient World*, Cambridge, Mass. 1972, 17-70; K.R. Veenhof (ed.), *Cuneiform Archives and Libraries* [*Uitgaven van het Nederlands Historisch-Archaeologisch Instituut te Istanbul* 57], Leiden 1986; J.A. Black and W.J. Tait, 'Archives and Libraries in the Ancient Near East', in Jack M. Sasson (ed.), *Civilizations of the Ancient Near East*, New York 1995, IV, 2197-2209. On archival filing methods in particular, see M. Weitemeyer, 'Archive and Library Technique in Ancient Mesopotamia', *Libri* 6 (1956) 217-238. On recent finds of archives and libraries dating from 1500 B.C. and after in the Near East, see O. Pedersén, *Archives and Libraries in the Near East 1500-300 B.C.*, Bethesda, Md. 1998.
60. Driessen, *The Scribes of the Room of the Chariot Tablets...*, 232.
61. So called because of the pictures of chariots incised on the tablets found there.
62. See A.J. Evans, 'Knossos: Summary Report of the Excavations in 1900', *BSA*

6 (1899-1900) 24; Driessen, *An Early Destruction...*, 64-66.

63. J. Driessen, 'The Scribes of the "Room of the Chariot Tablets"', in *Studies Bennett*, 123-165.
64. See J. Chadwick, 'The Archive of the Room of the Chariot Tablets at Knossos', in *Minutes of the London Seminar 12.10.1966*, 329-331; Id., 'The Archive of the Room of the Chariot Tablets at Knossos', *BICS* 14 (1967) 103-104.
65. For general information on the sealings see T. G. Palaima, 'Seal-Users and Script-Users/Nodules and Tablets at LM IB Hagia Triada' in *Archives Before Writing*, 307-337; J. Weingarten, 'The Sealing Bureaucracy of Mycenaean Knossos: The identification of some officials and their seals', in *Crète mycénienne*, 517-535.
66. On the *sillybos*, the more highly-developed form of label for papyrus rolls, see Ch. III.
67. On the sealings and the speculation concerning their uses, see Ruipérez and Melena, *Οἱ Μυκηναῖοι Ἕλληνες*, 60-62.
68. On the clay labels of the tablets found at Ugarit, see W. H. Van Soldt, 'Labels from Ugarit', *UF* 21 (1989) 375-388.

II

FROM HOMER
TO THE END OF
THE CLASSICAL PERIOD

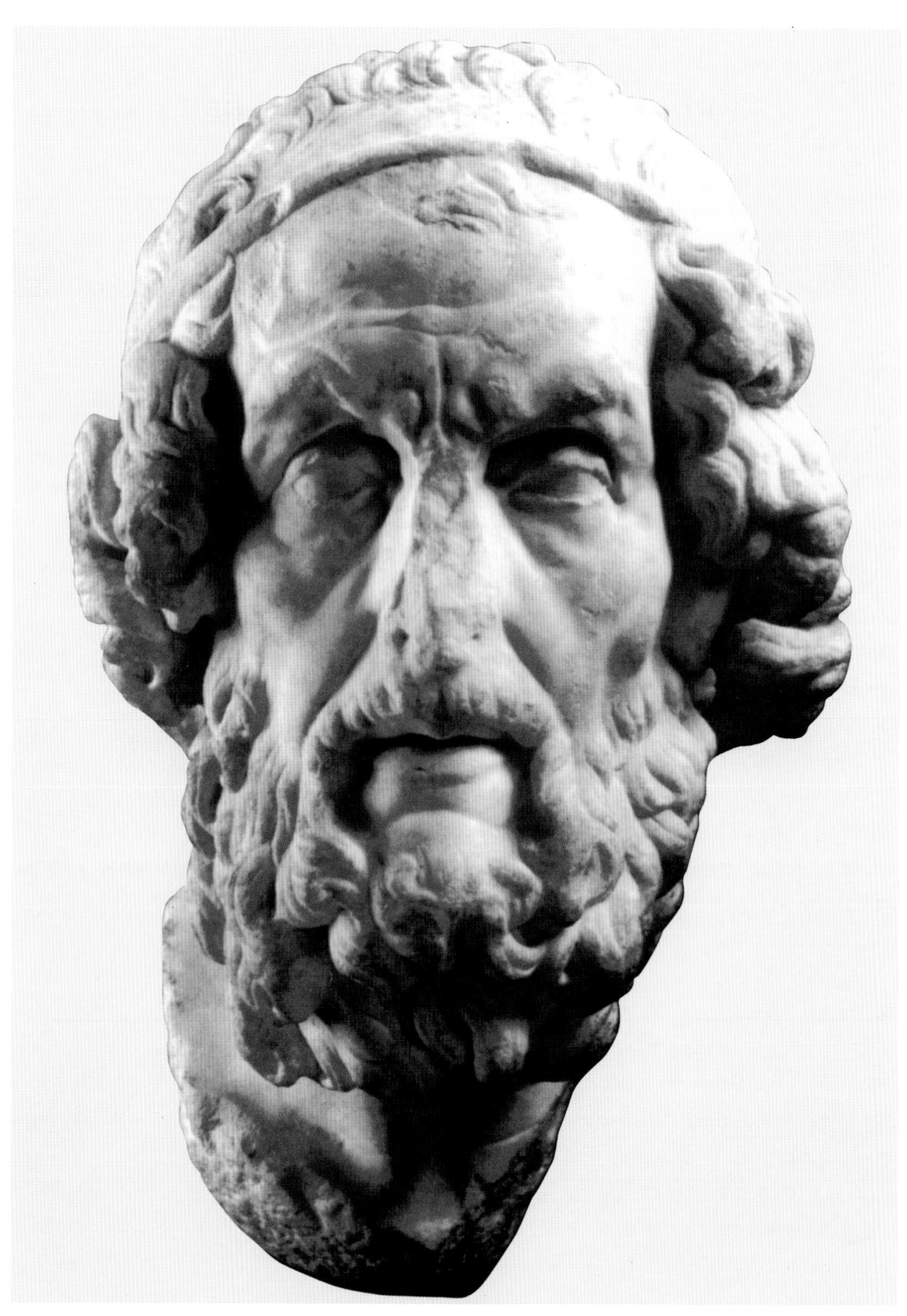

38. Head of Homer: marble copy.

FROM HOMER TO THE END OF THE CLASSICAL PERIOD

Public, Academic and Private Libraries in the Greek World

In dealing with the subject of literary writing and the crystallization of the alphabet in books, in ancient Greece and the Western world generally, the first obstacle one is faced with is the thorny one known as the 'Homeric question'. That is because, from the collapse of the Mycenaean world in about 1200 B.C. (when the art of writing appears to have been forgotten) until the time when rhapsodists started singing of the exploits of the Trojan War, everything we know about the Greek world and its traditions and customs is derived from archaeological evidence. Whether any written or oral literature existed in the Minoan and Mycenaean ages is a question that has yet to be answered, and consequently the place of the Homeric oral tradition in Greek literature is a matter of prime importance in the history of books. In fact, the story of Greek books and the circumstances that led the Greeks to collect written material in libraries starts with Homer and the tradition that grew up around his name, from antiquity to the present day.

Facts and presumptions about Homer's life

The Homeric question. When did Homer live? Herodotus says that he lived not more than four hundred years before his time: since we know that the great historian was writing in the middle of the fifth century, that would put Homer's lifetime in the middle of the ninth century, around 850 B.C. But by the Classical period Homer had already passed into the realm of myth: Philostratus thought he had lived in the twelfth century, while Eratosthenes, Aristotle, Aristarchus and Theopompus placed him a hundred years later, in the eleventh. Diogenes Laertius (3rd cent. A.D.), working from earlier biographical notes on poets and philosophers, seems to have concluded that Homer lived in the sixth century B.C., the time of Pisistratus and Solon.[1] The next point at issue is: did Homer compose both the *Iliad* and the *Odyssey*? This is a question that will probably never be answered. While many have gone so far as to maintain that Homer had no literary knowledge whatever, most literary scholars nowadays accept that he was a poetic genius who managed to give an age-old oral tradition a distinctive character that was due to the economy necessitated by the oral method of composition. Milman Parry and Albert Lord proved that both the *Iliad* and the *Odyssey* were basically oral compositions, regardless of the reasons that eventually led to their being written down.[2] Pursuing their line of thought, they concluded that those thousands of hexameters – 15,680 lines in the *Iliad* and 12,100 in the *Odyssey* – were not composed simply of individual words but of stock phrases, or groups of words adapted to the material of tradition and put together in such a way as fit into a hexameter. And so, for the heroes and gods of the Homeric epics – Achilles, Hector and Odysseus, Athena and Apollo and all the others – the bard used adjectives and verbs that were perfectly suited to the requirements of the metre. Thus it is clear that Homer had a 'phrase list' ready-formed in his mind and used his stock phrases again and again, with an admirable sense of good order and harmony.

Rhapsodists and the Homeric oral tradition

Furthermore, the fact that the Greek word *rhapsodos* (rhapsodist) comes from the verb *rhapto* (sew) and the noun *ode* (song) takes us straight to the poet who established this tradition: Homer 'stitched together' ready-made passages of poetry. The language of the Homeric epics, a mixture of early and later Aeolian and Ionian idioms, is best explained not as an agglomeration of different texts but as a language formed over the years by bards using long-established expressions and epithets which they perpetuated and adapted as the need arose, mainly in conformity with the dictates of the metre. After a long process of continual modification by rhapsodists, the *Iliad* and the *Odyssey* were eventually written down at an unknown date which is still in dispute among scholars. The language of the two epics was not the vernacular Greek of every use but a special language brought into being by the bardic tradition and passed on from one rhapsodist to another, from one generation to the next.[3]

In which period, then, did the events take place that Homer describes in his epics? Since Schliemann discovered Troy in 1870, raising hopes that Homer's works would prove to have been based on historical fact, archaeology has made such enormous strides that it is no longer possible for 'mythological' interpretations to be placed on archaeological finds: eleven cities of Troy succeeded one another on the historic hill which the ancient Greeks called Ilium (Ilion). In fact the Troy of what is known as 'Priam's treasure', that is Troy II, flourished at least a thousand years before the Trojan War, somewhere between 2500 and 2200 B.C. Not only was the Troy of the thirteenth or twelfth century a very ordinary town

39. The first edition of the complete works (Σωζόμενα) of Homer. Florence, Bartolomeo di Libri and [Demetrios Damilas], 1488/1489.

ἁρπαλέως ἀκέων, κακὰ δὲ μνηστῆρσι φύτευεν.
αὐτὰρ ἐπεὶ δείπνησε καὶ ἤραρε θυμὸν ἐδωδῇ,
καί οἱ πλησάμενος δῶκε σκύφος ᾧ περ ἔπινεν
οἴνου ἐμπλεῖον. ὁ δ' ἐδέξατο, χαῖρε δὲ θυμῷ.
καί μιν φωνήσας ἔπεα πτερόεντα προσηύδα.
ὦ φίλε, τίς γάρ σε πρίατο κτεάτεσσιν ἑοῖσιν.
ὧδε μάλ' ἀφνειὸς καὶ καρτερὸς ὡς ἀγορεύεις
φῂς δ' αὐτὸν φθίσθαι Ἀγαμέμνονος εἵνεκα τιμῆς.
εἰπέ μοι αἴ κέ ποθι γνώω τοιοῦτον ἐόντα
Ζεὺς γάρ που τό γε οἶδε καὶ ἀθάνατοι θεοὶ ἄλλοι
εἴ κέ μιν ἀγγείλαιμι ἰδών· ἐπὶ πολλὰ δ' ἀλήθην.
τὸν δ' ἠμείβετ' ἔπειτα συβώτης ὄρχαμος ἀνδρῶν
ὦ γέρον. οὔ τις κεῖνον ἀνὴρ ἀλαλήμενος ἐλθὼν
ἀγγέλλων πείσειε γυναῖκά τε καὶ φίλον υἱόν
ἀλλ' ἄλλως κομιδῆς κεχρημένοι ἄνδρες ἀλῆται.
ψεύδοντ' οὐδ' ἐθέλουσιν ἀληθέα μυθήσασθαι.
ὃς δέ κ' ἀλητεύων Ἰθάκης ἐς δῆμον ἵκηται
ἐλθὼν ἐς δέσποιναν ἐμὴν ἀπατήλια βάζει.
ἡ δ' εὖ δεξαμένη φιλέει καὶ ἕκαστα μεταλλᾷ.
καί οἱ ὀδυρομένῃ βλεφάρων ἄπο δάκρυα πίπτει
ἣ θέμις ἐστὶ γυναικὸς ἐπὴν πόσις ἄλλοθ' ὄληται.
αἶψά κε καὶ σὺ γεραιὲ ἔπος παρατεκτήναιο
εἴ τίς τοι χλαῖνάν τε χιτῶνά τε εἵματα δοίη
τοῦ δ' ἤδη μέλλουσι κύνες ταχέες τ' οἰωνοὶ
ῥινὸν ἀπ' ὀστεόφιν ἐρύσαι, ψυχὴ δὲ λέλοιπεν.
ἢ τόν γ' ἐν πόντῳ φάγον ἰχθύες. ὀστέα δ' αὐτοῦ
κεῖται ἐπ' ἠπείρου ψαμάθῳ εἰλυμένα πολλῇ
ὣς ὁ μὲν ἔνθ' ἀπόλωλε φίλοισι δὲ κήδε' ὀπίσσω
πᾶσιν. ἐμοὶ δὲ μάλιστα τετεύχαται, οὐ γὰρ ἔτ' ἄλλον
ἤπιον ὧδε ἄνακτα κιχήσομαι ὁππόσ' ἐπέλθω.
οὐδ' εἴ κεν πατρὸς καὶ μητέρος αὖτις ἵκωμαι
οἶκον. ὅθι πρῶτον γενόμην καί μ' ἔτρεφον αὐτοί.
οὐδέ νυ τῶν ἔτι τόσσον ὀδύρομαι ἱέμενός περ
ὀφθαλμοῖσιν ἰδέσθαι, ἐὼν ἐν πατρίδι γαίῃ
ἀλλά μ' Ὀδυσσῆος πόθος αἴνυται οἰχομένοιο
τὸν μὲν ἐγὼν ὦ ξεῖνε καὶ οὐ παρεόντ' ὀνομάζειν
αἰδέομαι. πέρι γάρ μ' ἐφίλει καὶ κήδετο θυμῷ.
ἀλλά μιν ἠθεῖον καλέω καὶ νόσφιν ἐόντα.
τὸν δ' αὖτε προσέειπε πολύτλας δῖος Ὀδυσσεύς.

of that period, and a fairly poor one, without the sort of formidable walls that would stand up to a ten-year siege by the combined armies of the Greeks; but we now know that that Troy was destroyed around 1275 B.C. by an earthquake, not sacked by a besieging army.[4] Hector himself, in the *Iliad* (XVIII.288-292), admits that Troy is no longer famed for its wealth as it used to be.

Literary scholars and archaeologists nowadays tend to agree that the Homeric world was entirely post-Mycenaean and that such Mycenaean elements as feature in it are rare, isolated, sporadic survivals. Is the Mycenaean world the one described by Homer? On this question, too, scholarly opinion is divided. The inference to be drawn from attempts to match Homer's subject matter with the archaeological finds is that in the *Iliad* and *Odyssey* Homer really was painting a picture of a much earlier society, the memory of which had been kept alive

40. Reconstruction of Troy VI (1700-1250 B.C.), with the royal palace in the acropolis and the rest of the town on the lower slopes.

in people's minds by the oral tradition; in fact some traditional customs would almost certainly have remained unchanged over the centuries. That does not mean, of course, that Homer actually gives an accurate description of Mycenaean Greece, especially considering that he would have had in his mind only a very confused idea of mainland Greece and many of the islands, including distant Crete. Some scholars have argued that the Catalogue of Ships in Book II of the *Iliad* is intended as a gazetteer of the Mycenaean world, so to speak, and – as we shall see – it is possible that the Catalogue became a bone of contention that led to the Homeric epics' being written down for the first time, in whole or in part.[5]

The historical background of Homer's world

A great many years passed between Homer's lifetime and the time when the rhapsodies were preserved in writing in a fixed form, and the ancients were uncertain not only about when he lived, but about where he came from as well. Seven city-states claimed the honour of being the birthplace of the blind bard, as he was called by the Greeks on the evidence of a Hellenistic portrait head of him, of which we have a Roman copy (Fig. 37). On the island of Chios, one of those seven, there is a rock carved into the shape of a seat which the local people still point out to visitors as 'Homer's Rock', from which he is alleged to have recited his verses. Chios was the birthplace of the Homeridae, a guild of rhapsodists who claimed to be directly descended from Homer and are said to have undertaken a commitment to perpetuate his poems: it may well be that they were at the root of the written tradition.[6]

41. Heinrich Schliemann. Engraving. Behind him are the Helios metope from the Temple of Athena at Hissarlik (Troy) (left) and the Lion Gate at Mycenae (right).

The 'legend' of the first edition of Homer. I have spent a little time discussing the Homeric question and the other subjects touched on above as an introduction to the world of Greek books, to draw attention to the origins of the written tradition as represented in the Homeric epics, in addition to its generally accepted connection with the first Greek public library. In Book VI of the *Iliad* we find Glaucus, one of the heroes fighting on the Trojan side, telling the story of his grandfather Bellerophon, who won eternal fame by slaying the Chimaera. Bellerophon, who had been sent to the king of Lycia bearing a message that contained his own death sentence: 'a folded tablet on which were incised a number of signs with a deadly meaning'.[7] This is the only reference to writing in Homer and the first such reference in Greek literature.

There are three significant items of information to be gleaned from this important line of verse. The first concerns the material on which the message was written: it was a tablet (*pinax*), that is a hinged pair of wooden boards coated with *maltha* (a mixture of wax and pitch), which is known to have been used a writing surface in the Mycenaean world from the middle of the second millennium B.C.[8] The second has to do with the type of script used – the 'signs' mentioned by Homer: these must have been Linear B symbols, since Homer was describing events that took place long before his time, and even at the time when he was composing his rhapsodies the alphabet had yet to be adopted by the Greeks. Thirdly, the fact that Bellerophon was the bearer of his own death sentence suggests that it was common knowledge that the only people who knew how to read and write in the Bronze Age were scribes and a small coterie of high-ranking dignitaries and officials.[9]

42. The tombs excavated by Schliemann at Troy. Engraving, 1881.

When were the Homeric epics preserved in writing in book form? In what oral form Homer passed them on to the Homeridae, and how that form compares with the text we have today, are questions that will remain forever unanswered. What increases the uncertainty is that these rhapsodies were composed for recitation to the rich and powerful in different parts of the Greek world and that the itinerant rhapsodists often adapted their language and wording to suit a particular audience. Be all that as it may, the Homeric epics were not preserved in writing in a fixed form before the middle of the eighth century B.C., when the alphabet came into general use in the Greek world.[10] The received wisdom on this subject is that the initiative of putting the *Iliad* and *Odyssey* on paper was taken in about 560 B.C. by Pisistratus, the 'tyrant' of Athens, for reasons connected with the dispute between Athens and Megara over Salamis.[11]

Pisistratus, founder of the first public library in Athens

An edition of Homer under Pisistratus(?). The story is as follows. In the sixth century B.C. the Athenians came into conflict with the Megarians over the sovereignty of Salamis, which had been a bone of contention since Solon's time. Pisistratus, the Athenian ruler, is said to have 'won great renown' in the fighting, and that helped him to establish himself in power.[12] The problem had arisen when the Megarians disputed the authenticity of Homer's 'Catalogue of Ships', which the Athenians cited as evidence that their association with the Salaminians dated back to before the Trojan War. The Megarians contended that the Athenians had corrupted the 'authentic text' by interpolating some extra lines to give added weight to their arguments.[13] But there was no authentic written text of the *Iliad* for either side to refer to in its own support, and so, for political rather than cultural reasons, Pisistratus took it upon himself to produce the first written edition of the Homeric epics. What is more, he undertook to pay an obol per line, even for lines that were repeated.[14]

43. Solon. Engraving, 19th c. Published by J. Wilks, London 1807.

Before drawing any conclusions or making any conjectures about the truth of this tradition, it is worth reviewing the literary evidence. Back in the early nineteenth century George Grote discussed the matter at some length in his *History of Greece*,[15] as did many other scholars. Grote was very scathing about the legend that Pisistratus had deposited an authentic Attic first edition of Homer's

Ille Troys in dardania regnauit et troyā condidit.

Anchises

Anchises ex dea venē sm̄ erro rez gētiliū genuit Eneaz. q̄ in Ytalia regnuit vt patuit.

Laomedon

Laomedō rex troye occidit ⁊ Ixiona filia eius capit ⁊ ducit i greciā ꝓpt̄ q̄ bella ğuissima secuta sunt et mala horrendissima

Troya regio minoris asie in q̃ Ilion fuit ciuitas cantatissima. Nōnunq̄ʒ vero ꝓ ipa vrbe troya ponitur. Et sm̄ homerū oīm que sub sole ac stellifero celo sunt vrbiū quidē insignissima est troya. Nūc aūt ingens Troya totiꝰ asie columē ita extincta est. vt vix vestigiū aliq̄ꝺ appareat. qꝺ Ouidiꝰ inq̄t. Jam seges est vbi troya fuit. Silr̄ virgilius. Campꝰ vbi troya fuit. Cū ea exusta lapides ⁊ quecunq̄ʒ alia inde ablata sunt. Talis finis humanaꝝ reꝝ. Tros aūt Erichtonij regis filius Anno quadragesimo iudicis aioth iam veteranꝰ dardaniā veniēs Troyā cōdidit. vir armoꝝ peritissimꝰ. ampliato regno ex suo noīe regionem q̄ prius dardania dicebat̄ Troyā appellauit. Dardanꝰ eñ fuit ex Ioue ⁊ electra filia Athlātis genita. Is ad phrigiā deuenit quā dardaniā nomīauit. Ex quo natꝰ Erichtoniꝰ ex eo tros qui iusticia ⁊ pietate laudabilis fuit: Isq̄ʒ vt memoriā sui noīs faceret Troyā appellari iussit. q̄ duos habuit filios. Ilion Asara. cunq̄ʒ primꝰ maioꝛ natu regnās troyā de suo noīe Iliū noīauit. Ilio laomedō fuit filius ex quo priamus natus est. Is troyā pꝰ suā primā diruptionē reformauit ⁊ exornauit. ac vrbē magnā ⁊ āpliora menia ac ꝓpugnacula ex lapidibꝰ marmoreis cū murꝭ altissimo extruxit ⁊ munitissimā reddidit. multitudinēq̄ʒ militū eē fec̄. ne ꝑ ignorātiā opp̄meret̄. vt priꝰ tp̄e laomedōtis opp̄ssa fuit. Regiā q̄ʒ edificauit ⁊ iouis statuā: ⁊ arā ꝯsecrauit. Ilio sex portas fecit. q̄rū h̄ sūt noīa. Anthenoidas. Ilia. Scea. Thymbria. Dardanides. Troyana Per mediū ciuitatis fluuiꝰ Xantꝰ decurrebat. Simois q̄ʒ fluuiꝰ ex Ida troyano mōte scaturiēs iuxta troyā decurrens. q̄ cū mari appropinq̄t̄ xanto cōmiscet̄. Et in paludē coactꝰ iuxta sigeum ꝓmontoriū in mare descendit Priamꝰ āt ex heccuba vxore hos hūit libos. Hectorē p̄io natū. Alexādrū: Deiphebū. Helenū. Troylū: Andromachā. Cassandrā: Polixenā. Pugnatū ē deiñ cū troyanis ꝑ grecos ānis. x. ⁊ mēsibꝰ sex. P̄io Esebon iudic̄ āno. cꝰ causaʒ dicūt. Cū alexāder q̄ Paris dictꝰ ē in Ida silua cū venatu abijssʒ i somnis Mercuriū ad-

Troya

Troyanum bellū decēnale primo Esebon siue Abesson iudicis anno (teste eusebio) surrexit. quo tpe sequētes claruerūt. Troya eīn quā Ilion tros regis troyanoꝝ filius amplissimā instaurauit mille ꝛ quingentis passibus a mari remota erat: vbi oīm rerum vbertas erat: Ipsa quippe que decēnalem grecorum obsidionem passa fuit: et ab eis tandē deleta.

Hercules

Hercules ille cū Jasone troyā vastauit que statim a priamo fuit reedificata. Idez hercules agonē olimpiacū cōstituit et bella multa cōfecit quē dicūt duodecim insignes et inhumanos pfecisse labores.

Menela⁹ Helena

Helena fuit vxor menelai regis ꝛ a pari de filio priami rapitur. ꝛ ad troyā pducitur. ꝓpter qd̄ troyanū bellū exortū. Ipsam tn̄ post troye excidium Greci menelao reddiderūt. ꝙ gaudēs nauim cū illa cōscendit patriam petitur⁹: sed tēpestatib⁹ acti in egiptū ad polibuz regez deuenere. Indeqz discedentes octo ānis errātes (vt testis est eusebi⁹) tandez in patriam redierunt.

Hector

Iste hector fuit pmo genitus priami ex hecuba vxore incōpabilis fortitudinis et strēnuitatis. Jō ob maximū ei⁹ militie fulgorem apud troyanos maxio in precio habitus est. Nā ob incredibilē ei⁹ prudētiā atqz fortitudinē nō solū parētes: sed et patriā nobilitate atqz gl'ia splēdidā fecit. hic ex Andromacha ꝯiuge plures genuit filios. E qb⁹ frāc⁹ vn⁹ fuit A ꝙ (vt ait vincēti⁹ hystorial' burgūd⁹) frāci originē habuere.

Paris

Paris qui et Alexāder dict⁹ est eiusdē hectoris frater: ex priamo ꝛ hecuba nat⁹: sb̄ specie legatiōis cū .xx. nauib⁹ in greciā mittitur Et a menelao hospicio suscipit. Cui⁹ cū aspexisset vxorez illaz. absente marito tandē cū oībus regijs thezauris abstulit et Troyam pduxit. Ex qua rapina bellum decēnale grecoꝝ aduersus troyanos susceptū est. Hic cū troyanis vrbem obsidentib⁹ multa strēnue gessisset: A pirrho achillis filio occisus fuit.

Agamenon

Agamenon fuit frater regis Menelai dux toti⁹ exercitus grecoꝝ. cōtra troyā bellauit. ꝙ tandem traditorie et turpissime capit. fuitqz Atrei regis fili⁹. ab omni exercitu imperator designatus. ad bellū pergens Clitemestram coniugez ex qua multos susceperat filios reliquit. Et apud troyam multos passus labores. ꝛ simultates principum pro quibus ab imperio depositus ꝛ illi palamedes suffect⁹ est. Quē cum vlixes occidisset ipse maiori gloria imperium reassumpsit. Tandez Troya capta et diruta cum ingenti preda et cassandra priami filia in patriam rediturus naues conscendit Uerum ꝛ ipse tempestate actus. ꝑ annū ferme errauit.

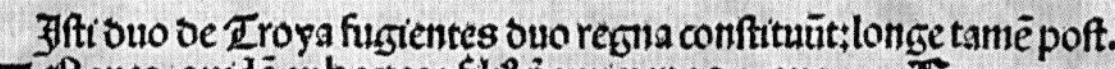

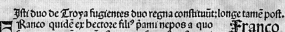

Isti duo de Troya fugientes duo regna constituūt; longe tamē post.

Franco

Franco quidē ex hectore fili⁹ priami nepos a quo francoꝝ nomē tractū est. a troya fugat⁹ postea tota Asia puagata in danubij ripis tandē puenit. Ibi cū aliqādiu cōsedisset. deinde locum querēs a cōmuni hominū societate seiunctū: ad thanai fluentia ꝛ paludes meotidas secessit. vbi Sicambriā condidit vrbem.

Turcus

Turcus fili⁹ Troili filij regis Priami. A ꝙ pplm ab eo descendentē. quidem turcos denoīari dicūt. Alij eoꝝ originē ex Scythia referunt.

works in a public library that he himself had founded. He was also critical of the readiness with which the legend had been accepted by such great textual scholars as Wolf and, more particularly, Müller and Lachmann. The earliest written reference to the Megarians' accusation of forgery probably occurs in the work of two Megarian historians of the fourth century B.C., Dieuchidas[16] and Hereas.[17] Neither of them ever described Pisistratus as a 'collector' of rhapsodies, but they did refer to additions to and corruptions of the Homeric text instigated by Solon or Pisistratus. The first writer to name Pisistratus as the publisher of Homer was Cicero (*De Oratore*, III.34) in the first century B.C., nearly three hundred years after the Megarian historians, and scholars have been debating the question ever since. Cicero's source may have been the grammarian and historian Asclepiades of Myrleia, a contemporary of his, who was living in Rome at the time of publication of his book *De Grammaticis*, a systematic history of literature.[18]

46. Thetis in Hephaestus's workshop. Red-figure kylix (interior) by the Foundry Painter, ca. *490-480* B.C.

The dispute over the traditional attribution set down in writing by Cicero actually has its roots much earlier. What is certain is that by the sixth century B.C. itinerant rhapsodists had made Homer's epics known in many Greek cities and that they took part in competitions, often with a large audience. According to Diogenes Laertius, Solon – who was something of a poet himself – had stressed the importance of the Homeric oeuvre when he was in power in Athens and had initiated the rhapsodists' competitions in the Panathenaea festival.[19] At any rate, whether Solon actually initiated the competitions or whether he had merely intended to do so and it was left to Pisistratus to put the idea into practice, what interests us here is that in the competitions Homer's

'Literary' disputes between Athens and Megara

☜

44-45. The first printed reconstruction of Troy and portraits of heroes of the Trojan War. From H. Schedel, Liber Chronicarum, *Nürnberg 1493, ff.* XXXVI-XXXVII.

works were recited in a specified order, and when one rhapsodist stepped down the next one had to carry on from the exact point where his predecessor had broken off. This implies that there existed a standard version of Homer, in writing and almost certainly generally accepted, which could be consulted by rhapsodists and judges alike. However, this does not necessarily mean that there was a published edition in existence.

The wording used by ancient authors writing about this innovation certainly supports the conclusion expressed above. According to Diogenes Laertius, Solon laid down that Homer's works were to be recited in a fixed order (*ἐξ ὑποβολῆς*),[20] and in the pseudo-Platonic dialogue *Hipparchus* we are told that they had to be recited 'in relay' (*ἐξ ὑπολήψεως*).[21] Although the phrases *ἐξ ὑποβολῆς* and *ἐξ ὑπολήψεως* do not have the same meaning, the implication in both cases is that there was a prompter whose job it was to make sure that the excerpts followed each other in the 'right' order according to the sequence of events in the narrative or a commonly accepted order of the rhapsodies, while it is clear that formerly each rhapsodist had recited his excerpt or excerpts in any order he chose.[22]

47. Achilles bandaging the wounded Patroclus. Red-figure kylix by the Sosias Painter, ca. *500* B.C. *Berlin, Archaeological Museum.*

Was there an 'authentic' Attic first edition of Homer?

The confusion created by conflicting anachronistic evidence concerning the existence of an authentic Attic copy of all Homer's work in about 570-560 B.C. is reflected in a vase-painting representing another side of Athenian cultural life. It is on a black-figure krater known as the François Vase and depicts a chariot-race at the funeral games in honour of the slain Patroclus. The painting is the work of the great artist Cleitias and the vase bears the signatures of both Cleitias and Ergotimus, the potter who made it. Of the five charioteers immortalized in the vase-painting, the only one mentioned in the 'canonical' version of the *Iliad* is Diomedes. On the evidence of other paintings on similar subjects, Cleitias and other artists of that period appear to have been unfamiliar with the event as described by Homer, or else not to have had access to a copy of Homer.[23]

The first public libraries. The tradition that Pisistratus was the first collector of the Homeric epics and that the texts were standardized in an Attic written edition, coupled with the comment by Athenaeus, who in his *Deipnosophistae* places Pisistratus immediately after Polycrates of Samos as one of the most important founders of libraries up to the time of Ptolemy II, has given rise to the hypothesis that a public library – and a major one by the standards of its day – did exist in sixth-century Athens.

Famous public and private libraries in Greece

The earliest list of founders of public, private and palace libraries in the Greek world – indeed the only such list that is known – is given by Athenaeus in his *Deipnosophistae* (I.3), written in Rome between A.D. 193 and 228.[24] The central figure of Athenaeus's book is one Larensius (P. Livius Larensis), who is said to have had so many Greek books that 'He outdoes all those who were renowned for their collections in the past, such as Polycrates of Samos,[25] Pisistratus the ruler of Athens, Euclides of Athens, Nicocrates of Cyprus, the kings of Pergamum, Euripides the poet, Aristotle the philosopher, Theophrastus and lastly Neleus, who preserved the books of those I have mentioned.' Athenaeus's list contains the only allusion to the formation of libraries by Polycrates of Samos, Euclides of Athens and Nicocrates of Cyprus. Another library dating from Solon's time was formed by Cleisthenes, the ruler of Sicyon, who, during a war with Argos, is said to have banned the recitation of Homer because of the frequent references to Argos in his work.[26]

Besides the reference to Pisistratus in Athenaeus's list and the presumed existence of a collection of all Homer's epics, there is other evidence to suggest that under Pisistratus and the Pisistratids, from about 570-560 onwards, steps really were taken to compile 'standard editions' of old and contemporary literature in books and to found a public library in Athens. According to Plutarch, Hereas (writing two hundred years later) accused Pisistratus of tampering with the text of Hesiod by deleting a whole line: presumably he was alluding to a written text that had existed in Pisistratus's time.[27] Onomacritus of Athens, a supporter of the Pisistratids, systematically collected the oracles of Musaeus, a

48. Fragment of an Attic red-figure vase depicting a symposium that is degenerating into a drunken orgy.
49. Dionysus and his wife Ariadne (centre) in a scene from a theatrical performance depicted on the Pronomos krater from southern Italy.

50. A bearded scribe, wearing a himation, seated on a stool: he was holding a stylus in his right hand. Athens, National Archaeological Museum.

mythical pupil of Orpheus, for editing and publication;[28] and Pisistratus's son Hipparchus, carrying on his father's tradition as a patron of art and literature, promoted the lyric poetry of Anacreon of Teos by inviting the poet to join his court in Athens.[29] It was again on the initiative of Hipparchus that Simonides of Ceos came to Athens.[30] For a time Simonides was rivalled as a lyric poet by Lasus of Hermione,[31] who also lived in Athens thanks to Hipparchus's patronage. Needless to say, the fact that all this evidence points in the same direction does not necessarily confirm the existence of a trend to lay down standard texts of epic and lyric poetry on papyrus rolls with the object of creating an 'academic' public library.

The fate of the first Athenian public library

According to Aulus Gellius, after the fall of the Pisistratid 'tyranny' the Athenians enlarged the library formed by Pisistratus[32] and apparently moved it to the Acropolis (if we assume that the prophecies collected by Pisistratus, which were kept on the Acropolis and were purloined by Cleomenes of Sparta, formed part of that library).[33] Gellius also tells us that the contents of Pisistratus's public library were taken to Persia as spoils of war after the sack of Athens in 480/479 B.C. Evidently the books were not dispersed, for Seleucus I Nicator returned them to Athens in about 280 B.C. after capturing Persepolis.[34] Many scholars believe that the reason why the Homeric recitation competition was suspended in the Panathenaea festival of 480 B.C. was that the written copy had been lost, and that the competition instituted under Pericles was of music and poetry more generally.[35]

The next question is: who were the textual scholars who undertook to edit Homer so as to create a tradition for an authentic Attic edition of his works in the sixth century B.C.? The answer is to be found in the work of Ioannes Tzetzes, written in the twelfth century of our own era. Tzetzes, in his *Prolegomena to Aristophanes*, where he writes about the Ptolemies' library in Alexandria, drawing on an unknown source, names the four people who were engaged by Pisistratus to prepare a recension of Homer's epics:[36] they were Epicongylus, Onomacritus of Athens, Zopyrus of Heraclia and Orpheus of Croton. Epicongylus is not known to us from any other source; Onomacritus was the poet who collected the oracles of Musaeus and had to leave Athens when he was caught forging them; Zopyrus is also otherwise unknown, unless he was the poet who wrote a prose account of the myth of Theseus; Orpheus of Croton, a poet of the sixth and fifth centuries B.C. at the Pisistratid court, was the author of an epic poem about the expedition of the Argonauts. Archaeology has yielded finds that may be connected with the tradition of the four editors: three statuettes of seated scribes at work (and a fragment of a fourth which may have belonged to the same set) were found on the Acropolis, and some believe they represent the four editors of the Homeric epics.[37] However, Pfeiffer (*Ἱστορία...*, 7) makes the point that no ancient source mentions the existence of an Attic copy of Homer, so the most we can assume is that the four scholar-poets in the age of Pisistratus were the first to arrange Homer's rhapsodies (the forty-eight 'books' of the *Iliad* and the *Odyssey*) in a fixed order, making some emendations to the text in the process.

The 'first editors' of Homer

Did the rhapsodists have their own private libraries or guild libraries? The rhapsodists, who had a decisive influence on the linguistic evolution of the epic and lyric tradition from the early sixth century onwards, were also instrumental in creating a 'literary sense', which led naturally to the transition from an oral to a written text. But let us start at the beginning.

At the beginning of the sixth century, during what is known as the Lyric Age, the epic poems handed down by rhapsodists from generation to generation came to be regarded as 'classics'. The possessors of that knowledge, namely the rhapsodists, were neither scholars nor men of letters, but when singing from memory about the Heroic Age they often had to interpret and elucidate passages according to their own lights, and sometimes to bring their own poetic talents into play. Moreover, the *Γένος Ἀριστοτέλους* and the *Vitae Aristotelis* provide ample testimony not only to their thorough knowledge of the Homeric epics and their proficiency as performers, but also to the public's universal acceptance of this role of theirs.

Did the rhapsodists of the sixth century possess technical aids, i.e. written texts, to help them to understand and study the old tradition of epic poetry?

To put it another way, did they use written glossaries of rare or obsolete words (*glossai*) found in the epics? Aristotle, in his *Poetics*, asserts that this was the case, for *glossai* were 'best suited to heroic verse'.[38] Quite possibly, in fact, the rhapsodists may have given explanations of and glosses on the words found in Homer, and clarifications of etymologically obscure words, of which they then made collections that served as 'grammar textbooks' of the oral tradition.[39]

Just as the rhapsodists were aware of the part they played in perpetuating the epic tradition, and later the lyric tradition too, from a certain point onwards they must have been equally aware that they were 'dependent' on written texts that were generally accepted as authoritative. An episode that sheds an interesting light on the exponents of the rhapsodic literature which came into being at the beginning of the sixth century is the case of Xenophanes of Colophon and the outcry provoked by his attitude to Homer.[40] This itinerant rhapsodist, who was himself a poet, travelled all over the Greek world, from Asia Minor to the Greek colonies in southern Italy. He is thought to have begun his career as a travelling rhapsodist reciting Homer, though there is no firm evidence for this. In time he developed into something of a homespun philosopher and strongly criticized Homer and Hesiod for portraying the gods as perpetrators of acts which humans consider immoral, such as theft, adultery and deception. The pious rhapsodist's censure gave rise to a spate of criticisms of Homer, so much so that Plato actually banished Homer from his ideal state on those very grounds,[41] and others reacted similarly. On the other hand, Xenophanes's strictures provoked other rhapsodists to rush to Homer's defence: one of those was Theagenes of Rhegium, who first mooted the principle of explanatory writings to interpret the motives behind the gods' actions.[42]

Rhapsodists take epic poetry to a wider public

What is certain is that all this 'literature' could not be sustained orally, and the more the rhapsodists acquired new audiences and continued to offer their own interpretations and linguistic variations, the more necessary it became for all that literary material to be set down in writing in a 'standard' version. Precisely when the rhapsodists came to realize that written texts were an essential aid to their professional reliability we do not know: most probably the process started in the sixth century. The only evidence we have touching on this subject is of no material relevance: it is a papyrus with a fragment of *The Persians* by Timotheus, dating from the second half of the fourth century B.C. It was found in a tomb at Abusir, near Memphis, with the mortal remains of a wandering minstrel, who had been buried with the chattels he would be wanting in the after life: his book, his knapsack and his staff. This papyrus book is in fact the oldest known Greek manuscript after the Derveni papyrus.[43]

The first written collections of philosophical works. By the sixth century B.C. there already existed written texts attributed to Orpheus, Musaeus and Epimenides. At about that time Orpheus was beginning to be regarded as the patron of various rites to do with life and death, and a number of theogonic poems of that period were attributed to him. It was in this way that metaphysics started to gain ground in the Greek world and some adherents of the Orphic doctrines professed Orphism as a religion, basing their beliefs on a corpus of sacred texts[44] written on a variety of materials about which nothing specific is known except for the famous gold plates found in southern Italy and Crete: these are plaques inscribed with the words of Bacchic, Orphic and Pythagorean burial rites.[45] The earliest historically documented written exposition of philosophical beliefs is mentioned by Diogenes Laertius, who states that at the end of the sixth century Heraclitus deposited a copy of his work subsequently known as *On Nature* (*Περί φύσεως*) in the temple of Artemis at his birthplace, Ephesus. about 150 years later this copy found its way into Aristotle's private library.[46] Whether the written text was in the form of a polyptych or a papyrus roll is unknown, but we do know that about 150 years later this very copy found its way into Aristotle's private library.[47]

The doctrines of 'natural philosophers' are set down in writing

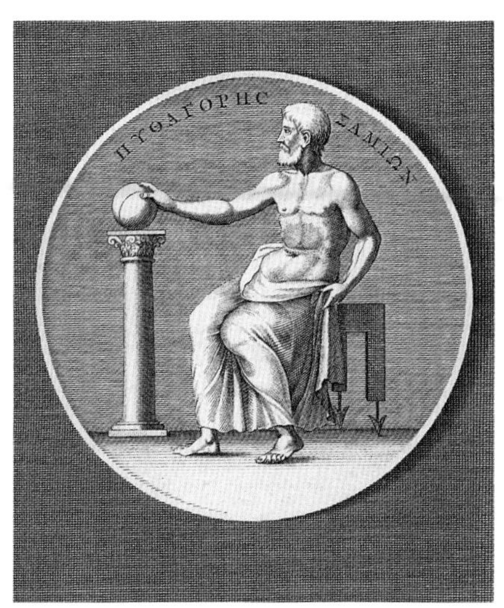

51. Pythagoras. Engraving from M. Meibonius, Diogenes Laertius, *Amsterdam 1698.*

At about the same time, in the last decades of the sixth century, two emigrants from Ionia, Xenophanes of Colophon and Pythagoras of Samos, started teaching philosophy in the Greek cities of Magna Graecia (southern Italy) and so inaugurated a new period of scholarly studies, the fruits of which their pupils preserved in book form after their death. Although Pythagoras did not write anything himself, and although his school of philosophy was esoteric and mystical in character, he inspired others to write a number of works based on his teaching: these were later gathered together in a book which was reproduced in numerous copies and before long was circulating beyond the confines of Magna Graecia.[48] Pythagoras emigrated to Croton in Magna Graecia between 540 and 522 B.C.: by an irony of fate he was sent into exile by the very man who is said to have founded the first public library on Samos, the 'tyrant' Polycrates. A disciple of Pythagoras's who preserved his teachings in writing was Philolaus of Croton, the teacher of Simmias of Thebes and Cebes, two young philosophers who subsequently studied under Socrates and thus form a connecting link between the Pythagorean tradition and the Athenian school. As we shall see, the written tradition of Pythagoras's teaching is connected with none other than Plato and his journeys to Magna Graecia when Dionysius I was ruler of Syracuse.[49]

52. *Heraclitus. Engraving from Meibonius,* Diogenes Laertius.

Another person connected with the form of papyrus books was Pherecydes of Syros, a sixth-century mythographer and theogonist, about whose friendship with Pythagoras a whole body of legend grew up over the centuries.[50] Diogenes Laertius relates that the book written by Pherecydes was still in existence in his own lifetime, the third century A.D.,[51] while Theopompus maintained that he was the first person to write about nature and the gods, and some say that he was the first to write a book in prose (*Seven Gulfs* or *Divine Mixture* or *Birth of the Gods*).[52] According to the lexicon called *Souda* ('Suidas'), he had a library containing some books written in other languages than Greek, including 'the secret books of the Phoenicians', and acquired most of his knowledge from his reading of books, not from Pythagoras.[53] Pherecydes bequeathed his books to Thales of Miletus: 'I have instructed my servants to send you my books when I am dead and buried. If you and other wise men approve of them, please publish them; if you don't approve of them, don't publish them.'[54]

From the oral to the written tradition. All the available evidence suggests that the era of books dawned in the Greek world in the early decades of the fifth century with the gradual decline not only of oral composition but of the oral tradition as well. From the third decade of the fifth century, references to writing and reading in poetry and the other arts are found more and more frequently. The image of the scribe and reader comes to be a symbol of the new era and little by little the written word supplants recitation and quotation from memory, which are often alluded to in the work of the three great tragedians, at least around 470 B.C.

53. Sophocles. Engraving, 19th c. 'Apud Fulvium Ursinum in marmore.'

54. Euripides. Engraving, 19th c. 'Apud Exc̃. D. Gasparum de Haro. et Gusman Catholicae Maiestatis.'

The age of the book dawns in Athens

Aeschylus, in *Prometheus Bound*,[55] gives us a Prometheus who presents himself as a bringer of culture, boasting that he has invented 'the combining of letters': 'Yes, and numbers, too, chiefest of sciences, I invented for [mankind], and the combining of letters, creative mother of the Muses' arts, with which to hold all things in memory.' In the *Eumenides*[56] he dares to state the view that the gods use divine 'mental writing tablets': 'For Hades is mighty in holding mortals to account under the earth, and he observes all things and within his mind inscribes them.' and Zeus himself has tablets on which mortals' misdeeds are recorded. It has been pointed out that the picture of Zeus with his divine tablets is suggestive of older oriental religious imagery, but Aeschylus actually follows the Hesiodic tradition, in which Justice, as Zeus's coadjutor, serves Zeus as his scribe: 'Justice, ... writing down the offences on Zeus's tablet.'[57] In *The Suppliant Women*, perhaps for the first time in Greek tragedy, Aeschylus implies that a book is something other than a tablet or tablets: 'Not on tablets is this inscribed, nor has it been sealed in folds of books.'[58] Sophocles uses the tablet image again in his earliest tragedy, *Triptolemus*: 'Put my words on the tablets of your mind.'[59] Finally, some fifty years later, Euripides again referred to these divine records: ''[60]

References to writing tablets in Classical Greek tragedy

Turning now to visual art, we find that Attic vase-painters drew no pictures of 'books' on black-figure vases and the earliest representation of a scribe is the statuette of a seated *deltographos* or 'tablet-writer' found on the Acropolis and dated to the late sixth or early fifth century (Fig. 49). Scenes with representations of inscribed rolls first appear on red-figure vases, which were painted during the period when the three great tragedians were writing (490-435 B.C.).[61] The best-known of these vase-paintings is on a kylix by Duris in

55. *Symposium at Agathon's house. From J. von Falke,* Hellas und Rom. Ein Culturgeschichte des classischen Alterthums, *Stuttgart [1880], 186-187.*

the Berlin Archaeological Museum, where all three branches of the school curriculum are depicted: in it we see a papyrus roll and also a diptych, i.e. a joined pair of tablets. The earliest representation of a papyrus is perhaps the one on a kylix by Onesimus (also known as the Good Panaitios), firmly dated to 490 B.C.: here the box on the floor at the reader's feet may be a portable bookcase of the type used by Alcibiades.[62]

In Athens, the growth of interest in books and the acquisition of private libraries[63] was apparently due to the influence of the philosophical schools in Ionia and Magna Graecia. It is to be dated to the period when the first tragedies were written and the vase-painters of Duris's generation were flourishing, that is the early decades of the fifth century: this period also coincided with the birth of Socrates (*ca.* 470). One of the Athenians' earliest contacts with books was in about 450, when Socrates and many others wished to listen to Zeno the Eleatic reading from his work on the occasion of his first visit to Athens with his teacher Parmenides. This piece of information is preserved by Plato himself in his dialogue *Parmenides*, where he describes Socrates criticizing Zeno's thinking.[64]

The role of the book is accepted. From the middle of the fifth century the spread of books gathered enormous momentum, with help from the sophists. This created a 'social problem' in which scholars were divided into two opposing camps, with Socrates in the vanguard of the trenchant critics of books.

Socrates's attitude to books

Socrates himself left no written work. What is more, he had something of an aversion to books and held them in scorn, believing that they could not be vehicles for productive dialogue, an argument propounded by Plato in *The Sophist*. However, he did acknowledge their beneficial role in the education of the young and the dissemination of knowledge generally. Most of what we known about Socrates's attitude to the written tradition that was growing up in his lifetime and to the diffusion of books in general comes from his most famous pupil, Plato; also from Xenophon, who was a member of his circle.

The earliest example of Socrates's disparagement of books, expressed with wry humour, was directed at Anaxagoras of Clazomenae, said to have been the first teacher of 'natural philosophy' in Athens (for an unbroken stretch of about thirty years from 460 B.C.). When he heard someone reading some interesting passages from the work by Anaxagoras known as *On Nature*, he sent out for a copy for himself, but his initial interest soon turned to disappointment with the intellectual capacity of its author. According to Plato in the *Apology*, he dismissed

56. Head of Socrates on an inscribed herm. Naples, Museo Archeologico Nazionale.

Anaxagoras's work with the mocking remark that his books were very cheap, as they could be bought for one drachma apiece.[65] Plato admitted that the sophists played a leading part in Athenian intellectual life in the last few years before the outbreak of the Peloponnesian War (431 B.C.) and singled Anaxagoras out for praise as the last of the 'natural philosophers' (*Hippias Major* 281c).

Yet Socrates's declared opposition to the written tradition and his doubts about the usefulness of books did not prevent him from consulting some kind of 'collection' of books. In fact, according to Xenophon, he was in the habit of studying the writings of earlier philosophers with his friends, making notes as he did so.[66] On the other hand, Euclides of Megara is said to have heard Socrates encouraging a slave to read aloud to his friend, which shows that he recognized that reading is of greater value when one's hearing is also brought into play. It is a fact that people in ancient Greece were in the habit of reading out loud, even when they were studying on their own: 'And if anyone else happens to be near the person reading, it will not be heard.'[67]

All the evidence suggests that systematic book production got under way in Athens around the middle of the fifth century. During the next few decades it mushroomed to such an extent – mainly as a result of the sophists' activities and with their encouragement – that their opponents became seriously concerned. The attitude of the educated public is illustrated by the following 'maieutic' dialogue between Socrates and the bookish Euthydemus (a namesake of an Athenian sophist), reported by Xenophon in his *Memorabilia*.[68]

> *'Tell me, Euthydemus,' he said, 'is it true that you have a large collection of books written by the wise men of the past?'*
> *'Yes, Socrates,' said Euthydemus. 'By Zeus, I have, and I am still collecting and will go on until I have got as many as I can.'*
> *'By Hera,' retorted Socrates, 'I congratulate you with all my heart because you value the treasures of wisdom above gold and silver. For you obviously believe that gold and silver do not improve men in any way, while the opinions of wise men enrich their possessors with virtue.'*
> *And Euthydemus was pleased to hear this, because he believed that Socrates thought he was on the road to wisdom.*

Dialogue about books between Socrates and Euthydemus

Euthydemus took Socrates's congratulations at their face value and really believed that his efforts to 'acquire wisdom' would help him in his political career; but Socrates, who was probably well aware of his interlocutor's inflated opinion of his own intellect, was presumably using this dialogue with the simple-minded book-lover to satirize the prevailing bibliomania, which the sophists' educational methods had implanted in the minds of the young by impressing upon them the importance of books for the acquisition of 'all learning'. His barbs were intended to puncture the pomposity of the rich young men who paid large sums to acquire wisdom from the sophists and thought that possessing books was an adequate substitute for true knowledge.

How the sophists helped to popularize books. The perception of books as indispensable tools for every educated person with an inquiring mind appears to have gained ground in Athens chiefly through the advocacy of the sophists from the middle of the fifth century onwards. But it did not really become firmly entrenched until the time of Aristotle (mid fourth century), and until then the value of books and their usefulness to education were hotly disputed, partly on account of their 'exploitation' by the sophists and partly because of the unregulated flood of new books pouring on to the market. Be that as it may, the sophists' contribution to higher education and the dissemination of knowledge in Athens was of seminal importance. It is no accident that before the fifth century no Athenian writer is heard of except Solon, whereas from 450 to 350 we know of hardly any writings that are not Athenian. For the whole of that fairly long period, therefore, when we think of scholarship and literature in the Greek world we think of Athens.

The sophists' educational philosophy

The sophists, who came from all parts of the Greek world and were in a way the successors of the itinerant rhapsodists, all taught for a time in Athens, the only city where we find them identifiable as such.[69] The most important of them were Protagoras of Abdera, Gorgias (from Sicily), Prodicus of Ceos, Hippias of Elis and Thrasymachus of Chalcedon in Asia Minor. Of the many minor sophists, such as the brothers Euthydemus and Dionysodorus, the most prominent were two Athenians, Antiphon and Critias. These first sophists were active for fifty years: from 450, when Protagoras probably arrived in Athens, to 399, when Socrates was put to death.

The difference of opinion that persists to this day concerning the true worth of the early sophists and the true nature of the education they provided is mainly due to the fact that the many once-famous treatises they wrote are lost to us almost in their entirety: if all the surviving fragments of their work were put together, it is doubtful whether they would fill twenty pages. So how did the sophists define themselves? They were not sages (*sophoi*, 'wise men', a word that denotes a quality of mind rather than a profession); nor were they philosophers (*philosophoi*, 'lovers of wisdom', which implies a seeking after truth – a concept that Plato stressed to differentiate between the sophists and himself). Thanks to Plato's scathing attacks on them, the word 'sophist' came to be a byword for casuistry. They were, of course, experts on the mental processes involved in the imparting of knowledge, and they were good at teaching their pupils how to think and speak. Their outlook on life is encapsulated in Thrasymachus's choice of epitaph for his tombstone: 'My homeland is Chalcedon and my profession is wisdom.'[70]

What, then, did the sophists set out to teach? To the Athenians of the fifth century, and indeed to all Greeks of the Classical period, the ability to speak well was a requirement for every citizen who wanted to succeed in public life, since all major decisions were reached by public debate; so the primary objective of the sophists' teaching was to impart skill in speaking, in other words rhetoric. Near the beginning of Plato's dialogue *Protagoras* (312d), Socrates asks the young Hippocrates what exactly he expects to be taught by the sophist he is going to consult ('On what subject does the sophist make a man talk eloquently?'). Later on in the dialogue, Protagoras himself says, 'I acknowledge myself to be a sophist and instructor of mankind.' The sophists' main aim was to teach civic virtue and sound judgment, in other words to give their pupils a proper education, and they asserted, in their rather provocative way, that they were able to achieve this by giving lessons in rhetoric. It is certainly true to say that not all of them were interested in humanistic values: rather, their object was to equip their pupils with the necessary technical expertise, mainly with regard to the structure of the language, and to give them a thorough grounding in the terms and concepts they used themselves.

Books as an educational aid for the sophists

Before 450 B.C. there was no provision in Athens for what we would now call higher education, and the sophists, who were following no precedent and had no competitors, felt that the academic and cultural training of the young was entirely in their hands.[71] Given their claim that they were able to give satisfactory and authoritative answers to all questions, there were no limits to the education they could offer. Moreover, the sophists' writings confirm the accusations of their critics: written in a style that belongs to the fringe of rhetoric, they present fragmentary or potted versions of opinions and assumptions then current in Athens. As professional teachers, the sophists were expected to provide their pupils with works by good poets (Plato, *Protagoras*, 325e), and before long they took to handing out copies of their own works as exemplars (Plato, *Phaedrus*, 266d) and writing classroom textbooks. That is the main reason why nearly all their books have perished, because they were intended for the use of their pupils rather than the general public. No matter how clever their lectures were, they were no more than what Thucydides calls 'prize essays designed to win the applause of the moment': in most of the books the sophists wrote, there is no sign of a desire to create something that posterity will treasure as a 'possession for all time'. They used books as their most powerful allies in the campaign to propagate their educational philosophy and as basic tools of their classroom work.

At the root of the conflict between the sophists on the one hand and Socrates and other intellectuals on the other was a question of principle: was it possible that everything the sophists promised could actually be delivered by teaching? And so the sophists' teaching methods led to the emergence of an opposing faction of furious antagonists, some of whom dismissed their very real contributions to education as being almost entirely valueless. Ironically enough, all we know about the controversy comes from the sophists' opponents, as their own writings were too slight to stand the test of time and give evidence in their defence.

Were Protagoras's books burnt?

Protagoras. For two of the sophists, Protagoras and Prodicus, we have testimony directly related to books. Protagoras of Abdera (*ca.* 490-420 B.C.), the leader of the professional sophists, arrived in Athens in the middle of the fifth century. There he taught with great success for forty years, making many firm friends but many enemies as well.[72] It may have been his close friendship with Pericles that persuaded the Athenian leader to start reading his speeches in court from a prepared text instead of speaking without notes, which until then had been the norm. Protagoras's most important contribution to philosophy was his doctrine that man is the measure of all things, but his most controversial work, which provoked a public outcry, was *On the Gods*. He is said to have read out this discourse for the first time at the home of either Euripides or Megaclides; but according to another informant one of his pupils, Archagoras the son of Theodotus, read it for him at the Lyceum. At all events, it stirred up great controversy, for at the beginning of the book Protagoras says he is unable to form any firm conclusions about the gods and cannot even decide whether they exist or not.[73] The Athenians charged him with blasphemy, according to Diogenes Laertius: not only did they sentence him to exile, but they sent a herald round the city to collect all the copies of his books they could find, and burnt them in the Agora.[74] If this is true, it is the first recorded case of censorship in ancient Greece.

Horae by Prodicus: an ancient best-seller

Prodicus. Prodicus of Ceos, perhaps the most able disciple of Protagoras, was admired by his contemporary Socrates, who regarded him as an authority on the differences between related words.[75] In fact Prodicus was excessively fussy about drawing distinctions between words of similar meaning, but what earned him the strictures and mockery of Socrates's circle was the exorbitant fee he charged for a single lesson – his 'fifty-drachma lecture', as Plato put it. In Plato's *Protagoras* Prodicus is portrayed giving a lesson while 'reclining with some sheepskins and other coverings thrown over him'.[76]

Prodicus's best-known treatise, entitled *Horae*, appeared in book form not later than 416 B.C. It was probably the enormous popularity of this book that provoked Aristophanes into equating books with sophists in the *Tagenistai*: 'This man has been corrupted either by a book or by Prodicus.' The very least one can deduce from the way he brackets the two together is that the sophists used books as a substitute for actual teaching. Prodicus and his *Horae* are mocked again in the *Symposium*, where Plato compares him with a learned man who wrote 'a wonderful panegyric on the usefulness of salt'.[77]

Though Plato may claim to have been the arch-critic of 'sophistry' and the man who expressed Socrates's opinion of the sophists' methods, the first 'public prosecutor' of the sophists was Aristophanes.[78] As early as 423, in *The Clouds*, he satirized not only the sophists, for their lessons in amorality, but also Socrates and his inner circle of disciples. In other words, he broadened the scope of his criticism to include all the intellectuals of his day and all who show off the knowledge they have acquired from their libraries.

Aristophanes: serious concerns about the indiscriminate proliferation of books

Aristophanes and his mockery of intellectuals. The epidemic of 'bad' books mentioned in *The Clouds* and again nine years later in *The Birds* (line 1288) typifies the satire and sarcasm that were prevalent in Athens in the last decades of the fifth century. Aristophanes shows us the young men rushing out first thing in the morning, like birds, to catch up with the latest news: 'Then they swoop off towards the notices and finally devour the decrees.' He was sufficiently disturbed by the spate of indiscriminate book-copying to comment wryly in *The Frogs* (line 1083) that Athens was suddenly 'swarming with clerks'; but that did not stop him telling the Athenians that tragedies, although undoubtedly written down originally for the purposes of staging a production, were also useful in book form for private reading and discussion. Aristophanes drew a sharp distinction between the sophists' books and the written texts of plays. It was his belief that the Athenians would never be in danger of lapsing into ignorance because the theatre was frequented by military servicemen and highly-educated 'readers of books able to understand the right points' (*The Frogs*, 1114), the implication being that most members of the audience came to the theatre armed with a copy of the play. Elsewhere (*The Frogs*, 52 ff.), he returns to the image of the studious reader when he describes Dionysus reading quietly to himself on board ship.

57. *Aristophanes. Engraving, 19th c. 'Apud Magnum Etruriae Ducem.'*

Plays that were not written for performance in competition may perhaps have been published in book form, either to make money or for purposes of publicity. While performances of tragedy were big events in Athenian social and political life, their texts were hunting-grounds for literary and philosophical critics. In *The Frogs* of Aristophanes (1182-95), Aeschylus criticizes two lines of Euripides's *Antigone* for failing to give an accurate description of the fate of Oedipus. Such fault-finding would hardly have been possible without a written text available for consultation, especially as it would not have been the only case of its kind. In any case, there is good evidence that the tragedians did indeed have private libraries: in *The Frogs* Aristophanes ridicules Euripides for his book-learning, poking fun at him also for his fine library and for employing a private scribe-cum-publisher: 'And next a dose of chatterjuice, distilled from books, I gave her.'[79] There was probably yet another reason for the barbs directed at Euripides: that he had attended the lectures not only of Anaxagoras but also, and worse still, of Protagoras and Prodicus.

59. Alcibiades. Engraving, 19th c. Published by J. Wilks, London 1807.

There was a story about Alcibiades and his thirst for books that was current in Aristophanes's time and must have remained in the repertoire of popular literary anecdotes for centuries thereafter, as it resurfaces in Aelian's *Historical Miscellany* (*Varia Historia*) in the second century A.D. Aelian found the story in the work of his contemporary Julius Pollux, who quoted it to illustrate the close relationship between book-lovers and booksellers in ancient Greece: 'Alcibiades was a great admirer of Homer. One day he went into a school and asked for a book of the *Iliad* [which he had presumably ordered]. When the master told him he had nothing of Homer's, he punched the man violently and walked off.' The inference is that the schoolmaster was earning money on the side by copying books and probably received the punch because he had not completed the

58. The Theatre of Dionysus in Athens. From J. von Falke, Hellas und Rom..., *172-173.*

work in time. Alcibiades called him an uneducated man and sneered that his pupils were bound to end up like him.[80] Aristophanes quarrelled with Alcibiades in or about 410 B.C., and it is very likely that he himself spread this story to show up the selfish greed of which he was always accusing Alcibiades, as in the *Tagenistai*.[81]

Aristophanes's anecdotes about books

The atmosphere conveyed by Aristophanes has been re-created in a 'period piece' by N. Hourmouziadis, who vividly and imaginatively recaptures the mood of a theatrical performance in the time of Socrates, as seen through the eyes of an Athenian by the name of Anthemocritus.[82] The only point I should like to add is that on his way down from the Hill of the Nymphs to the Theatre of Dionysus it is more than likely that Anthemocritus came across some itinerant vendors, perhaps including a bookseller or two. The passage already quoted from *The Frogs* (line 1114) confirms that theatregoers did have copies of the plays to read, but nothing whatever is known about the process of putting those written texts on the market. One thing we may be sure of is that it would have been no easy matter to follow the text while the play was in progress without having done some fairly thorough homework beforehand, as it took a good deal of practice to be able to follow the dialogue. The punctuation, if any, was rudimentary; words were still not separated by a space; and the system of accentuation, which would have made it much easier to tell where one word ended and the next began, was not devised until much later, in the Hellenistic period. In the written texts of the plays there was nothing to show which lines were spoken by which characters, extraordinary though that seems to us nowadays: usually the only indication of a change of speaker was a dash or colon at the beginning of the line. The confusion thus created was often compounded through repeated copying by careless copyists, as in the case of the only surviving manuscript of Menander's *The Misanthrope* (*Dyscolus*).[83]

Bookshops. Apparently the bookshops in the Athens Agora were well-known haunts of literary men towards the end of the fifth century. In *The Birds* (line 1288) the Athenians are portrayed as voracious readers who rush out to the Agora straight after breakfast to browse through law books, catch up on the latest publications and talk to their friends about the literary merits and defects of the books they have been reading. There were two words in use to denote a bookseller: one was the neutral *bibliopoles*, first used by Aristomenes Thyropoeus in *The Wizards* and then again by Theopompus in *Peace*, but Julius Pollux uses the rather more disparaging term *bibliokapelos* (a 'hawker' or 'peddler' of books). Their shops were in the Agora, at least from 425 B.C.[84] According to the comic playwright Eupolis, who refers to the place where books were sold, and to Xenophon in the *Apology* (399 B.C. or later), all the bookshops were concentrated near the area known as the Orchestra, a semicircle of level ground in the Agora, at the foot of the Acropolis, watched over by statues of the tyrannicides Harmodius and Aristogeiton, which might be seen as symbolic of the role of books in the service of democracy.[85] On the other hand, Nicophon, in his comedy *Cheirogastores* ('*Hand-to-mouth Toilers*'), classes booksellers in the same lowly category as fishmongers and charcoal-sellers.[86]

The first philosopher to have a teaching library

The first private library(?). By a curious irony, Plato, who questioned the importance of the written word and attacked the sophists and their book-centred approach to education, may be described as the first book-collector as such in the Greek world. His library was used as a teaching resource in the Academy and it may well have contained not only books by his contemporaries but also the writings of the Presocratic philosophers, to judge by his systematic study of writings relating to the theories of Pythagoras.

ΠΛΑΤΩΝ

60. Head of Plato. Roman copy, 1st c. B.C. Berlin, Archaeological Museum.

Plato's travels in search of books. Plato is known to have been introduced to Pythagoras's theories on his first visit to Magna Graecia, at a time when Pythagoreanism was enjoying a revival led by Archytas of Tarentum.[87] Plato went to Sicily when Syracuse was ruled by Dionysius I (405-367), then at the zenith of his power. He had an extremely stressful time with Dionysius,

61. Imaginary reconstruction of the gardens of Plato's Academy. Engraving from C. Frommel, Dreissig Ansichten Griechenlands zu den Werken griechischen Autoren, *Karlsruhe 1830.* ☞

with whom he got on very badly, and the only advantage he gained from his stay in Syracuse was the very generous stipend he received as long as he was in favour: this gave him the wherewithal to buy books.

The principal sources of information on Plato's library and its contents are Diogenes Laertius, who was an avid collector of material for his own books, and Satyrus, a biographer of the second century A.D. Satyrus, who enlivened his biographies – mostly of poets and philosophers – with all sorts of amusing anecdotes, says that Plato wrote to Dion (Dionysius I's brother-in-law) in Sicily, asking him to buy from Philolaus three books by Pythagoras priced at 100 minae (10,000 drachmae). It was said that he could afford this sum because Dionysius had given him more than eighty talents (480,000 drachmae).[88] However, according to the Alexandrian historian Hermippus of Smyrna, Plato bought these books himself in Sicily from relatives of Philolaus, paying forty Alexandrian minae for them; and a third version of the story has it that Plato was given the books as a reward for persuading Dionysius to release one of Philolaus's pupils from prison.[89]

62. Archytas. Engraving from Meibonius, Diogenes Laertius.

Another author whose work Plato looked for in Syracuse was Sophron, a fifth-century writer of mimes who had won a great reputation for himself. Plato, who regarded Sophron as an excellent mimographer, bought copies of his works and took them back with him to Athens, where they aroused great interest. It has been suggested that Plato may have modelled some of the characters in his dialogues on characters from Sophron's mimes, but this is probably an exaggeration, and Diogenes Laertius's story that Plato kept a copy of the mimes under his pillow is thought to be apocryphal.[90] The only other thing we know about Plato's book-buying spree is that, according to Proclus, he commissioned Heraclides Ponticus to procure for him the poems of Antimachus of Colophon.[91] A reasonable inference to be drawn from Plato's correspondence with Archytas, which contains allusions to certain *hypomnemata* ('memoirs' or 'commentaries') sent to Archytas by an unnamed writer from Myra, is that Archytas supplied Plato with books by earlier writers for his library. The form

Plato searches for books

in which these *hypomnemata* were written – on papyrus rolls or clay tablets – is not known.[92]

Plato himself, following the example of Pythagoras and Socrates, did not teach from a written text. In *Phaedrus* (275c) he belittles the importance of the written word, and in his seventh Epistle (341c-d) he confirms that he has never used written lecture notes: his teachings were, as Aristotle said, 'unwritten doctrines'. According to Diogenes Laertius once again, the only extant reference to the first time Plato's dialogues were edited and published in book form names one of his pupils, Philip of Opus, as their publisher. Philip produced an edition of the *Laws* at his teacher's dictation, with the help of the rough notes he had taken 'on wax' at Plato's lectures. Not content with merely reproducing Plato's words, Philip apparently took it upon himself to divide the work into twelve books and added a work of his own entitled *Epinomis*, which serves as an appendix to the *Laws*. Another of Plato's pupils, the mathematician Hermodorus of Syracuse, whose main interest – and the principal subject of his treatise *On Science* – was astral religion, nevertheless spent a great deal of time writing out numerous copies of Plato's dialogues, perhaps for publication. These books were sold even in far distant outposts of the Greek world such as Sicily, without Plato's consent, and brought in handsome profits.[93]

The first publishers of Plato's work

Rhetoric and books. To the Greeks of the Classical period, and especially to the Athenians of the fifth century, the ability to speak well was an essential requirement because, as we have seen, all major decisions were reached by public debate. It therefore occupied an important place in the educational philosophy of the sophists, one of whose primary objectives was to cultivate the art of public speaking, in other words rhetoric. Now the art of rhetoric, though oral in its application, is acquired first and foremost by means of the written word. And although concentration on rhetoric tended to compromise ethics, inasmuch as public speaking had become the be-all and end-all of success, there was one Athenian teacher – Isocrates, a pupil of Gorgias – who made it his purpose to reconcile rhetoric with the ethics of traditional criticism.

Isocrates. Isocrates was born in 436 B.C., when Athens was at the height of her power. At the age of about forty-six, in 390 or just after, about half a century after the emergence of the first great sophists, he opened a school which was destined to be extremely influential. He instituted a sophistical method of teaching that was aimed at providing an all-round education while taking political reality

RAPHAEL
SANTIVS
PINX
PIO SEXTO

IN AEDIBVS
VATICA
NIS
ONT. MAX.

into account. And, although he had had a sophistical education under Gorgias, the first manifesto of his new school – which was in tune with sophistical teaching methods – was nevertheless entitled *Against the Sophists*.

The speeches written for use in his rhetoric classes are models of eloquent rhetoric and straight thinking: they were composed with the object of demonstrating the power of words, which it was the purpose of his school to instil in its students.[94] Isocrates himself never denied the debt he owed to books: he describes his speech *On the Antidosis* as 'an oration intended to be read [to an actual audience]', and in it he acknowledges that when his works had been written out and distributed his reputation grew and students flocked to him.[95]

Isocrates acknowledges his debt to books

64. *Isocrates. Engraving, 19th c. 'Apud Magnum Etruriae Ducem in marmore.'*

Isocrates far outdid his predecessors Protagoras and Prodicus and chose to use books as one of his main tools in imparting rhetorical skills. Aristotle's remark (as reported by Dionysius of Halicarnassus) about the parcels of Isocrates's courtroom speeches to be found in the hands of booksellers may not have been so far from the truth, though one has to allow for a touch of hyperbole due to the rivalry between their two schools.[96] In his manifesto *Against the Sophists* he explains his views on philosophers, on the improvisation characteristic of courtroom oratory and on the false assertions of his opponents: 'I wrote and published a discourse,' he states explicitly, and he urges his followers 'to distribute my discourse among those who wish to have it'.[97] Although he was never in favour with philosophers, it was generally acknowledged that his speeches were not as blatantly propagandistic as those of the sophists, and even Plato recognized his qualities as a philosopher.

Demosthenes. As regards the other great ancient Greek orator, Demosthenes, who was born half a century after Isocrates in 384 B.C., little is known about

☜ 63. *Plato and Aristotle. Raphael, 'The School of Athens', intaglio reproduction, 19th c.*

his attitude to the written tradition, but we do know that he was deeply interested in everything to do with books.

Demosthenes saves Thucydides's work for posterity

Demosthenes trained his mind with the same self-discipline that helped him to overcome his physical infirmities: according to Cicero (*Brutus*, 121), he studied Plato without ever going to any of his lessons, and he also studied Isocrates and Thucydides, who greatly influenced him and instilled in him his passionate devotion to the greatness of Athens. That may have been the reason why he copied out the whole of Thucydides's *History*, either for friends or to order.[98] He is known to have given lessons in rhetoric and worked as a paid *logographos* (one who wrote speeches for litigants to deliver in court), but we do not know whether he was a talented calligrapher or whether he made money from his work as a copyist. Cicero's testimony agrees with that of Lucian, who said that Demosthenes himself had copied out most of the books in his possession and had made eight complete copies of Thucydides's *History*.

Zosimus, a historian from Ascalon or Gaza who lived in the fifth and early sixth centuries A.D., writes about the life of Demosthenes and mentions a great library that existed in Athens in his time (the fourth century B.C.). According to Zosimus, the library was burnt down and what was thought to be the only copy of Thucydides was destroyed with it; but fortunately Demosthenes had memorized it, and so the *History* survived.[99]

65. Demosthenes. Engraving, 19th c. Published by J. Wilks, London 1807.

The book trade in the Hellenic world. From the middle of the fifth century Athens was the intellectual driving force of the Greek world, 'an example to Greece', as Pericles put it in his funeral oration (Thucydides, II.41). And without a doubt it was the centre of the book trade in Greece, at least until near the end of the fourth century, considering that most of the books written from 450 B.C. onwards were of Athenian origin. One of the results of this cultural ferment was that an enormous mass of writing was made accessible to the gen-

eral public in book form, with slaves specially trained as copyists and readers (i.e. readers out loud) to help with the copying and oral transmission of the contents. There is every reason to believe that there was a considerable trade in those books between Athens and the rest of the Greek world, especially the members of the Athenian Alliance.

Xenophon in the *Anabasis*, describing the gruelling return journey of the Greek army from Persia, over the mountains to the Black Sea and then down through the Bosporus, mentions that on the coast at Salmydessus they came across a wrecked ship laden with crates containing household utensils and 'many books':[100] evidently those who had been studying in Athens liked to take home something to remind them of the bookish atmosphere there and of the importance of books and libraries in the preservation of knowledge. Memnon, in his lost *History* (extracts from which are preserved by Photios in his *Bibliotheca*), records that the Bithynian ruler Clearchus, on his return home after studying in Athens under Plato and Isocrates, founded a library in his own country not later than 364 B.C. Nor should we forget the publishing activities of Plato's pupil Hermodorus, who made money by selling books containing his teacher's dialogues.

67. Thucydides. Engraving, 19th c. 'Apud Fulvium Ursinum in marmore.'

Intellectual property. It is not easy to determine whether the concept of copyright was accepted in ancient Greece: that is to say, whether a testamentary bequest of a written work gave the legatee the intellectual property rights to that work, and, if so, how much protection that gave him (as, for example, in the case of Pherecydes, who bequeathed his books to Thales of Miletus with instructions to publish them if he approved of them).[101] But we do know that cases of piracy did occur, chiefly of books by authors who were dead or lived a long way away from Athens, or books of unattributed authorship. This is presumably the

66. Hadrianic Athens from the east. From J. von Falke, Hellas und Rom..., *106-107.*

main explanation for the fact that so many original texts – even the works of the three great tragedians – became corrupt in the last decade of the fourth century B.C.[102]

Quite possibly it was in that period that the publishing trade was born, the publisher being an educated man who took it upon himself to produce accurate copies of books which he would then market with the object of making money. Evidence in support of this hypothesis is to be found from the time of Anaxagoras, in the middle of the fifth century, and it leads me to believe that the books which Socrates sneered at because they could be bought for one drachma were not written by Anaxagoras in his own hand.[103] In the years immediately following the end of the Peloponnesian War (404 B.C.) we find references to slaves employed as scribes and even to specialized book-copyists, like those sent to Zeno, the founder of the Stoa, by Antigonus Gonatas.

Athens the centre of the book trade in the Greek world

Faced with all this evidence, one can only conclude that from the middle of the fifth century there must really have been 'as many private libraries as there were Athenian citizens'. This unlikely-sounding assertion is corroborated by Polybius, who says that in the third century B.C. there were so many private and public (i.e. school and gymnasium) libraries in Athens that the Sicilian historian Timaeus – whom Polybius mocks for his theoretical book-learning – spent fifty years listing them all after being sent into exile by the Syracusan ruler Agathocles.[104] Polybius mentions Timaeus's lengthy work (in thirty-eight books) on the history and geography of the Greek colonies in the west, for which almost all his material was drawn from books in the libraries of Athens.

The philosophy schools as centres of book learning in Athens. Although Athens was in the throes of a profound political and social crisis after finally losing the Peloponnesian War in 404, four important philosophy schools were founded in the fourth century by Plato, Aristotle, Epicurus and Zeno.

Plato's Academy

Plato. In 388 or soon after, Plato established his school in a grotto sacred to the Muses and the hero Academus or Hecademus, after whom it was named the Academy: as a school it lasted for more than nine hundred years.[105] Although he himself, following the example of Pythagoras, was an advocate of oral teaching, not only did he have a private library of his own (as we have seen), but his pupils and the teachers in the Academy gathered his 'unwritten doctrines' together and arranged them in order; and it may be that those 'unwritten doctrines' were published in book form shortly before Plato's death in 348/7 B.C.

Plato was succeeded as head of the Academy by Speusippus, who held the post until 339. Speusippus, too, had a fine library which was eventually acquired by Aristotle.[106] Speusippus was succeeded by Xenocrates of Chalcedon, and until the first century B.C. the principals of the Academy succeeded one another in orderly fashion without a break. The year 269 B.C., when Arcesilaus took over, marks the beginning of what is now known as the New (or Second, or Middle) Academy. Arcesilaus, who introduced new doctrines into the Academy's teaching, is said by Diogenes Laertius to have had all Plato's works in his library.[107] From 213 B.C., under Carneades of Cyrene, the Academy was embroiled in rivalry with the Stoics. After 87 B.C., when its teachers fled from Athens, the school went into a decline, and after a while it ceased to exist. However, Plutarch informs us that the word 'Academic' or 'Academician' remained in use for a long time thereafter.

It is beyond question that one of the resources of Plato's Academy was a well-stocked library, though little or nothing is known about its legal status or internal regulations, its contents or its eventual fate. Was it handed down into the ownership of each successive head of the school, or did Plato himself leave instructions on what was to be done with it after his death? One thing we do know is that Plato's immediate successor, Speusippus, had a fine library which was eventually acquired by Aristotle. Aristotle, in fact, was connected with the written word in the Academy in another capacity during his time there. According to an anecdote current in antiquity, he was nicknamed 'The Mind' or 'The Mind of the School'; or, in another version of the story, his nickname was 'The Reader'.[108] The post of Reader at the Academy was given to slaves specially trained for the work, since their public reading of unpublished works was tantamount to their publication.[109] Most of the young students at the Academy discovered what was written in books by hearing the books read aloud, but Aristotle was different: he read books for himself and, according to his own testimony, copied out passages into a commonplace book, just like a student nowadays. The anecdote mentioned above is of great interest, because it illustrates a fundamental difference between Plato and Aristotle: the nickname he gave Aristotle may perhaps have been meant disparagingly, to judge by Plato's unconcealed scorn of 'self-styled wise men' who 'feed upon opinion' (surely intended as a dig at Aristotle); but Aristotle was an obsessive questioner of the opinions of all other philosophers.[110]

68. Plato's Academy. Mosaic floor from Pompeii, 1st c. B.C. Naples, Museo Archeologico Nazionale.

Aristotle. The most famous alumnus of the Academy was Aristotle, who studied there from 368 until Plato's death in 348. In 335 he decided to give Plato's Academy some healthy competition and opened another school, which was at first called the Lyceum and later, at least from the time of his successor Theophrastus, the *Peripatos* or Peripatetic school.[111] At its peak, under Aristotle's successor Theophrastus, it was said to have had two thousand students. These two schools between them were responsible not only for preserving many of their founders' treatises and lectures, as well as earlier works of literature, but also for promoting awareness of the importance of books and private libraries to scholarly writing. Their teachers, and their students too, made a practice of collecting, filing and publishing their works on a scale that has never been equalled since by any philosophical school or movement in either the West or the East.

Aristotle's Lyceum and the Peripatetic school

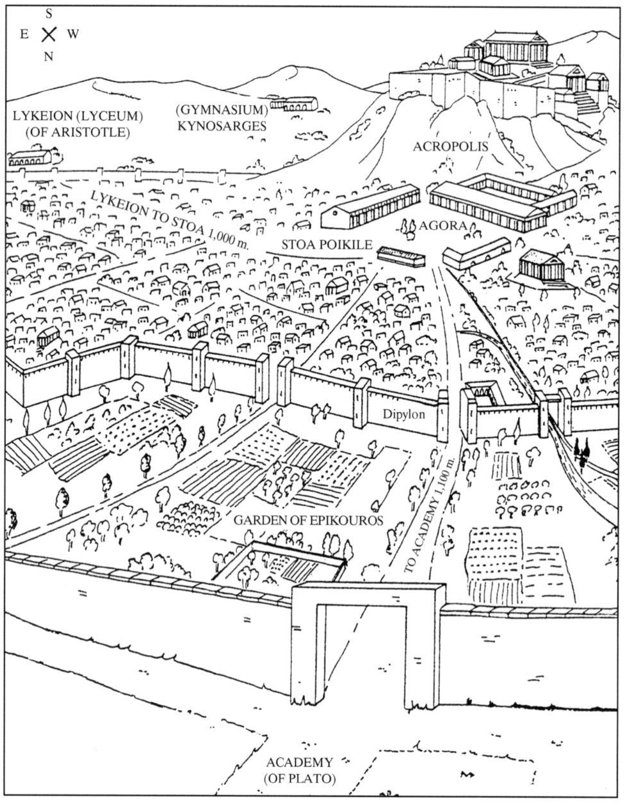

69. *Reconstruction drawing of Athens showing the positions of the philosophy schools. From M. Canto-Sperber, L. Brisson et al.,* La philosophie grecque, *Paris 1997.*

Epicurus. Epicurus was born on Samos of Athenian parents in 341 B.C. He went to Athens at the age of eighteen but accompanied his parents into exile soon afterwards and did not return until 306, bringing with him a large group of pupils. His philosophy school, which operated in competition with the Academy and the Lyceum, was situated in a garden near the Dipylon Gate, where he lived with his pupils in a community devoted to study. He wrote extensively and his philosophy was very influential in the Roman period, as attested by (among other things) the papyri of his book *On Nature* found at Herculaneum.[112] Epicurus bequeathed his library to Hermarchus, and his own writings alone filled three hundred papyrus rolls.[113]

The Garden of Epicurus at the Dipylon

Epicurus's immediate successor at the Garden, as it came to be called, was Hermarchus (271-240), who was followed by Polystratus. The last head of the school was Apollodorus of Athens (150-120 B.C.), nicknamed 'The Tyrant of the Garden'. Apollodorus was an extremely prolific writer, with over four hundred books to his name: among them was the first biography of Epicurus, now lost. In his *Collection of Doctrines* – which he wrote, to champion the superiority of Epicurus over Chrysippus (the head of the Stoic school), despite the latter's reputation for fecundity as a writer – he asserted that Epicurus's writings, which were entirely original, amounted to a great deal more than those of Chrysippus, whose work was full of quotations: if all the passages quoted from other writers are removed from Chrysippus's books, he concluded caustically, nothing is left but empty pages.[114]

Zeno's philosophy school in the Painted Stoa

As a community of students and research scholars, and also as a pattern for living, the Epicurean school exerted a powerful influence after its founder's death. Philodemus of Gadara transplanted Epicurus's teaching to Italy and quickly won a following that included Virgil, Horace and Lucretius.

70. *Zeno. Engraving from Meibonius,* Diogenes Laertius.

Zeno. Zeno, born at Citium in Cyprus in 333 or 334 B.C., may be said to have owed his standing as a philosopher to the bookshops of Athens. He first set foot in Athens after his ship was wrecked off the coast of Attica and spent his time in a bookshop, where he listening to the bookseller reading aloud from Xenophon's *Memorabilia*. He was very struck by what Xenophon said about Socrates and asked if men with such profound philosophical learning were still to be found. Just at that moment Crates of Thebes, the Cynic philosopher, happened to be passing and the bookseller introduced him to Zeno, who became his pupil.[115]

The Stoic school that he founded exerted a profound influence on later generations of philosophers and attracted students in large numbers from many parts of the world. It would seem that the teaching there was based on the written tradition, for Cleanthes, who succeeded Zeno as the head of the school, was said to have taken notes on his predecessor's lectures using oyster shells and the shoulder blades of oxen to write on, as he had no money to buy paper.[116] Zeno, unlike his successor, had a sizable private library, which he built up by having books copied for him not only by scribes sent to him by the Macedonian king Antigonus Gonatas, an ex-pupil of his,[117] but also by slaves whom he acquired after the Peloponnesian War owing to the increased demand for books. The Stoic school was so named after the Painted Stoa in the Athens Agora, lavishly decorated with paintings by Polygnotus, where he did most of his teaching, and made its reputation mainly in the fields of ethics and politics.[118] It was generally thought in antiquity that Zeno chose to teach in the Painted Stoa to cleanse the Agora of the stain left on it by the crimes of 'the Thirty', the oligarchs in power immediately after the Peloponnesian War, who murdered hundreds of Athenians there.

Zeno, the founder of the Stoa, was succeeded by Cleanthes (304-232 B.C.), who settled in Athens from the Troad. However, for the fullest statement of Stoic philosophy in all fields (logic, ethics, physics, politics) we are indebted to Chrysippus of Soli (281-208 B.C.). The Athenians recognized his importance: 'Without Chrysippus there would be no Stoa,' they would say later, which implies that Apollodorus was not being fair when he said that most of Chrysippus's work consisted of quotations from other writers. From the middle of the second century B.C. the Stoic school is often known as the Middle Stoa:[119] during this period Stoicism was taken up by scholarly patricians in Rome, with the result that passages from the writings of the early Stoics as well as the exponents of the Middle Stoa have been preserved in the work of Cicero, Plutarch, Sextus Empiricus and others. The name 'New Stoa' is used to describe the period starting in the early years of the Christian era, which is represented by Seneca the Philosopher (4 B.C. - A.D. 65), Epictetus (A.D. 60-140) and the philosopher emperor Marcus Aurelius (reigned 161-180), among others.

From the point of view of the history of books, what interests us most is Aristotle's private library: how it was formed, for what purposes it was used in the Lyceum, what eventually happened to it and what literary evidence we have for its history.

71. Aristotle. Marble head from a herm. Athens, National Archaeological Museum.

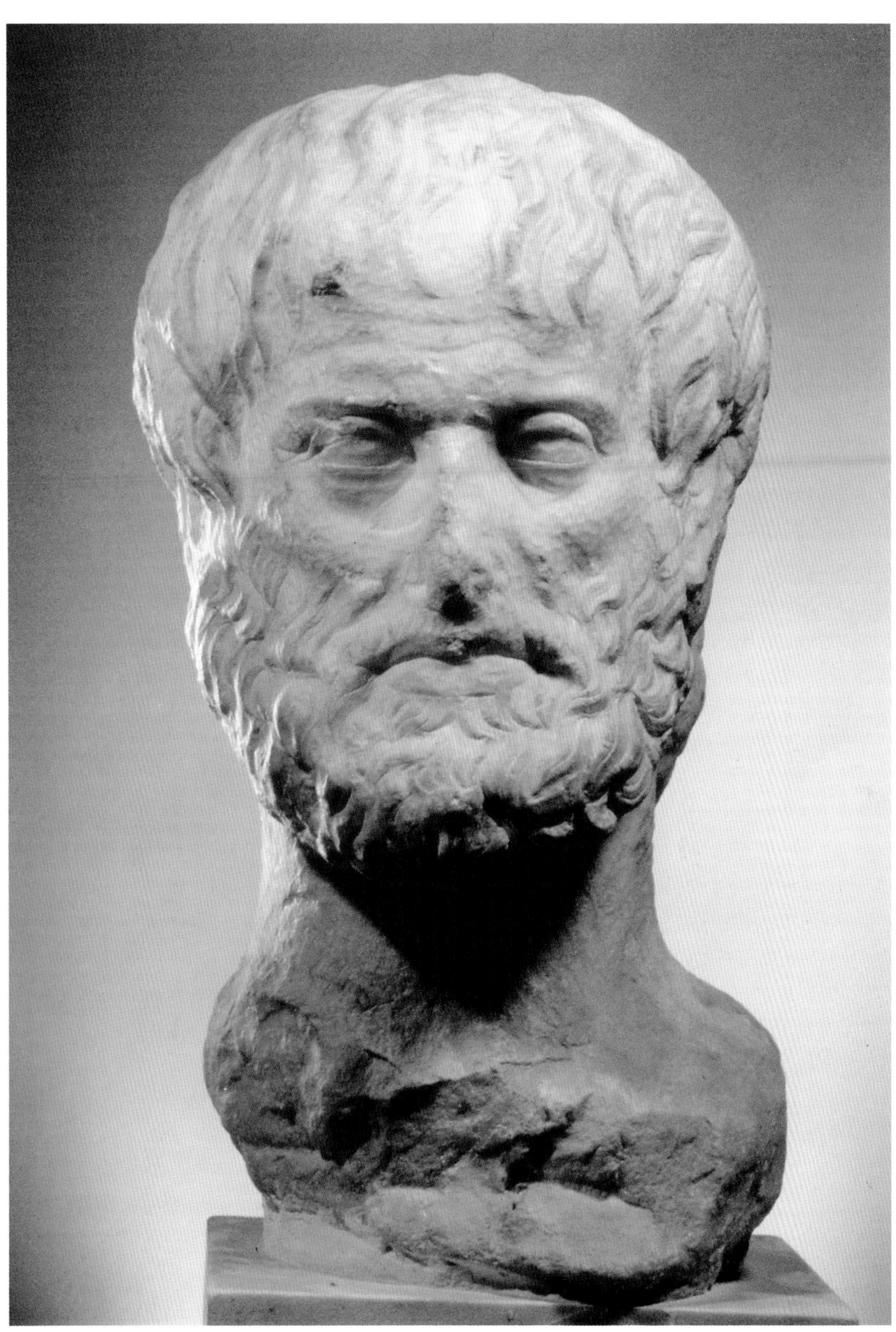

Aristotle's working methods. From the middle of the fourth century B.C. the importance of books as educational and research aids in the modern sense came to be established as a result of Aristotle's personality, the scientific character of his thought, his practice of questioning anything that could not be proved, the method of teaching at the Lyceum and the encyclopaedic learning he instilled into his students. Aristotle excelled all others in the catholicity of his knowledge and, unlike the sophists, he succeeded in classifying an enormous mass of material into categories, relying on his own philosophical principles and his constant collaboration with his pupils. Besides all this, he was the first great philosopher to make a scientific inventory of his work and he attached great importance to the written tradition.

Aristotle's library

Historical references to Aristotle's library. Strabo was the first writer to mention Aristotle's library, which he ranks as the greatest private library in ancient Greece and informs us that most of its contents were handed down to Aristotle's successors at the Lyceum to provide an infrastructure for its teaching programme.[120] Presumably Strabo was able to make this statement because he knew that Aristotle's library had contained books covering all branches of knowledge. The fame of the library and the memory of its eventful history had remained alive until his own time, and Cicero had been able to peruse books written by Aristotle in his own hand.

Aristotle buys books for his library

The formation of Aristotle's library. Alexander the Great, for whom Aristotle had prepared an edition of the *Iliad* (the famed 'casket Homer'[121]), had given his former tutor a grant of eight hundred talents, mainly so that he could enlarge his library;[122] and on his all-conquering march to the Middle East he sent back a great deal of valuable material for Aristotle's magnum opus on the constitutions of 158 cities.[123] Besides the books sent to him by Alexander, Aristotle had plenty of money with which to buy books for himself: he is known to have spent three talents on the works of Speusippus, Plato's successor as head of the Academy, totalling 43,475 lines.[124] As already mentioned, one of the books he is said to have had in his library was the only known copy of Heraclitus's *On Nature*, of which Heraclitus himself had deposited a copy in the temple of Artemis at Ephesus about 150 years earlier.[125] These are the only surviving testimonies to Aristotle's purchases of books for his private library.

72. Aristotle. Miniature from a manuscript of works by Aristotle and others, Rome 1457 (Cod. vindob. phil. gr. 64).

Aristotle's own works, as listed in the catalogue preserved by Diogenes Laertius, amounted to a total of 445,270 lines. According to Moraux's calculations, they filled approximately 550 papyrus rolls. Of these, the *Corpus Aristotelicum*, comprising the texts of the school lectures as published from the first century B.C. onwards and surviving to the present day, accounts for 106 books.[126]

Classification of Aristotle's library

It seems to me that there is enough evidence available to attempt to reconstruct the contents of Aristotle's library, classifying them into four categories: (a) his 'exoteric' works, (b) his 'esoteric' works, (c) reference works and (d) writings by other authors. To help us to do so, we have four catalogues of Aristotelian writings compiled in antiquity, the oldest being the one given by Diogenes Laertius. The question of its source, and whether it is derived from a post-Callimachus Alexandrian catalogue or from the Peripatetic school itself, is not merely a problem for textual scholars: it is directly connected with the fate of Aristotle's teaching books and the question whether some or all of the originals or copies of them came into the possession of the Ptolemies and were kept in the Universal Library.[127]

73. Aristotle and Alexander of Aphrodisias. Bronze plaquette by Ulocrino. London, Victoria and Albert Museum.

(a) The 'exoteric discourses', as Aristotle himself called them, are his writings intended for the general public rather than the students at the school. Many of them are polemics or refutations: one such is the *Protrepticus*, an answer to Isocrates's criticism of the teaching at the Academy. Also included in this category are the dialogue *Eudemus*, a work entitled *Alexander, or For the Colonists*, *Divisions* (*Diaireseis*), a series of treatises including *Reply to the Pythagoreans*, *To Zeno* and *To Gorgias*, and various other works. The 'exoteric' writings are the only ones that were published by Aristotle himself: only fragments of them survive.

(b) The 'esoteric', 'didactic' or 'acroamatic' works, which chiefly concern us here, represent the distillation of Aristotle's lectures at the Lyceum, and as such they are works that he was constantly revising and probably adding marginal notes and cross-references. They did not have titles in the sense in which we use the word today: the titles by which they are now known were given to them centuries after his death, probably in the first century B.C.[128] They include the *Analytica priora* and *Analytica posteriora*, the *Physics*, the *Nicomachean Ethics* and *Eudemian Ethics*, the *Topica*, *Rhetoric*, *Poetics* and other works.

(c) The third group comprises collections of reference material assembled by Aristotle for use in his continuing research: passages from books by other writers, classified by subject (in other words, systematically organized examples of scholarly work in various fields); catalogues and collections of data of various kinds; glossaries; jottings and passing thoughts; oral traditions recorded in writing; notes arising from his research on the Homeric tradition (*Homeric Questions*), Archilochus and Euripides; lists of names of persons, things and cities; and any other information that might enlarge his knowledge of persons and things.[129] In this category there would also have been books written by students at the Lyceum as part of their coursework, such as Theophrastus's *Doctrines of Natural Philosophers* (*Φυσικῶν δόξαι*).

(d) Lastly there were the books by other writers, which Aristotle had bought or otherwise obtained in order to accumulate a comprehensive store of knowledge, at least about the Greek intellectual tradition.[130]

The Lyceum library. At this point, while on the subject of Aristotle's library and the indisputable fact that he must have had access to a great deal of written material, a few words should be said about the Lyceum library, to draw a distinction between his strictly personal collection of books and that of the Lyceum – of which also he was the part owner. Reconstructing the contents of the Lyceum library can only be a matter of conjecture, as no ancient source tells us anything about how it was formed or what eventually happened to it, and what little we do know is based on only a few scattered items of evidence.[131]

The books in the Lyceum were kept in the temple of the Muses and the library must have been very well organized, considering that Ptolemy Philadelphus wanted to appoint the head of the Lyceum to organize the Alexandrian Library. The Lyceum library would doubtless have contained all sorts of writings by earlier philosophers and sophists, both published and unpublished, poetry and other literary works, factual treatises and a wide range of books on

the Greek intellectual and cultural tradition, as well as lecture notes, students' essays and dissertations and a mass of material waiting to be evaluated, edited and published.[132] This last category consisted mainly of educational works that Aristotle had set his most talented students and teachers to write: Eudemus[133] on the history of mathematics and astronomy, Meno[134] on the doctrines of early medical doctors, and Theophrastus[135] on the history of botany. Meanwhile Aristotle himself was constantly studying written documents of all kinds, even the official records of the city of Athens, to find out all he could about theatrical works and dithyrambs. It may indeed have been his comments on the textual authenticity of the plays that prompted Lycurgus, who was in charge of the public finances of Athens from 338 to 326, to have new, official editions of the works of the three great tragedians published. The new editions were deposited in the state archives (which perhaps served as a public library as well?) and from then on actors were required by law to follow the official texts.[136]

75. Lycurgus. Engraving, 19th c. Published by J. Wilks, London 1807.

The situation in the Lyceum changed completely in 322, just after the death of Alexander the Great, because Aristotle, who was generally regarded as pro-Macedonian and wished to avoid the risk of reprisals from the anti-Macedonian party, decided to leave Athens and went to live in his mother's house at Chalcis, in Euboea. There he spent the last months of his life in solitude, apart from the company of a few select pupils, and died in October 322 at the age of sixty-three. In drawing up his will he was careful to provide for his housekeeper Herpyllis, but he made no provision at all for the future of his library.[137] There is no evidence that he took any of the books from his private library

74. The Athens Agora. From J. von Falke, Hellas und Rom..., *108-109.*

with him to Chalcis. It is fair to surmise that he did take some (presumably some of the 'esoteric' writings), because it would have been strange if he had parted with something that was such an integral part of his inner life. Aristotle appointed Theophrastus, his favourite pupil and closest associate, to be his successor as head of the Lyceum: in the light of the subsequent course of events, it is fair to assume that it was to him that he entrusted the bulk of his teaching books.

Aristotle's successors at the Lyceum

Theophrastus and the Lyceum after Aristotle. Theophrastus, who was born *circa* 370 B.C. at Eressus on the island of Lesbos and lived to the age of eighty-five, was Aristotle's most gifted pupil. When Aristotle went into voluntary exile Theophrastus stayed on in Athens and, though not an Athenian citizen, managed with the help of his pupil Demetrius of Phalerum to take over the title to the school premises.

76. *Theophrastus. Engraving, 18th c.*

Diogenes Laertius wrote a *Life of Theophrastus* in which he included a catalogue of his writings.[138] His 221 works, each taking up from one to twenty-four books, added up to 232,808 lines and filled 466 papyrus rolls. Any attempt to reconstruct the contents of Theophrastus's private library has to take into account the vast amount of material he must have collected for the purposes of the ambitious publishing programme he had undertaken for Aristotle, including the writing of a history of philosophy from Thales to Plato (*Doctrines of Natural Philosophers*).

Theophrastus declined an invitation from Ptolemy I Soter to go to Alexandria to teach at the Museum and raise it to the same high academic standard as Aristotle's school,[139] preferring instead to stay on at the Peripatos ('The Walk'), as the Lyceum was known from his time on. Such was the fame and prestige of the Peripatetic school that at its peak it was said to have had two thousand students (Diog. Laer., V.37).

In his will, Theophrastus bequeathed 'the gardens, the Peripatos and all the buildings adjoining the gardens' to all who wished to study literature and philosophy there together.[140] The inference is that from Theophrastus's time onwards the library of the Peripatetic school was in some sense a collegiate library for the students, who were able to use books belonging to the principal and teachers. The teaching staff, of course, were allowed to take their own books with them if they left the school, as Dicaearchus[141] and Eudemus did. Evidently Eudemus inherited some of the autograph manuscripts of Aristotle's teaching books before going back to Rhodes to carry on his mentor's work there.[142] Theophrastus, unlike his teacher, left a will with a clause stipulating exactly what was to be done with the Peripatos library (and presumably his own library too): 'All the books [I leave] to Neleus.'[143] This bequest marks the beginning of the vicissitudes that overtook Aristotle's library.

The inheritors of Aristotle's original teaching books

Neleus. Neleus, who came from the small town of Scepsis in the Troad, is something of a mystery character: in fact, if his name were not connected with Aristotle's books we might know nothing at all about him. He was a student at Plato's Academy at the same time as Aristotle, and when Speusippus succeeded Plato he went with Aristotle to the court of Hermeias, a eunuch who had been a slave and had made himself ruler of the cities of Assus and Atarneus.[144]

But what was it that induced Theophrastus to bequeath his books to Neleus, an old man who was not a scholar and whose ability as a teacher – certainly at the level of the Peripatetic school – was open to question? The answer is unclear, but perhaps it had something to do with the friendship that had developed between Neleus and Aristotle at Assus and the support that Neleus enjoyed from Demetrius of Phalerum, the ruler of Athens.[145] Neleus, who was probably pulling strings behind the scenes, thought that, since Aristotle had left him his teaching books, he was sure to be appointed head of the Peripatetic school; but he was disappointed in his hopes, and when Demetrius Poliorcetes seized power in Athens in 307 he found himself out of favour with the Establishment. He retired in dudgeon to his native town, taking most of Aristotle's teaching books with him in revenge. He would then have been in his sixties.

This date marks the start of the chequered history of Aristotle's autograph manuscripts, as recorded by Strabo.[146] Theophrastus was followed as head of the Peripatetic school by Strato of Lampsacus (286-268), under whom the atmosphere at the school changed considerably. Strabo thought its decline was due to the loss or disappearance of Aristotle's lecture notes, and perhaps of Theophrastus's books as well.[147] This may not be the whole truth of the matter (and we have to remember that Strabo was writing two centuries after the event), but it is true that Strato's research interests were probably out of line with the traditional educational principles of the Peripatetic school.

Strato went to Alexandria at the invitation of Ptolemy II Philadelphus and spent some time there tutoring Ptolemy's son. On his return to Athens he probably acted as a link between the Athenian school and the Museum of Alexandria and, among other things, as an adviser on the enlargement of the Alexandrian Library. He was head of the Peripatetic school for eighteen years and bequeathed his own books – and those belonging to the school, or so it is said – to Lycon.[148]

The Peripatetic library under Theophrastus

Lycon of the Troad was not distinguished for his philosophical knowledge or brilliance. In the forty-four years that he was head of the Peripatos he broadened the curriculum and made improvements in the way the school was run, but he failed to revitalize philosophical studies. In his will he stipulated that after his death the school was to be run by a group of his friends (Amphion, the younger Lycon, Lycomachus and others), whom he exhorted to work together in harmony.[149] The library of the Peripatos and its principals is last heard of in connection with the elder Lycon, who left all his published works to his successor and namesake and his unpublished writings to Callinus, with instructions to edit and publish them.[150]

The eventful subsequent history of Aristotle's library. From the time when Neleus left Athens for his home town of Scepsis, the eventful history of the autograph manuscripts of Aristotle's teaching books reads like a novel.[151] Precisely how many books Neleus took with him when he left Athens, and which ones, are questions that cannot be answered. So, if any hypothesis is to be substantiated, we have to sift every grain of evidence from the sources and correlate it with the literary testimonies. Most important of all, we have to remember that the main sources for this story are Strabo and Cicero (who wrote in the first century B.C.), Plutarch (in the first and second centuries A.D.) and Athenaeus (*circa* A.D. 200).

Of all the questions raised by this curious episode in literary history, the one that probably needs to be answered first is this: from the time of Aristotle's death to the death of Theophrastus, were any or all of Aristotle's 'esoteric writings' published or at least copied in the Peripatos on Theophrastus's initiative, to make copies readily available and ensure that the school would not be completely deprived of its founder's teaching books? According to Strabo, the first Peripatetics after Theophrastus had no books at all apart from some of Aristotle's 'exoteric writings', which meant that serious philosophical discussion was impossible and all the teachers and students could do was to 'talk grandiloquently about commonplace propositions'.[152] The result was that later, when Aristotle's books were again available in Athens, the Peripatetics had to revise many of their opinions because so many mistakes had crept into the texts.[153] Strabo's testimony would be credible only if we accepted that throughout the forty years when Theophrastus was head of the school he had no access to Aristotle's teaching books – which is contradicted by the fact that Aristotle's autograph manuscripts were left to Neleus in Theophrastus's will – or else, just possibly, that Aristotle had bequeathed his teaching books to Neleus, who kept them under lock and key, which would mean that Theophrastus bequeathed only his own writings to Neleus.

77. *Aristotle in his library. From P. Gringore,* Les menus propos..., *Paris 1528.*

Was the Lyceum left without books?

Be all that as it may, the fact is that Neleus, on his return to Scepsis with the original manuscripts of Aristotle's teaching books, did nothing whatsoever about having them published: after all, he was not himself a scholar of any repute, and it seems that in any case he was not interested in doing so. The books stayed in the family until Neleus's descendants hid them in a cave to prevent them from falling into the hands of King Eumenes II of Pergamum, who was collecting books for his own library.[154]

The story told by Athenaeus is different: he says that Ptolemy II Philadelphus bought Aristotle's teaching books *and* the books that Theophrastus had bequeathed to Neleus and took them all, as well as many more that he had acquired in Athens and Rhodes, to the Library in Alexandria.[155] The subsequent course of events shows that this could not have been true, but it is possible that Neleus himself sold copies of the 'esoteric writings' – and perhaps some of the original manuscripts as well – to Ptolemy Philadelphus, and that they formed the basis for the development of the Alexandrian tradition of Aristotelian studies.[156]

If we accept one or other version of the story, we find ourselves faced with a crucial question: did the 'Universal Library' in Alexandria possess Aristotle's teaching books? The answer can perhaps be inferred from the relations between the Ptolemies and the Peripatetic school and the existence of the Alexandrian tradition of literary scholarship.[157] Ptolemy I Soter and his successor, Philadelphus, made it quite clear from the outset that they intended their Museum to have a special relationship with the Peripatos, their main object being to stress the Macedonian connection between Aristotle and his school and the great new centre of Hellenism, Alexandria. This is borne out by the invitations extended to Theophrastus and Strato to come and teach in Alexandria and help with the organization of the library, and by the fact that Demetrius of Phalerum was involved in planning the enlargement of the library. In any case, it would have been strange if the Ptolemies, in their efforts to create a treasury of the whole of the Greek intellectual tradition (and more besides), had not managed to obtain copies of at least some of Aristotle's teaching books. That they did have them is evident from the fact that Aristophanes of Byzantium wrote a book entitled *On Animals*, which was a compendium based on Aristotle's *History of Animals*, Theophrastus and the Paradoxographi,[158] and another book entitled *On Words*, which was based on Book III of Aristotle's *Rhetoric*.

Did the Alexandrians know Aristotle's didactic works?

Whatever the true facts of the case, the traditional story is that all(?) the original manuscripts of Aristotle's teaching books lay hidden and mouldering away for about two hundred years in the cave near Scepsis where they had been put for safe keeping by Neleus's descendants, before their fate became tied up with an opportunistic adventurer named Apellicon, who was active in Athens in the first century B.C.[159]

Apellicon. Towards the end of the second century B.C. there appeared on the Athenian intellectual scene a man named Apellicon, born at Teos in Asia Minor, who became a naturalized Athenian citizen. He was an eccentric who described himself as a Peripatetic philosopher (although the Peripatetic school was not functioning at the time) and enjoyed using his wealth to make a name for himself as a patron of literature.[160] He had a fine library, but his interests were entirely superficial: as Strabo (XIII.C.609) remarks, he was a bibliophile rather than a philosopher. To gratify his literary ambitions he went so far as to steal some original Attic decrees from the public archives, an offence for which he could well have been condemned to death. He managed to escape this penalty through the intervention of the city's ruler Athenion, an ancient Greek Cola di Rienzo, who took the Athenians into an alliance with Mithradates VI of Pontus so that they could fight under his leadership against the Romans. Apellicon won Athenion's friendship by appealing to the bond of their shared interest in Peripatetic philosophy, and as a result he was merely condemned to a brief period of exile from Athens.[161]

Apellicon brings Aristotle's original manuscripts back to Athens

Across the Aegean in the coastlands of Asia Minor, the last king of Pergamum, Attalus III Philometor, had bequeathed his kingdom to the Roman Senate on his death in 133 B.C. The strife that ensued, owing to the inability of the Romans to impose their rule on Pergamum, reduced the kingdom to a state of near-anarchy. When the Romans had eventually won control and Pergamum had been brought under Roman rule, certain descendants of Neleus remembered the cache of Aristotle's books and retrieved them with a view to selling them. Somehow Apellicon heard about this and lost no time in buying the books, for which he paid a handsome sum of money. And so what was left of Neleus's library – those of Aristotle's original manuscripts that had survived, and perhaps some other books too – found its way back to Athens. Apellicon was now able to set himself up as the fount of all knowledge, but he did at least have new copies made so that philosophers once again had access to them. So overweening was his vanity that in order to impress the Athenians he himself edited and published a work by Aristotle from an imperfect, moth-eaten manuscript, using his own imagination to fill in the missing parts.[162]

But the remnants of Aristotle's library were not to remain long in Apellicon's possession. Sulla, campaigning in Greece in the First Mithradatic War, encamped outside the walls of Athens and, after a long siege, captured the city in 86 B.C. Apellicon was killed and the spoils that Sulla carried back with him to Rome included Apellicon's library, or at least those of Aristotle's original teaching books that had survived.[163]

After 168 B.C., when Aemilius Paullus sacked the Macedonian royal library at Aegae and carried the books off to Rome, the biggest collections of books were owned by Roman patricians, many of whom were interested in and knowledgeable about Greece. Yet nearly a century later, in Sulla's time, there was still no 'book policy' in Rome: private libraries were few and far between and the first public library as such did not open until 39 B.C. This meant that a large number of important Greek books, brought to Rome as spoils of war from various victorious campaigns, failed to arouse interest even in scholarly circles.[164] Fortunately, however, Aristotle's books were not kept under lock and key in Sulla's villa, and so they came into the hands of two Greek men of letters whose names are connected with the beginning of the Aristotelian corpus as we now know it: Tyrannio first, and then Andronicus of Rhodes.

Tyrannio. Tyrannio the Elder, born at Amisus on the Black Sea coast of Asia Minor, studied under the celebrated grammarian Dionysius the Thracian. In the Third Mithradatic War he was taken prisoner, but fortunately for him his captor was Lucullus, a philhellene, who treated him kindly and took him under his wing in Rome so that he was able to move freely in the most illustrious Roman literary circles.

The greatest ancient Greek book-collector

Lucullus was a great book-lover who had gathered round him a coterie of Greeks with intellectual and artistic interests, and Tyrannio, thanks to his personality, won the friendship and patronage of a number of prominent Romans including Julius Caesar, Atticus and the great Cicero himself. Tyrannio was an Aristotelian and an avid bibliophile who, thanks to his friendship with these men, is said to have amassed a collection of 30,000 rolls. What is more, by cultivating the friendship of Sulla and his librarian he was allowed to use Sulla's library freely and even to borrow Aristotle's manuscripts.[165]

Tyrannio kept track of all the big book collections brought to Rome and took note of book sales, and in this way he acquired a great reputation for his knowledge of librarianship and the publishing trade. He gave Cicero valuable advice on the organization of his libraries and the writing of his great book on geography, based on Eratosthenes.[166] Besides collecting books for himself, Tyrannio made a serious effort to classify, edit and publish Aristotle's works, though he never completed the project.[167] Meanwhile Sulla died in 78 B.C. and all his books and other possessions were inherited by his son Faustus, who refused to lend out any of his books: anyone who wished to consult them had to go to Faustus's villa in person, with the result that his library became one of the centres of Roman intellectual life. It may have been there that Cicero had his first opportunity to read Aristotle's 'esoteric' writings.[168]

Faustus Sulla, having squandered his fortune and run into debt, had to sell off his property,[169] and evidently his books were among the possessions of his that were sold. Meanwhile he fought on the side of the aristocrats against Julius Caesar at Pharsala and Tapsus, was taken prisoner in Africa and was executed on Caesar's orders in 46 B.C. Whether his books and other possessions were sold before or after his death is not known; the outcome, however, on the evidence of Plutarch and the known facts, is that Tyrannio ended in possession of the original manuscripts of Aristotle's and Theophrastus's teaching books.

Roman intellectuals gain access to Aristotle's books

Tyrannio, who had intended to publish Aristotle's didactic works, abandoned his plan for some reason and, according to Plutarch, delegated it to Andronicus of Rhodes.[170] Andronicus completed the project between 40 and 20 B.C., according to Düring, and the first reference to this edition is found in the work of Dionysius of Halicarnassus, who was active in Rome after 30 B.C.[171]

Andronicus of Rhodes. Andronicus, a Peripatetic philosopher, was born on Rhodes and flourished in the first century B.C. There is a *fable convenue* to the effect that he was the eleventh head of the Peripatetic school, between 70 and 50 B.C., but this is a dubious story for which we have only the word of the Neoplatonist Elias of Alexandria, an unreliable source.[172] He studied on Rhodes, where the Aristotelian tradition founded by Aristotle's gifted pupil Eudemus still lived on, and he may have possessed some of the books from Eudemus's library. Andronicus was highly regarded for his thorough scholarship and his learning.[173] In Rome he mixed with a set of literary men and book-lovers with an interest in the Aristotelian tradition, and he found Aristotle's didactic works and books by other Peripatetics at Faustus's villa as well as copies of the didactic works in Lucullus's library.

The publishing project. The original manuscripts that Andronicus had in his hands needed a good deal of work before they were ready for publishing. There were no titles in the modern sense of the word: when Aristotle wished to refer to one of his own books he used various phrases that described its contents. Moreover, his method of working was to write numerous notes in the margins when he wished to alter the wording or modify his opinions, sometimes to such an extent that the final result amounted to a revised ver-

78. *Aristotle,* On Animals, *from the five-volume Aldine edition of the complete works,* Ἅπαντα, *Venice, Aldus Manutius, 1495-1498.*

ἈΡΙΣΤΟΤΕΛΟΥΣ ΠΕΡῚ ΖΩΩΝ ΜΟΡΙΩΝ ΤῸ ΠΡΩΤΟΝ.

Περὶ πᾶσαν θεωρίαν ἡ μέθοδον, ὁμοίως ταπεινοτέραν τε καὶ τιμιωτέραν, δύο φαίνονται τρόποι τῆς ἕξεως εἶναι· ὧν τὴν μὲν, ἐπιστήμην τοῦ πράγματος, καλῶς ἔχει προσαγορεύειν· τὴν δ' οἷον παιδείαν τινά. πεπαιδευμένου γάρ ἐστι κατὰ τρόπον, τὸ δύνασθαι κρίνειν εὐστόχως, τί καλῶς ἢ μὴ καλῶς ἀποδίδωσιν ὁ λέγων. τοιοῦτον γὰρ δή τινα καὶ τὸν ὅλως πεπαιδευμένον οἰόμεθ' εἶναι καὶ τὸ πεπαιδεῦσθαι, τὸ δύνασθαι ποιεῖν τὸ εἰρημένον. πλὴν τοῦτον μὲν, περὶ πάντων ὡς εἰπεῖν τινα κριτικὸν νομίζομεν ἕνα τὸν ἀριθμὸν ὄντα· τὸν δὲ, περί τινος φύσεως ἀφωρισμένης· εἴη γὰρ ἄν τις ἕτερος, τὸν αὐτὸν τρόπον διακείμενος τῷ εἰρημένῳ, περὶ ἓν μόριον· ὥστε δῆλον, ὅτι καὶ τῆς περὶ φύσεως ἱστορίας, δεῖ τινας ὑπάρχειν ὅρους τοιούτους πρὸς οὓς ἀναφέρων, ἀποδέξεται τὸν τρόπον τῶν δεικνυμένων, χωρὶς τοῦ, πῶς ἔχει τἀληθές· εἴτε οὕτως, εἴτε ἄλλως. λέγω δ' οἷον πότερον δεῖ, λαμβάνοντας μίαν ἑκάστην οὐσίαν, περὶ ταύτης διορίζειν καθ' αὑτήν· οἷον περὶ ἀνθρώπου φύσεως, ἢ λέοντος, ἢ βοός, ἢ καί τινος ἄλλου τοιούτου καθ' ἕκαστον προχειριζομένους, ἢ τὰ κοινῇ συμβεβηκότα πᾶσι κατά τι κοινὸν ὑποθεμένους· πολλὰ γὰρ ὑπάρχει ταὐτὰ γένεσιν ἑτέροις οὖσιν ἀλλήλων· οἷον ὕπνος· ἀναπνοή· αὔξησις· φθίσις· θάνατος· καὶ πρὸς τούτοις, ὅσα τοιαῦτα τῶν λοιπῶν παθῶν τε καὶ διαθέσεων· ἄδηλον γὰρ καὶ ἀδιόριστόν ἐστι λέγειν νῦν περὶ τούτων· φανερὸν δὲ ὅτι καὶ κατὰ μέρος μὲν λέγοντες, περὶ πολλῶν ἐροῦμεν πολλάκις ταὐτά· καὶ γὰρ ἵπποις καὶ κυσὶ καὶ ἀνθρώποις ὑπάρχει τῶν εἰρημένων ἕκαστον· ὥστε ἐὰν καθ' ἕκαστον τῶν συμβεβηκότων λέγῃ τις,

sion. Consequently the editor, in this case Andronicus, had to copy out all the marginal notes, cross-references and additions with the utmost care and weave them into the text in such a way as to make it read as smoothly as possible.

Deeper analysis of this matter belongs in the sphere of textual studies. The point of interest here is that the texts that have come down to us in the *Corpus Aristotelicum* must have been prepared from Aristotle's original manuscripts by an editor who did not omit or ignore anything he found in the marginal notes. Porphyry, who was faced with the same problem in preparing his edition of Plotinus, actually describes how Andronicus worked: 'He divided the works of Aristotle and Theophrastus into books [*pragmateiai*, "treatises"] by putting all writings on the same subject together under one title.'[174] Thus it was Andronicus who arranged Aristotle's writings thematically in the form in which we now know them.[175]

Andronicus's method of editing

Andronicus's recension presented the world with a new picture of the extent of Aristotle's philosophical writings, because now for the first time, three hundred years after the philosopher's death, his works were accessible in a form that permitted an overall view of his philosophy. Once the new edition had been published, multiple copies were doubtless made for the great libraries of the ancient Greek world and for the philosophy schools, opening the gates to a flood of commentaries and paraphrases written for the general reader.

Postscript. To conclude this chapter on the Classical period, having outlined the circumstances leading to the formation of the first private, public and academic libraries and the part played by those libraries in establishing the practice of scientific thinking through the teaching of the schools, it is worth devoting a little space to a short satire of much later date which is the only ancient Greek work exclusively devoted to the subject of books. Though not written until the second century A.D., it takes us back to the beginnings of the Greek written tradition, with Homer's references to Bellerophon, and keeps alive the traditions of the Classical period in Greece. It is strongly reminiscent of Socrates's dialogue with Euthydemus as immortalized by Xenophon, for it shows us that centuries later nothing had changed in the behaviour of ignorant bibliomanes. Its author, Lucian (A.D. 120-200), that mordant satirist of all human follies, aims his shafts at pompous bibliophiles and their dubious learning, using examples and anecdotes from his own time. It is entitled *To the Ignorant Book-Collector*.

95. See Turner, *Athenian Books*, 19 (Isocrates, *On the Antidosis*, 12).
96. Aristotle's disparaging comment led Cephisodorus, a loyal pupil of Isocrates, to take up the cudgels in defence of his teacher: see Dionysius of Halicarnassus, *Isocrates*, 18.
97. See Turner, *Athenian Books*, 19 (Isocrates, *On the Antidosis*, 193; *Panathenaicus*, 233).
98. See the quotation from Lucian (*To the Ignorant Book-Collector*, 4) on p. 129.
99. C. Müller (ed.), *Oratores Attici*, II, Paris 1848, 523.
100. Xenophon, *Anabasis*, VII.5: 'Here was a great find, beds and boxes and written books, and everything else which mariners carry in their wooden chests.' See also Kenyon, *op. cit.*, 23-24. Diogenes Laertius (IV.47), in his *Life of Bion of Borysthenes* (a philosopher from Borysthenes [Olbia] on the north coast of the Black Sea), states that Bion was sold into slavery with all his family when his father was convicted of some kind of tax fraud. On the death of the orator who had bought him, Bion inherited his property and decided to go to Athens to study philosophy, but before he left he burnt all the books bequeathed to him by his late master.
101. See p. 80.
102. See p. 118.
103. See p. 84.
104. Polybius, XII.25h. See also Lesky, *op. cit.*, 1000.
105. See H. Cherniss, *The Riddle of the Early Academy*, Berkeley 1945; Id., *Das Problem der frühen Akademie*, Heidelberg 1965. See also K. Gaiser, *Platons ungeschriebene Lehre* (with the testimonia and sources of information on the Academy and Plato's oral teaching), Stuttgart 1963. For a brief review of the philosophy schools in Athens see L. G. Benakis, 'Philosophy in Athens (from Anaxagoras to Damascius', in *Athens: From the Classical Period to the Present Day (5th century B.C. - A.D. 2000)*, ed. Ch. Bouras, M. B. Sakellariou, K. Sp. Staikos and Evi Touloupa, Athens 2003, 109-143.
106. Diog. Laer., IV.5: ' They comprise in all 43,475 lines. To him Timonides addresses his narrative.... Favorinus also in the second book of his *Memorabilia* relates that Aristotle purchased the works of Speusippus for three talents.'
107. Diog. Laer., IV.32-33: 'He would seem to have admired Plato, and he possessed copies of his works.'
108. John Philoponus, *Against Proclus on the Eternity of the World*, VI.27: 'Plato so admired his sagacity that he called him "The Mind of the School".' Also in the *Vita Marciana*, 7, which in this form is derived from the Arabic tradition, and more specifically from Ptolemy el-Garib. Philoponus's source for this item of information was probably the *Life of Ptolemy*. Quite possibly, when Plato gave this nickname to his favourite pupil, he was thinking of Epicharmus's words: "It is the Mind that sees and hears, all else is deaf and blind." See I. Düring, *Ὁ Ἀριστοτέλης, Παρουσίαση καί Ἑρμηνεία τῆς Σκέψης του* (= *Aristoteles. Darstellung und Interpretation seines Denkens*, tr. P. Kotzia-Panteli), I, Athens 1991, 51; Id., *Aristotle in the Ancient Biographical Tradition* [*Studia Graeca et Latina Gothoburgensia* 5], Göteborg 1957 (hereafter abbreviated as Düring, *Biog. Trad.*), 108-109.
109. Lycon, the successor of Strato of Lampsacus as head of the Lyceum (the *Peripatos* or Peripatetic school), left those of his books that had been read in public to his Reader (Diog. Laer., V.73). Strato, who had succeeded Theophrastus, had left a will in which he stated, 'Those books we have written': he was probably referring to the books that had been

written by him in his own hand and had not been published. Plato referred to books that were obtainable on the market as *δεδημοσιευμένα* (literally 'published'): see Plato, *The Sophist*, 232d; Düring, *Biog. Trad.*, 441.

110. Plato, *Phaedrus*, 248b ('they feed upon opinion'), 275b ('since they are not wise, but only think themselves wise').

111. On the Lyceum see p. 115. The most complete study is F. Wehrli, *Die Schule des Aristoteles*, 10 vols., Basel 1944-1959: I, *Dikaiarchos*, 1944; II, *Aristoxenos*, 1945; III, *Klearchos*, 1948; IV, *Demetrios von Phaleron*, 1949; V, *Straton von Lampsakos*, 1950; VI, *Lykon und Ariston von Keos*, 1952; VII, *Herakleides Pontikos*, 1953; VIII, *Eudemos von Rhodos*, 1955; IX, *Phainias von Eresos and others*, 1957; X, *Hieronymos von Rhodos and others* (with index), 1959. See also F. Grayeff, *Aristotle and his School: An Inquiry into the History of the Peripatos with a Commentary on Metaphysics Z, H, Λ and Θ*, London 1974, 49-68; J.P. Lynch, *Aristotle's School: A Study of a Greek Educational Institution*, Berkeley 1972.

112. On the Epicurean school see A. A. Long, *Hellenistic Philosophy: Stoics, Epicureans, Sceptics*, London 1974.

113. Diog. Laer., X.21: 'All my books to be given to Hermarchus.' Id., X.26: 'Epicurus was a most prolific author and eclipsed all before him in the number of his writings: for they amount to about three hundred rolls.'

114. Diog. Laer., VII.181: 'Apollodorus of Athens in his *Collection of Doctrines* [H. Usener, *Epicurea*, Leipzig 1887, 87], wishing to show that what Epicurus wrote with force and originality unaided by quotations was far greater in amount than the books of Chrysippus, says, to quote his exact words, "If one were to strip the books of Chrysippus of all extraneous quotations, his pages would be left bare." So much for Apollodorus.'

115. Diog. Laer., VII.2-3.

116. Diog. Laer., VII.174. Cleanthes the Stoic philosopher, who came from Assus in Asia Minor, was the subject of the following anecdote. An acquaintance remarked to him one day that he was looking old. 'Yes, I too am willing to go,' Cleanthes answered, 'but seeing that I am in the best of health and still able to write and read, I am content to wait.'

117. Diog. Laer., VII.36: 'Of the many disciples of Zeno the following are the most famous: Persaeus, son of Demetrius, of Citium, whom some call a pupil and others one of the household, one of those sent him by Antigonus to act as secretary....'

118. See J. H. Rist, *Stoic Philosophy*, Cambridge 1969; Long, *op. cit.*; M. Schofield, *Ἡ στωική ἰδέα τῆς πόλης* (= *The Stoic Idea of the City*, Cambridge 1991, tr. Chloe Balla), Athens 1997.

119. See A. Schmekel, *Die Philosophie der mittleren Stoa*, Berlin 1892; B. N. Tatakis, *Panétius de Rhodes, le fondateur du moyen Stoïcisme*, Paris 1931. The period after Chrysippus was marked by disputes between the Stoa and the Academy. Panaetius of Rhodes ushered in a new phase in the history of the school, when Stoic philosophy flowered anew among Roman intellectuals such as Scipio Aemilianus, Laelius and Cicero. This is the period that some modern scholars call the 'Middle Stoa'.

120. Strabo, XIII.C.608-609: 'Aristotle bequeathed his own library to Theophrastus, to whom he also left his school; and as far as I know he was the first man to collect books and the first to teach the kings of Egypt how to organize a library.' Cf. Athenaeus, I.3. See also p. 74 herein.

121. Of the several lives of Aristotle written by the Neoplatonists, only one mentions

Aristotle's alleged edition of the *Iliad*. There it is listed among his works after *Homeric Questions*: '... and the edition of the *Iliad* that he gave to Alexander.' The famous story of the 'casket Homer', which is accepted by some as fact but by others dismissed as fiction, is as follows. According to Plutarch (*Alexander*, VIII.2), the helmsman of Alexander's ship, Onesicritus – who was himself a historian, though not always reliable (Düring, *Ὁ Ἀριστοτέλης...*, I, 218, where his name is given as Onirocritus) – stated that Alexander always slept with his dagger and a copy of the *Iliad* 'edited by Aristotle, which people call "the casket copy" [*Ἀριστοτέλους διορθώσαντος ἣν ἐκ τοῦ νάρθηκος καλοῦσιν*]' under his pillow. Plutarch (*Alexander*, XXVI.1) explains this by saying that Alexander possessed a precious casket that had belonged to Darius himself, in which he kept a copy of the *Iliad*, and adds that it was no secret: 'This is attested by many trustworthy authorities.' Cf. Plutarch, *On the Fortune or the Virtue of Alexander*, I.4; Pliny the Elder, *Natural History*, VII.29 (30).

One of the Neoplatonic biographies of Aristotle mentions an edition of the *Iliad*, and Plutarch (perhaps following Onesicritus) refers to it as a version revised and amended by Aristotle himself. Aristotle's revision of the text is also mentioned by Strabo (XIII.C594), who confuses the issue still further by introducing other characters into the story: 'It is said that there exists an edited version of Homer's poems, the so-called "casket copy", which Alexander, with Callisthenes and Anaxarchus and other members of their circle, read and annotated to some extent.' See Callisthenes (*FGrHist* 124 T 10). On Anaxarchus see Wehrli, *op. cit.*, III, 67.

The conclusion to be drawn is that Alexander did indeed have a prized copy of the *Iliad* which he kept in a valuable case. He is known to have loved Homer and to have been a great admirer of Achilles, whom he took as his role model. Quite possibly Aristotle, when in Macedonia working on his *Homeric Questions* (see H. Hintenlang, *Untersuchungen zu den Homer-Aporien des Aristoteles* [dissertation], Heidelberg 1961), had a fair copy of the *Iliad* made for Alexander, and he may have read through it to correct the copyist's mistakes. This seems the most likely explanation, considering that there is no historical evidence that Aristotle ever edited the *Iliad* and brought out a new edition; furthermore, no such edition appears in the list of Aristotle's lost works (see P. Moraux, *Les listes anciennes des ouvrages d'Aristote*, Louvain 1951).

122. See W. D. Ross, *Ἀριστοτέλης* (= *Aristotle*, tr. Marilisa Mitsou), Athens 1993², 19.

123. Alexandrian book lists included under Aristotle's name a collection of 158 constitutions of cities with democratic, oligarchic, 'tyrannical' or aristocratic systems of government, which Aristotle arranged in the order in which he had treated them in Book IV of his *Politics*. It is doubtful whether that work was ever completed: of the sixty-two fragments of those constitutions that survive, mostly in notes by lexicographers and scholiasts of little value to the historian, only the *Constitution of the Athenians* (found in 1890) confirms the tradition of the existence of such a work, and its style, vocabulary and language are in many respects non-Aristotelian. See K. von Fritz and E. Kapp, *Aristotle's Constitution of Athens and Related Texts*, New York 1950; K. von Fritz, 'Die Bedeutung des Aristoteles für die Geschichtsschreibung', *Entretiens Fondation Hardt* 4 (1958) 86-128.

124. Diog. Laer., IV.4. See also p. 145 (n. 106) herein.

125. Diog. Laer., IX.6. See also pp. 79 and 139 (n. 46) herein.

126. According to Düring (*Ὁ Ἀριστοτέλης...*, I, 75-76), on the basis of the Alexandrian catalogue of Aristotle's works, Aristotle must have written about 550 books in the ancient sense of the word, i.e. papyrus rolls. And Moraux (*op. cit.*, 192), after checking through the books of the *Topica*, confirmed that the ancient information was correct. Given that an average book (papyrus roll) was equivalent to twenty printed pages, 550 books would be equivalent to 11,000 printed pages.

Aristotle's known works, all of which are included in the *Corpus Aristotelicum* although only a few are listed in the Alexandrian catalogue, fill 106 books. In Bekker's edition they take up 2,500 columns = 87,500 lines = 875,000 words.

127. See esp. Moraux, *op. cit.*; C. Lord, 'On the Early History of the Aristotelian Corpus', *AJP* 107 (1986) 137-161.

Four catalogues of Aristotle's written works are known: one from Diogenes Laertius, one from 'Anonyme de Ménage' and two from Arab writers. Neither Diogenes Laertius nor the anonymous compiler gives the slightest indication of the source of his list or of when it was compiled.

The catalogue given by Diogenes Laertius does not list all Aristotle's works, even though Diogenes claims that it does, since he himself, in the text, mentions some Aristotelian titles that are not included in his catalogue. Presumably his catalogue lists all the works given by his source, and the way the titles are listed makes it clear that he knew nothing about Andronicus's edition of the Corpus (see pp. 126-128).

It has been suggested that the source of Diogenes's catalogue was Hermippus, a grammarian and philosopher of the third century B.C., who studied under Callimachus in Alexandria and wrote his *Lives of Men Famous for their Learning* using the material provided by his master's *Pinakes* ('Tables', a catalogue of all Greek literature). Although that book is now lost, there is evidence to suggest that it consisted of separate biographies classified according to the kind of work for which their subjects were best known: lawgivers, the Seven Sages, magicians and so on. The fact that Hermippus based his work on the *Pinakes* (from which he quoted fairly lengthy extracts verbatim) suggests that what he was setting out to write was not a scientifically documented text but merely an anthology enlivened with anecdotes. If so, he could hardly be expected to have devoted time and effort to original research in quest of all Aristotle's works. He might, of course, have found a full list in the *Pinakes*, but in that case the titles would have been arranged under subject headings (and in alphabetical order within each subject), and one would therefore expect them to be in the same order in the catalogue of Diogenes Laertius. See J.S. Heibges, 'Hermippos [6]', in *RE*, 8/1 (1912), 845-852; F. Montanari, 'Hermippos aus Berytus', in *NP*, 5 (1998), 439-440; Moraux, *op. cit.*, 22 ff.

The *Vita Menagiana* ends with a catalogue of Aristotle's works, the first part of which bears many resemblances to that of Diogenes Laertius. And although the *Life of Aristotle* by 'Anonyme de Ménage' is virtually the same as the entry under 'Aristotle' in the *Onomatologos* of Hesychius of Miletus, its origin is still obscure because Hesychius's sources have not been traced. (On the *Vita Menagiana* see H. L. M. Flach, *Hesychii Milesii Onomatologi qua supersunt*, Leipzig 1883, 245-249.) It is therefore impossible, on this evidence, to establish a connection with the catalogue of Diogenes Laertius. The catalogue of 'Anonyme de Ménage' is divided into three parts: one contains 139 titles and is very similar to Diogenes's list; the second contains forty-six titles, some of which are duplicated in the first part; and the third has ten titles classified as spurious. See E. Heitz (ed.), *Aristotelis Fragmenta* [= *Aristotelis opera omnia*, IV.2], Paris 1869, 5-9. In the catalogue of 'Anonyme de Ménage', the first part has an appendix comprising two further sections: see Moraux, *op. cit.*, 249-288.

The two lists given by Arab writers, Ibn al-Qifṭī (1172-1248) in his *History of Learned Men* (on Ibn al-Qifṭī see Chapter III) and Ibn Abī Uṣeibi (†1236) in his *History of Medicine*, come not from Greek sources but from a Syriac version. Both these Arab writers name as their source a certain 'Ptolemy the Unknown', whom they distinguish from the author of the *Almagest*. Uṣeibi actually gives the original title of Ptolemy's work: *To Gallus, on the life of Aristotle, his history, his will and the list of his works* (see A. Baumstark, *Syrisch-arabische Biographien des Aristoteles* [dissertation], Heidelberg 1898, 14-15). The Ptolemy in question is the one called el-Garib.

Ptolemy el-Garib's catalogue differs from its predecessors in many particulars and we know that it was compiled after Andronicus had completed his editing and publishing project; in other words, the Aristotelian Corpus had already taken the form in which we know it today. Ptolemy's catalogue is of minor importance, chiefly because it is post-Andronicus and therefore tells us nothing about the contents of the Corpus before Andronicus went to work on it in the first century B.C. See Moraux, *op. cit.*, 289 ff.

The question remains: who compiled the catalogue of Aristotle's works retailed by Diogenes Laertius? In Moraux's opinion it was Ariston of Ceos, a philosopher of the third century B.C. (†226) who studied under Lycon, subsequently became head of the Peripatetic school and wrote a number of biographies of philosophers. See I. Düring, 'Ariston or Hermippus?', *Classica et Mediaevalia* 17 (1956) 11-12; Id., *Biog. Trad.*, 67-69. For a critical survey of the various hypotheses see P. Moraux, *Der Aristotelismus bei den Griechen von Andronikos bis Alexander von Aphrodisias*, I, Berlin 1973, 4; C. Lord, 'On the Early History...'.

128. On the editing and publishing of Aristotle's 'esoteric' writings see pp. 126-128.
129. From what we know of his method of working, Aristotle must at a fairly early stage have collected a good deal of varied material which he subsequently backed up with separate thematic collections: over a third of the entries in the Alexandrian catalogue are accounted for by works of this kind. See Düring, *'Ο Ἀριστοτέλης...*, I, 70-75 ("Στόχος καί μέθοδοι τῆς δουλειᾶς του").
130. See p. 112.
131. See p. 146 (n. 111).
132. Aristotle, *Topica*, 105b, 12: 'We should select also from the written handbooks.'
133. Eudemus of Rhodes, the fourth-century philosopher, was, with Theophrastus, one of Aristotle's favourite pupils. He took on the project of writing a history of various branches of learning: arithmetic, geometry, astronomy and perhaps theology. In recent times these three and other writers have come to be known as *doxographi*: see Diels, *Doxographi Graeci*.
134. Meno, a doctor and philosopher of the fourth century B.C., wrote a treatise for Aristotle summarizing the history of medical teaching down to about 370, with the title *Medical Collection* or

Menonian Medicine. The work itself is lost, but a few fragments survive on papyrus (Anonymus Londinensis): see W. H. S. Jones, *The Medical Writings of Anonymus Londiniensis*, Cambridge 1947.

135. Theophrastus, Aristotle's successor at the Lyceum, undertook to write a history of philosophy from Thales to Plato giving a survey of the beliefs of the 'natural philosophers': the finished work (now lost) filled eighteen books and was entitled *Doctrines of Natural Philosophers* (*Φυσικῶν σόξαι*). See O. Regenbogen, 'Theophrastos', in *RE*, suppl. 7 (1940), 1535 ff.

136. Pseudo-Plutarch, *Lives of Ten Orators*, VII.841F. See also A. Pickard-Cambridge, *The Dramatic Festivals of Athens*, 2nd edn. revised by J. Gould and D. M. Lewis, Oxford 1968; A. Wilhelm, *Urkunden dramatischer Aufführungen in Athen* [*Sonderschriften des Österr. Archäolog. Instituts in Wien* VI], Vienna 1906.

137. Diog. Laer, V.12-16. Aristotle's will has come down to us in two versions: one in Greek, as recorded by Diogenes Laertius, and the other a partial version in Arabic translation. The Greek version is based on the Alexandrian historian Hermippus, who used the archives of the Peripatetic school and probably drew on an unknown work by Ariston containing the wills of several of the Peripatetics. The Arabic translation can be traced back to Andronicus of Rhodes by way of Ptolemy el-Garib. Quite possibly Andronicus, who had had Aristotle's autograph manuscripts in his possession for a time, had found the original of his will among them. See Düring, *Biog. Trad.*, 238-241.

138. Diog. Laer., V.36-57 (catalogue, 42-50).

139. See Chapter III.

140. Diog. Laer., V.52. Theophrastus left money to Hipparchus to be used for rebuilding the *mouseion* and repairing the damage done by the Macedonians when they put down the Athenian rebellion (Plutarch, *Demetrius*, XXXIII, XXXIV, XLVI): See Diog. Laer., V.51: 'It is my wish that out of the trust funds at the disposal of Hipparchus the following appropriations should be made…'

141. See Grayeff, *op. cit.*, 69. The fourth-century philosopher Dicaearchus of Messene (Messana) in Sicily was born *circa* 340 B.C. and studied under Aristotle and Theophrastus. He travelled widely and was a prolific writer, one of his works being a history of Greek civilization (*Life in Greece*) in three books. His departure from the Peripatos was probably due to his disagreement with Aristotle and especially with Theophrastus over the orientation of research in the school. Dicaearchus thought it should be directed towards the active life, while Theophrastus was a supporter of the contemplative life: that, in fact, was the very reason why Cicero commended Theophrastus in his *Letters to Atticus* (II.16.3).

142. Eudemus was, with Theophrastus, one of Aristotle's favourite pupils. Apparently he left Athens when Theophrastus reopened the Lyceum four years after Aristotle's death and went back to his native island, Rhodes. Judging by the fact that a Peripatetic tradition came into being on Rhodes at that time and by the existence of a philosophy school there, perhaps founded by Eudemus himself, it would seem that he took copies of some of Aristotle's teaching books with him. Lengthy excerpts exist of a paraphrase of Aristotle's *Physics* that he wrote: see Wehrli, *op. cit.*, VIII (*Eudemos von Rhodos*, 1955).

143. Diog. Laer., V.52.

144. See D. E. W. Wormell, 'The Literary Tradition Concerning Hermias of Atarneus', *Yale Classical Studies* 5 (1928).

145. Aristotle mentions Neleus in the *Magna Moralia*, remarking that he and Lamprus

had been fellow-students when they learnt 'the art of writing': see Düring, *Ὁ Ἀριστοτέλης...*, II (Athens 1994) 217.

146. Strabo, XIII.C.609: 'Scepsis was the home town of the Socratic philosophers Erastus and Coriscus and also of Neleus the son of Coriscus: Neleus not only studied under Aristotle and Theophrastus but also inherited Theophrastus's library, which included that of Aristotle. At any rate, Aristotle bequeathed his own library to Theophrastus, to whom he also left his school; and as far as I know he was the first man to collect books and the first to teach the kings of Egypt how to organize a library. Theophrastus bequeathed the books to Neleus, and Neleus took them to Scepsis and bequeathed them to his heirs, ordinary people, who kept them locked up and not even carefully stored. But when they heard how determinedly the Attalid kings, to whom their city was subject, were looking for books to build up the library at Pergamum, they hid their books underground in a trench. Much later, when the books had been damaged by moisture and moths, their descendants sold Aristotle's and Theophrastus's books to Apellicon of Teos for a large sum of money. Now Apellicon was more interested in books than in philosophy; and so, in trying to restore the parts that had rotted away, he made new copies of the text, filling up the gaps incorrectly, and published the books full of errors. The result was that the earlier Peripatetics who came after Theophrastus had no books at all, except for a few, mostly "exoteric" works, and were therefore able to philosophize about nothing in a practical way, but only to talk grandiloquently about commonplace propositions; whereas, after the books in question had reappeared, the later Peripatetics, though better able to philosophize and Aristotelize, were forced to call most of their statements probabilities, because of the large number of errors. Rome also contributed much to this because, immediately after Apellicon's death, Sulla, who had captured Athens, carried off Apellicon's library and brought the books here [i.e. to Rome]. Tyrannio the grammarian, who was fond of Aristotle, then wheedled them out of the librarian, and so did certain booksellers, who used bad copyists and did not collate the texts: the same thing happens with other books that are copied for sale, both here and in Alexandria. But enough about these men.'

147. Strabo, XIII.C.609: 'The result was that the earlier Peripatetics who came after Theophrastus had no books at all, except for a few.'

148. Diog. Laer., V.58. See also Wehrli, *op. cit.*, V (*Straton von Lampsakos*, 1950). In his eighteen years as head of the Peripatos he may well have found that the shortage of suitable textbooks severely hampered his efforts to keep the school's teaching standards up to standard, especially if Neleus had inherited Theophrastus's as well as Aristotle's books and there were no copies available. On the other hand, quite possibly it was Strato's personal interest in physicalist theories, and not the lack of textbooks, that led to the shift in the Peripatetic school's educational philosophy.

149. Diog. Laer., V.70: 'I leave the Peripatos to such of my friends as choose to make use of it, to Bulo, Callinus, Ariston, Amphion, Lyco, Pytho, Aristomachus, Heracleus, Lycomedes, and my nephew Lyco.'

150. Diog. Laer., V.73: *Λύκων αὐτὸν καὶ παιδευσάτω ἀπὸ τοῦ νῦν χρόνου ἓξ ἔτη. καὶ Χάρητα ἀφίημι ἐλεύθερον· καὶ θρεψάτω Λύκων αὐτόν. καὶ δύο μνᾶς αὐτῷ δίδωμι καὶ τὰ ἐμὰ βιβλία τὰ ἀνεγνωσμένα· τὰ δ' ἀνέκδοτα Καλλίνῳ ὅπως ἐπιμελῶς αὐτὰ ἐκδῷ.*

151. Although the history of Aristotle's auto-

graph teaching books from the time they came into Neleus's possession reads like fiction, and although it is hard to believe that Andronicus, the eventual editor of those books, published them from manuscripts that had been lost for nearly three centuries, there is no evidence in any literary or other source to suggest that a different construction might be put on the testimony of the persons actually involved in the events and of contemporary historians.

The story of Aristotle's books is told by Strabo (XIII.C.608-609) and Plutarch (*Sulla*, XXVI). On the fate of Aristotle's private library, see also Düring, *Ὁ Ἀριστοτέλης...*, I, 93-101; L. Canfora, *Ἡ Χαμένη Βιβλιοθήκη τῆς Ἀλεξανδρείας* (= *La biblioteca scomparsa*, Palermo 1986, tr. F. Arvanitis), Athens 1989, 41-44; Grayeff, *op. cit.*, 71 ff.; N.J. Richardson, 'Aristotle and Hellenistic Scholarship', in O. Reverdin and B. Grange (eds.), *La philologie grecque à l'époque hellénistique et romaine* [*Entretiens sur l'antiquité classique* 40], Vandoeuvres/Geneva 1993, 7-38.

152. Strabo, XIII.C.609. Cf. Plutarch, *Sulla*, XXVI: 'The elder Peripatetics themselves appear to have been accomplished and learned men, but of the writings of Aristotle and Theophrastus they had no large or exact knowledge, because the bequest to Neleus of Scepsis (to whom Theophrastus bequeathed his books) fell into the hands of uncaring and ignorant men.'
153. Strabo, XIII.C.609: ' The later Peripatetics, though better able to philosophize and Aristotelize, were forced to call most of their statements probabilities, because of the large number of errors.'
154. Strabo, XIII.C.609: 'When they heard how determinedly the Attalid kings, to whom their city was subject, were looking for books to build up the library at Pergamum....'
155. Athenaeus, I.3a-b: 'Our King Ptolemy, surnamed Philadelphus, purchased them all from Neleus and transferred them, with those which he had procured at Athens and at Rhodes, to his beautiful capital, Alexandria.'
156. See n. 32 above.
157. Whether the catalogue of Aristotle's works in Diogenes Laertius was based on Hermippus or compiled by Ariston in the Peripatos, the literary scholars working in the Ptolemies' library would certainly have acquired a copy of it sooner or later. We should not forget that the centre of the book trade and the main hunting-ground for books was Athens, and it was there that the Ptolemies looked first when there was a book they wanted. See above, p. 101.
158. See Pfeiffer, *Ἱστορία...*, 206.
159. Strabo, XIII.C.609.
160. See A. Sperling, *Apellikon der Grammatiker und sein Verhältnis zum Judentum*, Dresden 1886.
161. See the fictional account by J. Bidez, *Un singulier naufrage littéraire dans l'antiquité*, Brussels 1943; Düring, *Biog. Trad.*, 382-395; A. Stahr, *Aristotelia*, I-II, Halle 1832.
162. Strabo, XIII.C.609: 'He published the books full of errors.'
163. Strabo, XIII.C.609. Cf. Plutarch, *Sulla*, XXVI: *Ἀναχθεὶς δὲ πάσαις ταῖς ναυσὶν ἐξ Ἐφέσου Τριταῖος ἐν Πειραιεῖ καθωρμίσθη, καὶ μυηθεὶς ἐξεῖλεν ἑαυτῷ τὴν Ἀπελλικῶνος τοῦ Τηΐου βιβλιοθήκην, ἐν ᾗ τὰ πλεῖστα τῶν Ἀριστοτέλους καὶ Θεοφράστου βιβλίων ἦν, οὔπω τότε σαφῶς γνωριζόμενα τοῖς πολλοῖς.*
164. On the first public library in Rome and the dawn of the 'age of the book' in the time of Atticus and Cicero, see Chapter III.
165. The biographical notes are from *Souda*, s.v. 'Tyrannion [the Elder]'. The estimate of the number of Tyrannio's books is the first numerical estimate of the size

of a private library in antiquity. See Moraux, *Der Aristotelismus...*, 33-44.

166. See Düring, *Ὁ Ἀριστοτέλης...*, I, 95-96. For Cicero's testimony see his *Epistulae ad Atticum*, II.6, IV.8a.

167. Düring, *Biog. Trad.*, 412-425.

168. Even in Cicero's time Aristotle was not widely read, and the first Greek to refer to him by name as one of the great philosophers was Dionysius of Halicarnassus, who was also the first person to quote a passage from the edition of Aristotle brought out by Andronicus. It was probably through Tyrannio that Cicero first made the acquaintance of some of Aristotle's didactic writings, before they were published by Andronicus. When he read Aristotle's writings he was bowled over by his style, which he described as 'a river of flowing gold' (Plutarch, *Cicero*, XXIV: *veniet flumen orationis aureum fundens Aristoteles*). In 45 B.C. he wrote in his dialogue *Hortensius*: 'You have to have your mind at full stretch when reading and interpreting Aristotle' (*magna etiam animi contentio adhibenda est explicando Aristotele si legas*.

Cicero read some of Aristotle's work in Lucullus's library, and recalls his meetings with Lucullus: cf. *Academica* II (*Lucullus*) XLVIII.148. In *De finibus bonorum et malorum* (III.III.10) he writes about a visit to the library after Lucullus's death: 'I came to borrow certain commentaries on Aristotle that I knew were here, to read while I have some free time.'

169. Plutarch, *Cicero*, XXVII: 'When Faustus Sulla, the son of Sulla the dictator (who had condemned so many citizens to death by putting up bills of proscription during his dictatorship), had got into debt and squandered so much of his fortune that he was forced to put out bills advertising his property for auction, Cicero told him that he liked these bills much better than those of his father.'

170. Plutarch, *Sulla*, XXVI: 'It is said that, when the collection was subsequently taken to Rome, Tyrannio the grammarian acquired most of the books, and that Andronicus of Rhodes, having been supplied with copies by him, published them and compiled the catalogues that are now current.'

171. See Düring, *Ὁ Ἀριστοτέλης...*, I, 98.

172. See Elias of Alexandria, *On the 'Categories'* (*CIAG*, XVIII.1, 113.17), in Düring, *Biog. Trad.* Elias, a Neoplatonist philosopher of the sixth century who studied at the Alexandrian school of Olympiodorus and Eutocius of Ascalon, was a commentator on Aristotle, fragments of whose work have been preserved by Byzantine scholiasts: see I. Hadot, 'Elias [2]', in *NP*, 3 (1997), 991. See also Chapter III on forgeries during the Alexandrian period.

173. See F. Littig, *Andronikos von Rhodos* (dissertation), Munich 1890; and all the relevant matter in Düring, *Biog. Trad.*, 412-425.

174. Porphyry, *Life of Plotinus*, XXIV.6-11: *ὁ δὲ τὰ Ἀριστοτέλους καὶ Θεοφράστου εἰς πραγματείας διεῖλε τὰς οἰκείας ὑποθέσεις εἰς ταυτὸν συναγαγών*. The material by Plotinus that Porphyry had to deal with consisted of untitled lecture notes. He therefore modelled himself on Andronicus's working methods, with which he was very familiar, as we can see from the passage quoted here.

175. See Düring, *Ὁ Ἀριστοτέλης...*, I, 98-99.

176. Lucian, *To the Ignorant Book-Collector*, 4 (see Loeb Classical Library, *Lucian*, III, 173-211).

III

HELLENISTIC PERIOD

The Universal Library of the Ptolemies in Alexandria

80. Imaginary reconstruction of the Museum, from the title page of Meibonius, Diogenes Laertius, *Amsterdam 1698.*

THE HELLENISTIC PERIOD

The Universal Library of the Ptolemies in Alexandria

At the mention of the Hellenistic period the first thing that comes into most people's minds is the Alexandrian Library, a symbol of the Greeks' cultural supremacy in the then known world and a unifying factor that helped to bind the Greeks together in a sort of commonwealth of independent states. Three main factors led to this astonishing accumulation of books: the opening-up of relations between the Greek world and the East, the passionate love of books displayed by the kings of the Ptolemaic dynasty and the rise to prominence of the new discipline of textual studies in literature.

Reasons for founding a 'Universal Library'

The historical background. On the untimely death of Alexander the Great in 323 B.C., about a year before the death of his teacher Aristotle, most Greeks gradually awoke to the awesome truth that the supremacy of Hellenism now extended almost to the furthest limits of the known world. Brought up on the idea of the Classical Greek city-state, and firmly believing that everything should be adapted to the human scale, they found the vastnesses of the East quite bewildering to contemplate. The familiar old order – the 'unity' of the Greek world, the Greek way of life – was rapidly falling apart, at least for those who settled in the East. Fortunately the struggle for supremacy among the Diadochi (the successors of Alexander the Great) did not have catastrophic consequences and did not completely break the underlying cohesion of the vast Greek empire.[1] However, the introduction of Hellenism into countries with a philosophical approach so very different from that of the Greeks created a new framework for intellectual activity. The Greek literary and philosophical tradition now found itself confronted by a way of thinking, particularly prevalent in Babylonia, Judaea and Egypt, in which mysticism and often symbolism featured largely, in contrast to the lucid and incisive thinking of the Greeks.[2] To ensure untroubled continuity in the everyday life of such a mixture of races it was essential for the Greeks to show a measure of understanding and respect for the religious and secular traditions of the

Near Eastern peoples, and so the creation of a 'universal library' seemed an obvious course of action.

It was on the linguistic level that the contact between the Greeks and the indigenous peoples worked most fruitfully, for the Greek language spread to all parts of the Near East and soon established itself as the region's lingua franca. Moreover, the Ptolemies not only despised the Egyptian language (Plutarch, *Antony*, XXVII) but refused to use their own Macedonian dialect and made a policy of promoting the 'purest' strain of Greek, namely the Attic

81. Alexander the Great saving the works of Homer. Engraving by Marcantonio Raimondi. Bibliothèque Nationale de France (Cabinet des Estampes).

dialect. One consequence of this policy was that large cultural centres were built around monumental libraries. Another was that a number of major works on the history and religious traditions of the Near Eastern peoples were translated into Greek – the Septuagint being the most obvious example – while others, such as the histories of Berossus and Manetho, were written in Greek.

By the time he died in 322, Aristotle had reduced a vast body of human knowledge to order and codified it all, discipline by discipline, with the help of the teachers at the Lyceum. It was now high time for all this literature to be subjected to critical study. The new trend first made its appearance in the south-eastern corner of the Greek world and its leading exponents tended to congregate in Alexandria, which the Ptolemies had made their capital in 320. Literary studies, which drew on the traditions of the Ionian and Attic Greeks, found in Alexandria the right conditions for their further development as a new academic discipline. Before long this new branch of learning, with its emphasis on criticism, had added greatly to the already large body of literature produced in the Classical period, and these commentaries in turn gave rise to a second generation of critical writings. Then again, because of the diligence of the literary critics and textual scholars, and because they kept finding that they needed new, accurate texts, the number of books required to fill a world library swelled to a total far beyond all expectations.

Alexander the Great: originator of the idea of a 'Universal Library'?

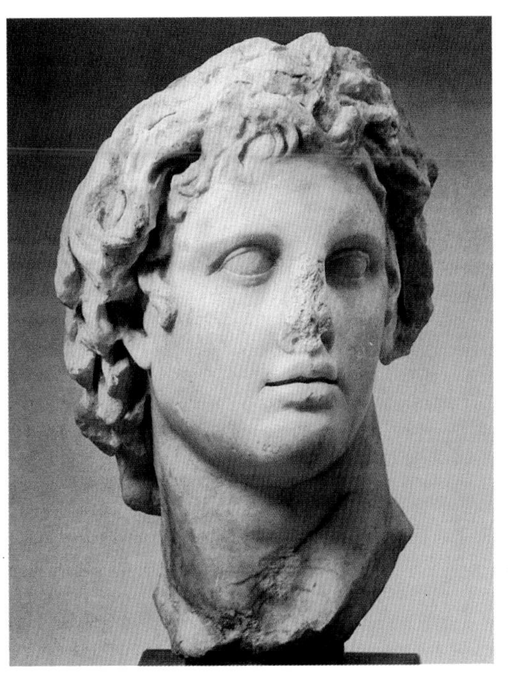

82. Marble head of Alexander the Great, 2nd c. B.C. Copenhagen, Ny Carlsberg Glyptotek.

But who was the person that first had the idea of founding a universal library? According to a Persian source and the tradition to which it gave rise, supported by Armenian testimony, the idea originated with none other than Alexander the Great.

The story given by the Persian source is connected with the sacred books of Zoroastrianism and the cultural traditions of the Achaemenids in general. It can be summed up as follows. The Sassanid dynasty of Persian kings (A.D. 226-642), whose official religion was Zoroastrianism, considered themselves to be the true successors of the ancient Achaemenid dynasty and wished to develop a cultural ideology clearly reflecting that continuity. On the fall of the Persian Empire to the Muslim Arabs, about half a century after the death of the great king Chosroes I (reigned 531-578), it was discovered that the 'treasury' of Zoroastrianism and Persian culture contained a chronicle of the transmission of philosophical, religious and scientific learning in Persia from the earliest times to the reign of Chosroes I. This chronicle survives both in the original version (in Middle Persian) and in numerous Arabic translations. The original version,

Greek translations of the Avesta

83. Alexander the Great and Diogenes, from Gisela M.A. Richter, The Portraits of the Greeks, *II, London 1965.*

written in the reign of Chosroes I, is in the book called the Dēnkard,[3] and the following passage comes from Book IV: 'Darius, son of Darius, gave orders that two copies of the Avesta and the Zend, as received by Zoroaster from Ormazd, were to be held in safe keeping. One copy was to be kept in the royal "treasury" and the other in the well-guarded archives. Volagases I(?) Arsaces ordered a directive to be sent out to the provinces with instructions that anything preserved intact from the Avesta, the Zend and any other authoritative teaching, whether oral or written, that existed anywhere in the Persian Empire in the form of a quotation from those two books, was to be preserved in the condition in which it was found: [this was necessary] because of the havoc wrought [on the royal archives] by the conquests of Alexander the Great and the depredations of the Macedonians.'

The other version of the chronicle – probably the first written translation into Arabic – is in the introduction to an Arabic translation of a treatise on astrology attributed to Zoroaster himself and entitled *The Book of Nativities* (*Kitāb al-Mawālīd*).[4] In it we find the following passage: 'I translated this text from the works of Zoroaster ... and I found no work by him ... dealing with philosophical studies.... Because when Alexander the Great conquered Dar-

Lucian gave this fable as a 'present' to a young man who had refused to lend him a book.[176] He derides his victim for being unable to distinguish between valuable ancient books and others being 'pushed' by booksellers, taunts him that he will never be able to call himself an educated man even if he buys all the autograph manuscripts of Demosthenes and the books looted from Athens by Sulla (after all, as the saying goes, an ape is an ape even if he has birth-tokens of gold) and sneers at him for being unable to see through sycophancy and not realizing that his friends are laughing at him behind his back for his vanity in always carrying about with him a beautiful roll with a gold knob and purple case. He compares the ignorant young book-collector with the tyrant Dionysius I of Syracuse, who wanted to write tragedies and paid an enormous sum of money for the writing tablet that Aeschylus had used in the belief that it would make him a great poet. Since you own so many copies of Homer, Lucian continues, why not read them: you will find they have practically nothing to say that applies to you, but let your mind dwell on that caricature of a man, the ugly and deformed Thersites, who thought that by putting on Achilles's armour he would be transformed into a handsome hero. Lucian also compares the foolish young man with Bellerophon, who carried with him a letter containing his own death sentence, and reminds him of the story of Demetrius the Cynic, who came across an ignorant man reading Euripides's *Bacchae* aloud in Corinth: when the reader reached the point where the messenger recounts Pentheus's horrible fate, Demetrius snatched the book away and tore it up in fury, exclaiming, 'It's better for Pentheus to be torn to pieces once and for all by me than over and over again by you!'

Lucian's satire on bibliophiles

79. Lucian. Engraving, 19th c. Published by J. Wilks, London 1807.

Notes

II
From Homer to the End of the Classical Period

NOTES

1. Herodotus II.53: 'Homer and Hesiod ... lived, as I believe, not more than four hundred years ago.' Diog. Laer., II.46, IX.18.
2. Milman Parry's pioneering studies, the fruits of exhaustive research on the power of the oral tradition among various peoples, started a revolution in the world of literary scholarship. His findings were incorporated into his doctoral dissertation for the Sorbonne (1928). Adam Parry, Milman's son, has written an excellent description of the spectacular evolution of his father's thinking, from his postgraduate thesis for the University of California at Berkeley in the early 1920s until his untimely death in 1935. See M. Parry, *The Making of Homeric Verse: The Collected Papers of Milman Parry*, ed. Adam Parry, Oxford 1971; A. B. Lord, *The Singers of Tales*, Cambridge, Mass. 1960.
3. On the Homeric oral tradition and other characteristics of the thinking and mode of expression based on orality, see W. J. Ong, *Προφορικότητα καί Ἐγγραμματοσύνη* (= *Orality and Literacy*, tr. Kostas Hadjikyriakou, ed. Theodoros Paradellis), Iraklion 1997, 19-32, 47 ff.
4. See G. E. Mylonas, 'Priam's Troy and the Date of its Fall', *Hesperia* 33 (1964) 352-380; M. Wood, *In Search of the Trojan War*, New York/Oxford 1985. On recent excavations at Troy, the dates of the successive cities, the archaeological finds and the mythological and the historical settings of the *Iliad*, see the exhibition catalogue entitled *Troia – Traum und Wirklichkeit*, ed. B. Theune-Grosskopf et al., Stuttgart 2001.
5. For a general discussion of the archaeological finds in relation to the descriptions of places and things for which Homer uses standard words and phrases, see Ione Mylonas-Shear, *Tales of Heroes: The Origins of the Homeric Texts*, New Rochelle/Athens 2000.
6. A band of bards known in antiquity as the Homeridae was regarded as the collective 'hereditary custodian' of Homer's epics. The tradition of the Homeridae already existed by the fifth century B.C. and lived on until near the end of the ancient era. See, for example: Pindar, *Nemean Odes*, II.1 ('Just as the Homeridae, the singers of verses stitched together, most often begin with Zeus as their prelude...'); Plato, *Phaedrus*, 252b ('But some of the Homeridae, I believe, repeat two verses on Love from the spurious poems of Homer'); Plato, *Republic*, X.599e ('"I think not," said Glaucon; "at any rate no one [similarly indebted to Homer] is mentioned even by the Homeridae themselves."'); Strabo, XIV.C.645 ('The Chians also claim Homer, setting forth as strong testimony that the men called Homeridae were descendants of Homer's family.'); Plutarch, *Moralia*, 496d-e. See also M. W. Edwards, *Homer, Poet of the Iliad*, Baltimore/London 1987, 26; C. H. Whitman, *Homer and the Heroic Tradition*, Cambridge, Mass./London 1958, 81.
7. *Iliad*, VI.168-169. Whether Bellerophon himself knew how to read and write is a moot point. If he did not, it is reasonable to assume that illiteracy was the general rule even among Greeks of his class. The Greek princes' ignorance of writing is apparent from the scene where two of the heroes imprint their mark and then draw lots out of a helmet (*Iliad*, III.315-317). See R. Bellamy, 'Bellerophon's Tablet', *CJ* 84 (1988-1989) 289-307; A. Ford, *Homer, The Poetry of the Past*, Ithaca/London 1992, 13, 137.
8. See above, p. 57 (n. 53).
9. See above, p. 52 (n. 10).

10. On the archaeological evidence for dating the world of Homer's epics to the eighth century or later, see G. S. Kirk (ed.), *The Iliad: A Commentary*, Cambridge 1985-1993 (vols. I-II by G. S. Kirk, 1985-1990, vol. III by J. B. Hainsworth, 1993, vol. IV by R. Janko, 1992, vol. V by M. W. Edwards, 1991). See also O. Taplin, *Homeric Soundings: The Shaping of the Iliad*, Oxford 1992, 33-35; E. F. Cook, *The Odyssey in Athens: Myths of Cultural Origins*, Ithaca/London 1995; G. Nagy, *Poetry as Performance: Homer and Beyond*, Cambridge 1996, 101; J. P. Crielaard, 'Homer, History and Archaeology: Some Remarks on the Date of the Homeric World', in *Homeric Questions: Essays in Philology, Ancient History and Archaeology, including the papers of a conference organized by the Netherlands Institute at Athens (15 May 1993)*, Amsterdam 1995, 273-275; A. J. Graham, 'The *Odyssey*, History and Women', in Beth Cohen (ed.), *The Distaff Side: Representing the Female in Homer's Odyssey*, Oxford/New York 1995, 3-17.

The Phoenician alphabet is thought to have been introduced into Greece in the tenth and ninth centuries, although some scholars would place its first introduction in the eleventh century. The eighth century is generally accepted as the *terminus ante quem* for its first appearance in Greece, and the middle of that century as the date when it came into general use. The case for dating its introduction before the eighth century is based mainly on the following evidence:

(a) By the end of the eighth century the alphabet is found in a well-developed form (in an inscription from the Dipylon Gate), which implies that it had already been in use for a long time.

(b) In the eighth century the Chalcidians took with them to southern Italy a well-developed alphabet (the Western alphabet), which is generally agreed to have evolved into the Latin alphabet.

(c) The alphabet must have been introduced during the period when trade between the Phoenicians and Greeks was flourishing, that is from the twelfth to the ninth century.

(d) The letters of the early Greek alphabet resemble those of the Phoenician alphabet of the eleventh to ninth centuries, not those found in later (eighth-century) inscriptions.

(e) The transmission of the *Iliad* and *Odyssey* – a total of over 25,000 lines of verse – from generation to generation is seen by some scholars as proof that they must have been written down at an early stage, probably at the time of their composition.

(f) We have ancient testimony to the fact that the names of victors in the Olympic Games were recorded in writing from as early as 776 B.C.

(g) The explanation for the absence of extant inscriptions dating from before the eighth century (leaving a gap from 1200 to 720 B.C.) may be either (i) simply that no inscriptions from that period have been found as yet, or (ii) that they were written on wood, hides, papyrus or some other material not resistant to decay in the Greek climate.

See M. Guarducci, *Epigrafia Greca*, 3 vols., Rome 1967, 1969, 1974; L. H. Jeffery, *The Local Scripts of Archaic Greece*, Oxford 1990[2]; A. Sigalas, *Ἱστορία τῆς ἑλληνικῆς γραφῆς*, Thessaloniki 1974[2]; J. T. Hooker (ed.), *Reading the Past: Ancient Writing from Cuneiform to the Alphabet*, London 1993; G. Babiniotis, *Συνοπτική Ἱστορία τῆς Ἑλληνικῆς Γλώσσας*, Athens 2002[5].

11. See R. Pfeiffer, *Ἱστορία τῆς Κλασσικῆς Φιλολογίας. Ἀπό τῶν Ἀρχῶν μέχρι τοῦ τέλους τῶν Ἑλληνιστικῶν Χρόνων* (= *History of Classical Scholarship: From the Beginnings*

to the End of the Hellenistic Age, Oxford 1968, tr. P. Xenos et al.), Athens 1972, 6 ff.; A. Lesky, *Ἱστορία τῆς ἀρχαίας Ἑλληνικῆς Λογοτεχνίας* (= *Geschichte der griechischen Literatur*, Bern 1957/58, tr. A. G. Tsopanakis), Thessaloniki 1983, 73; H. Berve, *Die Tyrannis bei den Griechen*, II, Munich 1967, 41-63.

12. [Aristotle], *Constitution of the Athenians*, XIV.1.4: 'Pisistratus, being thought to be an extreme advocate of the people, and having won great fame in the war against Megara....'
13. *Iliad*, II.558. The story of this episode was current in the ancient tradition, and Aristotle (*Rhetoric*, I.15) attaches some weight to it. See also Plutarch, *Solon*, 10; Diog. Laer., I.48: 'And lest it should be thought that he had acquired Salamis by force only and not of right, he opened certain graves and showed that the dead were buried with their faces to the east, as was the custom of burial among the Athenians; further, that the tombs themselves faced the east, and that the inscriptions graven upon them named the deceased by their demes, which is a style peculiar to Athens. Some authors assert that in Homer's catalogue of the ships, after the line "Ajax had brought twelve ships from Salamis" Solon inserted one of his own: "and he beached them where the Athenian contingent was stationed" [*Iliad*, II.557-558].'

    On the historicity of the incident, see A. Andrewes, 'The Growth of the Athenian State' and 'The Tyranny of Pisistratus', in *CAH*, III.3, Cambridge 1982², 372-374, 392-416; M. J. Apthorp, *The Manuscript Evidence for Interpolation in Homer*, Heidelberg 1980, 169-170; J. A. Davison, 'Peisistratus and Homer', *TAPA* 86 (1955) 1-21.
14. Scholia on Dionysus the Thracian: I. Bekker, *Anecdota Graeca*, Berlin 1816, II, 768 and II, 767: *ἦν δέ, ὥς φασιν, ἀπολόμενα τὰ τοῦ Ὁμήρου· τότε γὰρ οὐ γραφῇ παρεδίδοτο, ἀλλὰ μόνῃ διδασκαλίᾳ καὶ ὡς ἂν μνήμῃ μόνῃ ἐφυλάττετο. Πεισίστρατος δέ τις Ἀθηναίων τύραννος, ἐν ἅπασιν ὢν εὐγενής, καὶ ἓν τοῦτο θαυμαστὸν ἐβουλεύσατο ἠθέλησε γὰρ καὶ τὴν Ὁμήρου ποίησιν ἔγγραφον διαφυλάττεσθαι. Προθεὶς δὲ ἀγῶνα δημοτελῆ καὶ κηρύξας καὶ ἄδειαν τοῖς εἰδόσι καὶ βουλομένοις τὰ Ὁμήρου ἐπιδείκνυσθαι, καὶ μισθὸν τάξας στίχου ἑκάστου ὀβολόν, συνήγαγεν ὁλοσχερεῖς τὰς λέξεις καὶ παρέδωκεν ἀνθρώποις σοφοῖς καὶ ἐπιστήμοσιν καὶ ἐκήρυξεν ἐν πάσῃ τῇ Ἑλλάδι τὸν ἔχοντα Ὁμηρικοὺς στίχους ἀγαγεῖν πρὸς αὐτόν, ἐπὶ μισθῷ ὡρισμένῳ καθ' ἕκαστον στίχον.*

    According to Lilian Jeffery (*op. cit.*, 57), the minimum daily wage in fifteenth-century Athens was two obols, which is what Pisistratus was offering for the 'publication' of two lines of Homer; and a sheet of papyrus then cost eight obols: see below, p. 141 (n. 65).
15. G. Grote, *A History of Greece; From the Earliest Period to the Close of the Generation Contemporary with Alexander the Great*, II, London 1872⁴, 86-96. See also Pfeiffer, *op. cit.*, 6-10.
16. The only known work by Dieuchidas is *Megarica*, in at least five books: see P. Kroh, *Λεξικό Ἀρχαίων συγγραφέων Ἑλλήνων καί Λατίνων*, tr. and ed. by D. Lypourlis and L. Tromaras, Thessaloniki 1996, 141.
17. Hereas, whose work was probably entitled *Megarica*, wrote history with an anti-Athenian slant and was keen to refute the Athenians' claims against Megara. Like Dieuchidas, he mentions Pisistratus's alleged interpolation in the *Iliad* (II.546-558).
18. Asclepiades of Myrleia in Bithynia, a grammarian and historian, lived around 100 B.C. He may have been a pupil of Dionysius the Thracian and he worked for a time in Rome before moving on to Spain. Most of his works were commentaries on poets (Homer, Pindar and Aratus of Soli, among others).
19. Some fragments of Solon's poetry have

been preserved by Diogenes Laertius, who says (I.61): 'He is undoubtedly the author of the laws which bear his name; of speeches, and of poems in elegiac metre, namely, counsels addressed to himself, on Salamis and on the Athenian constitution, five thousand lines in all, not to mention poems in iambic metre and epodes.' According to Kroh's calculations, about three hundred of the 5,000 lines of his work have come down to us through being quoted by other authors.

20. Diog. Laer. I.57: 'He has provided that the public recitations of Homer shall follow in fixed order: thus the second reciter must begin from the place where the first left off.'
21. Pseudo-Plato, *Hipparchus*, 228b: '[Hipparchus] first brought the poems of Homer into this country and made the rhapsodists at the Panathenaea recite them in relay, one following on after another, as they still do now.'
22. The probable key to the question of what exactly it was that Solon tried to establish and what was the innovation he introduced into the recitation of Homer lies in the construction we put on the phrases *ἐξ ὑποβολῆς* and *ἐξ ὑπολήψεως*. According to Grote (*op. cit.*, 88), Hermann's interpretation is the most satisfactory.

   The word *ὑποβολεύς* is a technical term meaning a person who assists the actors in a theatrical performance (Plutarch, *Praecepta gerendae reipublicae*, 816). The noun *ὑποβολή* and the verb *ὑποβάλλειν* both refer to the act of prompting a speaker's memory and reminding him of the correct order and sequence of the original text (Xenophon, *Cyropaedia*, III.3.37: *ἐξ ὑποβολῆς*). If this reading is correct, the word *ὑποβολή* does not necessarily refer to the order in which the rhapsodists recited: it could be equally applicable to a single rhapsodist. The noun *ὑπόληψις* means taking up where another left off.

   For the fact that the recitation of passages from Homer was a regular feature of the Panathenaea festival we have the testimony of – among others – the fourth-century orator Lycurgus in his speech *Against Leocrates*, 102: 'I should also like to commend Homer to you. Your fathers considered him such a fine poet that they passed a law that he, alone of all the poets, should have his works recited every four years at the Panathenaea.'
23. The chariot-race is described in Book XXIII of the *Iliad*, 272-650: 'Son of Atreus and Achaean men-at-arms, these are the prizes that await the winning charioteers....' See Mylonas-Shear, *op. cit.*, 99. One of the few known vases by the potter and painter Nearchus, who was contemporary with Cleitias and one of the best Attic vase-painters, is a cantharus with a picture of Achilles with his horses: in it the horses' names are given as Chaetus and Eutheias, rather than the famous pair of Xanthus and Balius mentioned in the *Iliad*. For a reproduction of the painting see I. Th. Kakridis, *Ἑλληνική Μυθολογία. Τρωικός Πόλεμος*, V, Athens 1986, 43 (Fig. 29).
24. Athenaeus, *Deipnosophistae*, I.3: *Ὑπὸ τῆς τῶν πολλῶν ἀφιλοκαλίας. ἦν δέ, φησί, καὶ βιβλίων κτῆσις αὐτῷ ἀρχαίων Ἑλληνικῶν τοσαύτη ὡς ὑπερβάλλειν πάντας τοὺς ἐπὶ συναγωγῇ τεθαυμασμένους, Πολυκράτην τε τὸν Σάμιον καὶ Πεισίστρατον τὸν Ἀθηναίων τυραννήσαντα Εὐκλείδην τε τὸν καὶ αὐτὸν Ἀθηναῖον καὶ Νικοκράτην τὸν Κύπριον ἔτι τε τοὺς Περγάμου βασιλέας Εὐριπίδην τε τὸν ποιητὴν Ἀριστοτέλην τε τὸν φιλόσοφον καὶ Θεόφραστον καὶ τὸν τὰ τούτων διατηρήσαντα βιβλία Νηλέα· παρ' οὗ πάντα, φησί, πριάμενος ὁ ἡμεδαπὸς βασιλεὺς Πτολεμαῖος, Φιλάδελφος δὲ ἐπίκλην, μετὰ τῶν Ἀθήνηθεν καὶ τῶν ἀπό Ρόδου εἰς τὴν καλὴν Ἀλεξάνδρειαν μετήγαγε. διόπερ ἐκεῖνα τῶν Ἀντιφάνους ἐρεῖ τις εἰς αὐτόν*. See J. A. Davison, 'Literature and Literacy in Ancient Greece', *Phoenix* 16 (1962) 152.

25. Polycrates seized power probably about 532 B.C. and died in 522. His court was a gathering-place for men of learning and culture, including the physician Democedes and poets such as Ibycus and Anacreon. Another who frequented Polycrates's court was Cynaethus of Chios, a rhapsodist active around 500 B.C., who ran a school for rhapsodists. Scholiasts on Pindar accused Cynaethus and his associates of altering Homer's words, and some of them credited Cynaethus with the authorship of the *Hymn to Apollo*. As a member of the Homeridae, Cynaethus was almost certainly the first rhapsodist to recite Homer's works in Syracuse, Sicily. See *Scholia Vetera in Pindari carmina*, ed. A.B. Drachmann, III, Leipzig 1927 (*Nemean Odes*, II.1); R. Janko, *Homer, Hesiod and the Hymns: Diachronic Development in Epic Diction*, Cambridge 1982, 112-114; W. Burkert, 'Kynaithos, Polycrates and the Homeric Hymn to Apollo', in *Arktouros: Hellenic Studies presented to Bernard M. W. Knox*, ed. G. W. Bowersock, W. Burkert and M. C. J. Putnam, Berlin/New York 1979, 53-62. More generally, see Berve, *op. cit.*, II, 107-114.
26. Herodotus, V.67. Davison (Literature and Literacy...', 152) takes the view that Cleisthenes's library was formed for reasons of political expediency.
27. Plutarch, *Theseus*, 20: '"Dreadful indeed was his [Theseus'] passion for Aigle, the daughter of Panopeus." This verse Pisistratus deleted from the poems of Hesiod, according to Hereas of Megara, just as he inserted into Homer's "Book of the Dead" the verse....'
28. Onomacritus, an Athenian poet of the sixth and fifth centuries, was chiefly interested in collecting the oracles of Musaeus, but Lasus of Hermione exposed him as a forger of the oracles, and so he had to leave Athens and went to Susa in about 486 B.C. See Herodotus, VII.6.3: '... an Athenian named Onomacritus, a diviner who had edited the oracles of Musaeus. The Pisistratids, who had not been on good terms with him, had since made up the quarrel. This man had been expelled from Athens by Hipparchus, the son of Pisistratus, when he was caught by Lasus of Hermione in the act of interpolating into the writings of Musaeus a prophecy that the islands off Lemnos would disappear into the sea.'
29. [Aristotle], *Constitution of the Athenians*, XVIII; Pseudo-Plato, *Hipparchus*, 228b-c; J. M. Edmonds, *Greek Elegy and Iambus*, I, Cambridge, Mass. 1968, 25.
30. Simonides of Ceos, a lyric poet of the sixth and fifth centuries B.C., was born *circa* 556 and had already won fame in Greece and Asia Minor as a writer of panegyrics and *epinikia* before being invited to Athens. In Athens he entered numerous dithyrambic competitions and, by his own account, won fifty-six victories with male choruses.
31. Lasus of Hermione in the Argolid, a sixth-century lyric poet, was held in the highest repute from the time when he exposed the forgery of Onomacritus: see F. W. Schneidewin, *De Laso Hermionensi*, Göttingen 1842-1843.
32. See Aulus Gellius, *Noctes Atticae*, VII.XVII.1-2: 'Libros Athenis disciplinarum liberalium publice ad legendum praebendos primus posuisse dicitur Pisistratus tyrannus. Deinceps studiosius accuratiusque ipsi Athenienses auxerunt; sed omnem illam postea librorum copiam Xerxes, Athenarum potitus, urbe ipsa praeter arcem incensa, abstulit asportavitque in Persas. Eos porro libros universos multis post tempestatibus Seleucus rex, qui Nicanor appellatus est, referendos Athenas curavit.'
33. Herodotus, V.90: 'It was from the Acropolis of Athens that Cleomenes took the prophecies, which had formerly been in the possession of the Pisistratids. When the latter were exiled, they left them in the

temple, from where they were retrieved by Cleomenes.'

34. See n. 32 above. Besides the books from Pisistratus's library, the statues of Harmodius and Aristogeiton, the 'tyrannicides', were also returned to Athens: see Gellius, VII.XVII.1-2; Pausanias, I.8.5.
35. On the Panathenaea festival and Hipparchus's regulations for the music contests, see J. A. Davison, 'Notes on the Panathenaea', *JHS* 78 (1958) 23-42; Id., 'Addenda to Notes on the Panathenaea', *JHS* 82 (1962) 141-142; J. Neils, *Goddess and Polis: The Panathenaic Festival in Ancient Athens* (with contributions by E. J. W. Barber, D. G. Kyle, B. S. Ridgway and H. A. Shapiro), Princeton 1991; E. Simon, *Festivals of Attica*, Madison/London 1983.
36. See Chapter III.
37. Three of the broken statuettes were published by Humfry Payne in his book *Archaic Marble Sculpture from the Acropolis*, London 1936. On the question of their date, see M. S. Brouskari, *The Acropolis Museum: A Descriptive Catalogue*, Athens 1974: Dr. Brouskari, who identified the object held by one of the figures (inv. no. 144) as a box containing writing implements, dates them to *ca.* 520 and 510-500 B.C. More generally, see H. L. Alford, *The Seated Figure in Archaic Greek Sculpture*, Los Angeles 1978, 396-408. The fragment of the head of the biggest and best-preserved statuette was identified by Ismene Triandi: see her paper "Παρατηρήσεις σέ δύο ὁμάδες γλυπτῶν τοῦ τέλους τοῦ 6ου αἰώνα ἀπό τήν Ἀκρόπολη" in *The Archaeology of Athens and Attica under the Democracy: Proceedings of an International Conference celebrating 2500 years since the birth of Democracy in Greece, held in the American School of Classical Studies at Athens, December 4-6, 1992*, ed. W. D. E. Coulson, O. Palagia, T. L. Shear, Jr., H. A. Shapiro and F. J. Frost [*Oxbow Monograph* 37], Oxford 1994, 83-86; Ead., *Τό Μουσεῖο τῆς Ἀκροπόλεως*, Athens 1998, 199-205.
38. Aristotle, *Poetics*, 1459a ff. *αἱ δὲ γλῶτται τοῖς ἡρωικοῖς*. See also K. Latte, 'Glossographika', *Philologos* 80 (1925) 125 ff.
39. Pfeiffer, *op. cit.*, 9-13.
40. Xenophanes of Colophon flourished in the sixth century B.C. A self-styled philosopher (fr. B 8), he made his living by writing poetry, which he usually recited himself. He was a perceptive and critical observer who learnt from what he saw on his travels, and so he progressed from poetry to philosophy. See S. M. Untersteiner, *Senofane*, Florence 1956; A. Kelesidou-Galanou, *Ἡ κάθαρση τῆς θεότητας στή φιλοσοφία τοῦ Ξενοφάνη* (dissertation), Athens 1969.
41. Plato, *Republic*, II.378d: 'But stories about Hera being tied up by her son, or Hephaestus being flung out of Heaven by his father for trying to save his mother from a beating, or any of Homer's battles of the gods, are things that cannot be admitted into our city, whether their intention is allegorical or not.' See also E. A. Havelock, *Preface to Plato*, Cambridge, Mass. 1963, 115.
42. Pfeiffer, *op. cit.*, 11-14; F. Buffière, *Les mythes d'Homère et la pensée grecque*, Paris 1956.
43. The oldest extant Greek manuscript is the papyrus discovered at Derveni, near Thessaloniki, in 1962. It contains an allegorical commentary on a theogony attributed to Orpheus, evidently written by an anonymous grammarian familiar with the thinking of Anaxagoras and Diogenes of Apollonia. It was found, charred, in a grave of 330 B.C. and is to be published by K. Tsantsanoglou and G. Parasoglou. Cf. W. Burkert, 'La genèse des choses et des mots: Le papyrus de Derveni entre Anaxagore et Cratyle', *Études Philosophiques* 25 (1970) 443-455. According to J. Irigoin in his paper 'Les deux plus an-

ciens livres grecs', *Revue des études grecques* 75 (1962) XXIV-XXV (Conclusion), the Derveni papyrus is two or three decades older than *The Persians* of Timotheus: he dates it to the middle of the fourth century, in the reign of Philip II of Macedon. The papyrus found by L. Liangouras in 1981 (*Archaiologikon Deltion* 36 (1981) 47) in a cist grave known as the musician's grave, because wooden tools for making musical instruments were buried with the body, has still not been dated or even read.

44. Not enough prominence has been given to the pre-Socratic philosophers' role in the development and dissemination of books in the Greek-speaking world, especially Athens. If more of their writings had survived, we might know more about the form of 'book' in which the earliest works of Greek literature, such as Hesiod's *Theogony*, the Orphic Hymns and the writings of Pherecydes of Syros, were handed down to succeeding generations. On this period see: H. Diels, *Doxographi Graeci*, Berlin 1879; Id., *Die Fragmente der Vorsokratiker*, ed. W. Kranz, Berlin 1951-1954; W. K. C. Guthrie, *A History of Greek Philosophy*, 6 vols., Cambridge 1962-1981; G.S. Kirk, J. E. Raven and M. Schofield, *Οί Προσωκρατικοί Φιλόσοφοι* (= *The Presocratic Philosophers*, 2nd edn., Cambridge 1983, tr. D. Kurtovik), Athens 1988 (hereafter abbreviated as *KRS*).

45. Works attributed to Orpheus and his pupil Musaeus were circulating in book form as early as the sixth century B.C., and the text of a theogonic poem attributed to Epimenides had apparently been written down by then (*KRS*, 38). See I. M. Linforth, *The Arts of Orpheus*, Berkeley 1941; W. K. C. Guthrie, *The Greeks and Their Gods*, London 1950. Guthrie takes the view that the Orphic texts had already been written down in a sacred book by the sixth century. Orpheus was generally believed to have lived before Homer, and the Orphics based the authenticity of their doctrines on the written tradition (*ta biblia*, 'the books'): see *KRS*, 228, 478.

46. Diog. Laer., IX.6: 'As to the work which passes as his, it is a continuous treatise *On Nature*, but is divided into three discourses.... This book he deposited in the temple of Artemis and, according to some, he deliberately made it the more obscure in order that none but adepts should approach it.' See also E. G. Turner, *Athenian Books in the Fifth and Fourth Centuries B.C.*, London 1952, 17. The end of Heraclitus's active life as a philosopher is usually dated around 480 B.C. *On Nature* had the reputation in antiquity of being written in a crabbed style, so much so that Diogenes Laertius (IX.13) comments that not even those most conversant with literature could understand what it really meant. Hieronymus of Rhodes records that in the fourth century B.C. the satirical poet Scythinus of Teos undertook to summarize Heraclitus's doctrines in verse. Heraclitus was the subject of many epigrams, one of which satirizes the style in which *On Nature* was written: 'Do not be in too great a hurry to get to the end of the book written by Heraclitus of Ephesus: the path is hard to travel' (Diog. Laer., IX.16).

47. See below, p. 148 (n. 125).

48. The unwritten 'doctrines' of Pythagoras, as they are described by Plato in *Timaeus* and *Philebus*, left a gap which was filled by numerous works containing references to his life and teaching: see W. D. Ross, *Plato's Theory of Ideas*, Oxford 1951, Chs. 9-16. Most of those works are unreliable and owe much to their authors' imagination, the only reliable ones being those published by Philolaus and Archytas: see *KRS*, 221-245. Josephus, writing in the first century A.D., states in his treatise *Against Apion* (I.167) that the most reliable

of the many authors who wrote about Pythagoras's doctrines was Hermippus of Smyrna: see *KRS*, 478.

49. See Lesky, *op. cit.*, 671-727. On Plato's library see p. 93 herein. A text showing an affinity to the Pythagorean tradition, or at least some similarities, is a written doxography of earlier date attributed to Orpheus, which was in use in the time of Pythagoras's pupils.
50. See *KRS*, 64-83.
51. Diog. Laer., I.119: 'There is preserved a work by Pherecydes of Syros, a work which begins thus....'
52. Diog. Laer., I.116: 'Theopompus says that he was the first to write [in Greek] about nature and the gods.' See also *Souda*, s.v. Pherecydes: 'Some record that he was the first to publish a composition in prose.'
53. *Souda*, s.v. Pherecydes: 'There is a story that Pythagoras was taught by him, but that he himself had no teacher and taught himself after acquiring the secret books of the Phoenicians.'
54. Diog. Laer., I.122: *ἐπέσκηψα δ' ὧν τοῖσιν οἰκιήτῃσιν, ἐπήν με καταθάψωσιν, ἐς σὲ τὴν γραφὴν ἐνέγκαι. σὺ δὲ ἢν δοκιμώσῃς σὺν τοῖς ἄλλοις σοφοῖς, οὕτω μιν φῆνον. ἢν δὲ οὐ δοκιμώσητε, μὴ φήνῃς.*
55. Aeschylus, *Prometheus Bound*, 460 ff. Further on in the play (788 ff.), Prometheus says to Io, 'First will I declare your much-vexed wandering, and may you engrave it on the recording tablets of your mind.'
56. Aeschylus, *Eumenides*, 273-275.
57. Aeschylus, *Aetnae*(?), *ca.* 470 B.C. = Oxyrrhynchus Papyrus XX (1952), 2256, fr. 9a 21, ed. E. Lobel. E. Fraenkel, in *Eranos* 52 (1954) 64 ff., recognized this as a fragment of a play intended for performance at the festival in honour of Hieron I of Syracuse, the founder of the city of Aetna: cf. F. Solmsen, 'The Tablets of Zeus', *Classical Quarterly* 38 (1944) 27-30.
58. Aeschylus, *The Suppliant Women*, 946 ff.
59. Sophocles, fr. 597 P.
60. Euripides, *Melanippe*, fr. 506 N[2].
61. See F. Winter, 'Schulunterricht auf griechischen Vasenbildern', *Bonner Jahrbücher* 123 (1916) 275-285, esp. 281; also the detailed study by J. D. Beazley of an unpublished vase painted in the style of Duris and eight other representations of inscribed rolls in his paper 'Hymn to Hermes', *AJA* 52 (1948) 336 ff. According to E. Pöhlmann in his book *Griechische Musikfragmente*, Nürnberg 1960, 83 ff., certain signs written on the inside of the rolls are passages of musical notation: R. P. Winnington Ingram (*Gnomon* 33 [1961] 693) believes them to be poems.
62. See p. 274.
63. Useful information on libraries and Greek books in the Classical period is to be found in the following works: K. Dziatzko, *Untersuchungen über ausgewählte Kapitel des antiken Buchwesens*, Leipzig 1900; J. W. Clark, *The Care of Books: An essay on the development of libraries and their fittings from the earliest times to the end of the eighteenth century*, Cambridge 1901, 5; J. W. Thompson, *Ancient Libraries*, Berkeley 1940, 17-25 (='Libraries of Ancient Greece'); H. L. Pinner, *The World of Books in Classical Antiquity*, Leiden 1948; C. Wendel, 'Das griechisch-römische Altertum' (completed by W. Göber), in F. Milkau and G. Leyh (eds.), *Handbuch der Bibliothekswissenschaft*, III.1, Wiesbaden 1955, 51 ff.; E. G. Turner, *Athenian Books in the Fifth and Fourth Centuries B.C.*, London 1952; F. G. Kenyon, *Books and Readers in Ancient Greece and Rome*, Oxford 1951; E. Bethe, *Buch und Bild im Altertum*, Amsterdam 1964; J. Platthy, *Sources on the Earliest Greek Libraries with the Testimonia*, Amsterdam 1968; M. Burzachechi, 'Ricerche epigrafiche sulle antiche bibliotheche del mondo greco', *Rendiconti dell' Accademia dei Lincei* 18 (1963) 75 ff. and 39 (1984) 307 ff.; H. A. Thompson, 'The Libraries of

Ancient Athens', in N.C. Wilkie and W.D.E. Coulson (eds.), *Contributions to Aegean Archaeology: Studies in Honor of William A. McDonald*, Minneapolis 1985, 295-297; T. Kleberg, 'La Grecia a l'epoca ellenistica', in G. Cavallo (ed.), *Libri editori e pubblico nel mondo antico*, Rome/Bari 1989, 27-39; H. Blanck, *Τό βιβλίο στήν ἀρχαιότητα* (= *Das Buch in der Antike*, Munich 1992, tr. D.G. Georgovasilis and M. Pfreimter), Athens 1994, 176-204; K.Sp. Staikos, *The Great Libraries from Antiquity to the Renaissance (3000 B.C. to A.D. 1600)*, (=*Βιβλιοθήκη. Ἀπό τήν Ἀρχαιότητα ἕως τήν Ἀναγέννηση (3000 π.Χ. - 1600 μ.Χ.)*, tr. T. Cullen), New Castle, Del./London 2000, 29-55; J. Irigoin, *Le livre grec des origines à la Renaissance*, Paris 2001; W. Hoepfner (ed.), *Antike Bibliotheken*, Mainz 2002, 19-29.

64. Plato, *Parmenides* 127c: 'Socrates and many others with him went there because they wanted to hear Zeno's writings, which had been brought to Athens for the first time by them. Socrates was then very young. So Zeno himself read aloud to them, and Parmenides was not in the house.' Cf. Diog. Laer., IX.21-23. Parmenides, a brilliant pupil of Xenophanes, is extolled by Plutarch (*To Colotes* 1114b) for the soundness of his book on ancient 'natural philosophy' (i.e. natural science) and the fact that he did not plagiarize other writers' works. See *KRS*, 246-270.

65. Plato, *Apology*, 26d-e: 'You must have a very poor opinion of the judges, and think them very unlettered men, if you imagine that they do not know that the works of Anaxagoras of Clazomenae are full of these doctrines. And so young men learn these things from me, which they can buy sometimes in the orchestra for a drachma at most, and laugh Socrates to scorn if he pretended that these doctrines, which are very peculiar doctrines too, were his.' Plato asserts that Socrates grasped all of Anaxagoras's beliefs at a single reading.

According to the calculations of A.H.M. Jones (*KRS*, 489), the drachma was equal in value to a day's work by one slave. This means that a book selling at one drachma (= 6 obols) took less than a day to copy out, since the slave's owner had to defray the expenses of one day's board and lodging for the slave, amounting to four obols, which would leave him two obols to cover the cost of the papyrus plus his profit.

The cost of papyrus in the closing years of the fifth century can only be calculated approximately: it is known that the commissioners of the Erechtheum kept their accounts on papyrus rolls for which they paid one drachma and two obols each, but we do not know the length of the rolls. See Turner, *op. cit.*, 21; R. Flacelière, *Ὁ Δημόσιος καί Ἰδιωτικός Βίος τῶν Ἀρχαίων Ἑλλήνων* (= *La vie quotidienne en Grèce au siècle de Périclès*, Paris 1959, tr. G.D. Vandoros), Athens 1990, 151 ff. Lilian Jeffery agrees that a roll of papyrus cost eight obols: see n. 14 above. On bookshops see p. 144 (n. 85).

66. Xenophon, *Memorabilia* I.6.14: 'To this Socrates replied: ... And the treasures that the wise men of old have left us in their writings I open and explore with my friends. If we come on any good thing, we extract it, and we set much store on being useful to one another.' Further evidence for the existence of private libraries is provided by a passage in Plato's *Critias* (113a-b): 'You must not be surprised if you should perhaps hear Hellenic names given to foreigners. I will tell you the reason for this: Solon, who was intending to use the tale for his poem, enquired into the meaning of the names, and found that the early Egyptians in writing them down had translated them into their own language, and he recovered the meaning of the several names and when copying them out

again translated them into our language. My great-grandfather, Dropides, had the original writing, which is still in my possession, and was carefully studied by me when I was a child. Therefore if you hear names such as are used in this country, you must not be surprised, for I have told how they came to be introduced.'

67. Antiphanes, *Sappho*: see Th. Koch (ed.), *Comicorum Graecorum Fragmenta*, I, Leipzig 1881, fr. 196. Cf. Plato, *Theaetetus*, 143a-b; Xenophon, *Symposium*, IV.27. The change from reading aloud to reading silently would not have taken place overnight. It may perhaps have been Aristotle who made silent reading the norm (cf. Kenyon, *op. cit.*, 21), but I believe it had probably been standard practice since about the beginning of the fourth century.
68. Xenophon, *Memorabilia*, IV.2.8-10. Euthydemus, the son of Diocles, is mentioned in the *Symposium*, 222b (*Kleine Pauly*, II, 446).
69. Out of the extensive literature on the early sophists, some of the most important works are: R. Pfeiffer, 'Die Sophisten, ihre Zeitgenossen und Schüler im fünften und vierten Jahrhundert', in C. J. Classen (ed.), *Sophistik*, Darmstadt 1976, 170-219; N. M. Skouteropoulos, *Ἡ Ἀρχαία Σοφιστική: Τά σωζόμενα ἀποσπάσματα* (fragments edited, translated into Modern Greek and annotated by —), Athens 1991; W. K. C. Guthrie, *Οἱ Σοφιστές* (= *The Sophists*, Cambridge 1971, tr. D. Tsekourakis), Athens 1991; Jacqueline de Romilly, *Οἱ Μεγάλοι Σοφιστές στήν Ἀθήνα τοῦ Περικλῆ* (= *Les grands sophistes dans l'Athènes de Périclès*, Paris 1988, tr. F. I. Kakridis), Athens 1994.
70. A8: *Πατρὶς Χαλκηδών· ἡ δὲ τέχνη σοφία.*
71. On education in antiquity see the classic work by H.-I. Marrou, *Ἱστορία τῆς Ἐκπαιδεύσεως κατά τήν Ἀρχαιότητα* (= *Histoire de l'éducation dans l'antiquité*, Paris 1948, tr. Th. Fotinopoulos), Athens 1961; also M. A. Manacorda, 'Scuola e insegnanti', in M. Vegetti (ed.), *Oralità, scrittura, spettácolo*, Turin 1983.
72. *Souda*, s.v. 'Protagoras of Abdera'; Guthrie, *Οἱ Σοφιστές*, 38. Protagoras must have been in Athens in 443, for in that year Pericles commissioned him to draft the constitution of Thurii, a colony in southern Italy founded in 444/443 B.C. Cf. K. M. Dietz, *Protagoras von Abdeira: Untersuchungen zu seinem Denken*, Bonn 1976.
73. See Turner, *op. cit.*, 18. According to a scholiast on Plato's *Republic* (X.600c), Protagoras was the first teacher to demand money from his pupils and was therefore known as 'Speech for Hire'. It was he who classified the branches of learning into two groups, one comprising arithmetic, astronomy, geometry and music and the other grammar, rhetoric and logic, constituting respectively the quadrivium and the trivium of the seven 'liberal arts' of the Middle Ages. See Marrou, *op. cit.*, 89, 97.
74. Diog. Laer., IX.51: *διὰ ταύτην δὲ τὴν ἀρχὴν τοῦ συγγράμματος ἐξεβλήθη πρὸς Ἀθηναίων. καὶ τὰ βιβλία αὐτοῦ κατέκαυσαν ἐν τῇ ἀγορᾷ ὑπὸ κήρυκι ἀναλεξάμενοι παρ' ἑκάστου τῶν κεκτημένων.* The sentence of exile on Protagoras and the burning of his books are said to have been part of a campaign against atheism launched in Athens in the mid fifth century, aimed initially at Socrates, in the course of which Anaxagoras and Diagoras of Melos were also prosecuted for impiety: see E. Derenne, *Les procès d'impiété intentés aux philosophes au Vème et au IVème siècles*, Liège 1930. However, serious doubts have been cast on the accuracy of Diogenes Laertius's facts: see C. W. Müller, 'Protagoras über die Götter', *Hermes* 95 (1967) 140-159; Skouteropoulos, *op. cit.*, 41.

Eusebius, in his *De Evangelica Praeparatione* (XIV.3.7), records the testimony of Porphyry (3rd cent. A.D.) that books by Protagoras were available in his time even though the works of pre-Platonic writers were in general very scarce: see Skouteropoulos, *op. cit.*, 100-101.

75. *Souda*, s.v. 'Prodicus of Ceos'; Guthrie, *Οἱ Σοφιστές*, 73 ff.; Skouteropoulos, *op. cit.*, 286-335.
76. Plato, *Hippias Major*, 282c-d: 'Our friend Prodicus has often come here in a public capacity, and the last time he came here in a public capacity from Ceos, just lately, he made a great reputation for himself by his speaking before the Boule [Senate]; and in his private capacity he made an astonishing amount of money by giving exhibitions and associating with the young; but not one of those ancients ever thought fit to extract money as payment for his wisdom or to give exhibitions among people of various places.' In Plato's *Theaetetus* (151b) Socrates explains the difference between his own educational method and the passive teaching of the sophists and sends to Prodicus any would-be student who appears to have no embryonic ideas in his mind waiting to be 'delivered' by the maieutic method. In *Cratylus* (384b) Socrates acknowledges the importance of learning about words but remarks ironically that if only he had attended Prodicus's 'fifty-drachma lecture' he would have had a thorough understanding of the correct meaning of words; unfortunately, though, he has heard only the 'one-drachma lesson'. The latter figure brings to mind the selling price of Anaxagoras's book.

    Another leading sophist notorious for his exorbitant fees was Gorgias (*c.* 483-376), from Leontini in Sicily, who was said to charge his pupils a hundred minae (= 10,000 drachmae!) per lesson.
77. The *Horae* deals with the birth of religion as mankind's reaction to living conditions on earth, culminating in the dilemma confronting Heracles when Virtue and Pleasure appeared before him and invited him to choose between them: he opted for the arduous path of Virtue in preference to the transient delights of Pleasure. The *Horae* must have come out not later than 416 B.C. as it is mentioned in Plato's *Symposium*, which is set in that year. The 'learned man' to whom Plato likens Prodicus may be Polycrates, a sophist who later wrote a savage attack on Socrates, for Polycrates was the author of panegyrics on cooking-pots, mice and pebbles.
78. See de Romilly, *op. cit.*, 59, 72-73, 75, 79, 206.
79. *The Frogs*, 943. Here Aristophanes may have been mocking Euripides not only for his bookishness but also for having studied under Gorgias: see Aulus Gellius, XV.XX.4.
80. Aelian, *Varia Historia*, XIII.38: *Ἰσχυρῶς Ὅμηρον ἐθαύμαζεν Ἀλκιβιάδης, καί ποτε διδασκαλείῳ παίδων προσελθὼν ῥαψῳδίαν Ἰλιάδος ᾔτει. τοῦ δὲ διδασκάλου μηδὲν ἔχειν Ὁμήρου φήσαντος, ἐντρίψας αὐτῷ κόνδυλον εὖ μάλα στερεὸν παρῆλθεν, ἐνδειξάμενος ὅτι ἐκεῖνος ἀπαίδευτός ἐστι καὶ τοιούτους ἀποφαίνει τοὺς παῖδας.* Cf. Plutarch, *Alcibiades*, VII.1: 'Once, when he was past his boyhood, he accosted a school-teacher and asked him for a book of Homer. The teacher replied that he had nothing of Homer's, whereupon Alcibiades gave him a blow with his fist and went his way.'
81. The world of the sophists forms the background to Aristophanes's *Tagenistai* ('the Fryers'), a comedy of which only fragments survive and which seems to be about various well-known Athenian rakes, notably Alcibiades: see Jacqueline de Romilly's recent monograph *Ἀλκιβιάδης* (= *Alcibiadès*, tr. Athina-Babi Athanasiou and Katerina Miliaressi), Athens 1995, 51, 107.
82. N. Hourmouziadis, *Ἕνας Ἀθηναῖος θεατής στά ἐν ἄστει Διονύσια*, Athens 1988.
83. On Greek palaeography see esp.: E. G. Turner, *Ἑλληνικοί Πάπυροι: Εἰσαγωγή στή*

μελέτη καί τή χρήση τῶν παπύρινων κειμένων (= *Greek Papyri: An Introduction*, Oxford 1968, tr. G. M. Parasoglou), Athens 1981, 81, 166; L. D. Reynolds and N. G. Wilson, *Ἀντιγραφεῖς καί Φιλόλογοι: Τό ἱστορικό τῆς παράδοσης τῶν κλασικῶν κειμένων* (= *Scribes and Scholars: A guide to the transmission of Greek and Latin literature*, 2nd edn., London 1975, tr. N. M. Panayotakis), Athens 1981, 19; E. Mioni, *Εἰσαγωγή στήν Ἑλληνική Παλαιογραφία* (= *Introduzione alla Paleografia Greca*, Padua 1973, tr. N. M. Panayotakis), Athens 1977, 45-53 (and, on Menander, 32). What made it even more difficult to read the texts was that the old alphabet – in which, for example, the letter *ε* was also used for *ει* and *η* – was still in use right down to 403 B.C.

84. Aristomenes Thyropoeus, *The Wizards* (*Goetes*), fragment quoted by Julius Pollux (Polydeuces): see Th. Koch (ed.), *Comicorum Graecorum Fragmenta*, I, Leipzig 1881, 691 (fr. 9).
85. Archaeological evidence concerning the purposes for which the Orchestra was used in the fifth century, brought to light by the Agora excavations, suggests that John Camp's hypothesis regarding the construction of the bookshops is almost certainly correct: namely that they were little more than roofed wooden stalls, perhaps built by scaffolders, not unlike the bookstalls on the Left Bank in Paris or at the Monastiraki flea market in Athens. They may have been either permanent or temporary, and in fact it is quite likely that when theatrical performances were put on for the Dionysia or other festivals the bookstalls were moved bodily to the theatre. See H. A. Thompson and R. E. Wycherley, *The Athenian Agora*, XIV, Princeton 1972, 126-127.
86. Athenaeus, III.126e-f: 'Let me ask you, my friend, what Nicophon, poet of the Old Comedy, has to say in *Hand-to-mouth Toilers*. For I find him also mentioning spoons when he says: "Anchovy-peddlers, charcoal-peddlers, dried-fig-peddlers, hide-peddlers, barley-peddlers, spoon-peddlers, book-peddlers, sieve-peddlers, sweet-cake-peddlers, seed-peddlers."'
87. Lesky, *op. cit.*, 703 ff.
88. Diog. Laer., III.9: *λέγουσι δέ τινες, ὧν ἐστι καὶ Σάτυρος ὅτι Δίωνι ἀπέστειλεν εἰς Σικελίαν ὠνήσασθαι τρία βιβλία Πυθαγορικὰ παρὰ Φιλολάου μνῶν ἑκατόν. καὶ γὰρ ἐν εὐπορίᾳ φασίν, ἣν παρὰ Διονυσίου λαβὼν ὑπὲρ τὰ ὀγδοήκοντα τάλαντα.*

    Aristippus of Cyrene also received a sum of money from Dionysius, the ruler of Syracuse, who was keen to attract philosophers to his court. When criticized for his conduct, Aristippus retorted, 'Well, I need money, Plato needs books!' (Diog. Laer., II.81).
89. Diog. Laer., VIII.85: *ἕτεροι δὲ λέγουσι τὸν Πλάτωνα λαβεῖν αὐτὰ παρὰ Διονυσίου παραιτησάμενον ἐκ τῆς φυλακῆς νεανίσκον ἀπηγμένον τῶν τοῦ Φιλολάου μαθητῶν.*
90. Diog. Laer., III.18: 'Plato, it seems, was the first to bring to Athens the mimes of Sophron which had been neglected, and to draw characters in the style of that writer; a copy of the mimes, they say, was actually found under his pillow.'
91. Proclus, *Commentary on 'Timaeus'*, 21c.
92. Diog. Laer., VIII.81: 'Plato to Archytas, greeting. I was overjoyed to get the memoirs which you sent, and I am very greatly pleased with the writer of them.'
93. Zenobius, V.6. See also J. W. Thompson, 'Libraries of Ancient Greece', 19; Kleberg, *op. cit.*, 30.
94. On Isocrates's teaching methods see Marrou, *op. cit.*, 130 ff.; W. Jaeger, *Παιδεία: Ἡ μόρφωσις τοῦ Ἕλληνος ἀνθρώπου* (= *Paideia. Die Formung des griechischen Menschen*, tr. G. P. Verrios), III, Athens 1974, 128 ff.; de Romilly, *Οἱ Μεγάλοι Σοφιστές...*, 93-94, 118-119.

ius's realms he ordered all these writings to be translated into Greek. And then, on his orders, not only were all the originals from Darius's treasury burnt, but all the people suspected of possibly having similar books in their possession were put to death.' And, according to a third version, 'Alexander the Great ordered those writings in the archives and treasuries of Istahar [Persepolis] to be copied and translated into Greek and Coptic.'[5]

These stories about Alexander's depredations and the translations of Persian works into Greek come from the popular tradition of the late Sassanid period (early seventh century) and are told in writing in the various versions and adaptations of the *Book of Rulers* (*Ḫwadāy-nāmag/Ḫudāy-nāma*).[6]

According to an old Armenian tradition, in about 150 B.C. a Chaldaean named Mar Abas Katina went to Nineveh on a mission for the first Armenian king, Valascase, to look through the archives there for material relating to the history of the Armenians. There he found a book starting with the following words (in Greek): 'This book, translated from Chaldaean into Greek on Alexander's orders, tells the true history of our ancestors.'[7]

Alexander the Great's 'library'

Neither the Persian nor the Armenian tradition necessarily substantiates the theory that Alexander the Great actually conceived the idea of establishing a Universal Library, even though they imply that he definitely intended to have at least the written tradition of the East translated and made known to the Greeks. His reading and discussion of books with his teacher Aristotle had deepened his appreciation of such matters: it seems that not only did he have a private library, but on his all-conquering march he managed to make time for reading: as Plutarch informs us, 'When he was in upper Asia, since he had no other books, he ordered Harpalus to send him some; and Harpalus sent him Philistus's histories, many of the plays of Euripides, Sophocles, and Aeschylus and some dithyrambic odes by Telestes and Philoxenus.'[8] What is more, Alexander had not only given Aristotle a generous grant to buy books but had also supplied him with the material he needed for writing the *Politics*. Given that he was driven by boundless ambition, the splendid libraries he found in the palaces at Persepolis, Babylon, Nineveh and elsewhere, full of books written in unknown languages and scripts, would naturally have given him the idea of gathering them all together into a Greek library universal in its scope. This hypothesis is supported by the fact that Ptolemy I Soter, the founder of the Universal Library at Alexandria, was one of Alexander's clos-

84. Plan of ancient Alexandria, after G. Botti (1898). ☞

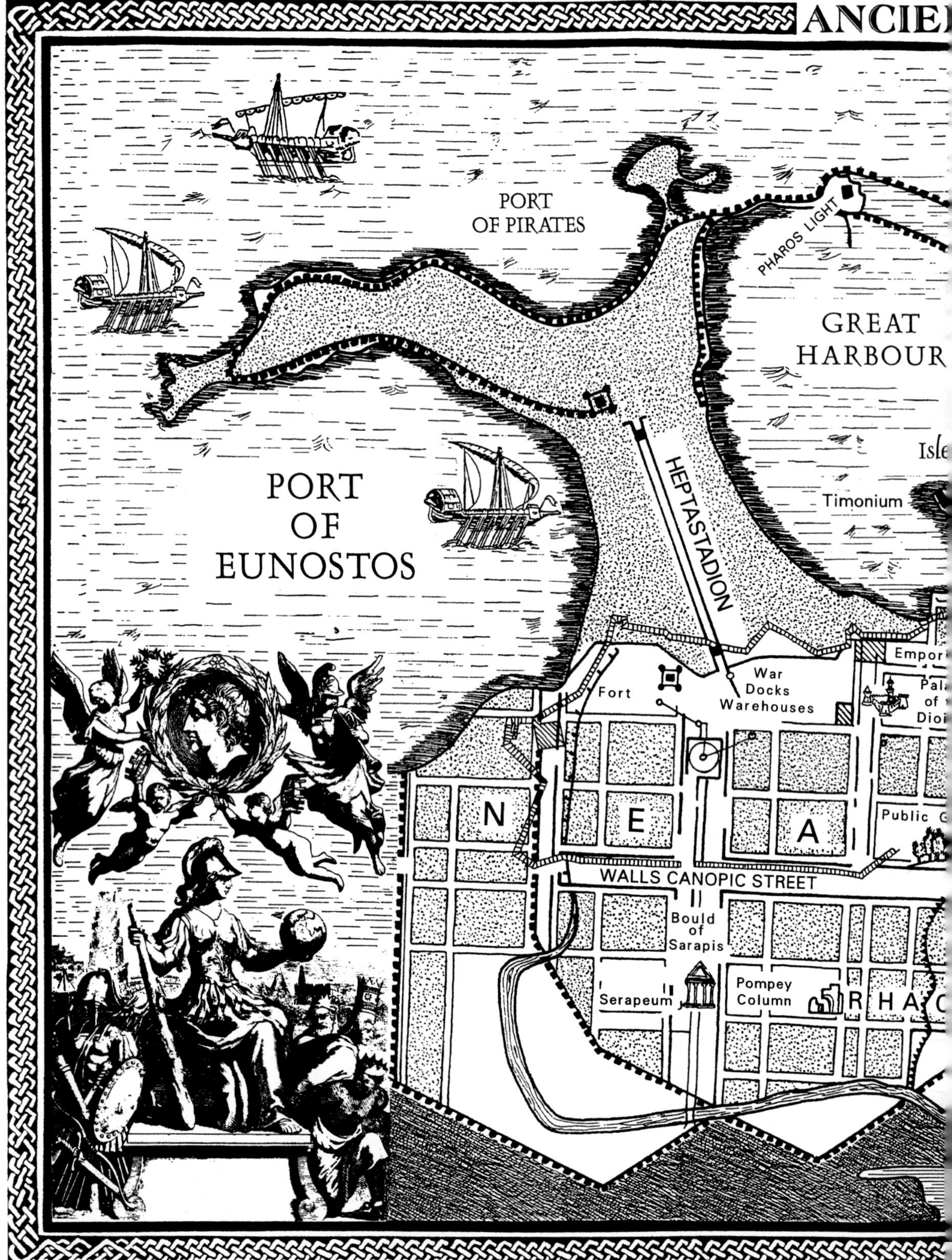

PORT
OF PIRATES
PHAROS LIGHT
GREAT
HARBOUR
PORT
OF
EUNOSTOS
HEPTASTADION
Timonium
Fort
War
Docks
Warehouses
N
E
A
WALLS CANOPIC STREET
Bould
of
Sarapis
Serapeum
Pompey
Column

ALEXANDRIA

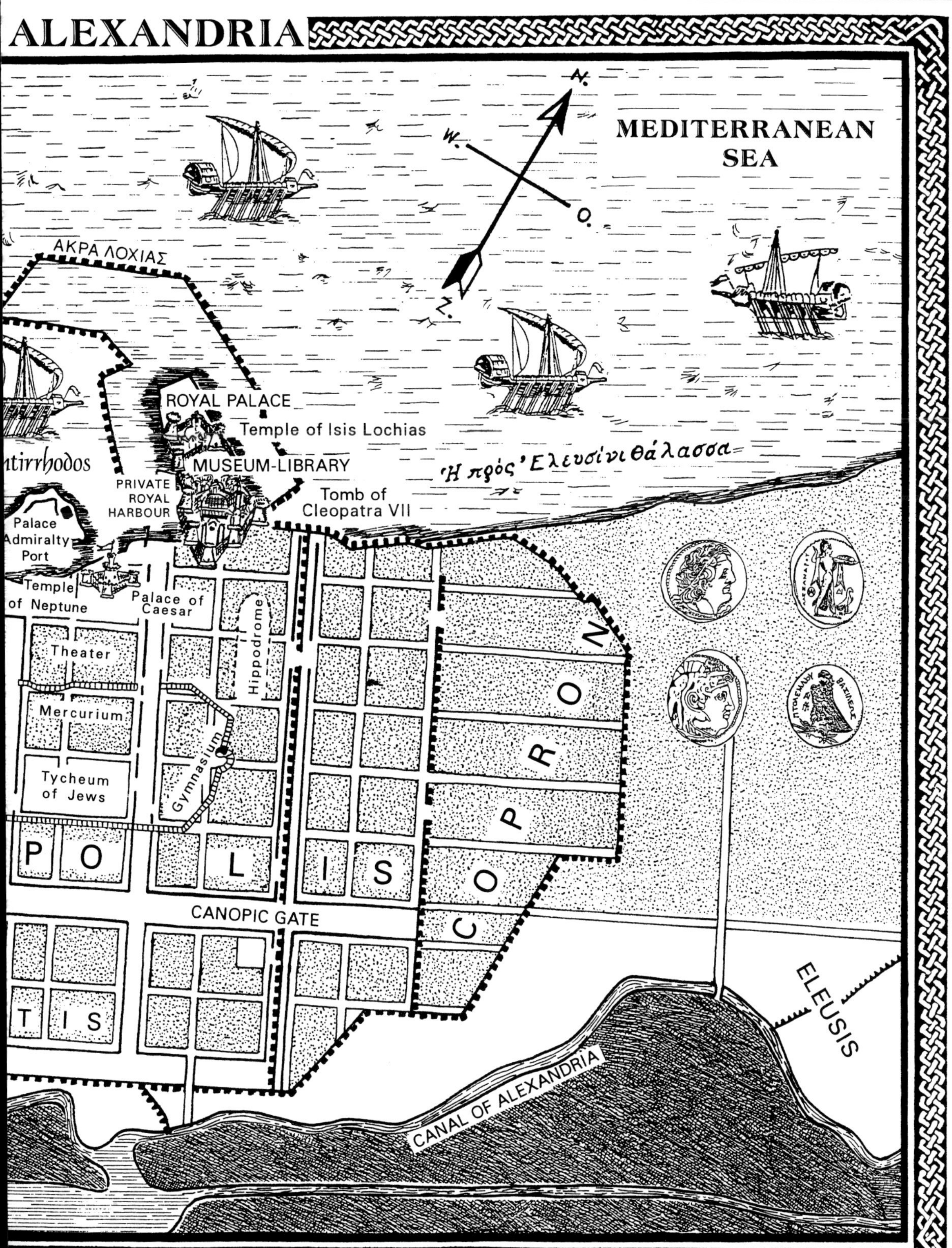

MEDITERRANEAN SEA
N.
W.
O.
Z.
ΑΚΡΑ ΛΟΧΙΑΣ
ROYAL PALACE
Temple of Isis Lochias
ntirrhodos
MUSEUM-LIBRARY
Ἡ πρὸς Ἐλευσῖνι θάλασσα
PRIVATE ROYAL HARBOUR
Tomb of Cleopatra VII
Palace Admiralty Port
Temple of Neptune
Palace of Caesar
Theater
Hippodrome
Mercurium
Tycheum of Jews
Gymnasium
BRUCHION
P O L I S
CANOPIC GATE
COPRON
T I S
ELEUSIS
CANAL OF ALEXANDRIA

est associates – so much so that Alexander had probably confided his dearest aspirations to him. That, at any rate, seems not too much to infer from the fact that Ptolemy wrote a biography of the Macedonian conqueror, now lost, in which he would doubtless have explained Alexander's actions and plans.[9]

Alexandria, the Ptolemies' capital city

Ptolemy I Soter, founder of the Library. Ptolemy Soter († 283 B.C.), a son of Lagus and Arsinoe, was said by some to have been related to the Macedonian royal family, an innuendo which was meant to suggest that he was an illegitimate son of Philip II. He had great respect and affection for Alexander and all he stood for. On Alexander's death Ptolemy transported his mortal remains to Alexandria and had a mausoleum built in his honour.[10] In the struggle between Alexander's would-be successors Ptolemy showed great circumspection and diplomatic acumen. He strengthened his own kingdom by acquiring a number of small territories of strategic importance, including Cyrene, Cos and Cyprus,[11] and he kept out of the fighting among his rivals, notably Perdiccas and Antigonus, each of whom hoped to emerge as sole inheritor of the whole of Alexander's empire. This wise man, a general, diplomat and peacemaker, made it his aim to establish Alexandria as the cultural centre of the Greek world.[12] The Museum, the Universal Library, the library of the Serapeum, his attempt to transfer the Peripatetic school to Alexandria and his policy of attracting the most prominent scholars and artists to his capital established a tradition which was respected and followed, sometimes with enthusiasm and sometimes half-heartedly, by all subsequent rulers of Egypt down to Cleopatra.

85. Ptolemy I Soter. Engraving, 19th c.

The sources. The written sources and other evidence and the various theories put forward concerning the establishment, growth and final destruction of the Alexandrian Library are full of contradictions and often (especially with regard to its destruction) verging on the realm of myth. This means that the only possible approach to the subject is to identify all those concerned in its foundation; to follow the progress of the Greek literary scholars who worked in the Museum, especially those who became its Master; to trace the course of its enlargement; and, of course, to inquire into the ultimate fate of its books. The first point that has to be made is that the Library was an integral part of the Museum and was not open to the public. The principal sources for the history of the Museum and Library are: a 'letter' written by a man calling himself Aristeas; Strabo; Galen; Ioannes Tzetzes; the *Lives* of the various Directors of the Library, as given by *Souda*; and references in the writings of scholars who visited Alexandria, such as Aphthonius and Epiphanius.

86. Strabo. Engraving, 18th c.

The Museum. The idea of opening a *Mouseion*, that is a cultural centre to serve the Muses, did not originate with Ptolemy I, for several similar centres existed in the Greek world, some of them with roots going back to Pythagoras and his circle. The most highly-developed example was the *mouseion*[13] in the Peripatos in the form in which it existed under Theophrastus, that is to say a centre of specialized teaching and research – an academy, in other words – with lecture rooms, a library and scientific instruments for the study of natural phenomena as well as courtyards, colonnaded galleries, garden walks and numerous statues of gods and mortals, and with the sanctuary and altar at the centre. Diogenes Laertius (V.51) quotes a passage from Theophrastus's will which hints at its appearance: 'I

The greatest 'university' of the Hellenistic period

should like the money entrusted to Hipparchus to be used as follows. First, work on the *mouseion* and the statues of the goddesses is to be completed, and anything else necessary for their embellishment is to be done. Secondly, the bust of Aristotle and the other votive offerings that used to be in the sanctuary are to be re-erected. The small stoa adjoining the *mouseion* is to be rebuilt, at least as handsomely as it was before, and the tablets with the maps of the world are to be replaced in the lower stoa. Lastly, the altar is to be repaired and made as beautiful and elegant as possible.'

The character of the Museum

The person Ptolemy I originally wanted to organize and run the Museum was Theophrastus, Aristotle's successor, and accordingly he asked him to leave the Peripatos and move to Alexandria (Diog. Laer., V.8). However, as we saw in the last chapter, he declined the king's invitation, preferring to stay on with the two thousand students at the Peripatos. Evidently Ptolemy then followed the advice of Demetrius of Phalerum concerning the organization of the Museum. His ambition was to establish a Panhellenic centre of education and scholarship, and with that object in view he invited eminent scholars from all over the Greek world: Philetas from Cos, Zenodotus from Ephesus, Strato and Demetrius of Phalerum from Athens, to name only a few.

Unfortunately the historical sources for Ptolemy I's reign, such as Hecataeus of Abdera[14] and Manetho in their histories both entitled *Aegyptiaca*, make only passing references to the Museum, while Herondas in the third century B.C., who does mention the Museum as one of the sights of Alexandria,[15] adds nothing to our knowledge of it. The Museum as a whole was apparently crown land. Strabo, who visited Alexandria in the first century B.C.,[16] gives a fairly laconic description of it. It occupied part of the *basileion* or *basileia*, that is to say the palace grounds, which accounted for at least a quarter of the city's total area. The main building, a splendid edifice with colonnades and paved walks connecting it to the palace, was surrounded by all sorts of outbuildings and an 'exedra' (here a sort of open-air theatre). There was also a religious side to its character, inasmuch as it was presided over by a priest (the Priest of the Museum) appointed by the king himself. The only other member of the Museum's administrative staff mentioned by the sources was the *Epistates* (Superintendent), who was probably in charge of administration, finance and general management.[17] The brevity of Strabo's description may be due in part to the fact that Aristonicus of Alexandria had written a book all about the Museum, which was in existence in Strabo's time but is now lost.[18]

The members of the Museum. The academic community of the Museum is described by Strabo as an 'assembly' (*synodos*), and we know from other sources that the members of this unusual self-contained community received various privileges and substantial grants and amenities to enable them to concentrate on their work of serving the Muses without worrying about the necessities of everyday life. They were given free board and lodging, tax exemptions, high salaries and enough servants to look after their needs.[19] Their privileged treatment provoked a good deal of comment from the Alexandrian *literati*, and they often came in for scathing criticism and sarcastic gibes directed not only at their soft and easy lives but also at the poor quality of their work. Timon of Phlius (*ca.* 320-230 B.C.), a Sceptic philosopher and pupil of Pyrrho, railed against those who made their living by 'scribbling endlessly and waging a constant war of words with each other in the Muses' birdcage';[20] and he cast aspersions on the quality of the editorial work of Zenodotus – and by implication all the scholars of the Museum – by advising Aratus of Soli, the author of a poem entitled *Phenomena*, to 'go back to the old copies of Homer instead of using the newly-corrected versions'.[21] In effect the members of the Museum lived in a gilded prison, because even when they went out of the building they were still in the palace grounds, which they were hardly ever allowed to leave. Aristophanes of Byzantium, for example – the Director of the Library and a most distinguished member of the Museum – was arrested and imprisoned when it was discovered that he was planning to leave the Museum for the court of Eumenes II at Pergamum.[22]

Mockery of members of the Museum

The exchanges of raillery and derogatory stories between the members of the Museum and outside scholars were nothing new in the Greek world, of course: in a way, they were a continuation of the wrangling and logic-chopping characteristic of Athens in the fourth century B.C. The only difference was that instead of Socrates, Plato and Aristophanes attacking the sophists' practices we now find the 'old guard' at odds with the exponents of the new literary studies and members of the Museum coterie.

Little is known about the duties of the scholars of the Museum, except that the Directors of the Library usually doubled as tutors to members of the royal family. For example, there is no evidence as to whether the literary scholars (*philologoi*, as Strabo calls them)[23] had fixed teaching hours, whether each one had a set group of students under his personal supervision, or whether they gave regular lectures. The only thing that can be said with any certainty is that the bulk of their scholastic and literary work was concerned with arranging, evaluating, classifying and expanding a vast mass of material covering the entire corpus of every genre of poetry, the philosophy teaching books of Aristotle, Theophrastus and the Peripatetics and every other branch of literature and learning. Judging by Euclid's work and the tradition that grew up around it in the time of Ptolemy the geographer, as well as the advances made in medical science by Herophilus of Chalcedon, it would appear that anatomy, mathematics, astronomy and medicine were all included in the Museum's curriculum.[24] In other words the Museum was more or less a university in the modern sense of the word, and it was set in an exceptionally elegant environment rich in amenities: the main university building and the Library were surrounded by auxiliary buildings of all kinds, interconnected with a network of colonnades, courtyards, paved walks and open-air lecture areas (in addition to the indoor lecture rooms), and there were botanical and zoological gardens for the observation of plants and animals. It was in this part of the palace grounds, and in the functional context of the Museum, that the Library came into being.[25]

The beginning of the Library's tradition

87. Demetrius of Phalerum. Engraving of a marble bust.

Towards a Universal Library. The first person known to have been directly connected with the preparations and planning of the Library, if not of the Museum as such, was Demetrius of Phalerum,[26] for Strabo's statement that the Ptolemies appointed Aristotle to organize the Library is baseless.[27] Following Theophrastus's refusal to move to Alexandria[28] and the brief stay of Strato of Lampsacus in Egypt,[29] Demetrius of Phalerum – who went to Alexandria seeking asylum as a political refugee – was the only member of the Peripatetic school to become one of Ptolemy I's close advisers.

Demetrius of Phalerum. Demetrius of Phalerum, a man of wide learning with an incisive intellect, was a firm believer in the political importance of encouraging literature and the arts in any organized society. He was born at Phalerum, near Athens, *circa* 350 B.C., studied under Aristotle, became a close friend of Theophrastus's and attained such a high level of philosophical learning and rhetorical skill that he was singled out for commendation by Cicero. He made his appearance on the political scene in 325 B.C., by which time Attic orators had lost their ascendancy, and consequently he quickly won the fame he longed for. In politics he was something of an adventurer and fickle in his loyalties, for at the drop of a hat he switched from the anti-Macedonian democratic party and became a leader of the oligarchic faction. In this capacity he won favour with Cassander, the ruler of Macedonia, and governed Athens as his viceroy for ten years from 317. His uninterrupted period of rule won him a large following in the city: his devotion to the ideals of the Peripatetic school and the innovations he introduced to foster literature made him extremely popular. He also breathed new vigour into the theatre, which had been in the doldrums because the state was no longer able to subsidize costly productions, and this was another reason why the Athenians idolized him. But the atmosphere of prosperity and well-being was rudely shattered in 307, when Demetrius Poliorcetes sailed into Piraeus harbour with his fleet and roused the Athenian democrats to rebellion, forcing the viceroy to flee to Thebes and from there, in about 297, to Egypt, to escape the death penalty.

88. Aristeas. Engraving from Aristeae Historia, *Oxford 1692.*

Once in Alexandria, it is beyond question that he was accepted into Ptolemy I's innermost circle and quite possible that he too, like Strato, provided a link between the Peripatos in Athens and the Museum in Alexandria; but, important though his contribution may have been, he was never Director of the Library (as is often asserted) and no historical source makes it clear whether he was ever appointed to any official post. The only source that says anything to that effect is the so-called 'Letter of Aristeas', a narrative written more than a hundred years after his death.

The 'Letter of Aristeas'. Aristeas's letter (*Aristeae ad Philocratem epistula*)[30] has to be approached with circumspection and its value assessed from two different angles: as it concerns the Library and as it concerns the relations between Greeks and Jews, especially in Alexandria. Although its authenticity is disputed, it is the oldest extant source of information – and the only one apart from the Prolegomena of Tzetzes – concerning the thinking behind the formation and enlargement of the Library, and all the indications are that the main facts stated in it are not far from the truth. The letter also attests to the first cultural contacts between the Greeks and the Jews and signals the birth of a substantial body of Hellenistic Jewish literature.[31]

The Jews come into contact with Greek literature

Aristeas, the supposed author of the 'Letter', who describes himself as a Greek at the court of Ptolemy II Philadelphus (285/3-247 B.C.), was a Jew who was perhaps deliberately setting out to glorify the Hellenistic tradition of Jewish religion and literature in order to strengthen the cultural links between the Greeks and the Jewish community in Alexandria. The document is a narrative in the form of a letter from Aristeas to his 'brother' Philocrates, who was probably not a real person.[32] It is thought to have been written between 180 and 145 B.C. – perhaps in 160, during the reign of Ptolemy VI Philometor – as a straight narrative, and was probably not put into epistolary form until much later. A full reading of the 'Letter' makes it clear that the author's primary purpose in writing was not to give an account of history of the Universal Library. Aristeas, who praises the Ptolemies for their initiative in making the literature and cultural traditions of the Near Eastern peoples better known by having them translated into an international language, Greek, takes the opportunity to discourse at length on the teachings of the Torah, preparing the ground for a comprehensive survey of the Jewish scriptures with the object of making them known to the rest of the world.[33] In his 'Letter', which sets out the historical background of the links between Jews and Greeks, he discusses the whole question with the utmost diplomacy, first acknowledging the importance of Greek learning and ending with a glowing panegyric to Judaism. Not surprisingly, various hypotheses have been put forward in answer to the questions raised by the 'Letter': what was Aristeas's purpose in writing it; to what readership it was addressed; whether it was apologetic or propagandistic in character, or neither of these; and, in general, what ideology lay behind it. The conclusions to be drawn are that the writer was an educated Jew, familiar with Greek learning and influenced by the Greek philosophy and literature of his own time, who wished to give Jewish readers an account of the translation of the Septuagint and showed great respect for the Greeks and their civilization. His ultimate objective was to bring the Jews and the Greeks closer together.

According to Aristeas,[34] Demetrius of Phalerum had been given *carte blanche* to manage the Library as he saw fit and he urged Ptolemy to visit the Library regularly to keep himself informed about new accessions and general progress. At one of their meetings Demetrius reported that the Library already had 200,000 books and estimated that a total of 500,000 would be needed to complete the project. Ptolemy therefore entered into correspondence with kings and princes everywhere, asking them to send him copies of all the books (by poets, prose writers, sophists, physicians, historians and magi) that they had in their libraries and archives.

Ptolemy – Aristeas does not specify which one – was particularly interested in acquiring entire libraries. In his reports Demetrius advised the king to extend his book search to the Jewish world: he reminded him of the authoritative standing of Hecataeus of Abdera (the author of *Aegyptiaca*, which contained a good

89. Imaginary reconstruction of the Pharos at Alexandria. Engraving, 18th c.

deal of information on Jewish history) and gave it as his opinion that the Library should have copies of all Jewish books in existence. On one of Ptolemy's visits to the Library Demetrius told him that if the Library were to acquire works of Jewish literature – the king having by then agreed to the proposal – they would have to be translated into Greek from Hebrew and not (as the received wisdom was at that time) from Syriac. In a display of magnanimity, Ptolemy II freed more than a hundred thousand Jews who had been taken prisoner during his Syrian campaign and were living in Alexandria. In return for this gesture of goodwill Ptolemy asked Eleazar, the high priest of Jerusalem, to send him a team of Greek-speaking Jewish scholars to translate the scriptures. Eleazar gladly complied: Aristeas made a special journey to Jerusalem to see about it, and the high priest nominated six scholars from each of the twelve tribes of Israel.

The translation of the Septuagint

Ptolemy welcomed the Jewish scholars with the utmost courtesy and entertained them to a banquet where he satisfied himself of the breadth of their learning by engaging them in penetrating discussions on a wide variety of topics. The Jewish translators were not accommodated in the Museum but in special quarters of their own on the offshore islet of Pharos. Demetrius visited them there regularly, taking his own grammarians along with him to check their work, which they finished in exactly seventy-two days. The translation of the Septuagint (as it is called because it was translated by (approximately) seventy scholars, known as the Seventy or the LXX) was a demonstration of the king's determination to acquire all the books in the known world both in their original languages and in Greek translation, or at least in abridged Greek versions, for which he engaged foreign translators from various countries with a good knowledge of Greek.

Irrespective of speculation concerning the political expediency served by the 'Letter of Aristeas', its accuracy is called in question by a comparison with the known facts. In the first place, as we shall see, the official list of the Directors of the Library gives Zenodotus as the first holder of the post: Demetrius of Phalerum is not mentioned at all. References to Ptolemy in the Letter sometimes mean Ptolemy I Soter and sometimes Ptolemy II Philadelphus; but when Philadelphus ascended the throne Demetrius of Phalerum fell out of favour because he had not supported his claim to the throne, and so he was exiled to Upper Egypt, where he died *circa* 280 B.C. The dating of the Septuagint to the reign of Ptolemy I is clearly wrong: given that the translation was made in the middle of the second century B.C. (at about the time when the Letter was written), it is probably to be explained in the context of the surge of writing in Greek on subjects connected with Judaism – by Jewish writers for Jewish readers – that occurred in Alexandria in the second century.[35]

The 'Letter of Aristeas' was very popular not only in the Ptolemaic period but also much later, in the Christian era. It was still current and may still have been considered a reliable source even in the twelfth century, the time of Ioannes Tzetzes, who used material from it in writing about the Alexandrian Library in his *Prolegomena to Aristophanes*. An excerpt from a Latin adaptation of the Prolegomena by an anonymous fifteenth-century humanist is also extant in a manuscript of scholia on plays by Plautus.

The *Prolegomena to Aristophanes*. It would appear that the sources used by Ioannes Tzetzes for the Prolegomena to his commentary on three comedies by Aristophanes[36] included another work or works, now lost, in addition to the 'Letter of Aristeas'. In connection with the Library, Tzetzes mentions three literary scholars who belonged to the famous group of seven tragedians known as The Pleiad,[37] a group formed for the purpose of classifying, cataloguing and commenting on the works of the ancient tragedians. Alexander of Pleuron[38] was commissioned to edit the tragedies and satyric dramas for publication, Lycophron of Chalcis[39] was to edit the comedies, and Zenodotus undertook the onerous task of editing Homer and other poets. In the Prolegomena, Tzetzes goes back to the tradition that Pisistratus conceived the idea of editing and publishing Homer, and he offers the additional information that Pisistratus engaged four scholars, Onomacritus of Athens, Epicongylus, Zopyrus of Heraclia and Orpheus of Croton, to carry out the project.[40]

Statistics on the size of the Library

Demetrius of Phalerum, according to Tzetzes, was instructed by Ptolemy II [*sic*] to collect copies of all the books in the world, which were to be kept in two libraries in Alexandria. Here, then, we find a reference to a second library, described as being 'outside the palace' and attached to the Temple of Serapis (the Serapeum) in the Rhachotis or Rhacotis district of Alexandria. This much smaller library, which was open to the public, eventually contained only 42,800 books, whereas the Great Library in the palace grounds had 400,000 'composite' rolls and another 90,000 'unmixed' rolls.[41] The information is said by Tzetzes to come from Callimachus himself, who had been entrusted with the task of sorting, classifying and indexing the books. When the books, brought from many different countries and written in many different languages, had all been gathered together, Ptolemy had them translated by linguists fluent in Greek and the other language involved in each case.

The Plautine Scholium. An excerpt from a fifteenth-century Italian humanist's Latin version of the Prolegomena of Tzetzes,[42] which appears in a commentary on Plautus, has nothing new to say about the Library. The anonymous Italian omits all reference to the Jews and the translation of the Septuagint, but he does have the passage about Demetrius of Phalerum helping Ptolemy Philadelphus and the allusion to the second library which occurs in Tzetzes. He describes Callimachus as a man of the court and royal librarian (*aulicus regius bibliothecarius*): perhaps this was simply a mistranslation.

Before going on to a fuller discussion of the reliable authorities and the known facts about the life and works of the Library's first organizers, let us take a look at the small library attached to the Temple of Serapis.

The library of the Serapeum. Serapis, the new god whose cult was introduced by the Ptolemies (in fact by Ptolemy I Soter), symbolized the union between the sacred bull Apis and the goddess Osiris, and as such he came to be worshipped under the name of Osiris-Apis or Osorapis. However, although the Egyptians continued to call him Osorapis, the Greeks preferred the name Serapis or Sarapis, which they found more euphonious.[43] Of all the temples built in his honour throughout Egypt, the most splendid was the one in the Rhachotis district of Alexandria.

The 'subsidiary' library in the Serapeum

According to the Prolegomena of Tzetzes, the temple was built in the reign of Ptolemy II Philadelphus, but excavations on the site – which have been under way for years – have brought to light some inscribed plaques stating that its founder was Ptolemy III Euergetes (246-221 B.C.)[44] The existence of this library is also known from the work of fourth-century ecclesiastical authors, including Epiphanius[45] and Aphthonius,[46] both of whom had been there. Epiphanius states that the Septuagint was kept in the 'first library' and that a smaller library known as the 'subsidiary' (*θυγατρική*, literally 'daughter library') was built later at the Serapeum.[47] Aphthonius, who visited the temple in the middle of the fourth century, speaks of 'chambers' (*sekoi*) on either side of the 'stoas' and of 'treasuries' or 'storerooms' (*tameia*) full of books (in other words small book-lined rooms or carrels facing the stoas) accessible to 'those who are keen to study'.[48] The Serapeum library may have been founded by Ptolemy III, who had studied under Apollonius Rhodius and was very keen to obtain copies of ancient writings, but the question remains open.

90.The main gateway leading in to the temple at Edfu: architecture of the Ptolemaic period.

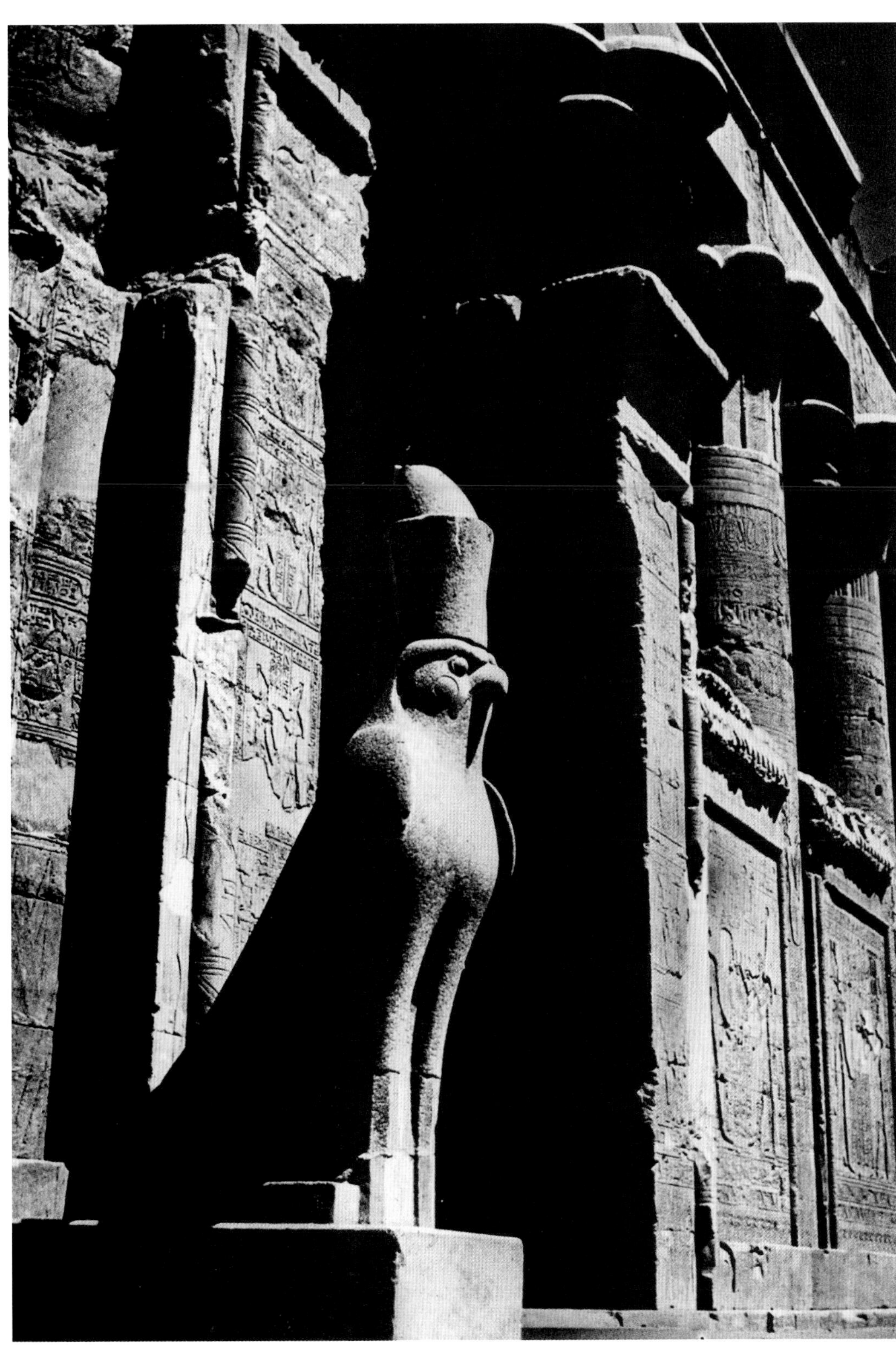

Given that the Universal Library had a peculiar status and was run more or less as a study centre for copyists and textual scholars, it is a reasonable surmise that the Serapeum library was a public library containing copies of literary works in their final edited form.

According to contemporary historians, the destruction or partial destruction of the Serapeum was a consequence of a change in the Eastern Roman Empire's policy towards pagan religions. As a result of the triumph of Christianity and its adoption as the official religion of the Empire, many pagan temples were converted into churches. The new policy was applied with increased severity in the reign of Emperor Theodosius the Great (379-395), who persecuted the pagans ruthlessly, and his edict of 391 implicitly legalized the demolition of all the ancient temples in Alexandria.

91. Statue of Serapis, late Antonine period (A.D. 180-190). Iraklion Archaeological Museum.

Bishop Theophilus of Alexandria, who implemented the anti-pagan policy with fanatical enthusiasm, incited the Christians to attack the Temple of Serapis, seen by many as the quintessential symbol of paganism in the city, and the mob obliged by looting and destroying it utterly: according to the historian Theodoretus, 'The temple was razed to the ground,' while Eunapius, another historian, says that nothing of it was left intact except the foundations – and those only because the massive blocks of stone were too heavy to move. When the destruction was complete, Theophilus had a Christian church built on the site.[49]

Aphthonius, who died in 393, says nothing in the account of his visit to the Serapeum to suggest that what he saw was a building that had been sacked; one can only suppose, therefore, that the mob directed its fury only at temple buildings and not at sanctuaries in their entirety, or else that Aphthonius visited Alexandria before 391. The relevant passage in his work runs as follows: 'Chambers are built in the stoas. Some are storerooms for books: they are open to those who are keen to study, and they induce the whole city to acquire learning.' There were also some of those studies or reading rooms that made Alexandria into the philosophical capital of the Greek world, and other chambers were used for 'the worship of the ancient gods'.

Historians such as Polybius inform us that the Serapeum was an imposing building which, in accordance with the Egyptian architectural tradition, looked more like a fortress than a temple, and that it was situated on a hilltop – an 'acropolis of Alexandria', so to speak.

In the traditional story of the founding of the Universal Library, based mainly on the 'Letter of Aristeas' and the Prolegomena of Tzetzes, there is just one central figure: Demetrius of Phalerum. However, thanks to one of the Oxyrrhynchus papyri (Pap. Oxy. 1241), which lists the Directors of the Library, we are not fettered by Aristeas's narrative: in fact, since we know about the lives and works of those scholars, it is possible to reconstruct the atmosphere and aims of the Universal Library over a period of about two hundred years by viewing them from a different angle.

The succession of Directors of the Library

The Directors of the Library. The first person mentioned in connection with the Library is none other than Aristotle, who, according to Strabo (as we have seen), advised the kings of Egypt on the best way of forming a library. However, this statement must be treated with circumspection, as it can hardly be made to tally with the dates: Aristotle died only eighteen months after Alexander the Great and before Ptolemy I made Alexandria his capital in 320 B.C. Therefore the introduction of Aristotle's name at the beginning of the traditional account of the Directors of the Library must reflect the Ptolemies' determination to ensure that they themselves, the Museum and the Museum's scholars were associated with the Peripatos. Yet, as we have seen, Theophrastus refused to move to Alexandria while Strato stayed there for only a short time before returning to Athens to resume his duties as head of the Peripatos. The author of the 'Letter of Aristeas' mentions only Demetrius of Phalerum but, assuming that the 'Letter' was written around 160 B.C., the writer must have known the names of the Directors of the Library up to that time: Zenodotus, Apollonius Rhodius, Eratosthenes, Aristophanes of Byzantium, Apollonius Eidographus, Aristarchus and Cydas. Of the grammarians mentioned in the Oxyrrhynchus papyrus – Ammonius, Zenodotus, Diocles and Apollodorus – nothing is said to indicate the precise nature of their connections with the Library. Another person attested as having been Director of the Library, though after the 'Letter' was written, was Onesander of Paphos,[50] son of Nausicrates: according to an inscription from Cyprus, he held the post from 88 B.C. It is mainly from the *Lives*[51] of those scholars, and also of course from what we know of their work, that we can form some idea of their enormous achievements in the field of literary scholarship, in which they were certainly assisted by a host of anonymous grammarians, textual scholars and copyists.

The first official Director of the Library

Zenodotus. Zenodotus, born at Ephesus, was active in the second half of the third century B.C.[52] After studying under Philetas he succeeded his teacher as tutor to the royal family and was then appointed Director of the Library by Ptolemy I. He remained in the post during the reign of his ex-pupil, Ptolemy Philadelphus, with the title of 'Head of the Libraries [*sic*] in Alexandria'. This was the title held by all the Directors of the Library, as the term *bibliophylax*, which one would expect to mean 'custodian of the books', and which Tzetzes seems to have used in this sense, meant 'keeper of the government archives' in the Ptolemaic period.[53]

Nothing is known about the work Zenodotus did for the library except that, according to *Souda*, he was the first scholar of the Museum to undertake the task of producing a complete critical edition of Homer.[54] The precise extent and nature of his work on Homer we cannot say: Tzetzes is of no help here, as he merely remarks, 'The theatrical works were revised, as I have said, by Alexander [of Pleuron] and Lycophron, the poetry first by Zenodotus and then by Aristarchus.'[55] However, quite possibly he was the first person to make textual emendations to Homer's works, considering that we find Aristarchus subsequently rejecting Homeric words from Zenodotus's edition when he himself was making his recension.

In the Prolegomena of Tzetzes the thorny question of Pisistratus's first edition of Homer[56] raises its head once again, although three hundred years had elapsed between the time of Pisistratus and the time of Zenodotus. To recapitulate briefly, it was said that in the sixth century B.C. there was probably an official text of Homer deposited in the public library in Athens, and that this was the text that rhapsodists had to follow in their recitations at the Panathenaea festival. But in ancient literature there is no evidence whatsoever for the existence of a sixth-century 'Attic' edition that was generally accepted in the Greek world, and so the earliest known published edition remains that of Antimachus of Colophon, produced at the end of the fifth century B.C.

The Ptolemaic papyrus tradition gives us some clues as to the approach Zenodotus adopted in his work on Homer, as we know he had access to a large number of copies from cities far and wide, including Sinope, Chios, Massalia (Marseille) and Argos.[57] From those he selected one version that seemed to provide the best basis for his recension, and he then went through the whole text, comparing the different versions of the passages that needed emendation and sometimes deleting whole lines, until he finally arrived at what came to be known as the Zenodotus edition.[58] Academic rivalry being what is, there were some who suggested that Zenodotus had had access to the 'Attic' manuscript and had relied chiefly on that in preparing his edition, and that the Alexandrian literary scholars had concealed the fact because they felt that it would detract from their reputation.

On Zenodotus's death, Apollonius Rhodius was appointed Director of the Library.

The quarrel between Apollonius and Callimachus

Apollonius Rhodius. Apollonius was born in Alexandria between 295 and 290 B.C. and was called Rhodius because he spent most of his life on the island of Rhodes.[59] He was taught by Callimachus in Alexandria and must have taken over as Director of the Library between 270 and 260. As holder of that post he tutored the future king Ptolemy III Euergetes (reigned 247-222). He was the greatest poet of his day, his best-known work being the *Argonautica*, the longest extant post-Homeric epic poem.

The pupil-teacher relationship between Apollonius and Callimachus deteriorated after the pupil grew up, and indeed this may have been the main reason for Apollonius's decision to leave Alexandria and settle in Rhodes. The cause of the quarrel between them was Callimachus's attitude towards the *Argonautica* and 'long-winded' epic poetry in general, which was cool at best and openly hostile at worst.[60] Actually, although Callimachus never regarded Apollonius as his main adversary – except on the somewhat dubious evidence of his poem *Ibis*[61] – it is beyond question that scholarly backbiting was the order of the day in the Museum, even among its most respected members.

Eratosthenes. Apollonius Rhodius was succeeded as Director of the Library by Eratosthenes, who was also said to have had Callimachus as his teacher. Eratosthenes was born at Cyrene in 295/290 B.C. (or later?) and died at a great age near the end of the century. Before becoming Director of the Library he had studied in Athens under Zeno, Ariston and Arcesilaus when the last-named was head of Plato's Academy.[62] In about 246 Ptolemy III Euergetes invited him to Alexandria to take over from Apollonius, and he combined his duties as librarian with those of tutor to the royal family.

Poet, textual scholar and scientist

Eratosthenes's achievements in literature, science and the arts(?) demonstrate his versatility and polymathy: he was, in fact, one of the last intellectual all-rounders. Poet, critic and brilliant mathematician – to judge by the fact that the great Archimedes dedicated the 'poem' called *The Cattle Problem* to him in recognition of his mathematical accomplishments[63] – he founded the science of critical chronology with reference to the ancient past. Among his other interests were historical geography and the collecting and listing of technical terms used in various practical occupations, as exemplified in his book *Architectonicus* (*The Master Builder*). He called himself a *philologos*,[64] thus coining the term that exactly describes the principal work of the scholars in the Museum.

The wide scope of Eratosthenes's work was undoubtedly made possible by the huge quantity of material he had at his disposal, especially as Callimachus had by that time nearly completed the task of classifying and cataloguing that material in his *Pinakes* (see p. 186). Perhaps, too, in his official capacity as Director of the Library, he supported the expansion of the Museum's research programme into other branches of learning.

The master of textual scholarship

Aristophanes of Byzantium. Eratosthenes was succeeded as Director of the Library by Aristophanes of Byzantium, a pupil of his who had also studied under Zenodotus and Callimachus.[65] He was born at Byzantium between 258 and 255 B.C. and died in 180 B.C. When he took over the running of the Library, perhaps on the death of Eratosthenes (between 196 and 193), Ptolemy V Epiphanes was on the Egyptian throne.[66]

Aristophanes's work as a textual scholar was of major importance. The rules of accentuation and punctuation that he applied to the work of earlier writers, in combination with the fact that he was able to collate many differ-

92. *Fragment of an Oxyrrhynchus papyrus with part of the* Hellenica, *the continuation of Thucydides's* History *(Pap. Oxy. 1843). British Museum.*

ent manuscripts thanks to the enormous number of books in the Library, made it possible for him to produce exemplary first editions. He also succeeded in changing the prevailing attitude towards literary studies by persuading his contemporaries to overcome their suspicion of revised texts and their ingrained preference for the 'old copies', a suspicion exemplified by Timon of Phlius and his implied sneer at Zenodotus's recension of Homer.[67] Aristophanes compiled a glossary entitled *Words (Lexeis)* containing a wealth of learning on dialect and usage; he edited tragedies and comedies (both Old and New Comedy); and he compiled a collection of proverbs for which he searched mostly in the comedies to find the originals, although he recognized that they were usually derived from colloquial speech. He had an unbounded admiration for Menander, whom he ranked second only to Homer, and he was in the habit of exclaiming, 'O Menander and Life, which of you imitated the other?'[68] But that did nor prevent him from compiling a list of parallel passages in which he noted Menander's borrowings from other writers – the earliest known book on the subject of plagiarism.[69] Lastly, he corrected and supplemented Callimachus's great catalogue, the *Pinakes*. His book was entitled *On* [or *A Supplement to*] *the 'Pinakes' of Callimachus*.

Alexandrian anecdotes

It is worth mentioning two incidents that shed some light on Aristophanes's life in the Museum and on life in Alexandria generally. One was quite serious: shortly after 197 Aristophanes was invited to the court of King Eumenes II of Pergamum to take charge of the new Royal Library there. Apparently Aristophanes was seriously considering the offer, for reasons best known to himself, but as soon as the news of his plans to escape from the Museum leaked out he was arrested and imprisoned to prevent his leaving.[70] The other was not so much an incident as a rather bizarre anecdote: it was said that Aristophanes and an elephant were rivals in love, because both of them were enamoured of a certain flower-girl in the city.[71] Preposterous though this sounds, there were apparently a lot of stories circulating in Alexandria about elephants being attracted by the fragrance of the flowers that were made up into wreaths and sold on the streets,[72] and Aristophanes himself tells a similar story in his book *On Animals*.

Apollonius Eidographus. Apollonius, who succeeded Aristophanes of Byzantium as Director of the Library not later than 180 B.C., was born in Alexandria at a time when Egypt had started sinking into a social, economic and political decline.[73] Very little is known about his life and work. The epithet Eidographus ('the Classifier')[74] was given to him because he classified lyric poems according to the musical mode (Dorian, Phrygian, Lydian, etc.) for which they were written.[75]

Aristarchus. The last Director of the Library with a literary education before the Roman period, as far as we know, was Aristarchus of Samothrace, who was born *circa* 216 and died *circa* 144 B.C.[76] Aristarchus spent most of his life in Alexandria in the reign of Ptolemy VI Philometor (180-145) as tutor to the royal family, one of his pupils being Philometor's brother, the future king Ptolemy VIII (Euergetes II). Aristarchus gathered a large circle of pupils around him, forming a sort of school, and his writings quickly won him a large following that included Apollodorus of Athens, Ammonius of Alexandria and Dionysius the Thracian.[77]

The art of literary interpretation

Aristarchus was regarded as an authoritative critic and interpreter of ancient poetry, especially Homer, whose work he interpreted on the basis of the poet's own words: in other words, he relied on internal evidence. He further expanded the system of critical symbols and made a comparative study of all branches of the tradition to produce a text that was as authentic as possible. Unlike most editors of that time, who delivered their notes on the text orally in the lecture room, he wrote lengthy and intelligent commentaries (*hypomnemata*) on the works he edited. *Souda* states that he wrote over eight hundred books of commentaries alone, but it may be that the figure refers to his total output, which is known to have included original monographs (*syngrammata*).

About Aristarchus's private life in the Museum's academic circles nothing is known: although jokes and anecdotes were commonly told about even the most highly-respected members of the Museum, no stories about him have come down to us, apart from the comment made by Callistratus, a pupil of Aristophanes of Byzantium, that he neglected his appearance and was always badly dressed.[78]

The first crisis in the world of literary studies. Ptolemy VI, who died in 145 B.C., was succeeded by his son, who came to the throne as Ptolemy VII and was given the epithet of Neos Philopator. A year later Ptolemy VII was murdered on the orders of his paternal uncle on the very day when the latter married the former's mother. The usurper, Ptolemy VIII, was officially known as Euergetes (Benefactor) II, but the intellectuals nicknamed him Kakergetes (Malefactor) or Physkon (Pot-Belly), the latter being an echo of the nickname given by Alcaeus to Pittacus, the hated ruler of Lesbos in the seventh century B.C.[79] Ptolemy VIII persecuted all the late king's friends, including even Aristarchus, with the result that many of Aristarchus's pupils and many of the younger generation of scholars and intellectuals left Alexandria to look for greener pastures outside Egypt, chiefly at Pergamum, Athens and Rhodes. Aristarchus chose to settle in Cyprus but died there very soon afterwards, perhaps in 144.

The 'brain drain' of literary scholars from Alexandria

This 'brain drain' led to the first crisis in the history of literary studies. The all-round decline in the standards of scholarship in Alexandria was typified by the appointment of an army officer named Cydas as Director of the Library.[80] Yet, although Ptolemy VIII was a licentious, boorish and generally odious individual, he was a former pupil of Aristarchus and still took an interest in literature and learning generally, as the twenty-four books of his *Memoirs* prove.[81] The Museum remained operational throughout his reign, as did the libraries in the palace and the Serapeum. After Cydas, the Oxyrrhynchus papyrus mentions four grammarians who flourished under Ptolemy IX (Soter II), who reigned from 120 to 80 B.C. (including a period spent in exile). Their names are given as Ammonius, Zenodotus, Diocles and Apollodorus, but, as we have seen, it is not clear precisely what position they held in the Museum or the Library.[82]

Be that as it may, the last director of the Library in the Ptolemaic period, as far as we can tell, was Onesander. According to an inscription found at Paphos, Onesander backed Ptolemy IX during his exile in Cyprus and, when Ptolemy returned to Alexandria in 88 B.C., he appointed Onesander to be his personal priest and Director of the Great Library (*τεταγμένος ἐπὶ τῆς Ἀλεξανδρείας μεγάλης βιβλιοθήκης*) in recognition of his services.[83]

Before closing this section on the lives and works of the Directors of the Library, something must be said about the man who, although he never actually held that post, was for decades the *éminence grise* of the Library and may in fact have held the formal position of royal librarian (*regius bibliothecarius*): Callimachus.

Callimachus. Callimachus was born at Cyrene shortly before 300 B.C. Though he came from an aristocratic family, as a young man he was obliged to earn his living by giving lessons in Alexandria.[84] The great turning-point in his life came when Ptolemy II Philadelphus engaged him to classify and catalogue the vast number of books in the Library. Having unrestricted access to this wealth of material, and being by nature exceptionally industrious as well as very talented, he soon established himself as the outstanding personality of his generation. He is now considered the most important poet of the Hellenistic period and one of the major figures of Graeco-Roman literature. He was active for at least thirty-five years, from 280 to 245, and he died at a ripe old age, probably *circa* 240. According to *Souda* he wrote more than eight hundred books of poetry and prose. His work on the cataloguing of the papyrus rolls in the Library and, more especially, on the compilation of the *Pinakes* (see next page) substantiates his reputation for enormous literary learning.

An indefatigable literary scholar in the service of the Library

Callimachus was never Director of the Library, and the statement in the Plautine Scholium that he was the royal librarian (*regius bibliothecarius*)[85] is nor corroborated by any other source. However, he may have held some official position in the hierarchy of the Library: the fact that nothing is known about the structure of the Library staff does not mean that there was not a large team of experts in various fields, each with his own title and specific duties, to help with the running of the Library.

93. Callimachus, from P. Giovio, Elogia virorum litteris illustrium, *Basel 1577.*

Creating a library classification system. It is not known whether Callimachus had a model of library organization to work on when he tackled that mountain of unsorted papyrus rolls: whether perhaps he was following a classification method used by Aristotle or Theophrastus in the Lyceum library, or whether he knew anything about the system used for classifying the clay tablets in the great libraries of Babylonia, Assyria and Persia.[86] At all events, Callimachus was assigned the task of putting into order everything written before the third century B.C.; at the same time he was expected to pass judgment on the textual integrity of the various editions of literary works in the Library, some of which existed in multiple copies, and also if possible to decide on the authorship of unattributed works or of two or more works bearing the same title. It may be that his own numerous historical, geographical, paradoxographical and antiquarian writings grew from seeds planted when he was compiling the *Pinakes* or that they were written to help him in his cataloguing project. That is something we cannot know, but, as we shall see, those writings – such as the *Collection of Marvels*, the *Collection of Curious Stories* and *The Settling of Islands and Cities and their Changes of Name* – would certainly have served as excellent reference works for the biographical notes included in the *Pinakes*.

The *Pinakes*. What Callimachus set out to do was to compile a comprehensive 'bibliographical' list of authors and their works that would also serve as a library catalogue. The result was the *Pinakes* ('Tables', i.e. catalogues), whose full title was *Tables of all those who were eminent in every branch of learning and of their writings, in 120 books*.[87] Only fragments of the *Pinakes* survive, but they are enough to give us a good idea of the philosophy underlying the method of their arrangement. First of all, what Callimachus called 'every branch of learning' was divided into separate classes of literature: three of these – rhetoric, law and miscellaneous writings – are expressly attested, while the others – poetry, philosophy, history, medicine and so on – are implied.[88] These classes were then subdivided into genres: poetry, for example, was divided into epic, lyric, tragedy and comedy. Within each genre the authors were arranged in alphabetical order, and each author was identified by a brief biographical note. Similarly, within the works of each author, the titles were probably listed alphabetically. The title was written at the end of the papyrus roll, or, if the title was not given, the work was identified by the *incipit* (the first line of the text), which was used to identify the work precisely even where there was a title.[89] Occasionally, too, the total number of lines in the book was written both in the *Pinakes* and at the end of the roll, and sometimes the scribe would write notes in verse rather like a colophon, as in the case of Menander's play *The Man from Sicyon* (3rd cent. B.C.).[90]

The philosophy underlying the Pinakes

The storage arrangements for all these writings would presumably have been ordered by Callimachus in such a way as to follow the catalogue classification system, and the architectural layout of the library would have had to be designed to facilitate not only the permanent storage of the books but also the preparatory work of editing and copying.[91]

The editing and copying centre. The staff required for an editing and copying centre in a Universal Library of the third century B.C., such as the Alexandrian Library, would not have been limited to the Directors of the Library

(Zenodotus, Eratosthenes and the rest), senior figures like Demetrius of Phalerum and Callimachus, and eminent scholars such as Alexander of Pleuron and Lycophron of Chalcis: a huge team of specialists in various fields would also have been needed. The information at our disposal about the philosophy underlying the formation of the Universal Library is scanty and some of it comes from unreliable sources, but I think it is enough for us to reconstruct the pattern of a normal working day at the Library.

Besides the Director, the management of the Library would have consisted of a team of textual scholars assisted by the appropriate administrative personnel and working in co-operation with the official 'librarian', perhaps, from Callimachus's time onwards. These would have constituted the executive staff responsible for making policy decisions concerning the enlargement and arrangement of the Library. From a certain point on, the structure of the *Pinakes* would have provided the guidelines both for the acquisition of books that the Library did not possess and for the textual emendation of books that needed revision and editing. Grammarians and literary scholars gathered information and all kinds of other material for the compilation of anthologies and commentaries, for the purpose of creating an up-to-date encyclopaedia. The object of adopting an alphabetical arrangement and giving explanatory notes on 'every branch of learning', with geographical descriptions and maps of the earth and the heavens, was to create a 'grid of knowledge' in which the answers to all questions and problems could be found. This intellectual treasure-hunt embraced practical as well as theoretical areas of knowledge: medicine, mechanics, mathematics, zoology and botany were all integral parts of the research programme.

Organization of the editing and copying centre

From the time when a royal decree was issued ordering that copies were to be made of books carried on every ship putting into the port of Alexandria, the Library acquired an annexe, both for practical reasons and for the sake of security. An imposing edifice on the waterfront was set aside for this purpose and the necessary structural alterations were made. Under the terms of the decree, scholars were to pick out all books that fell within the scope of the Library's accessions policy and copies of them were to be made. The copies were then returned to the owners, while the originals – known as the 'books from the ships' – were kept in the appropriate section of the Library. This would have been a never-ending occupation, as Alexandria was the busiest port in the Mediterranean in the Ptolemaic period, and there must have been a large staff of grammarians, high-speed copyists, administrators and clerks to deal with the exchange of books between ship and shore, as well as a warehouse full of clean sheets of papyrus.

Another project of primary importance from the time of the first two Ptolemies was that of appraising foreign literary works, both secular and religious, and having them translated into Greek. Persons from all over the Near East with a good knowledge of Greek and an excellent command of their own languages were set to work collecting and copying out catalogues of the books and tablets in public and palace libraries and other libraries attached to religious institutions from Persepolis to Egypt, from the depths of India to Latium in Italy. And the departments mentioned above were assisted by workers with general and specialized skills: manufacturers and repairers of papyrus rolls, label-writers and so on, not to mention librarians to look after the bookcases, which were spread over several buildings and occupied an area of at least 5,000 square metres. Which brings us to the subject of the number of books in the Library.

The growth of the Library. The only information we have about the size of the Library comes from three main sources, which were followed (with some variations) by later historians. The earliest is the 'Letter of Aristeas', the second is Aulus Gellius in *Noctes Atticae*, and the third is the source – now lost – that Tzetzes drew on for his *Prolegomena to Aristophanes*. According to Aristeas, the Library already had 200,000 rolls in the time of Demetrius of Phalerum, in other words before the death of Ptolemy I in 283 B.C.[92] Gellius, writing in the second century A.D. about the war between Julius Caesar and Achillas for the possession of Alexandria, states that more than 700,000 books were burnt through the carelessness of the Roman soldiers.[93] Tzetzes, writing in the twelfth century, says that the palace library contained 490,000 rolls, of which 400,000 were 'composite' and 90,000 'unmixed'.[94] Quite possibly, considering that these figures appear to be close to the truth, they may be derived from reliable sources now unknown. What is certain is that the Library did have a stock of several hundred thousand rolls, and when all the reliable contemporary evidence is evaluated it is reasonable to suggest that the highest figure of all – 700,000 rolls – does not sound excessive and may even be an underestimate.

The number of books in the Library

The classification system in use in the Library. From what we know of the Ptolemies' intention of collecting all books in all languages, we can formulate a working hypothesis to reconstruct the classification system in use in the Library, with the twofold object of establishing how close to the truth the received statistics on the size of the Library really are and, if possible, working out the planning and layout of the rooms.

First of all, the stock of books was divided into three main categories:

94. Imaginary reconstruction of the Universal Library at Alexandria. From H. Goll, Die Weisen und Gelehrten des Alterthums, *II, Leipzig 1876.*

ALEX

DRIA

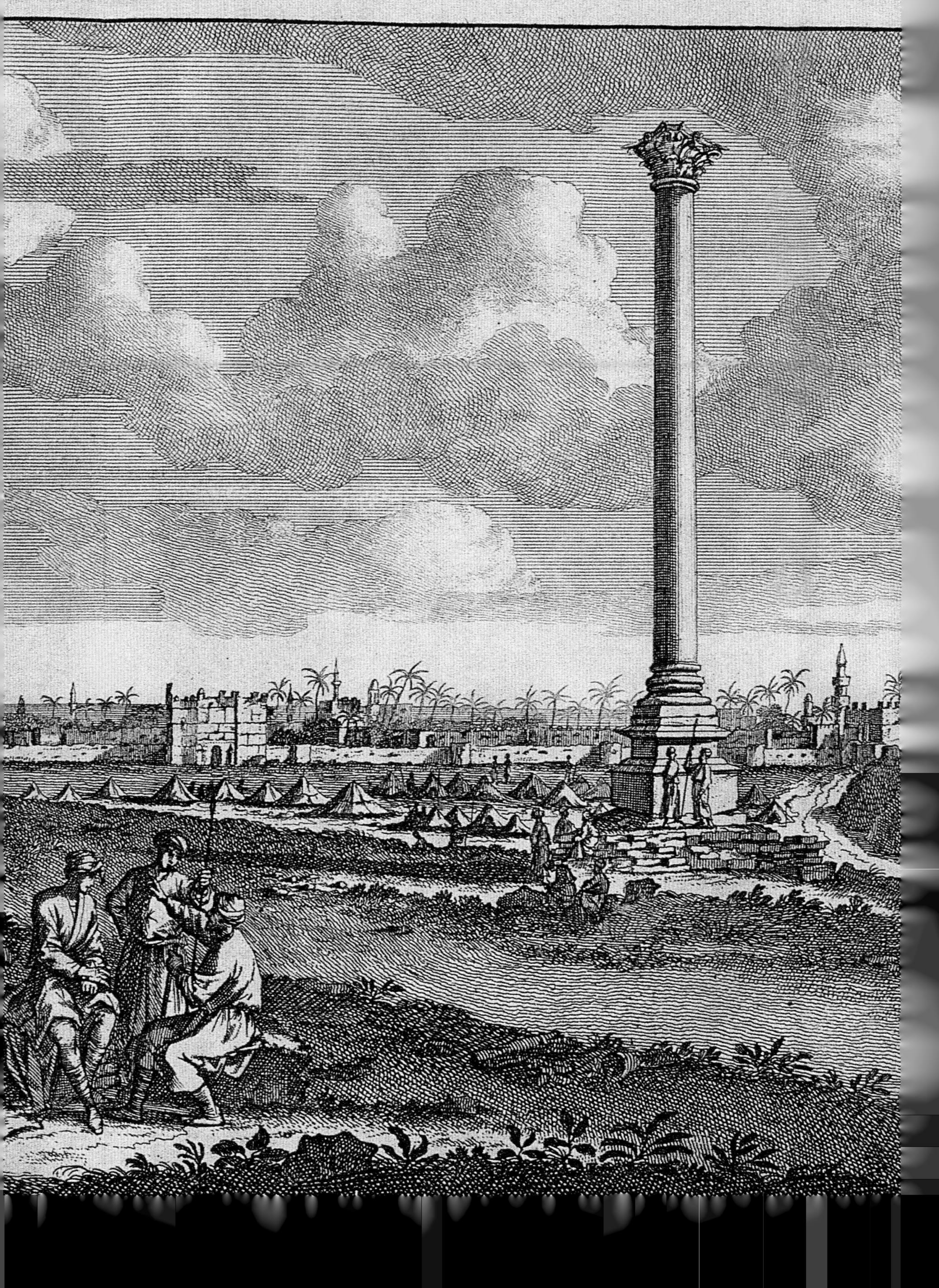

(a) History books, edited literary works and new works of Ptolemaic literature, which were classified in bibliographical order in the *Pinakes*;

(b) All kinds of papyrus rolls that were used for purposes of comparison, excerpts and sundry other writings such as letters, almanacs, descriptions, biographical notes, maps and so on;

(c) Foreign works, comprising original writings in foreign languages and those of them that had been selected for translation into Greek: this category might be described as the other half of a bilingual library.

The classification system in use in the Library.

(a) It would seem that one of the primary concerns of the Directors of the Library, from the very outset, was to gather copies of every written work in every branch of Greek literature and to build up a representative collection – a 'Greek library' – covering everything from Homer and other epics to the literature of their own time. Most of the epic poems and plays are known to have been corrupted by careless copying well before 330 B.C., with the result that reliable new copies were urgently needed – so much so that Aristotle persuaded Lycurgus to issue a decree ordering revised editions of the tragedies to be made and the new editions to be deposited in the Athenian state archives as 'official copies'.[95] In the Alexandrian Library, from the time of Zenodotus, its first Director, Homer and other epic poetry were treated with even greater respect and urgency than drama. To facilitate the necessary textual research, copies of Homer were sought from all over the Greek world and were known by the name of the city they came from: the copy from Massalia (Marseille), from Sinope, from Argos, from Chios.[96] Another method of classification, 'by person', may have signified that the manuscript had belonged to the person named or been emended by him: thus there were copies labelled 'of Zenodotus' (*Ζηνοδότου* or *Ζηνοδότειος*) or 'from the ships, emended by Mnemon of Side' (*τῶν ἐκ πλοίων κατὰ διορθωτὴν Μνήμονα Σιδήτην*).[97] To help them in their work, the Directors and their assistants wrote glossaries, explanatory notes, comments, registers and lists of useful facts of all kinds.

Textual emendation was not the only reason for making new copies. The innovations introduced by Aristophanes of Byzantium in the way of writing Greek, with spaces between words and with accents, diacritics and punctuation marks, made it necessary for the entire corpus of Greek literature to be written out afresh, in copies that were easier to read as well as being more reliable.[98]

☞ *95.The Ptolemaic acropolis of Alexandria. From C. Le Brun,* Voyage au Levant, *Paris 1714, 96.*

(b) The second category consisted of a mass of disparate material, often unsorted and existing in multiple copies, from every corner of the greater Greek world, to be used as the basis for textual studies. Depending on their quality, these documents were either sent on as authentic manuscripts to be included among the official books in the main collection of the 'Greek library', or else filed somehow. At first, this category also included all the various books bought at book sales, those donated to the Library, those that had been confiscated or borrowed from provincial libraries and other big public libraries, and the books from the ships.

The Alexandrian scholars tried to bring together under broad subject headings every branch of knowledge and everything that might provide material for their research, such as letters and writings in epistolary form, wills, cultural traditions, biographical notes on statesmen and intellectuals, descriptive writing, public records, diaries and logbooks, travel books, maps, plans and diagrams, as well as descriptions of the traditions and customs of the inhabitants of Greek cities everywhere.

(c) Although there is no firm evidence from the time of Ptolemy Soter that the Universal Library made systematic and thorough efforts to collect literary and 'scientific' works of the Middle Eastern peoples and translate them into Greek, there are indications which suggest that such a project was carried out, if only selectively, until about the end of the second century B.C. The testimony of Mar Abas Katina concerning Alexander's keenness to find out about the history of the Chaldaeans, taken together with the fact that the works of Zoroaster were translated from Persian into Greek, seem to imply that Alexander's successors were no more willing to ignore their subject peoples' political and cultural heritage than he had been.[99] Further evidence of their interest is to be seen in the two books written for Greek readers in the third century B.C. by Manetho and Berossus, perhaps commissioned by Ptolemy II and Antiochus I, and in the translation of the Old Testament by the LXX, and also in the fact that Hermippus is said to have worked on Zoroastrian writings.

A Greek book on the cultural history of the Egyptians

Manetho. Manetho, who is of particular interest in the present context, was a priest from Sebennytus in Egypt in the third century B.C. In his capacity as a high priest at Heliopolis he was instrumental in propagating the cult of Serapis. He also wrote an extremely enlightening work in Greek: a history of Egypt in three books entitled *Aegyptiaca*, starting in the age of myth and legend and going down to the Thirtieth Dynasty (343 B.C.).[100] Manetho drew his material from books that he found in Egyptian temples, including chronological records of important events and lists of the Pharaohs with the dates of their reign, and from other books intended more for the popular reader. It is worth remembering that Greek interest in the knowledge accumulated by Egyptian priests dates from at least as far back as the time of Pythagoras, Solon, Herodotus and Plato, and quite possibly the scholars of the Museum made a serious attempt to evaluate the written tradition of the Middle East in the fields of mathematics and astronomy.

A Chaldaean in the service of Antiochus I Soter

Berossus. A priest of Baal from Babylon, also active in the third century, was Berossus, who wrote a historical work entitled *Babyloniaca* or *Chaldaica* and dedicated it to Antiochus I Soter.[101] In it he describes the creation of the world and the great flood and writes about the ancient kings and dynasties before Alexander. According to his own calculations, his book covers a period of 468,215 years. It was based on archival tablets from Babylonian and other libraries in Mesopotamia.

Pliny the Elder informs us that Hermippus, a philosopher and grammarian who studied under Callimachus, added *indices* (summaries) to the rolls of Zoroaster's Persian verses,[102] probably inspired by his teacher's *Pinakes* and perhaps hoping to outdo his achievement, since the writings attributed to Zoroaster amounted to a total of two million lines. If we are to believe a statement by Georgios Synkellos whose accuracy is disputed, Eratosthenes translated chronological tables from the Egyptian archives and compiled a list of the kings of Egypt.[103] And Tzetzes informs us that the Library contained all the major works of Latin literature from as early as the reign of Philadelphus.[104]

How much ancient Greek literature has survived? The statistical figures mentioned earlier are those handed down by tradition, but we have to ask ourselves how much they actually mean. If we work on the hypothesis that the Ptolemies continued enlarging the Library systematically and with undiminished zeal down to the time of Cleopatra VII, with the object of collecting the whole of Greek literature in reliable editions, the question that arises next is whether we know enough to answer the first question. On the basis of direct and indirect evidence, the number of writers in the ancient Greek world – from the mythical Orpheus to Ariston and his contemporaries, including anonymous poets whose existence is known from quoted excerpts from their epics, such as the authors of *The Fall of Oechalia*, the *Thebaid*, the *Telegony* and the *Titanomachy* – is estimated at a thousand, with a margin of error of only about one per cent. Their works, whether extant in whole or in part or known only from allusions by other writers, would have filled approximately fifty thousand papyrus rolls. Wilamowitz believed that only a fifth of 'Classical' Greek literature had survived to modern times: if so, the Directors of the Library would have expected 'the whole of Greek literature' to amount to some 250,000 rolls. To these we must add the multiple copies they possessed of some works such as Homer's epics, Pindar's epinician odes and the plays of the three great tragedians, among many others, which makes it obvious that the true total must have been far higher and would have kept on rising, so that any estimate can only be conjectural.

Evidence of lost works

The fact is that our knowledge of the books written in the Classical and Hellenistic periods is extremely limited. A few examples will suffice to show just how little we actually know, even about great poets and philosophers and their contemporaries.

Astydamas, a tragedian of the fourth century B.C., is said to have written 240 plays, of which we know the titles of eight, plus four others doubtfully attributed to him. His contemporary Alexis, a dramatist of the Middle Comedy, wrote 245 plays, according to *Souda*: only fragments of a few of these have come down to us, and the titles of 130 are known. The number of commentaries and other books written by Aristarchus, the Director of the Library, is said to have totalled eight hundred, but so far the surviving fragments have not been gathered together in a corpus. Aristoxenus, a philosopher and musicologist of the fourth century B.C., is said to have been the author of 453 written works and compositions: of these, the only one to have survived complete is his *Elements of Harmonics* in three books. Didymus of Alexandria was known to the scholars of the Museum as *Chalkenteros* ('Brazen-guts'), on account of his indefatigable industry, or *Bibliolathas* ('Forgetter of books') because he had written so many that he could not remember them all: his total output was said to have been between 3,800 and 4,000 rolls! Of the ninety-two plays by Euripides, the Alexandrian scholars knew only seventy-five, and of those only eighteen (seventeen tragedies and a satyric drama) have survived. The 221 works by Aristotle's pupil Theophrastus added up to a total of 232,808 lines and filled 466 papyrus rolls, according to the catalogue given by Diogenes Laertius. The younger Carcinus, a tragedian of the fourth century B.C., who spent many years at the court of Dionysius II of Syracuse, wrote 160 plays and won eleven victories: that is exactly the number of titles of his works that are known today. Clitomachus, a philosopher of the second century B.C. who studied under Carneades and took notes of his teacher's lectures, is credited with about four hundred written works of his own. Menander wrote about 109 plays and, although the titles of ninety-six of them are known, only two have come down to us in good condition. Another comic playwright of the fourth and third centuries B.C., Philemon the elder, who was born at Syracuse but lived and worked in Athens, is said to have written ninety-seven plays. Finally, incredible though it may sound, Choerilus, a tragedian of the sixth century B.C., had 160 plays to his name.

One work that shows up the paucity of our knowledge of the Middle and New Comedy is the *Deipnosophistae* of Athenaeus, completed in A.D. 238 in thirty books, of which we have a tenth-century abridgement in fifteen books. In it Athenaeus mentions the names of about eight hundred authors and more than 1,200 titles of works now lost – and he is said to have got his raw material from Alexandria.

Statistics on the size of major libraries

At this point something should be said about the comparative figures available relating to the size of great monumental libraries from the first century B.C. onwards, and for major private libraries. According to Strabo, in about 30 B.C. a Greek slave in Rome, Tyrannio, had a private library of 30,000 rolls.[105] The collection of a virtually unknown Roman named Serenus Sammonicus, who bequeathed his father's library to Emperor Gordian II, contained not less than 62,000 rolls.[106] According to *Souda*, Marcus Mettius Epaphroditus also had a collection of 30,000 books, the same size as Tyrannio's. Another extremely valuable library was that of Larensius (P. Livius Larensis), which, according to Athenaeus (I.3), was renowned for the number and quality of its books. Lastly, Plutarch, in his *Life of Antony*, says that Antony gave Cleopatra 200,000 volumes from the Attalids' royal library at Pergamum.

The Ptolemies scour the world for books. The bibliomania of the Ptolemies, especially Soter, Philadelphus and Euergetes I, was without precedent in the history of books. And from the early second century B.C., when Eumenes II of Pergamum set out to create a library that would rival that of the Ptolemies, the search for rare and hitherto unknown books developed into an extravagant treasure-hunt which encouraged forgeries and pseudepigraphy.

Galen, born in A.D. 130 at Pergamum, the home of the library that was Alexandria's great rival, tells a number of stories that were still current in his time. The Ptolemies, he says, were so determined not only to collect as many thousands of manuscripts as possible but also to have nothing but first-class copies (he is probably referring to Euergetes I in particular) that on one occasion they borrowed from Athens the official copies of the three great tragedians' works, putting down the exorbitant sum of fifteen talents as a deposit to guarantee their safe return; but instead they chose to lose their deposit by keeping those historic manuscripts, commissioned by Lycurgus (*ca.* 330 B.C.) in accordance with Aristotle's advice, and sending back the copies they had made.[107] From then on a market came into being for books for which bibliophiles were willing to pay a premium, not only on account of their contents and their textual authenticity but also because of their previous ownership. Galen tells us of forgers who made big profits by selling all kinds of spurious manuscripts, some containing what were supposedly adaptations or expanded versions of older books, others that were forgeries from start to finish.[108] Great expertise, a sharp mind and a good deal of time were often needed to unmask these forgeries because the authentic and spurious passages were woven together with great ingenuity, as attested by Olympiodorus,[109] John Philoponus[110] and the Neoplatonist Elias of Alexandria:[111] the later scholiasts on Aristotle are cases in point.

Forgeries, pseudepigraphy and imaginary literature

Olympiodorus tells us how books were forged in the Ptolemaic period: 'In the past spurious books came into existence in three ways: either through the vanity of kings, or through the partiality of pupils [towards their teachers], or through homonymy. But let us see how the vanity of kings came to be a cause of the existence of spurious books. It should be explained that in the old days kings loved the written word and so, out of vanity, they were eager to obtain books by ancient writers. For example, Iobates, King of Libya, was a great admirer of Pythagoras, the Ptolemy called Philadelphus admired Aristotle, and Pisistratus, the ruler of Athens, admired Homer; and so they offered money to obtain their works. Consequently there were many avaricious people who either wrote books themselves or acquired any books that happened to come their way, passing them off as the work of earlier writers, and offered them to the rulers in order to claim the promised bounty. And that was how it happened, as already mentioned, that spurious books sometimes came into existence as a result of the vanity of kings.'

An extreme example of the completely spurious work produced during this period is connected with a certain Cratippus, according to Marcellinus (whose source was Didymus).[112] This Cratippus, a namesake of the Athenian historian, wrote a 'literary-historical' composition in which he claimed to be a contemporary of Thucydides and to have compiled a chronicle of events that the latter had not mentioned in his *History*. He even wrote about Thucydides's tomb, a subject that was then topical thanks to the archaeological descriptions of Athens written by Polemon of Ilium. Then, to puzzle the experts checking the authenticity of his narrative, he added the name of Zopyrus, a younger writer, as the co-author. Didymus, who had studied Thucydides, dismissed Cratippus and Zopyrus as 'foolish windbags'.[113] Nevertheless, Dionysius of Halicarnassus and (later) Plutarch both accepted Cratippus as a contemporary of Thucydides and the author of the *Hellenica*(?).

96.Plutarch. Engraving, 18th c.

From the first crisis in literary studies to the time of Cleopatra. The onset of the Alexandrian Library's real troubles is probably to be dated to the year 144 B.C., when Ptolemy VIII murdered his nephew Ptolemy VII. The Museum and the Library continued to function, but the departure of the literary scholars for Rhodes, Athens or Pergamum deprived the Museum of its driving force. The later Ptolemies' diminished interest in books – which was not total philistinism, for Plutarch tells us that Cleopatra herself had intellectual accomplishments unusual in a queen – was not the only reason for the downturn in the fortunes of the Library: more important than this were the drastic political changes that had been taking place in the Mediterranean region. Since 168 B.C. Rome had been steadily extending her ascendancy over Egypt, in 146 Carthage had been destroyed, and in the same year Greece had become a Roman province. And although this first crisis in the history of literary studies did not raise an insurmountable barrier to the new academic discipline, it

97. 'Cleopatra's Needle' standing amid the ruins of the Library and Museum.

did shift its focal point from Alexandria to other Greek cities and eventually to Rome, which became the new centre of the book trade in the Mediterranean from the end of the first century B.C.

Political developments taking place in the middle of the first century B.C. marked the beginning of the end of the Ptolemaic period, at least as far as the Universal Library was concerned. In 48 B.C. Julius Caesar arrived in Alexandria at the invitation of the young King Ptolemy XIII, brother of Cleopatra VII. His involvement in the dispute between Ptolemy and Cleopatra, the two children of Ptolemy XI Auletes (80-51 B.C.) who had succeeded their father as joint rulers, created such a furore in Ptolemy's entourage that the young king's all-powerful general Achillas and the eunuch Pothinus hatched a conspiracy against Caesar. Their plot was nipped in the bud and Pothinus was imprisoned and executed. However, Achillas managed to escape, raised a formidable army (including a number of Roman deserters) and besieged Caesar by land and sea. Caesar put up a stout resistance and went on to the counterattack: from the top of the sea walls overlooking the harbour he set fire to sixty of Ptolemy's ships anchored there. The conflagration spread rapidly to the dockyard installations and the warehouses and other buildings on the waterfront.[114]

Was Caesar responsible for the burning of the Library? If it ever proves possible for archaeologists to excavate the palace grounds and the foundations of the various buildings there, including the Library, we may learn more about the truth of the story that the fire spread to the palace area, and whether or not the Museum was burnt down. But until that happens we have to make do with conjectures, forming our own judgment on the evidence given by historians and geographers of Caesar's time.

Caesar's Alexandrian War

The only writer who actually witnessed the events of the Alexandrian War was Julius Caesar himself, who recorded them in his memoirs (which, however, were probably written by his staff officer Aulus Hirtius).[115] Hirtius wrote an account of the war (*Bellum Alexandrinum*) as a continuation of Caesar's unfinished *Commentarii de bello civili*, which cover the years 49-48 B.C. only. Caesar's memoirs provided a valuable source of material, until at least the time of Suetonius in the second century A.D., for historians such as Livy, Nicolaus of Damascus, Tacitus, Dio Cassius and Orosius. Livy, who was alive at the time of the Alexandrian War and described it in his monumental history *Ab urbe condita*, is of no help as the relevant part of his 142-volume work is lost.

Seneca and Lucan, writing in the first and second centuries A.D., drew their material from Livy but gave a different slant to the events they describe, perhaps because of their ideological objection to the Empire. Seneca was the first to assert that forty thousand books were burnt in the course of the hostilities,[116] while Plutarch, in his *Life of Caesar* written towards the end of the first century A.D., has this to say: 'When the enemy tried to cut off his fleet, [Caesar] was forced to avert the danger by using fire, and this spread from the dockyards and destroyed the Great Library.'[117] Aulus Gellius, an antiquarian of the second century A.D., mentions in *Noctes Atticae* that more than 700,000 books were burnt when the city was sacked.[118] And Dio Cassius, writing in the early third century, states in his account of those events: 'Many places were set on fire, with the result that the docks and the storehouses of grain, among other buildings, were burned, and also the library, whose volumes, it is said, were of the greatest number and excellence.'[119] Ammianus Marcellinus (fourth century A.D.) repeats Gellius's assertion that a priceless library of 700,000 books was burnt.[120] And Orosius in the fifth century, probably following Seneca, states that 400,000 papyrus books were destroyed during the siege.[121]

98. Alexander the Great and Julius Caesar: 'Allegory of Victory'. Engraving by an unknown artist. Rome, Istituto Nazionale per la Grafica, Fe 91362.

Strabo, who spent four years in Alexandria not much more than twenty years after the siege (24-20 B.C.), gives a perfunctory description of the city's main sights, including the harbour, the theatre, temples, the Sema (Alexander's tomb) and the Museum, yet he does not even mention the Library, nor does he say anything about devastation caused by a great fire in the city.

What are we to make of these hopelessly brief descriptions of the Univer-

sal Library and the contradictory reports of what happened to it during Caesar's stay in Alexandria? Although no certainty is possible, we can at least make some conjectures by examining all the factual and circumstantial evidence that might shed some light on the truth. The first point to note is that, strange though it may seem, not one description of the Museum or the Library written in the Ptolemaic period has come down to us – if indeed any such description was ever written. The earliest surviving reference dates from Strabo's stay in Alexandria (24-20 B.C.). Strabo writes about the Museum as if he has never been there himself. All he says about its architectural design is that there is a main building with stoas and an 'exedra' (here a sort of theatre or lecture hall). He says nothing about the Library – neither the Royal Library nor the subsidiary library in the Serapeum, even though the latter is known to have existed until A.D. 391. What can be the reason for Strabo's silence, even if the Universal Library had been irreparably damaged? After all, he was a great book-lover, so much so that he devoted space in his *Geography* to an account of the fate of Aristotle's original manuscripts.

The conflicting evidence concerning the destruction of books in the Great Library – with the number of books burnt ranging from 40,000 in the earliest sources to 400,000 or even 700,000 later – is probably due to a misreading of Livy, who was probably the first to quantify the loss.

The story of the burning of the Library

Strabo, as we have seen, makes no mention of damage done in the palace grounds or elsewhere by a conflagration during the Alexandrian War: not until about a hundred years later do we first hear of the story of the burning of the city and the destruction of the Library's priceless books. Dio Cassius, who specifies the buildings that were burnt down, including one that was used for storing books, was presumably referring to buildings in the immediate vicinity of the docks. Given that Livy describes the book warehouse as *pulcherrimum monumentum* and that Orosius says that that building was in the port area, the inference is that the buildings mentioned by Dio Cassius were on the waterfront of the royal harbour.

When Dio Cassius says that 'books of excellent quality' were burnt, he is presumably referring to the materials of which they were made, rather than to their content. It is not unlikely that there was an annexe of the Royal Library, a scriptorium where the 'books from the ships' were copied, down by the

99. Imaginary reconstruction of the city in flames during Caesar's Alexandrian War in 48 B.C. From H. Goll, Die Weisen und Gelehrten des Alterthums.

docks, and that the same building was subsequently used for other, similar purposes, perhaps as a warehouse for papyrus rolls destined for export.[122] Then we have to consider the meaning of the word *apothekai* (translated above as warehouses) in the context of books and the places where books were sorted: were these buildings part of the main library complex or were they warehouses in the port? The answer, it seems to me, is to be sought in the architecture of that building or those buildings.[123] The numerical statistics sound like figures handed down by legend or popular tradition: the 40,000 papyri mentioned by Seneca are subsequently multiplied tenfold to 400,000 and then nearly doubled again to the 700,000 of Gellius. Later writers perpetuated different versions of the story taken from different sources: Orosius follows Seneca's erroneous account, Isidore of Seville that of Gellius.

Mention should be made here of something that is not a conjecture but a fact which shows how Caesar's ideas were moulded by the role of the Universal Library in the Greek world. On his return to Rome, Caesar appointed Varro to superintend the planning and implementation of a project to create the first public library in Rome.[124] Varro himself did not manage to complete his cherished project, but C. Asinius Pollio built a bilingual library – one with separate Greek and Latin sections in a building with two wings – on which construction work started in 39 B.C.[125] It is not known whether Caesar had conceived the idea in Alexandria, nor whether he himself had had time to begin making preparations for the despatch of Greek books and unused papyrus rolls for the projected public library in Rome.

Egypt as the Roman Emperors' 'private property'

Egypt as a Roman province. From the time of Caesar's death and the arrival of Mark Antony on the political scene down to Cleopatra's death in 30 B.C., the only extant reference to the Alexandrian Library is to be found in Plutarch's *Life of Antony*. According to a source quoted by Plutarch with reservations as to its reliability, Antony gave Cleopatra 200,000 volumes from the Pergamum Library.[126]

On the death of the last queen of the Ptolemaic dynasty, Egypt came under the sway of Rome and the character of the Library altered radically. Although Augustus wrote in the famous record of his career known as the *Res gestae* that he had 'added Egypt to the dominions of the Roman people', Egypt was never a Roman province in the same sense as all the other provinces but was administered more or less as the Emperor's private property. Broadly speaking, Roman Egypt was governed by a well-organized, centralized administration backed by an army strong enough to deal with marauding raids by the nomadic desert tribes and maintain law and order in the cities within the framework of a society in which the Greeks, in particular, enjoyed special privileges at the expense of the indigenous Egyptians and their culture.[127] About the organization of the archival libraries (i.e. public record offices) a good deal is known, as it is also about the innovations introduced by the Romans into the Ptolemies' very highly-developed bureaucratic machine;[128] however, it is possible to infer from indirect evidence that the Library and the Museum were turned into a sort of 'imperial foundation' (since even the priest who was Master of the Museum was appointed by the Emperor himself) and that the Museum kept its name and functioned as an educational establishment.[129]

The library in the Sebasteum

On the demise of the Republic and the inauguration of the Empire, the Romans made a major change in the organization of the library by creating separate sections for Greek and Latin books: in other words they introduced the concept of the bilingual library (*diplobibliotheke*), which was to remain the norm until the Early Byzantine period. The idea probably originated with Julius Caesar or Varro but was not put into practice until after Caesar's death, by Pollio in 39 B.C.[130] The purpose of this innovation was to focus attention on the Romans' cultural background and history and to persuade the Greeks, a people noted for their intellectual curiosity, to learn the 'barbaric' Latin language and discover that Latin literature deserved respect. To remind the people of Egypt and visitors to Alexandria that the land of the Pharaohs and Ptolemies was now a Roman province, in 12 B.C. Augustus built a temple dedicated to Julius the God, with a bilingual library next to it.[131] The temple came to be known as the Sebasteum (from *Sebastos*, the Greek rendering of *Augustus*, the title given to the Roman emperors). It stood in a magnificent precinct on a hill, surrounded by peristyle courtyards and adorned with statuary and other works of art, and was perhaps intended to replace the public library of the Serapeum and the Museum library in accordance with the new cultural policy. The ultimate objective of this move was to erase from public memory the symbolism of the Alexandrian Library as the intellectual centre of Mediterranean civilization. It is likely that thousands of papyrus rolls were moved to the new library, and in the course of time, as the enforcement of the library rules became more lax, many rare copies may have found their way into the hands of booksellers.

Nevertheless, even in the first century A.D. it would seem that Alexandria still possessed the finest collection of Greek literature – and perhaps of Latin literature too, because when the Palatine Library in Rome was burnt down by Nero or Titus a team of experts was sent to Alexandria by Domitian to make new copies of the books that had been destroyed. Suetonius, the source of this piece of information, also mentions that Emperor Claudius enlarged the Museum, but without making it clear whether Claudius was following the example of his predecessors, who had made regular improvements to the Museum's facilities.[132]

The linguistic tradition. The annexation of Egypt by the Romans did not alter the linguistic tradition forced upon the country by the Ptolemies, a tradition that would have affected the production and distribution of Greek books. Numerically, the Roman administrators in Egypt were a negligible minority, and so Greek was retained as the official language of the government. The use of Latin was compulsory for the Roman army and for all official documents (such as birth certificates and wills) relating to Roman citizens. And in spite of Caracalla's edict of A.D. 212 and Diocletian's attempts to bring Egypt into line with the administrative methods employed in other Roman provinces, Latin never managed to conquer more than a few strongholds of the Greek language: the rest held out until fully a century after the Arab conquest of 642.[133]

Caracalla avenges the 'assassination' of Alexander the Great

Caracalla is the central figure in a story related by Dio Cassius which illustrates the great influence exerted even in Roman imperial circles by the Museum and the Library, whose roots went back to Aristotle and the Lyceum by way of no less a person than Alexander the Great. According to the Greek historian, Caracalla was a passionate admirer of Alexander the Great: he used weapons and drinking goblets that were said to have belonged to him, erected statues of him in army camps and in Rome itself and formed a phalanx composed entirely of Macedonian soldiers. But even this was not enough to satisfy his obsession with Alexander, so he conceived the idea of writing to inform the Senate that Alexander had been reincarnated in the person of the Augustus (i.e. Caracalla himself) in order to live out the rest of his time on earth, which had been so cruelly cut short. Being particularly obsessed by the circumstances of his hero's death, for which he actually convinced himself that Aristotle had been ultimately responsible, Caracalla determined to take revenge and threatened the Aristotelians of the Alexandrian school that he would burn all their books[134] and deprive the Museum scholars of their entitlement to free board and other privileges.

Incidental information about scholars of the Museum. There are innumerable papyri written during the Roman period in the form of letters, accounts and reports of various kinds which contain fascinating snippets of information about some of the scholars of the Museum and their bookish interests. In A.D. 155, for example, we learn that there was a piece of land at Euhemeria in the Faiyûm belonging to Julius Asclepiades, 'philosopher' (i.e. a member of the philosophy department of the Museum), which implies that the Museum was still functioning as an educational institution;[135] in the year 198 or 227 another scholar of the Museum, Valerius Titanianus, owned a property at Philadelphia; and an honorific inscription in the city of Antinoe, probably of the third century, promulgates a decree of the local council in honour of the Platonic philosopher Flavius Marcius Se[verianus?] Dionysodorus, one of the scholars maintained tax-free at the Museum.[136] From this it would appear that in the Roman period the Museum was still basically unchanged since the time of Ptolemy I and that its scholars were still being supported by the old system of 'royal' welfare. Even more interesting is a papyrus of A.D. 173 with a letter mentioning that a certain Valerius Diodorus, 'a former writer of commentaries and member of the Museum', had discussed books and the best way of obtaining them with two men named Polion and Harpocration.[137] Diodorus, Polion and Harpocration were Alexandrian literary scholars who were particularly interested in the Attic orators, Harpocration being best known as the compiler of the *Lexicon of the Ten Orators*.[138]

The Museum in the Roman period

Another invaluable item of information to be gleaned from letters written in Alexandria in the second century A.D. concerns the cost of copying manuscripts. A statement of account, probably from Oxyrrhynchus, lists the fees paid to a scribe for copying books, including a sum of twelve drachmae for copying Aristophanes's *Plutus*, an unspecified work and *Thyestes* by Sophocles. Other entries refer to two different rates of pay: one of 28 drachmae per 10,000 lines and a cheaper rate of 20 drachmae and 4 obols for the same number of lines.[139] These statistics are extremely interesting for the light they throw on the differences between Rome and Alexandria in the business of book production and marketing. In Rome the book trade relied on the services of a pool of highly-trained slaves and substantial export sales, whereas in Alexandria publishing was evidently not organized on a business footing, and books – or at least those that were not especially popular with the general reader – were to be found only in the homes of a few literary men.[140]

Relations between publishers and scribes

The strife caused by Christianity. The Christians of Egypt were always given to heretical tendencies with a pronounced leaning towards Gnosticism, and in the first century A.D., through the influence of Philo Judaeus, they developed a Greek-language Judaic philosophy whereby Egypt came to be a centre for reconciliation between paganism and the new faith of Christianity. A typical instance of this coexistence is to be seen in the fact that the Museum continued to function side by side with the great Christian Catechetic School founded by Pantaenus, with which the illustrious names of Clement of Alexandria and Origen were closely associated. Even so, the transition from paganism to Christianity was a complex process that lasted for more than four hundred years in the Eastern Mediterranean. In this often turbulent period the book-loving public came under great pressure, especially now that the international book trade had been reorganized on the Roman model, with catastrophic consequences thereafter for Greek books and the Classical tradition generally.

From Zenobia to Diocletian. The first armed conflict in Alexandria after Caesar's Alexandrian War in 47 B.C. was due to the protracted warfare waged by Queen Zenobia of Palmyra and her allies against Emperor Aurelian (*c.* A.D. 272-275). Zenobia captured Alexandria and, having done so, she naturally took an interest in the Museum and the rich store of books in the city's libraries, as she was noted for her encyclopaedic learning: she was equally at home in Greek, Latin, Syriac and Egyptian and had written a brief history of the peoples of the East. When Aurelian forced Palmyra into submission in 272, he recaptured Alexandria. In the course of the fighting the Bruchium quarter of the city, which included the palace and the Museum, was badly damaged: according to Ammianus Marcellinus (XXII.16.15), it was razed to the ground.[141]

Zenobia captures Alexandria

The accession of Diocles (who preferred to be known as Diocletian) to the Roman imperial throne marks the beginning of what one might call a Pre-Byzantine period. The administrative reforms introduced by the new Emperor (284-305) ushered in a formative period of history, and the redistribution of power between the Roman provinces eventually worked to the advantage of the peoples of the East. But Diocletian's reign was marred by persecution of the Christians and mutual suspicion between Christians and pagans. The

100. Reconstruction of the central area of Alexandria in the Hellenistic period, viewed from the Canopic Way. Watercolour by J.-P. Golvin, from Alexandria Rediscovered, *London 1998.*

rapid spread of Christianity did not proceed as peacefully in all the Roman provinces as it did in Alexandria. During this peculiar period the signals reaching Nicomedia, Diocletian's capital, were confusing and contradictory: the suspicion shown by the Christians for the pagans; the picture of desolation presented by the Gardens of Epicurus, the Stoa of the Stoics and the other philosophical schools; and the fact that the Romans went so far as to condemn the works of no less a person than Cicero, which were submitted to the Senate for censorship.[142] North Africa was up in arms from the banks of the Nile to the Atlas Mountains, and L. Elpidius Achillaeus seized control of Alexandria. Diocletian chose to start his campaign against the rebels in Egypt and in 296 he laid siege to Alexandria, which fell to him after holding out for eight months. No historical records survive to tell us whether or not the fighting over the city resulted in further damage to the monuments and cultural treasures of the Ptolemies.

Diocletian's reforms

The Byzantine period. The whole of Egypt went to the Eastern Roman Empire without bloodshed, but the familiar atmosphere of classicism and scholarly learning no longer existed even in the Ptolemies' old capital. And although Patriarch Cyril of Alexandria failed to have the city's school of philosophy closed down, the lasting influence of monasticism, combined with the agitation of the indigenous population against economic oppression, created a climate that posed a permanent threat to Hellenism. For the fourth century we are again without sources, apart from the accounts of their visits to the Serapeum library given by Epiphanius and Aphthonius, and so one can only hypothesize about this period.

As a general rule, whenever any new royal library is founded it tends to supplant all its predecessors, assuming that it covers the same range of subjects. Unfortunately we have practically no information about the books that went into the new 'imperial' library founded by Constantius II in Constantinople in 357 mainly for the purpose of collecting works of classical literature. The only point of which we can be fairly certain is that not all the necessary books were to be found in Constantinople, because only a few years earlier Constantine the Great, needing fifty copies of the Scriptures, had had to order them from Eusebius's scriptorium in Caesarea.[143] It seems likely that valuable

The library of Emperor Constantius II

101. The Bible, a fourth-century manuscript written in majuscule ('Codex B'). Vatican Library (Vat. gr. 1209, F. 12492).

ΚΑΙΤΗΣΓΗΣΟΤΙΕΚΡΥ
ΨΑΣΤΑΥΤΑΑΠΟΣΟΦΩΝ
ΚΑΙΣΥΝΕΤΩΝΚΑΙΑΠΕ
ΚΑΛΥΨΑΣΑΥΤΑΝΗΠΙ
ΟΙΣΝΑΙΟΠΑΤΗΡΟΤΙΟΥ
ΤΩΣΕΥΔΟΚΙΑΕΓΕΝΕΤΟ
ΕΜΠΡΟΣΘΕΝΣΟΥ ΠΑΝ
ΤΑΜΟΙΠΑΡΕΔΟΘΗΥΠΟ
ΤΟΥΠΑΤΡΟΣΜΟΥΚΑΙ
ΟΥΔΕΙΣΕΠΙΓΙΝΩΣΚΕΙ
ΤΟΝΥΙΟΝΕΙΜΗΟΠΑΤΗΡ
ΟΥΔΕΤΟΝΠΑΤΕΡΑΤΙΣ
ΕΠΙΓΙΝΩΣΚΕΙΕΙΜΗΟ
ΥΙΟΣΚΑΙΩΕΑΝΒΟΥΛΗ
ΤΑΙΟΥΙΟΣΑΠΟΚΑΛΥΨΑΙ
ΟΕ ΔΕΥΤΕΠΡΟΣΜΕΠΑΝΤΕΣ
ΟΙΚΟΠΙΩΝΤΕΣΚΑΙΠΕ
ΦΟΡΤΙΣΜΕΝΟΙΚΑΓΩ
ΑΝΑΠΑΥΣΩΥΜΑΣΑΡΑ
ΤΕΤΟΝΖΥΓΟΝΜΟΥΕΦΥ
ΜΑΣΚΑΙΜΑΘΕΤΕΑΠΕ
ΜΟΥΟΤΙΠΡΑΥΣΕΙΜΙΚΑΙ
ΤΑΠΕΙΝΟΣΤΗΚΑΡΔΙΑ
ΚΑΙΕΥΡΗΣΕΤΑΙΑΝΑΠΑΥ
ΣΙΝΤΑΙΣΨΥΧΑΙΣΥΜΩΝ
ΟΓΑΡΖΥΓΟΣΜΟΥΧΡΗ
ΣΤΟΣΚΑΙΤΟΦΟΡΤΙΟΝ
ΜΟΥΕΛΑΦΡΟΝΕΣΤΙΝ
ΟϚ ΕΝΕΚΕΙΝΩΤΩΚΑΙΡΩ 12
ΕΠΟΡΕΥΘΗΟΙΣΤΟΙΣΣΑΒ
ΒΑΤΟΙΣΔΙΑΤΩΝΣΠΟΡΙ
ΜΩΝΟΙΔΕΜΑΘΗΤΑΙΑΥ
ΤΟΥΕΠΕΙΝΑΣΑΝΚΑΙΗΡ
ΞΑΝΤΟΤΙΛΛΕΙΝΣΤΑΧΥ
ΑΣΚΑΙΕΣΘΙΕΙΝΟΙΔΕΦΑ
ΡΙΣΑΙΟΙΙΔΟΝΤΕΣΕΙΠΑΝ
ΑΥΤΩΙΔΟΥΟΙΜΑΘΗΤΑΙ
ΣΟΥΠΟΙΟΥΣΙΝΟΟΥΚΕ
ΞΕΣΤΙΝΠΟΙΕΙΝΕΝΣΑΒ
ΒΑΤΩ ΟΔΕΕΙΠΕΝΑΥ
ΤΟΙΣΟΥΚΑΝΕΓΝΩΤΕ
ΤΙΕΠΟΙΗΣΕΝΔΑΥΕΙΔ

ΟΤΕΕΠΕΙΝΑΣΕΝ ΚΑΙΟΙΜΕ
ΤΑΥΤΟΥΠΩΣΕΙΣΗΛΘΕ
ΕΙΣΤΟΝΟΙΚΟΝΤΟΥΘΥ
ΚΑΙΤΟΥΣΑΡΤΟΥΣΤΗΣ
ΠΡΟΘΕΣΕΩΣΕΦΑΓΟΝ
ΟΟΥΚΕΞΟΝΗΝΑΥΤΩΦΑ
ΓΕΙΝΟΥΔΕΤΟΙΣΜΕΤΑΥ
ΤΟΥΕΙΜΗΤΟΙΣΙΕΡΕΥΣΙ
ΜΟΝΟΙΣ ΗΟΥΚΑΝΕΓΝΩ
ΤΕΕΝΤΩΝΟΜΩΟΤΙΤΟΙΣ
ΣΑΒΒΑΣΙΝΟΙΙΕΡΕΙΣΕΝ
ΤΩΙΕΡΩΤΟΣΑΒΒΑΤΟΝ
ΒΕΒΗΛΟΥΣΙΝ ΚΑΙΑΝΑΙΤΙ
ΟΙΕΙΣΙΝ ΛΕΓΩΔΕΥΜΙΝ
ΟΤΙΤΟΥΙΕΡΟΥΜΕΙΖΟΝ
ΕΣΤΙΝΩΔΕ ΕΙΔΕΕΓΝΩ
ΚΕΙΤΕΤΙΕΣΤΙΝΕΛΕΟΣ
ΘΕΛΩΚΑΙΟΥΘΥΣΙΑΝΟΥ
ΚΑΝΚΑΤΕΔΙΚΑΣΑΤΕΤΟΥΣ
ΑΝΑΙΤΙΟΥΣΚΥΡΙΟΣΓΑΡ
ΕΣΤΙΝ ΤΟΥΣΑΒΒΑΤΟΥ
ΟΥΙΟΣΤΟΥΑΝΘΡΩΠΟΥ
ΟΖ ΚΑΙΜΕΤΑΒΑΣΕΚΕΙΘΕΝ
ΗΛΘΕΝΕΙΣΤΗΝΣΥΝΑΓΩ
ΓΗΝΑΥΤΩΝΚΑΙΙΔΟΥΑΝ
ΘΡΩΠΟΣΧΕΙΡΑΕΧΩΝ
ΞΗΡΑΝ ΚΑΙΕΠΗΡΩΤΗΣΑΝ
ΑΥΤΟΝΛΕΓΟΝΤΕΣΕΙΕ
ΞΕΣΤΙΤΟΙΣΣΑΒΒΑΣΙΘΕ
ΡΑΠΕΥΕΙΝΙΝΑΚΑΤΗΓΟ
ΡΗΣΩΣΙΑΥΤΟΥ ΟΔΕΕΙ
ΠΕΝΑΥΤΟΙΣΤΙΣΕΣΤΑΙ
ΕΞΥΜΩΝΑΝΘΡΩΠΟΣ
ΟΣΕΞΕΙΠΡΟΒΑΤΟΝΕΝΚΑΙ
ΕΑΝΕΜΠΕΣΗΤΟΥΤΟΤΟΙΣ
ΣΑΒΒΑΣΙΕΙΣΒΟΘΥΝΟΝ
ΟΥΧΙΚΡΑΤΗΣΕΙΑΥΤΟΚΑΙ
ΕΓΕΡΕΙΠΟΣΩΟΥΝΔΙΑ
ΦΕΡΕΙΑΝΘΡΩΠΟΣΠΡΟ
ΒΑΤΟΥΩΣΤΕΕΞΕΣΤΙΝ
ΤΟΙΣΣΑΒΒΑΣΙΝΚΑΛΩΣ
ΠΟΙΕΙΝ ΤΟΤΕΛΕΓΕΙΤΩ

ΑΝΘΡΩΠΩΕΚΤΕΙΝΟΝ
ΣΟΥΤΗΝΧΕΙΡΑΚΑΙΕΞΕ
ΤΕΙΝΕΝ ΚΑΙΑΠΕΚΑΤΕΣΤΑ
ΘΗΥΓΙΗΣΩΣΗΑΛΛΗ
ΟΗ ΕΞΕΛΘΟΝΤΕΣΔΕΟΙΦΑ
ΡΕΙΣΑΙΟΙΣΥΜΒΟΥΛΙΟΝ
ΕΛΑΒΟΝΚΑΤΑΥΤΟΥΟ
ΠΩΣΑΥΤΟΝΑΠΟΛΕΣΩ
ΣΙΝ ΟΔΕΙΣΓΝΟΥΣΑΝΕ
ΧΩΡΗΣΕΝΕΚΕΙΘΕΝΚΑΙ
ΗΚΟΛΟΥΘΗΣΑΝΑΥΤΩ
ΠΟΛΛΟΙΚΑΙΕΘΕΡΑΠΕΥ
ΣΕΝΑΥΤΟΥΣΠΑΝΤΑΣ
ΚΑΙΕΠΕΤΙΜΗΣΕΝΑΥ
ΤΟΙΣΙΝΑΜΗΦΑΝΕΡΟΝ
ΑΥΤΟΝΠΟΙΗΣΩΣΙΝΙΝΑ
ΠΛΗΡΩΘΗΤΟΡΗΘΕΝΔΙΑ
ΗΣΑΙΟΥΤΟΥΠΡΟΦΗ
ΤΟΥΛΕΓΟΝΤΟΣ ΙΔΟΥΟ
ΠΑΙΣΜΟΥΟΝΗΡΕΤΙΣΑΟ
ΑΓΑΠΗΤΟΣΜΟΥΟΝΕΥΔΟ
ΚΗΣΕΝΗΨΥΧΗΜΟΥΘΗ
ΣΩΤΟΠΝΕΥΜΑΜΟΥΕΠΑΥ
ΤΟΝΚΑΙΚΡΙΣΙΝΤΟΙΣΕΘΝΕ
ΣΙΝΑΠΑΓΓΕΛΕΙΟΥΚΕΡΙ
ΣΕΙΟΥΔΕΚΡΑΥΓΑΣΕΙΟΥ
ΔΕΑΚΟΥΣΕΙΤΙΣΕΝΤΑΙΣ
ΠΛΑΤΕΙΑΙΣΤΗΝΦΩΝΗΝ
ΑΥΤΟΥΚΑΛΑΜΟΝΣΥΝ
ΤΕΤΡΙΜΜΕΝΟΝΟΥΚΑ
ΤΕΑΞΕΙΚΑΙΛΙΝΟΝΤΥΦΟ
ΜΕΝΟΝΟΥΣΒΕΣΕΙΕΩΣ
ΑΝΕΚΒΑΛΗΕΙΣΝΕΙΚΟΣ
ΤΗΝΚΡΙΣΙΝΚΑΙΤΩΟΝΟ
ΜΑΤΙΑΥΤΟΥΕΘΝΗΕΛ
ΟΘ ΠΙΟΥΣΙΝ ΤΟΤΕΠΡΟΣΗ
ΝΕΓΚΑΝΑΥΤΩΔΑΙΜΟ
ΝΙΖΟΜΕΝΟΝΤΥΦΛΟΝ
ΚΑΙΚΩΦΟΝΚΑΙΕΘΕΡΑ
ΠΕΥΣΕΝΑΥΤΟΝΩΣΤΕ
ΤΟΝΚΩΦΟΝΛΑΛΕΙΝΚΑΙ
ΒΛΕΠΕΙΝΚΑΙΕΞΙΣΤΑΝΤΟ

books were taken from what remained of the Ptolemies' Great Library in order to build up the new 'imperial' library in Constantinople.

The papyrus roll is superseded

From the roll to the codex. The Roman and Early Byzantine periods witnessed a major innovation in book production that was later to have a decisive impact on the interior architecture of libraries. This was the invention of the codex – a book in the form in which we know it today, consisting of quires of folded sheets – which eventually consigned the papyrus roll to oblivion. The changeover was a gradual process that took several centuries to complete, and during the second and third centuries the codex and the roll were both in common use.[144] It is worth spending a little time on this important development, because in my opinion it was one of the main factors affecting the fate of the innumerable papyrus rolls in the Library. Once the codex had finally come into its own, papyrus rolls were no longer used for copying literary works. Theological treatises, a new category of writing, were usually published in codex form from the outset. As more and more works of the ancient tradition were transferred to the newer and much more convenient format, even the rarest of the old rolls lost much of their value until at last they were of interest only as museum pieces. It may be no exaggeration to say that papyrus rolls containing classical writings eventually came to be worth no more than the material they were written on, or even less, because the papyrus needed to be processed before it could be reused. At the same time as the codex was superseding the roll, another new development in book production was taking place: this was the replacement of papyrus by parchment. The first signs of this change had been seen as early as the first century A.D., when education spread so rapidly in the Roman Empire that papyrus could no longer be produced in sufficient quantities to keep up with demand. At first parchment was used as a substitute for papyrus, but a great drought in the reign of Tiberius (A.D. 14-37) reversed their relative positions and paved the way for the general acceptance of parchment as a standard writing material.[145] Throughout this period the balance was steadily tilting from papyrus to parchment, as it was from the roll to the codex.[146]

These changes in book production followed very different patterns in Christian religious writing and in secular literature. When C.H. Roberts published his account of the development of the codex in 1955, he noted that not one of the surviving early texts of the Greek New Testament on papyrus was written on the recto of a roll. Of the 111 then known biblical manuscripts in Greek dating from before the end of the fourth century, 99 were codices; and those of them that were Christian in origin (in other words, those that did not contain the Old Testament only) and could be dated to the turn of the second to third centuries were all papyrus codices.[147] Roberts concludes: 'When the Christian bible ... first makes its appearance in history, the books of which it is composed are always written on papyrus and in codex form.' Although many more examples of early Christian literature have been found since then, Roberts's finding still holds good. In classical (i.e. pagan) literature the percentages are different, and only in the fourth century do we find a big swing in favour of the codex. This means that in Alexandria there was no systematic drive to copy the classics from papyrus to parchment before the fourth century, and therefore the Library's original stocks remained unchanged.[148]

The discovery of Aristotle's Constitution of the Athenians

It must also be remembered that Egypt had a monopoly of papyrus, though this does not mean that everybody in Egypt could afford to use it: for instance, there is a copy of Aristotle's *Constitution of the Athenians* written on the back of some private farm accounts.[149] There is also evidence of people going to the trouble of rubbing out an entire document so as to reuse the papyrus:[150] such a twice-used papyrus is called a palimpsest, which literally means 'rubbed clean again'. Impecunious priests, Roman soldiers, civil servants and (of course) schoolboys in Egypt used all kinds of available material to write on, such as potsherds and even linen mummy wrappings. These remarks about the change in the format of books and the availability of writing materials are relevant to our theme inasmuch as they may shed some light on the question whether the Great Library underwent a process of 'peaceful spoliation', with books being stolen simply for the value of the material of which they were made.[151] However, isolated incidents, the general climate of the age and the attitude to books can only be matters of conjecture.

The last piece of historical evidence prior to the Arabs' capture of Alexandria that may be relevant to the Ptolemies' original collection of books takes us to the year 415, when, as already mentioned, Bishop Theophilus stirred up the Christians to launch an unprecedented campaign against the pagans. The rampaging crowds made their way to the Serapeum and devastated it, perhaps destroying it completely: certainly they looted its remaining votive offerings and ornaments and perhaps even what was left of the subsidiary library. This frenzied outburst of hooliganism aimed at destroying all trace of the pagan tradition reached its climax in 415 with the lynching of Hypatia, a philosophy teacher prominent in Alexandrian life who was the daughter of the Neoplatonist mathematician Theon, the last known member of the Museum.[152]

The destruction of the Library: the Arab version. The alternative account of the complete destruction of the Library, or of a collection of books that had belonged to the initial nucleus of the Library, is connected with the fall of Alexandria to the Arabs in 642.

When Emir Amru ('Amr ibn al-'Aç) had captured Alexandria, he wrote a letter to Caliph Omar ('Umar), mentioned in the *Chronicle* of the Christian Arab historian Eutychios,[153] in which he reported: 'I have taken the great city of the West and I have no words to describe its wealth and beauty. I will merely say that it has 4,000 villas, 4,000 public bath-houses, 400 theatres and places of entertainment, 12,000 greengrocers' shops and 40,000 Jewish subjects. The city was captured by force of arms, with no capitulation. The faithful cannot wait to enjoy the fruits of victory.' Amru, however, was a cultivated man: he did not let his troops sack Alexandria, he refused to be stung into taking reprisals by the Byzantine army's repeated attempts to recapture the city, and he abided by his promise to keep Alexandria 'open to all comers, like a harlot's house', going so far as to demolish a large section of the city walls. What is more, on the very spot where he had managed to persuade his army to refrain from looting, he erected a mosque which he called the Mosque of Clemency.

Arab travellers in Alexandria

Caliph Omar and the burning of the books. It was not until the thirteenth century, some six hundred years after the Arab conquest of Alexandria, that two eminent Arab writers, 'Abd al-Latîf of Baghdad and Ibn Qifṭī, made any further reference to the Ptolemies' Universal Library and the burning of its books. Al-Latîf, a distinguished doctor who visited Syria and Egypt in 1200, wrote a highly imaginative account of his impressions of Alexandria. In a passage presumably based on popular local tradition and his own conjectures, he mentions a place with a stoa where Aristotle and his successors had taught, and also an educational centre established by Alexander the Great containing the Library, which was burnt by Emir Amru on the orders of Caliph Omar.[154]

Ibn al-Qifṭī (1172-1248), a native of Upper Egypt, held various diplomatic and political posts, but his real bent was for scholarship. He wrote a number of historical works, many of them now lost, of which the *History of Learned Men* is generally considered to be the most important.[155]

In that book Ibn al-Qifṭī chronicles the destruction of what was left of the Universal Library in a story whose protagonist is a certain John Grammaticus,[156] an Alexandrian who had studied under a certain Severus and had been a Coptic priest. This John was present at the fall of his native city to the Arabs. He was personally acquainted with the conqueror, Emir Amru, and respected his wisdom, and he himself impressed the Emir with his erudition. At one of their meetings Philoponus summoned up the courage to ask Amru a favour: 'Now that all the city's treasures are yours,' he said, 'I should like to ask you for certain things that are of no use to you but valuable to me.' On being asked what those things were, John replied that he was referring to 'books full of wisdom' in the royal treasury. Amru then expressed a wish to learn more about the person who had conceived the idea of founding the library, so John told him its history, following the account given in the 'Letter of Aristeas' and mentioning Ptolemy Philadelphus and Demetrius of Phalerum. Amru had no objection to John's request but told him that he would first have to ask permission from his Caliph. Omar's answer was terse: 'If the contents of the books accord with the Book of Allah, we do not need them, because in that case the Book of Allah is more than enough. If, on the other hand, they contain anything contrary to the Book of Allah, there is no need to keep them. Proceed with their destruction.' In obedience to the Caliph's orders, the Emir distributed the books to all the public bath-houses in Alexandria (four thousand of them, according to Eutychios) to be used as fuel for heating the water, and we are told it took six months to burn them all. Of the books that remained in the Ptolemies' royal library, the only ones exempted from the order for destruction were the works of Aristotle.

Caliph Omar's pithy verdict on the books

Ibn al-Qifṭī's chronicle of the burning of the Royal Library by the Arabs was repeated in whole or in part by later writers in the East, though it did not become known in Europe until the seventeenth century. A.J. Butler attempted to clear up the whole matter in a book written at the beginning of the twentieth century: he challenged the accuracy of the chronicle, and his line of argument has won many supporters as well as adversaries. However, M. el-Abbadi, in his recent book on the Alexandrian Library, sets out his reasons for believing that the story should be neither accepted nor rejected in its entirety, arguing that it is more constructive to judge the narrative on more than one plane and to follow the oldest tradition.

The first paragraph of Ibn al-Qifṭī's narrative deals with the life and personality of John Grammaticus (whose biographical particulars match those of John Philoponus) and is based on a work written in the tenth century by Ibn al-Nadim. Although Ibn al-Nadim gives a detailed account of the life of John Grammaticus and mentions that he knew Amru, he says nothing about the treasures of the Royal Library. The second paragraph, which describes the founding of the Library by Ptolemy Philadelphus, is taken from an earlier work by Isaac the Monk, which Ibn al-Nadim quotes elsewhere in his book. Isaac's paragraph is the same, word for word, as the corresponding passage in Ioannes Tzetzes's *Prolegomena to Aristophanes* (twelfth century). However, the third paragraph, about Amru's letter to Omar, the Caliph's reply ordering the books to be burnt and the arrangements for selling off the papyrus, is not found in any earlier source.

It seems to me that the answer to the question of the accuracy of Ibn al-Qifṭī's narrative is to be sought in the cultural relations between Greeks and Arabs from the time of the Ummayad dynasty. The main features of these cultural relations, which developed from the seventh to the tenth century, are as follows.

Cultural relations between Greeks and Arabs

The principal point of contact between the two cultures was in the area of language, as Greek was the mother tongue of much of the indigenous population of Syria and Palestine after the Arab conquests and throughout the period of the Ummayad dynasty's rule (661-750), and probably for some time thereafter. Greek was also the lingua franca of commerce (used by merchants in the course of their business) and of educated Christian clergymen, especially the Melkites.[157] Contracts and other documents written in Greek and Arabic attest to the prevailing bilingualism, which was undoubtedly the norm in other countries besides Egypt in the seventh and eighth centuries. Greek was the first language of very many civil servants and grammarians, Arabs as well as Greeks. Even in Damascus, the Ummayad capital, the caliphs employed Greek and Arab Christians to run their administration. The most famous Greek-speaking Arab, John of Damascus, was an adviser to Caliph 'Abd al-Malik.[158]

As regards the cultural alignment of all these Greek-speaking groups that surrounded the Ummayads and virtually controlled the administration, it exactly reflected the cultural and religious character of Constantinople. However, after the Abbasid dynasty came to power in the middle of the eighth century, the situation was radically altered by the cultural initiatives and reforms of the new caliphs, notably al-Mansur, Harun ar-Rashid and al-Mamun. Al-Mamun declared all-out war on the Byzantines and backed the military confrontation with ideological propaganda to the effect that the Byzantines were inferior to the Muslims, not only because they were infidels

102. Commentary on the Koran, Tabriz, between 1210 and 1255.

بسم الله الرحمن الرحيم
بنام خداى مهربان بخشاينده
الحمد لله رب العالمين
سپاس خدايرا خداوند جهانيان
الرحمن الرحيم مالك
خداى مهربان بخشاينده پادشاه

but more particularly because on the cultural plane they had proved themselves unworthy successors of the ancient Greeks. Using this rationale, he clothed his anti-Byzantine policy in a pro-Hellenic cloak, citing the drive for Greek-Arabic translations[159] as proof of the fact that the Arabs were willing recipients of ancient Greek learning.

The drive for Greek-Arabic translations

The drive for Greek-Arabic translations, directed from Baghdad, coincided and was closely associated with the move of the Abbasid dynasty to the new capital as rulers of a world empire.[160] Between the middle of the eighth and the middle of the tenth century nearly all the Greek-language secular works then available in the eastern territories of the Byzantine Empire and the Near East, with the exception of literature and history, were translated into Arabic. This phenomenon was not confined to an intellectual élite at the caliphs' court in Baghdad but was a characteristic feature of Abbasid society: caliphs and princes, high officers of state, merchants and bankers, grammarians and scholars all made important contributions to the movement. Their involvement was all the more necessary inasmuch as a great deal of money was needed to finance the programme: most of it was provided by al-Mamun, of course, but some came from private individuals.[161]

Aristotle the philosophical model for the Arabs

The strongest cultural and intellectual links between the Greeks and the Islamic world were in the field of philosophy. The adherents of *falsafa* (literally 'philosophy', but more specifically Greek philosophy) tried to transplant the anthropocentric thinking of Aristotelianism to the Muslim world in opposition to the apocalyptic and unimaginably strict interpretation of the world offered by Islam. Ambivalence is a feature of all Arab philosophy, which tends to swing between the intellectual reasoning of the Greeks and the revelations contained in the Koran. The leaning towards the Greek philosophical model was expressed rationally in the sciences: those who made a study of philosophy devoted some of their attention to medicine (invariably) and also perhaps to astronomy, chemistry or mathematics. Averroës (Ibn Rushd), one of the great names in Arab philosophy – along with al-Kindi, al-Farabi, Avicenna (Ibn Sina) and al-Ghazali – wrote in the preface to Aristotle's *Acroasis Physica*: 'The author of this book is Aristotle, son of Nicomachus, the wisest of the Greeks. He it was who founded logic, physics and metaphysics. I say that he was their founder, because everything on those subjects ... written before him was unworthy of consideration.... Of those who have come after him – right down to our own time, that is to say in the last 1,500 years or so – not one can claim to have added anything to what he wrote, nor to have found any error worth speaking of in his writings.' These words, written by Averroës in the twelfth century, encapsulate Aristotelian philosophy and elevate it to the level of the prophetic revelations in the Koran, compelling the Arab philosophers who admired Aristotle to conduct a continuous dialogue between reason and faith.[162]

Caliph al-Mamun's 'House of Wisdom'

The Abbasid caliphs, especially al-Mansur and al-Mamun, initiated other cultural projects as well: these include the 'House of Wisdom' (*buyut al-hikma*) and al-Mamun's private library. It may be that the House of Wisdom was the place where books were translated from Greek into Arabic, but there is not enough reliable evidence to support this conclusion. More probably it was a repository of the Sassanid administrative tradition: that is to say, it was probably a centre for translations from Persian into Arabic and a library of the Sassanid cultural and historical tradition. Quite possibly it also housed the fine library built up by Caliph al-Mamun.[163] Ibn al-Nadim states that he found there (i.e. in al-Mamun's library) rare manuscripts of great historical importance, and he adds that it contained all manner of valuable old books, including some written in strange alphabets.

Caliph al-Mamun is also associated with Leo the Mathematician, according to a dubious Byzantine source which alleges that the Caliph conceived the idea of offering the Byzantine philosopher a fabulous sum of money if he would come to live in Baghdad. The story could well be pure legend,[164] and the same can be said of the reputedly reliable report given by Ibn al-Nadim in his *Kitab al-Fihrist* (*Index*) that the Byzantines burnt fifteen consignments of books by Archimedes. Stories about the destruction of great libraries or about secret storehouses of wisdom 'kept under lock and key' – stories in which fact and imagination are interwoven, which border on the realm of legend and serve propaganda purposes – abounded in the period round about the tenth century. Ibn al-Nadim himself, in the *Kitab al-Fihrist* (Ibn al-Qifṭi's primary source for the stories about John Grammaticus and the founding of the Library by Ptolemy Philadelphus), mentions another abandoned library which he found in a monumental ancient temple two or three days' journey from Constantinople – again referring to the same period, the late tenth century.[165] As regards the bibliological tradition of the Arabs, it is said that Caliph al-Hakim II of Cordoba (971-976) had a library of 400,000 manuscripts, all listed in a catalogue that ran to forty-four volumes.[166] Even if there is an element of exaggeration in these figures, there was nothing in the Byzantine or Western world that could begin to compare with them: St. Christodoulos, the founder of the library

Information about Byzantine and Arab libraries

on Patmos, had only 220 manuscripts, and there were only nine hundred in the collection of Charles V of France.[167] It is true, of course, that the cost of books in the Arab world was much lower than in the West, as the Muslims had been using paper for their manuscripts (having learnt the technique of paper-making from the Chinese) since the middle of the ninth century.[168]

Ibn al-Qifṭī's account of the burning of what remained of the Universal Library is not corroborated by any other reliable source. Most probably it reflects the growth of opposition to the drive for Greek-Arabic translations and was invented to supply historical grounds for questioning the soundness of that decision: al-Qifṭī had every reason to present Omar (who was widely respected for his learning) as one who would have disapproved of the translating programme, because his epigrammatic verdict on the value of Greek literature was tantamount to outright condemnation.

Epilogue. One question remains. What eventually happened to the only library that ever set out to be a 'universal library'? Before drawing any conclusions, let us sum up what the sources have to say about the Library.

Unfortunately there is no reliable extant source that gives a full account of the thinking underlying the initial formation of the Library by Ptolemy Soter and Ptolemy Philadelphus or its enlargement by their successors; nor do we have any detailed description of the Library and the rest of the Museum. About the organization and size of the Library very little is known, apart from the names of the Directors from Zenodotus to Cydas listed in the Oxyrrhynchus papyrus. The number of books in the Library and the nature of the collections can only be matters of conjecture.

Until the time of Cleopatra and the fall of Alexandria to Julius Caesar, the Library, the Museum and the whole palace complex would appear to have been undamaged by fire or any other agency. There is no contemporary documentary evidence for the burning of the Library during the Alexandrian War between Caesar and Ptolemy XIII, and the truth is probably that a large number of books were destroyed in buildings in the docks that belonged to the Crown. Whether Augustus – who built a bilingual library in the precinct of the splendid temple of Julius the God – carried off some of the Library's books, and whether the Roman emperors took books from the Alexandrian Library to enrich their own city's bilingual libraries, we do not know.

Whatever damage may have been done to the city when it was besieged by

Aurelian (272) and then by Diocletian (297-298), no firm conclusions can be drawn concerning the extent of the damage, if any, to the Museum and the Library. Epiphanius and Aphthonius, who visited the Serapeum library in the fourth century A.D., were simply recording their impressions as ordinary travellers and shed no further light on the matter. The sacking of the Temple of Serapis during the riots instigated by Bishop Theophilus in 391 is not in dispute, but once again the sources say nothing about what happened to its library. As for Ibn al-Qifṭī's story of the burning of the Universal Library at the time of the Arab conquest in 642 and Caliph Omar's pithy verdict on the books, that is probably fictitious and may have been intended to shore up an ideology.

My personal view of the matter, assuming that there was no other catastrophe of which we have no historical record, is that the Ptolemies' Universal Library in Alexandria suffered the fate that sooner or later befalls every library when it ceases to reflect and fulfil its original purpose and gradually becomes run down and depleted. Finally it succumbs to the inexorable law of nature: progressive decay leading to extinction.

Notes

III
Hellenistic Period

The Universal Library of the Ptolemies in Alexandria

NOTES

1. On the history of the struggle between the Diadochi I have consulted the pioneering work by J. G. Droysen, *Ἱστορία τῶν Διαδόχων τοῦ Μεγάλου Ἀλεξάνδρου* (= *Geschichte des Hellenismus: Geschichte der Epigonen*, Gotha, 1843, tr. and annotated by Renos I. Apostolidis), new edn., 2 vols., Athens 1992 (an updated edition by I. R. and S. R. Apostolidis incorporating the latest findings of historical, archaeological and literary research). On the historical background to the Hellenistic period and the transition from the fourth to the third century, see M. Rostovtzeff, *The Social and Economic History of the Hellenistic World*, 3 vols., Oxford 1941.
2. J. G. Herder, in the eighteenth century, was one of the first to draw attention to the influence of Oriental epic poetry and philosophy on Greek thought. Since then the decipherment of the great Sumerian, Egyptian and Babylonian epics and theogonies has cast light on many of the probable points of contact. Martin West has pointed out certain elements in Hesiod's work that appear to be drawn from the Sumerian 'Moral Precepts' of Shuruppak, the Egyptian 'Moral Precepts' and the Babylonian 'Counsels of Wisdom', which would place Hesiod in this current of Oriental literature: see M. L. West (ed.), *Hesiod: Theogony*, Oxford 1966, 74; Id. (ed.), *Hesiod: Works and Days*, Oxford 1978, 172-177. It is thought that experts from the Near East may have helped the Alexandrians to classify works of literature by introducing them to the 'Babylonian methods': see G. Zuntz, *The Text of the Epistles: A disquisition upon the Corpus Paulinum*, London 1953, 270 ff. For further reading on this subject see C. H. Gordon, Homer and Bible: The origin and character of East Mediterranean literature, Ventnor, N. J. 1967.
3. For a translation of the Dēnkard see M. Shaki, 'The Dēnkard Account of the Zoroastrian Scriptures', *Archív Orientální* 49 (1981) 114-125, which is based on R. C. Zaehner, *The Dawn and Twilight of Zoroastrianism*, New York 1961, 175-177.
4. The treatise attributed to Zoroaster exists under several different titles. For a description of the extant manuscripts and their contents see *GAS*, VII, 85-86.
5. According to this third version, as soon as the copies had been made, Alexander gave orders to burn the Persian originals, whether written in the ordinary script or the official calligraphic script (kaštağ). Once he had recorded all the necessary information relating to the sciences (astronomy, medicine, etc.) and the properties of the heavenly bodies, he sent all those 'books' to Egypt, together with any other cultural or scholarly trophies he came across on his way through Persia.
6. On the *Book of Rulers* and the translations of it, see A. Christensen, *L'Iran sous les Sassanides*, Copenhagen 1944², 59-62, 71; Mary Boyce, 'Middle Persian Literature', in *Handbuch der Orientalistik*, 1.4: *Iranistik*, 2: *Literatur*, 1, ed. B. Spuler, Leiden 1968, 57-59.
7. See F. Macler, 'Extraits de la Chronique de Maribas Kaldoyo (Mar Abas Katina[?])', *Journal Asiatique* (May-June 1903) 491 ff. That Alexander wanted his empire to be truly multicultural we know from his general Ptolemy (the future King Ptolemy I), who was present at the great reconciliation conference that Alexander called at Opis on the Tigris after the mutiny in the Macedonian army had been put down. At that public banquet, which Arrian says was at-

tended by a total of 9,000 Greeks and Persians (the term 'Persians' being used to mean Asians generally) who wished to offer sacrifices to the gods together, Alexander made a speech appealing for concord and unity between the Macedonians and the Persians, whom he called upon to live together as subjects of a multinational commonwealth. Arrian records Alexander's speech as it had come down to him from Ptolemy, and the same episode is recounted in different words by Plutarch (*On the Fortune or the Virtue of Alexander*) and Strabo, both of whom followed the account given by Eratosthenes of Cyrene, the scholarly Director of the Library.

8. Plutarch, *Alexander*, VIII.
9. Another story from the same source (Macler, *op. cit.*, 533), also on the subject of books, conflicts sharply with the Greek tradition: it is said that when Seleucus I Nicator mounted Xerxes's throne in Babylon the first thing he did was to burn all the books he found there, in all the languages of the world, so that thenceforward time would be reckoned as starting with him. According to the Greek sources, Seleucus rescued the contents of the first Athenian public library, which Xerxes had carried off in 484 (see above, p. 76).

   It is interesting to note that a similar story is told of a king in China, Si Huang Ti of the Ch'in dynasty, who united the Six Kingdoms under his rule. This first Emperor of China, in the period when the Great Wall was being built, is said to have given orders that all books written before his time were to be burnt. The event is dated to 245 B.C., that is to say during the reign of King Attalus I of Pergamum. See J. Delorme, *Παγκόσμια Χρονολογική Ἱστορία* (= *Chronologie des civilisations*, tr. and ed. K. Dokou et al.), I, Athens 1985, 130. A fuller account is given by J. L. Borges in *Διερευνήσεις* (= *Otras inquisiciones*, tr. A. Kyriakidis), Athens 1990, 11-114 (= «Τό Τεῖχος καί τά Βιβλία»). Borges took the story from Pope's *Dunciad*.
10. In the last years of his reign Ptolemy I started taking an interest in history and wrote the most reliable and circumstantial account of Alexander's exploits. Unfortunately only fragments of his narrative survive, and those only in the work of Arrian, who says little or nothing about the cultural aspirations that were so dear to Alexander's heart. See *FGrHist* 138, with notes by Jacoby (1930); C. B. Welles, 'The Reliability of Ptolemy as an Historian', in *Miscellanea di studi alessandrini in memoria di Augusto Rostagni*, Turin 1963, 101-106. See also H. Strasburger, *Ptolemaios und Alexander*, Leipzig 1934; and, more generally: J. P. Mahaffy, *A History of Egypt under the Ptolemaic Dynasty*, London 1898; P. M. Fraser, *Ptolemaic Alexandria*, 3 vols., Oxford 1972.
11. These new possessions of Ptolemy's, together with Samos (which Ptolemy II acquired in 280), were of more than merely military significance: their great cultural traditions did much to give Alexandria the universal status the Ptolemies wanted for it, at least on the cultural plane. Samos had been the centre of an influential circle of poets as early as the middle of the sixth century, when Polycrates was the island's ruler. Cos, where Ptolemy Philadelphus was born, was well known for its medical school and was also the birthplace of Philetas, a pioneer of literary studies, while Cyrene was the native country of Callimachus and Eratosthenes. Cyrene, Cyprus and Rhodes, which between them supplied Alexandria with a number of prominent literary scholars, retained their political autonomy and served as places of refuge when the world of literary scholarship was shaken by its first crisis in 145 B.C.
12. There is no direct evidence of Ptolemy's

ambitions for Alexandria as a centre of scholarship and culture, unless we count a passage in which Strabo (XIV.C.673) compares the educational and philosophical institutions of Ptolemy's capital with those of Tarsus and other cities: 'The people of Tarsus have devoted themselves so eagerly, not only to philosophy, but to the whole round of education in general, that they have surpassed Athens, Alexandria and any other place that can be named where there have been schools and lectures by philosophers. But it is different from other cities in that the men who study there are all local people, and foreigners are not inclined to sojourn there; nor do those local people stay there, but they complete their education abroad; and when they have completed it they are pleased to live abroad, and few go back home. But the opposite is the case with the other cities which I have just mentioned except Alexandria: for many people go to those other cities and spend time there with pleasure, but you would not see many of the local citizens either going abroad to study or keen to study in their own native city. In the case of the Alexandrians, however, both things are true, for they admit many foreigners and also send a good number of their own citizens abroad. Furthermore, the city of Tarsus has all kinds of schools of rhetoric, and in general it not only has a flourishing population but is also very powerful, thus keeping up the reputation of the mother city.'

13. The term *mouseion* or *museum* was applied to a number of centres serving a variety of purposes. Some were shrines erected in memory of well-known poets, usually in their birthplaces, like the 'Museum of Homer' at Smyrna or the heroön of Archilochus on Paros (see N. M. Kontoleon, «Ἀρχίλοχος καί Πάρος», *Ἐπετηρίς τῆς Ἑταιρείας Κυκλαδικῶν Μελετῶν* 5 (1965) 53-103); some were associated with burials, like the *mouseion* in honour of Andragoras (see C. Boyancé, 'Le culte des Muses chez les philosophes grecs', *Bibliothèque des Écoles Françaises d'Athènes et de Rome* 141 (1937) 329 ff.); and some were educational centres, the most obvious examples being the Peripatetic school and the *mouseion* at Stagira. In comparison with these last there was nothing new about the Alexandria Museum in conception, but only in the matter of its size and organization. There can be no doubt that Aristotle's Lyceum, as developed by Theophrastus, was the original on which it was modelled. On the various activities that went on in the Museum see Boyancé, *op. cit.*; and, more generally, see G. Parthey, *Das alexandrische Museum*, Berlin 1838; E. Müller-Graupa, «Μουσεῖον», in *RE*, 16 (1933), 797-821; Fraser, *op. cit.*, I, 305-317.
14. Hecataeus of Abdera (or of Teos, of which Abdera was a colony), a philosopher and historian of civilization who flourished around 300 B.C., spent some time in Egypt in Ptolemy Soter's reign. He was officially commissioned to write a history of Egypt (*Aegyptiaca*) as a work of propaganda to encourage friendlier relations between the Greeks and the Egyptians. This work is lost, except for fragments preserved in Book I of the *Bibliotheca* of Diodorus Siculus. It was a historical survey written on the basis of first-hand experience, laying more than usual emphasis on cultural history and leaving the reader in no doubt as to the political motivation behind its writing. To the Greeks, Egypt was a country of immemorial antiquity with a strongly mystical culture; so it is described as an ideal polity with best possible form of government, a 'constitutional' monarchy.

Hans Lewy, in his paper 'Aristotle and the Jewish Sage according to Clearchos of Soli', *Harvard Theological Review* 31 (1938)

217, states that Hecataeus accompanied Ptolemy I on his second Syrian campaign in 312 B.C. and that he was probably the first Greek to make personal friends among the Palestinian Jews: see E.J. Bickerman, *The Jews in the Greek Age*, Cambridge, Mass./London 1988, 16-18, 27, 142, 224, 231.

According to B. Schaller, 'Hekataios von Abdera über die Juden. Zur Frage der Echtheit und der Datierung', *Zeitschrift für die neutestamentliche Wissenschaft und die Kunde der älteren Kirche* 54 (1963) 15-31, the passages attributed to Hecataeus that are preserved by Josephus (*Against Apion*, I.87) are spurious, written by an unknown Greek historian and philosopher who knew the writer of the 'Letter of Aristeas'.

15. Herondas (as Athenaeus calls him) or Herodas was a poet of the third century B.C. whose name suggests that he may have been of Dorian extraction. The setting of two of his poems seems to indicate that he was a native of Cos, or that he lived there. The king referred to in one of his poems was presumably Ptolemy III Euergetes, who reigned from 246 to 221 B.C. Herondas describes Alexandria in a scene in one of his mimes (I.26-33), where a bawd tries to seduce a virtuous woman whose husband is away in Egypt: 'There is the goddess's house. Everything that exists or comes to pass is to be found in Egypt: wealth, athletic facilities, power, a good climate, fame, sights worth seeing, learned men, gold, young men, the sanctuary of the divine brethren [i.e. the Ptolemies], a worthy king, the house of the Muses, wine, all good things that you could ever want, women...'
16. Strabo, XVII.C.793-794: 'Within the royal quarter lies the Museum, which has a covered walk and an exedra and a large building containing the refectory of the scholars who belong to the Museum. This community has common funds and there is a priest in charge of the Museum, who was formerly appointed by the kings but now by Caesar [Augustus].'
17. F. Durrbach (ed.), *Choix d'inscriptions de Délos*, I, Paris 1921, 151-153 (No. 90) (*ca.* 125 B.C.): 'Chrysermus, son of Heraclitus, of Alexandria, "Kinsman" of King Ptolemy, exegete, head of the medical corps and *Epistates* of the Museum.' Cf. Fraser, *op. cit.*, I, 316, II, 179 (n. 31).
18. Aristonicus, a grammarian who lived in Augustus's reign, was probably the son of Ptolemy the grammarian. In most of his books he expatiated on the critical symbols used by Aristarchus in his recensions.
19. The Museum had its own treasury and its funds came direct from the royal exchequer. The bursar may been the *Epistates* of the Museum, or so it has been inferred on the evidence of a dedicatory inscription on Delos in honour of a certain Chrysermus, a member of a prominent Alexandrian family who held that post. His job would have been to collect taxes, make disbursements and monitor expenditure. See W. Otto, *Priester und Tempel im hellenistischen Ägypten*, I, Rome 1971, 42; Fraser, *op. cit.*, I, 316-317. The main evidence for the members' free board and lodging comes from the Cornell papyrus of *ca.* 220 B.C., published by N. Lewis in his paper 'The Non-Scholar Members of the Alexandrian Museum', *Mnemosyne*, 4th ser., 16 (1963) 257-261.
20. Timon was well-known in antiquity for his *Silloi* (literally 'squint-eyed verses'), which were three books of poems in hexameters ridiculing all doctrinaire philosophers. See Athenaeus, I.22d: 'Timon of Phlius, the satirist, calls the Museum a birdcage, to ridocule the philosophers who made their living there because they were fed like the most valuable birds in a coop: "There are many people in populous Egypt who make a livelihood by scribbling endlessly and waging a constant war of words with each other in the Muses' birdcage."'

21. Diog. Laer., IX.113: *πῶς τὴν τοῦ Ὁμήρου ποίησιν ἀσφαλῆ κτήσαιτο, τὸν δὲ εἰπεῖν, «εἰ τοῖς ἀρχαίοις ἀντιγράφοις ἐντυγχάνοι καὶ μὲ τοῖς ἤδη διωρθωμένοις»·* See also U. von Wilamowitz-Moellendorf, *Antigonos von Karystos* [*Philologische Untersuchungen*, IV], Berlin 1881, 43.
22. See p. 182.
23. See K. M. Abbott, «Φιλόλογος», in *RE*, 19/2 (1938), 2510-2514. See also the exhaustive study by H. Kuch, *Φιλόλογος. Untersuchung eines Wortes von seinem ersten Auftreten in der Tradition bis zur ersten überlieferten lexikalischen Festlegung* [*Schriften der Sektion für Altertumswissenschaft* 48], Berlin 1965, 30 ff. Kuch traces the use of the word *philologos* back to Plato's time, when it was used of philosophers, rhetoricians and mathematicians.
24. On the advances made in mathematics, astronomy, mechanics and medicine by scientists working in Alexandria, see Fraser, *op. cit.*, I, 336-446.
25. See Parthey, *op. cit.* The main works on the Universal Library of Alexandria are: C. Wendel, 'Das griechisch-römische Altertum' (completed by W. Göber), in F. Milkau and G. Leyh (eds.), *Handbuch der Bibliothekswissenschaft*, III.1, Wiesbaden 1955, 62-82; E. A. Parsons, *The Alexandrian Library, Glory of the Hellenic World: Its Rise, Antiquities, and Destructions*, New York 1967[3]; Fraser, *op. cit.*, I, 312-335; L. Canfora, *Ἡ Χαμένη Βιβλιοθήκη τῆς Ἀλεξανδρείας* (= *La biblioteca scomparsa*, Palermo 1986, tr. F. Arvanitis), Athens 1989; M. el-Abbadi, *Ἡ Ἀρχαία Βιβλιοθήκη τῆς Ἀλεξανδρείας. Ἡ Ζωή καί ἡ Μοίρα της* (= *The Life and Fate of the Ancient Library of Alexandria*, Paris 1990, tr. Lena Kassimi), Athens 1998; K. Sp. Staikos, *The Great Libraries from Antiquity to the Renaissance (3000 B.C. to A.D. 1600)* (= *Βιβλιοθήκη. Ἀπό τήν Ἀρχαιότητα ἕως τήν Ἀναγέννηση (3000 π.Χ. - 1600 μ.Χ.)*, tr. T. Cullen), New Castle, Del./London 2000, 57-89. See also R. M. MacLeod (ed.), *The Library of Alexandria: Centre of Learning in the Ancient World*, London/New York 2001[2]; and the volume published to commemorate the opening of the new Bibliotheca Alexandrina in Alexandria: L. Giard and C. Jacob (eds.), *Des Alexandries*, I: *Du livre au texte*, Paris 2001.
26. On Demetrius of Phalerum see E. Martini, 'Demetrios von Phaleron', in *RE*, 4 (1901), 2817-2841; E. Bayer, 'Demetrius Phalereus', *Tübinger Beiträge zur Altertumswissenschaft* 36 (1942) 105 ff.; F. Wehrli, 'Demetrios von Phaleron', in *RE*, suppl. 11 (1968), 514-522. A catalogue of his works is given by Diogenes Laertius (V.80).
27. Strabo, XIII.C.608.
28. Diog. Laer., V.37. See also F. Wehrli, *Die Schule des Aristoteles*, IV: *Demetrios von Phaleron*, Basel 1949.
29. Diog. Laer., V.58. See also Wehrli, *op. cit.*, V: *Straton von Lampsakos*, Basel 1950. Diogenes Laertius also mentions that Ptolemy I's son (the future king Ptolemy II Philadelphus) paid Strato eighty talents for tutoring members of the royal family. After Theophrastus's death the atmosphere at the Peripatos changed considerably under his successor Strato, who was head of the school from 286 to 268. Strabo (see Chapter II) thought its decline was due to the loss or disappearance of Aristotle's lecture notes and Theophrastus's books. This may not be the whole truth of the matter (and of course we have to remember that Strabo was writing two centuries after the event), but it is a fact that Strato, who was Ptolemy Philadelphus's tutor and acted as a link between the Athenian school and the Museum of Alexandria after his return to Athens, did find that the shortage of suitable textbooks severely hampered his efforts to keep the school's teaching standards up to the level maintained by Theophrastus.

30. The first edition of the letter published in modern times was that of P. Wendland in *Aristeae ad Philocratem epistula*, Leipzig 1900. Wendland's edition was used as the basis for subsequent translations and commentaries: see, for example, the more recent edition by A. Pelletier, *Lettre d'Aristée à Philocrate* [*Sources Chrétiennes* 89], Paris 1962. The first person to challenge the authenticity of the letter was the Spanish humanist Ludovicus Vives in his notes on St. Augustine's *De civitate Dei*, which he edited and published in 1522 (Basel, J. Froben) together with Erasmus's letter *To the Reader* (see *La Correspondance d'Érasme*, tr. and ed. P.S. Allen, H.M. Allen and H.W. Garrod, V, 1976, 148-152, Letter 1309).
31. See the standard work by E. Schürer, *The History of the Jewish People in the Age of Jesus Christ (175 B.C.-A.D. 135)*, new English version revised and edited by Geza Vermes et al., I-III, Edinburgh 1987-1995; V. Tcherikover, *Hellenistic Civilization and the Jews*, Philadelphia 1959; M. Hengel, *Judaism and Hellenism: Studies in their encounter in Palestine during the Early Hellenistic period*, London 1974; Id., 'The Ideology of the Letter of Aristeas', *Harvard Theological Review* 51 (1958) 59-85.
32. Given that the 'Letter of Aristeas' was not actually a letter written by one man to his brother, the presumption is that it was published in book form. Furthermore, considering that narratives in epistolary form were very popular in the Christian era, it is fair to assume that they were widely read in the author's lifetime too, mainly by Jews. If so, the events described by Aristeas cannot be fictitious, as they could easily be checked by the literary scholars of the Library. The matters in dispute are two: Demetrius of Phalerum's position as official librarian and the statistics relating to the number of books in the Library. Obviously Aristeas was not particularly bothered about specifying Demetrius's precise position, and it may well be that he was commonly believed to have been Director of the Library because of his association with Aristotle's Lyceum. About the size of the library there can be no argument, as the figure given by Aristeas is reasonable by the standards of the day.
33. The Jews attached great importance to the translation into Greek of the Torah, the whole body of the Jewish sacred writings and tradition, as it contained teachings of universal application which needed to available in an international language: see Bickerman, *The Jews in the Greek Age*, 101-116 ('The Greek Torah'); N. Walter, 'Jewish-Greek Literature of the Greek Period', in the *Cambridge History of Judaism*, II: *The Hellenistic Age*, ed. W.D. Davies and L. Finkelstein, Cambridge 1990, 385-408; G. Dorival, M. Harl and O. Munnich, *La Bible grecque des Septante. Du judaïsme hellénistique au christianisme ancien*, Paris 1994[2]; G. Dorival, 'La fixation du canon de la Bible. Entre Jérusalem et Alexandrie', in Giard and Jacob, *Des Alexandries*, I, 115-134.
34. Eusebius of Caesarea, *De Evangelica Praeparatione*, VIII.2.1-5.11: '*Demetrius of Phalerum, having been placed in charge of the king's library, was given substantial funds to collect all the books in the world. Some he bought and others he copied, until eventually he had accomplished the king's project so far as it was in his power. Once, when I [Aristeas] was present, the king asked him how many books there were, and he answered, "More than two hundred thousand, your majesty, and I will do my best to reach a total of five hundred thousand before long. And I have been told that the law books of the Jews are also worth copying and deserve a place in your library." "What is to prevent you from doing that?" asked the king. "Everything you need is at your disposal." "They need to be translated, too," answered Demetrius, "be-*

cause in Judaea they use special characters, as the Egyptians do in their writing, and they have a language of a kind peculiar to them. They are reputed to use Syriac, but that is not so: their language is quite different." When the king was in possession of all the facts of the matter, he ordered a letter to be written to the high priest of the Jews, so that the aforesaid project might be put into effect.'

A little further on, he adds:

'Once this had been done, he told Demetrius to prepare a report on the transcription of the Jewish books; for those kings arranged everything by means of decrees and with great attention to detail, without leaving anything to chance. That is how I have been able to make copies of the report and the letters, as well as details of the number of items sent and the amount of work that had gone into each of them, taking into consideration the magnificence and skilled workmanship of each one. Here is a copy of the report.'

LETTER FROM DEMETRIUS OF PHALERUM TO PTOLEMY, KING OF EGYPT

'"To His Majesty the King, from Demetrius. On receiving your command, O King, that the books still needed to make the library complete be collected and that the damaged books be suitably repaired, I have treated this as a matter demanding my full attention and I now present my report. We are still missing the law books of the Jews, as well as a few other books. They are in the Hebrew language and script and are written carelessly and inaccurately, according to experts on the subject, since they have not had the benefit of royal patronage. You need to have properly edited copies of those, too, because that Law is superior in wisdom and free from all blemish, inasmuch as it is of divine origin. That is why prose writers and poets and so many historians have avoided mentioning the said books and the men who have regulated their lives in accordance with them, because the teachings they contain are 'hallowed and august', to use the words of Hecataeus of Abdera. Therefore, if you agree, O King, a letter will be written to the high priest of Jerusalem asking him to send six elders from each tribe – all exceedingly upright men and well versed in their Law – so that we may ascertain the points on which the majority of them are in agreement and, having thus obtained an accurate translation, we can put it in a conspicuous place in a manner worthy of the subject and of your intentions. May you prosper always."

'When this report had been presented, the king ordered a letter to be written to Eleazar about the matter, mentioning the release of prisoners that had taken place. He also donated fifty talents of gold, seventy talents of silver and a considerable quantity of gemstones for the manufacture of wine-mixing bowls and drinking bowls and a table and libation vessels – with orders to the guardians of the treasury to let the artists choose any materials they might require for the purpose – and a hundred talents in cash to cover the cost of sacrifices and other expenses. I shall tell you about the workmanship of these articles when I have given you the copies of the letters.

'The king's letter ran as follows:

LETTER FROM KING PTOLEMY TO THE HIGH PRIEST ELEAZAR

'"From King Ptolemy to the high priest Eleazar, greetings and salutation. There are many Jews living in our country, of whom some were driven out of Jerusalem by the Persians at the time of their conquest, while others came to Egypt as prisoners of war with my father, who placed many of them in the army and paid them higher wages than usual, and when he had proved the loyalty of their leaders he built fortresses and manned them with Jews so that they might instil fear and

respect into the native Egyptians. And I, since I ascended the throne, have shown great kindness to all my subjects, and more particularly to your compatriots. I have set more than a hundred thousand prisoners free, paying their owners the proper market price for them, and if ever your people have been harmed through the passions of the mob, I have made due reparation, motivated by a desire to act piously and to make a thank offering to the supreme god for preserving my kingdom in peace and the greatest glory in all the world. Moreover, those of your people who were in the prime of life I have drafted into my army; those who were fit to be in my personal retinue and worthy of the confidence of the court, I have established in official positions. Now, therefore, since I am anxious to show my gratitude to these men and to the Jews throughout the world and their descendants, I have decided to have your Law translated into Greek from the Hebrew language which you use, so that these books may be added to the other royal books in my library. I shall take it as a kindness on your part and a regard for my zeal if you will select six elders from each of your tribes, upright men experienced in your Law and skilled at interpreting and translating it, so that we can arrive at a rendering on which the majority agree; for this research is of the highest possible importance. I hope to win great renown by the accomplishment of this work. With this end in view I have sent Andreas, one of my senior bodyguards, and Aristeas – both men whom I hold in high esteem – to discuss the matter with you and to bring you a hundred talents of silver as a votive offering for the temple and the sacrifices and other rites. If you will write and tell me of your wishes in this matter, you will be doing me a great favour and making a gesture of friendship, and all your wishes shall be carried out as speedily as possible. Farewell."

'To this letter Eleazar replied appropriately as follows:

LETTER FROM THE HIGH PRIEST ELEAZAR TO KING PTOLEMY

'"Eleazar the high priest sends greetings to King Ptolemy, his true friend. I pray that you are in good health, and Queen Arsinoe your sister and your children likewise: if so, all is well. I also am well. On receiving your letter, I was delighted to read of your intentions and your fine project. I summoned all the people and read it to them that they might know of your devotion to our God; and I showed them the cups which you sent, twenty of gold and thirty of silver, and the five mixing-bowls and the offering table, and the hundred talents of silver to pay for the offering of sacrifices and the purchase of materials needed for the maintenance of the temple. These gifts were brought to me by Andreas, one of your honoured servants, and by Aristeas, both good men and true, distinguished by their learning and altogether worthy to be the representatives of your high principles and sense of justice. These men delivered your message to me and received from me an answer in agreement with your letter. I will consent to everything that serves your purpose, unusual though your request may be, in token of my friendship and affection, for you have bestowed great and unforgettable benefits upon our compatriots in many ways. Immediately, therefore, I offered sacrifices on behalf of you, your sister, your children and your friends, and all the people prayed that your plans might always prosper, and that Almighty God might preserve your kingdom in peace with honour. So that the translation of the holy Law might profit you and be completed successfully, in the presence of all the people I selected six elders from each tribe, all good men and true, and I have sent them to you with a copy of our Law. It will be a kindness, O righteous King, if you will give orders for the men to be restored to us in safety as soon as the translation of the Law is completed. Farewell."

Later on, after saying a great deal about the project, he adds, in these very words:

'After the books had been read, the priests, the elders from the team of translators, the elders of the Jewish community and the leaders of the people stood up and said, "Since so excellent and sacred and altogether accurate a translation has been made, it is right that it should remain just as it is, without any alteration whatsoever." When all present had shown their approval by acclamation, they told them to pronounce a curse in accordance with their custom upon any one who should make any alteration, either by adding anything or making any change whatsoever to the words that had been written, or by omitting anything. This was a wise thing to do, to ensure that the book would remain unchanged forever. When the king was informed of this he was overjoyed, for he felt that the project he had initiated had been safely carried out. The whole book was read out to him and he was full of admiration for the lawgiver's intelligence. Then said he to Demetrius, "How is it that no historian or poet has ever thought it worth mentioning so wonderful an achievement?" Demetrius answered, 'Because the Law is sacred and of divine origin. What is more, some people who did think of doing so were struck down by God and therefore gave up the idea." In fact, he added, Theopompus had told him that he had been driven out of his mind for more than thirty days because he had intended to insert in his history some passages from the earlier and less reliable translations of the Law. When he prayed to God to explain why the misfortune had befallen him, it was revealed to him in a dream that out of idle curiosity he was intending to communicate sacred truths to laymen, and that if he desisted he would recover his health. "And I myself have heard from the lips of Theodectes, one of the tragic poets, that when he was about to insert some passages from the Book in one of his plays, he was afflicted with cataract in both his eyes. Realizing what was the probable reason for his affliction, he prayed to God for many days and his sight was restored." Having heard Demetrius's explanation, as I have just said, the king did homage and ordered that great care should be taken of the books, and that they should be guarded religiously.'

So much for my extracts from the aforesaid text. So let us now look also at the constitution of the Mosaic law, as recorded by men famed among those people. First of all I shall cite what Philo says concerning the Jews' exodus from Egypt under Moses' leadership, taken from the first of the works that he calls Hypothetica, where, arguing in defence of the Jews as if he were addressing their accusers, he says the following.

35. In the second century B.C. the Jews of Alexandria became so thoroughly Hellenized that a body of Jewish literature in Greek came into existence. Evidently the purpose of these writings was to create a wider readership for matters relating to Judaism by writing about them in Greek literary genres, such as poetry and tragedy, and to comment on certain problems peculiar to Judaic Greek literature, to judge by the works of Demetrius the historian (*On the Kings in Judaea*), the poet Philo the Elder (*On Jerusalem*) and other writers. See J. Freudenthal, *Hellenistische Studien*, II: *Alexander Polyhistor und die von ihm erhaltenen Reste jüdäischer und samaritanischer Geschichtwerke II*, Breslau 1875, 81; Methodios G. Fougeas (Bishop of Pisidia), *Ἡ Ἑλληνιστική Ἰουδαϊκή Παράδοση*, Athens 1995, 167-183.
36. The Prolegomena to Tzetzes's *Commentary on Aristophanes* survives in three versions with slight variations between them: see G. Kaibel, 'Die Prolegomena Περί Κωμῳδίας', *Abhandlungen der Göttinger Gesellschaft der Wissenschaften*, N.F., II 4 (1898) 4. See also the exhaustive discussion by C. Wendel, 'Tzetzes', in *RE*, $7A_2$ (1948), 1973 ff.; and

the edition by W. J. W. Koster, *Scholia in Aristophanem*, IV/I, Groningen 1960, XX; also H. Hunger, *Βυζαντινή Λογοτεχνία. Ἡ λόγια κοσμική γραμματεία τῶν Βυζαντινῶν* (= *Die höchsprachliche profane Literatur der Byzantiner*, Munich 1978, tr. G. Ch. Makris et al.), II, Athens 1992, 446-447.

Prolegomena: 'Alexander of Aetolia, Lycophron of Chalcis and Zenodotus of Ephesus were set to work together by the royal command of King Ptolemy Philadelphus: Alexander edited the tragedies, Lycophron the comedies and Zenodotus the works of Homer and the other poets. For the said King Ptolemy, a great lover of learning in the truest sense and a most excellent person who desired everything that was good by way of spectacle and deed and word, set Demetrius of Phalerum and other elders to collect books from all countries and bring them to Alexandria, using funds from the royal treasury. He then deposited these books in two libraries, of which the one outside the palace grounds contained 42,800 and the one in the palace grounds contained 400,000 composite and 90,000 simple, unmixed books. This is recorded by Callimachus, who was then a young courtier and compiled a catalogue of the books when they had been revised. Eratosthenes, a contemporary of his, was put in charge of this great library by the king. Within a short time the books had been collected and corrected under the supervision of Callimachus and Eratosthenes, as I have said, even until the death of Ptolemy Philadelphus. Then, since all the Greek books and those of other nations – including the Jews – had been gathered together, that munificent king, being a seven-mouthed river of gold, had the foreign books rendered into the Greek script and language by learned men of the appropriate nationality who had a perfect knowledge of Greek. For the translation of the Hebrew books he commissioned seventy-two learned Jews with a mastery of both languages.'

37. The earliest known use of the name 'Pleiad' in this connection is in Strabo (XIV.C.675): 'An excellent tragic poet, one of those numbered among the Pleiad.' The name recurs in literary history centuries later, when it was used of the group of French poets that formed round Ronsard in 1563, soon after the foundation of the Collège Royal, which Guillaume Budé dubbed 'the new Museum'.
38. Alexander, a native of Pleuron in Aetolia, worked for Ptolemy Philadelphus and was invited to the Macedonian court, with Aratus of Soli and others, by Antigonus Gonatas (276-240/39 B.C.). He was instructed to edit the tragedies and satyric dramas in the Library, and he himself wrote epics, elegiacs, epigrams, mimes and plays. See R. Pfeiffer, *Ἱστορία τῆς Κλασσικῆς Φιλολογίας. Ἀπό τῶν Ἀρχῶν μέχρι τοῦ τέλους τῶν Ἑλληνιστικῶν Χρόνων* (= *History of Classical Scholarship: From the beginnings to the end of the Hellenistic age*, Oxford 1968, tr. P. Xenos et al.), Athens 1972, 140-141; P. E. Easterling and B. M. W. Knox, *Ἱστορία τῆς ἀρχαίας Ἑλληνικῆς Λογοτεχνίας* (= *The Cambridge History of Classical Literature*, I: *Greek Literature*, tr. N. Konomis et al.), Athens 1994, 1026.
39. Although Lycophron is known to have written a number of tragedies, mostly on mythological subjects, the few surviving fragments of his work nearly all come from a satyric drama lampooning the contemporary philosopher Menedemus of Eretria and his circle. He was commissioned to write a treatise *On Comedy* as an aid to the arrangement of the comedies in the Library. See Pfeiffer, *op. cit.*, 141-142; Easterling and Knox, *op. cit.*, 1026-1027.
40. See pp. 75-77.
41. G. Kaibel (ed.), *Comicorum Graecorum*

Fragmenta, Berlin 1899, 19. The meaning of the terms 'composite' and 'unmixed' has been discussed at length by T. Birt in his book *Das antike Buchwesen*, Berlin 1882, 484, 490. F. Schmidt (*Die Pinakes des Kallimachos*, Kiel 1924, 37-38) arrived at a different conclusion from Birt, namely that a 'composite' roll was one containing more than one work by the same or different authors, while an 'unmixed' roll contained a single work or part thereof: this seems a more reasonable interpretation. There is good evidence to suggest that by the Hellenistic period, if not before, there already existed books (i.e. papyrus rolls) containing more than one complete work: see Diog. Laer., VI.15: 'The surviving works [of Antisthenes] are in ten volumes. The first contains: *On Expression, or Styles of Speaking*; *Ajax, or The Speech of Ajax*; *The Defence of Orestes*; etc., etc.' See also E. G. Turner, *Athenian Books in the Fifth and Fourth Centuries B.C.*, London 1952, 15; F. G. Kenyon, *Books and Readers in Ancient Greece and Rome*, Oxford 1951, 50 ff.

42. It was called the *Scholium Plautinum* by F. Osann, who discovered the Plautus manuscript in the Collegio Romano in 1819. It was Dindorf who first suggested that the mysterious author 'Caecius' was to be identified with Tzetzes: see W. J. W. Koster, 'Scholium Plautinum plene editum', *Mnemosyne*, 4th ser., 14 (1961) 23 ff. On this worthless Latin adaptation see also Wendel, 'Tzetzes'.
43. See H. I. Bell, *Cults and Creeds in Graeco-Roman Egypt*, Liverpool 1953, 18 ff.
44. See A. Rowe, *The Discovery of the Famous Temple and Enclosure of Sarapis at Alexandria* [*Annales du Service des Antiquités de l'Égypte*, Suppl. 12], Cairo 1946. On subsequent discoveries see P. M. Fraser, 'Two Studies on the Cult of Sarapis in the Hellenistic World', in *Opuscula Atheniensia*, III, Lund 1960, 1-54.
45. Epiphanius of Salamis, a Greek ecclesiastical writer from Judaea, lived in the fourth century. He entered the monastic life in Egypt at an early age, subsequently founded a monastery in his birthplace, of which he was the abbot, and from 367 was Bishop of Constantia (Salamis) in Cyprus.
46. Aphthonius of Antioch, a pupil of Libanius, taught rhetoric in Athens in the fourth century. His *Progymnasmata* (speeches written as exercises for his students) are lost, but they were very influential in the Byzantine period.
47. Epiphanius, *On Weights and Measures* (*PG* 43, 256): '... in the first library, built in the Bruchium. Later, a second library was founded in the Serapeum: it was smaller than the first and was called the daughter library, and in it were kept the writings of Aquila, Symmachus and Theodotion and others, two hundred and fifty years on.'
48. Aphthonius, *Progymnasmata* (ed. H. Rabe, *Rhetores Graeci*, X, Leipzig 1926, 40): 'Chambers are built in the stoas. Some are storerooms for books: they are open to those who are keen to study, and they induce the whole city to acquire learning. Others are established in honour of the ancient gods.'
49. Rufinus, *Ecclesiastical History*, II.23-30; Socrates, *Ecclesiastical History*, V.16; Sozomenus, *Ecclesiastical History*, VII.15; Theodoretus, *Ecclesiastical History*, V.22.
50. See p. 237 (n. 83).
51. The *Lives* (*Vitae*) of the scholars and poets mentioned in the *Onomatologos* of Hesychius and in *Souda* were published by A. Westermann in his *Vitarum Scriptores Graeci*, Braunschweig 1845.
52. On Zenodotus see Westermann, *op. cit.*, 369.
53. The problems arising in connection with the post of librarian and the use of the term *bibliophylax* are discussed at length in Fraser, *Ptolemaic Alexandria*, I, 320 ff.

See also E. G. Turner, *Ἑλληνικοί πάπυροι: Εἰσαγωγή στή μελέτη καί τή χρήση τῶν παπυρικῶν κειμένων* (= *Greek Papyri: An Introduction*, Oxford 1968, tr. G. M. Parasoglou), Athens 1981, 180, 190-191.

54. On Zenodotus's editing of Homer see Pfeiffer, *op. cit.*, 124 ff.
55. See Kaibel, *Comicorum...*, 24.
56. See pp. 76-77.
57. See p. 192.
58. See Fraser, *Ptolemaic Alexandria*, II, 447-448.
59. See Pfeiffer, *op. cit.*, 167 ff.
60. On Apollonius's relations with his teacher see E. Eichgrün, *Kallimachos und Apollonios Rhodios* (doctoral dissertation), Berlin 1961, 279.
61. See *Souda*, s.v. Callimachus: 'Ibis (this is a poem deliberately made obscure and abusive, addressed to one Ibis, who was an enemy of Callimachus: he was in fact Apollonius, who wrote the *Argonautica*).'
62. See Pfeiffer, *op. cit.*, 181 ff.
63. See R. C. Archibald, 'The Cattle Problem of Archimedes', *American Mathematic Monthly* 25 (1918) 411-414; B. L. van der Waerden, *Science Awakening*, Groningen: Noordhoff, 1954, 208.
64. See n. 23 above.
65. See Pfeiffer, *op. cit.*, 204 ff.
66. The normal practice was for a new Director of the Library to take over on the death of his predecessor, but it is not known whether Eratosthenes, who was eighty when he died, held the post until his death.
67. See p. 167.
68. Comedy was defined by the Peripatetics as 'the imitation of life': see Pfeiffer, *op. cit.* 227. See A. Rostagni, 'I Bibliotecari Alessandrini', in his *Scritti minori*, I, Turin 1955, 230, 339.
69. See K. Ziegler, 'Plagiat', in *RE*, 20/2 (1950), 1956-1957 and, on Aristophanes of Byzantium, col. 1979.
70. *Souda*: 'Having been prepared to consider going to Eumenes, he was thrown into prison.' It is in connection with this episode that the name of Pergamum makes its first appearance in the history of literary studies.
71. Pliny, *Natural History*, VIII.13; Plutarch, *Moralia*, 972 D (*On Intelligence in Animals*).
72. Aelian, *On the Nature of Animals* VII.43, XIII.8. The Ptolemies were animal-lovers, and two of them (Philadelphus and Euergetes II) had their own private zoos, but whether that fact has any relevance to the story of the flower-loving elephants is hard to say. Diodorus Siculus (III.36) has a passage about the capture of a large snake for Ptolemy Philadelphus and adds that the king was always keen to obtain rare animals in order to study their habits.
73. A. Rostagni ('I Bibliotecari Alessandrini', in his *Scritti minori*, II.1, Turin 1956, 185 ff.) makes a case for putting Apollonius Eidographus as the next Director of the Library after Eratosthenes.
74. On the meaning of the word *eidos*, from which the epithet Eidographus is derived, see *Μέγα Ἐτυμολογικόν*, ed. Fredericus Sylburgius, Heidelberg, Hieronymus Commelinus, 1594, col. 295.
75. On the musical modes see C. von Jan (ed.), *Musici Scriptores Graeci*, Leipzig 1895, 308 ff.
76. See Pfeiffer, *op. cit.*, 251 ff.
77. According to *Souda* he had about forty pupils.
78. Athenaeus, I.21.
79. See Strabo, XVII.C.795; Plutarch, *Coriolanus*, XI.
80. Pap. Oxy. 1241, II.16. M. Launey, in his paper 'Recherches sur les armées hellénistiques', *Bibliothèque des Écoles Françaises d'Athènes et de Rome* 169 (1949/50) 273, 1163, identifies Cydas as a Cretan on the strength of his name. See also Fraser, *Ptolemaic Alexandria*, II, 491.

81. *FGrHist*, 234 F 11.
82. Pap. Oxy. 1241, II.17 ff. On the identity of these four grammarians see Fraser, *Ptolemaic Alexandria*, II, 391-392. It is interesting to note that Diocles and Apollodorus are given as the names of the two benefactors who endowed a library on Rhodes or more probably on Cos, in an inscription of the second century B.C.: see p. 260.
83. T. B. Mitford, 'The Hellenistic Inscriptions of Old Paphos', *BSA* 56 (1961) 40, No. 110: 'The city of the Paphians [dedicates] to Paphian Aphrodite [this statue of] Onesander, son of Nausicrates, royal "Kinsman", priest for life of the divine king Ptolemy Soter and of the sanctuary of the Ptolemaeum founded by him, Secretary of the city of the Paphians and Director (*tetagmenos*) of the Great Library in Alexandria.' G. Pasquali takes the view that Onesander was 'vice-librarian', meaning that he did not perform his duties as Librarian in Alexandria but simply held the honorary title while living in Cyprus: see *Enciclopedia Italiana*, s.v. 'Biblioteca', p. 943. This may explain why his name does not appear in the Oxyrrhynchus papyrus.
84. See Pfeiffer, *op. cit.*, 146-180; A. Lesky, *Ἱστορία τῆς ἀρχαίας Ἑλληνικῆς Λογοτεχνίας* (= *Geschichte der griechischen Literatur*, Bern 1957/58, tr. A. G. Tsopanaki), Thessaloniki 1983, 968-991; Easterling and Knox, *op. cit.*, 1029 (for up-to-date bibliography). See also R. Pfeiffer, *Callimachus*, 2 vols., Oxford 1949-1953; Fraser, *Ptolemaic Alexandria*, I, 717-793 ('The Horizon of Callimachus').
85. See p. 174.
86. Recent excavations in Mesopotamia have brought to light dozens of archival libraries dating from as far back as the Sumerian era. Not only have thousands of clay tablets been discovered intact, but in many cases, as at Ebla and Nippur, their relative positions in the archive rooms have given us a good idea of how they were classified and arranged. See K. R. Veenhof (ed.), *Cuneiform Archives and Libraries [Uitgaven van het Nederlands Historisch-Archaeologisch Instituut te Istanbul* 57], Leiden 1986; and for a general review of libraries in the Near East before the Alexandrian Library see D. T. Potts, 'Before Alexandria: Libraries in the Ancient Near East', in MacLeod, *The Library of Alexandria*, 19-33.
87. The source of the information that Callimachus compiled the *Pinakes* is once again Tzetzes, who says, '... and Callimachus later wrote up the tables of [the books].' On the figure of 120 books of *Pinakes* see the biographical notes on Callimachus in Hesychius and *Souda*.
88. On the *Pinakes* see F. Schmidt, *Die Pinakes des Kallimachos*, Kiel 1924; Wendel, 'Das griechisch-römische Altertum', 69 ff.; O. Regenbogen, «Πίναξ» in *RE*, 20 (1950), 1423-1438; P. Moraux, *Les listes anciennes des ouvrages d'Aristote*, Louvain 1951, 221 ff.
89. See R. P. Oliver, 'The First Medicean MS of Tacitus and the Titulature of Ancient Books', *TAPA* 82 (1951) 232 ff.
90. See A. Blanchard and A. Bataille (eds.), 'Fragments sur papyrus du *Sikyonios* de Ménandre', *Recherches de Papyrologie* 3 (1964) 161 (Pap. Sorb. 2272, col. XXI, Pl. XIII).
91. See Chapter V.
92. See p. 171.
93. Aulus Gellius, *Noctes Atticae*, VII.XVII.3: 'Subsequently an enormous quantity of books, nearly seven hundred thousand volumes, was either acquired or written [i.e. copied from other manuscripts] in Egypt under the kings known as the Ptolemies; but these were all burnt when the city was sacked during the first Alexandrian War, not intentionally or by anyone's order, but accidentally by the auxiliary soldiers.'
94. See p. 173.

95. See p. 110.
96. J. La Roche, *Die homerische Textkritik im Alterthum*, Leipzig 1866, 18 ff.; Fraser, *Ptolemaic Alexandria*, II, 483 (n. 163).
97. According to Galen, the use of Mnemon of Side's name to identify the papyrus is capable of being interpreted in three different ways. Some authorities on the subject maintain that Mnemon borrowed from the Library a copy of Book III of *On Epidemics* by Hippocrates, which he returned with annotations that he had made on the text. Others assert that Mnemon had brought the copy in question with him from Pamphylia, that it had been appropriated for the Library under the terms of Ptolemy's decree, and that he had been given a new copy in its place. The third explanation is that the identification tag meant simply that it had belonged to Mnemon.

    Galen, *Commentary I on Hippocrates 'On Epidemics' III* (XVII a 605-606): 'Some say that [Mnemon] borrowed from the Great Library of Alexandria the third book of Hippocrates *On Epidemics*, which he wanted to read, and that he returned it with additions that he had made using a similar kind of ink and similar handwriting to the original. Others say that he had brought that copy, already annotated, with him from Pamphylia, and that Ptolemy, the then king of Egypt, who had a passion for acquiring books, had ordered it to be confiscated: for he had ordered that all books on ships arriving in Alexandria were to be brought to him and copied into new books, and that the copies were to be given to the owners whose books had been brought to him on their arrival, while the originals were to be deposited in the library: these were labelled "From the ships". They say that one such was the third book of *On Epidemics*, which was inscribed "From the ships, emended by Mnemon of Side". And others say that the inscription did not refer to the person who had emended it, but that it simply gave the name of Mnemon, for in the same way the king's servants wrote the owners' names in all the other books arriving by sea, because the books were not usually taken straight to the library but were first stored temporarily in other buildings, piled up in heaps.'
98. For a brief review of the subject see L. D. Reynolds and N. G. Wilson, *Ἀντιγραφεῖς καί Φιλόλογοι: Τό ἱστορικό τῆς παράδοσης τῶν κλασικῶν κειμένων* (= *Scribes and Scholars: A guide to the transmission of Greek and Latin literature*, 2nd edn., London 1975, tr. N. M. Panayotakis), Athens 1981, 26-32; Turner, *Ἑλληνικοί Πάπυροι*, 152 ff.; E. Mioni, *Εἰσαγωγή στήν Ἑλληνική Παλαιογραφία* (= *Introduzione alla Paleografia Greca*, Padua 1973, tr. N. M. Panayotakis), Athens 1977, 45-53.
99. See pp. 160-161.
100. Manetho was a major figure in Ptolemaic intellectual life, of particular significance in that he was the first Egyptian to write in Greek. Although there is no firm evidence that he spent most of his life in Alexandria, he certainly knew the work of Greek historians, probably including Hecataeus: see Fraser, *Ptolemaic Alexandria*, I, 505-509.
101. Berossus probably wrote his history between 280 and 261 B.C. On the school of astrology he is said to have opened on Cos, see Fraser, *Ptolemaic Alexandria*, II, 728 (n. 96).
102. Callimachus's pupil Hermippus of Smyrna was the main source used by Diogenes Laertius (V.78) in writing his lives of the Peripatetic philosophers. The only authority for the allegation that Hermippus embarked on such a project is Pliny the Elder (*Natural History* XXX.4): 'Hermippus, a most studious writer about every aspect of magic, and an exponent

of two million verses composed by Zoroaster, added summaries too to his rolls.' [The word *index*, translated here as 'summary', might be a mere title or a brief list of contents, or both.]

103. On the pseudo-Eratosthenic list of Egyptian kings given by Synkellos, see *FGrHist* 244 (Apollodorus), F 85: *ὧν τὴν γνῶσίν φησιν ὁ Ἐρατοσθένης λαβὼν ἐν Αἰγυπτιακοῖς ὑπομνήμασι <σὺν> καὶ ὀνόματι κατὰ πρόσταξιν βασιλικὴν τῆς Ἑλλάδι φωνῆς περίφρασιν οὕτως.* Cf. Fraser, *Ptolemaic Alexandria*, II, 487 (n. 182).

104. Synkellos, 516.3: 'After Ptolemy the son of Lagus was killed by lightning (as already mentioned) in the battle with the Galatians, the Egyptian throne passed to his son Ptolemy Philadelphus, a man of great learning on every subject and an indefatigable worker. Philadelphus collected the books by all Greek writers as well as Chaldaeans, Egyptians and Romans, had the foreign works translated into Greek and amassed a hundred thousand books in the libraries he founded in Alexandria.'

105. On Tyrannio see p. 125.

106. See *Scriptores Historiae Augustae*, 'Gordianus', XVIII.2.

107. Pseudo-Plutarch, *Lives of Ten Orators* VII.841F. On the borrowing of the copies from Athens, see Galen, *Commentary II on Hippocrates 'On Epidemics'* III (XVII a 608): 'That that Ptolemy was very keen to acquire books is well attested by what he did to the Athenians. Having put down a deposit of fifteen talents of silver as security, he borrowed the works of Sophocles, Euripides and Aeschylus for the sole purpose of copying them, after which they were to be returned in good condition. He then made new copies on paper of the best quality, but he kept the copies he had borrowed from the Athenians and sent them the new copies he had made, asking them to keep the fifteen talents and to accept the new books in lieu of the old ones they had sent him. As for the Athenians, even if he had not sent them the new books but had kept the old ones, they would have been powerless to do anything else.... They therefore accepted the new copies and kept the silver.'

108. Galen thought that Plato believed *On the Nature of Mankind* to be genuine (Plato, *Phaedrus*, 270c-d) and that he must have been in a good position to know, since he lived at about the same time as Hippocrates's pupils. Galen himself, however, states that *On the Nature of Mankind* was by Polybus (Hippocrates's pupil and son-in-law), not by the master himself; and he continues (*Commentary on Hippocrates 'On the Nature of Mankind'* II [XV 105]): 'Moreover, Plato was almost a contemporary of Hippocrates's pupils, and among them the name of the person who owned a book was written as if it were the name of the author. Before the time of the kings of Alexandria and Pergamum who were avid collectors of old books, a written work was never falsely attributed. But when people who brought them books by old writers started being paid, they brought a great many books with false ascriptions. But those kings lived after Alexander's death, whereas Plato had written the titles of works before Alexander's reign, and in those days the titles and ascriptions were never falsified: the name of the actual author was given in the front matter of each book.'

109. Olympiodorus, *Prolegomena* (*CIAG*, XII.1, p. 13): *ἐνοθεύοντο τοίνυν τὰ βιβλία τὸ παλαιὸν κατὰ τρεῖς τρόπους· ἢ διὰ φιλοτιμίαν τῶν βασιλέων ἢ διὰ εὔνοιαν τῶν μαθητῶν ἢ διὰ ὁμωνυμίαν. ἀλλ εἰ δοκεῖ μάθωμεν πῶς τὸ τῶν βασιλέων φιλότιμον αἴτιον ἦν τοῦ τὰς βίβλους νοθεύεσθαι. ἰστέον τοίνυν ὅτι οἱ παλαιοὶ βασιλεῖς ἐρασταὶ ὄντες λόγων ἔσπευδον διὰ φιλοτι-*

μίας συναγαγεῖν τὰ τῶν ἀρχαίων συγγράμματα, οὕτως οὖν Ἰοβάτης ὁ τῆς Λιβύης βασιλεὺς ἐραστὴς ἐγένετο τῶν Πυθαγορικῶν συγγραμμάτων καὶ Πτολεμαῖος ὁ ἐπίκλην Φιλάδελφος τῶν Ἀριστοτελικῶν καὶ Πεισίστρατος ὁ τῶν Ἀθηναίων τύραννος τῶν Ὁμηρικῶν <καὶ> χρημάτων δωρεαῖς ἔσπευδον ταῦτα συναγαγεῖν πολλοὶ οὖν χρημάτων ὀρεγόμενοι ἔσπευδον ἢ συγγράψασθαι ἤγουν καὶ τὰ τυχόντα συναγαγεῖν καὶ ἐπιγράφειν τοῖς τῶν ἀρχαιοτέρων ὀνόμασι καὶ προσφέρειν καὶ καρποῦσθαι δωρεὰς διὰ τούτου μνηστευόμενον. καὶ συνέβαινε, ὡς προείπομεν, νοθεύεσθαι τὰ βιβλία <Ἔσθ ὅτε> διὰ φιλοτιμίαν βασιλέως.

110. Philoponus (*Commentary on Aristotle's 'Categories'*, *CIAG*, XIII.1) gives three reasons for the misattribution and forging of works supposedly by Aristotle: 'There has been more than one person called Aristotle.... His pupils Eudemus and Phanias and Theophrastus wrote books entitled "Categories" and "On Interpretation" and "Analytica", following their teacher's example.... And the third reason is that Ptolemy Philadelphus is said to have been very keen on Aristotle's writings and other writings as well, and to have given money to anyone who brought him any work by Aristotle; and consequently there were some who, to make money, attached the philosopher's name to books which they then brought to him.'

111. Elias, *On the 'Categories'* (*CIAG*, XVIII.1): 'Consequently one has to seek out the authentic text because of the corruptions. For forgeries and spurious writings can come into being in five ways. It may be that pupils ascribe their own works to their teachers out of gratitude, as in the case of the books that are said to be by Pythagoras but are actually by Socratics or Pythagoreans. Or it may be due to the vanity of kings: since King Iobates of Libya collected the works of Pythagoras, and Ptolemy those of Aristotle, there were some people who, to make money, took any manuscripts they happened to find and made them look worn and decayed so that the patina of age would make them appear authentic. Or it may be due to the existence of two or more authors with the same name or books with the same title. For example, the Stagirite Aristotle was not the only person of that name: there were other Aristotles as well, such as the gymnastics teacher nicknamed Mythos, and later the teacher Alexander, who was like a second Aristotle, and the writings of all those others are thought to be by the Stagirite.'

112. Marcellinus, *Life of Thucydides*, 31-34.

113. *Ibid.*, 33-34: 'I myself think Zopyrus is talking nonsense when he says that Thucydides died in Thrace, even if Cratippus does believe it to be true. And it is utterly ridiculous to maintain, as he and others do, that Timaeus is buried in Italy.' Thucydides's unfinished *History* was quickly followed by a rash of 'continuations' and imitations. Xenophon's *Hellenica* starts exactly where Thucydides leaves off, in 411 B.C., and was continued first by Cratippus of Athens (*Hellenica*?), who carried on the narrative probably to 394, and then by Theopompus (*Hellenica*, in twelve books).

114. For an analytical account of the Alexandrian War and the effects of the siege on the city of Alexandria, see P. Graindor, *La guerre d'Alexandrie. Receuil de travaux publiés par la Faculté des Lettres (septième fascicule)*, Cairo 1931.

115. Aulus Hirtius was Julius Caesar's chief of staff (*ca.* 54 B.C.), praetor (46 B.C.) and finally, having been appointed proconsul (45 B.C.), governor of Gaul. At Caesar's prompting he wrote a polemic against Cato, and after Caesar's death he set out to complete his memoirs. Hirtius

wrote a record of the events of 51-50 B.C. which was incorporated as Book VIII of Caesar's *Commentarii de bello Gallico*.

116. Seneca, *De animi tranquillitate*, IX.5: 'Forty thousand books were burnt at Alexandria. Let someone else praise this library as the most noble monument to the wealth of kings, as did Titus Livius, who says that it was the most distinguished achievement of the good taste and solicitude of kings.' It is not certain whether Seneca wrote 'forty thousand' (*quadraginta milia*) or 'four hundred thousand' (*quadringenta milia*).

117. Plutarch, *Caesar*, XLIX.3: *δεύτερον δὲ περικοπτόμενος τὸν στόλον ἠναγκάσθη διὰ πυρὸς ἀπώσασθαι τὸν κίνδυνον, ὃ καὶ τὴν μεγάλην βιβλιοθήκην ἐκ τῶν νεωρίων ἐπινεμόμενον διέφθειρε.*

118. Gellius, VII.XVII.3: 'Subsequently an enormous quantity of books, nearly seven hundred thousand volumes, was either acquired or written [i.e. copied from other manuscripts] in Egypt under the kings known as the Ptolemies; but these were all burnt when the city was sacked during the first Alexandrian War, not intentionally or by anyone's order, but accidentally by the auxiliary soldiers.'

119. Dio Cassius, *Roman History*, XLII.38.2: *πολλὰ δὲ καὶ κατεπίμπρατο, ὥστε ἄλλα τε καὶ τὸ νεώριον τάς τε ἀποθήκας καὶ τοῦ σίτου καὶ τῶν βίβλων, πλείστων δὴ καὶ ἀρίστων, ὥς φασι, γενομένων, καυθῆναι.*

120. Ammianus Marcellinus, XXII.16.13: 'In this there were invaluable libraries; and, according to the unanimous testimony of old records, seven hundred thousand books collected by the unremitting energy of the Ptolemaic kings were burnt in the Alexandrian War, when the city was sacked under the dictator Caesar.'

121. Orosius, *Historiae adversus paganos*, VI.15.31-32: 'In the battle itself, the royal fleet, which happened to be drawn up on shore, was ordered to be burnt. The fire, when it spread to part of the city, burnt four hundred thousand books which happened to be stored in a building nearby: that was a remarkable monument to the zeal and interest of our ancestors who had collected so many works – and such great works – by men renowned for their learning. In this connection, although today there exist in the temples bookcases which I myself have seen and which I am told were emptied by our own men in our own time when these temples were plundered (and this is the truth), nevertheless it is believed more honourably that other books were collected to emulate the ancient interest in studies, rather than that there was at that time another library which was separate from the four hundred thousand books and consequently escaped destruction.

122. See p. 187.

123. See Chapter V.

124. Marcus Terentius Varro (116-27 B.C.) was noted for his wide learning, good taste and original mind. Politician and soldier, poet, historian and orator, he was a major figure in contemporary Roman life, as he introduced Greek research methods into Roman scholarship.

When one considers the extremely broad scope of his work, it is easy to see why he was chosen to write *De bibliothecis*, a book that may perhaps have dealt with the methods of librarianship in use in the great Hellenistic libraries, just when the idea of creating the first public library in Rome was on the point of coming to fruition. *De bibliothecis* is now lost.

125. Very little is known about the library started by Pollio. It formed part of a complex of public buildings in the Atrium Libertatis and consisted of separate Greek and Latin sections (Pliny, *Nat. Hist.*, VII.115, XXXV.10, XXXVI.33), as Cae-

sar had wished. As a personal friend of Mark Antony's, Pollio was able to move about freely in those dangerous times. Such was his love of literature that he retired from public life to devote himself to writing. He used his spoils from a campaign against the Parthians in Dalmatia to fund the building of the library, which was completed shortly after 39 B.C.

126. See p. 256.
127. See H. I. Bell, *Egypt from Alexander the Great to the Arab Conquest*, Oxford 1948, 65 ff.
128. We know from Ptolemaic tradition that even in the first century of Roman rule every nome had its own public library or public records office. In A.D. 72 these regional record offices were divided into 'archives of public documents and records' and 'archives of property records': see Turner, *Ἑλληνικοί πάπυροι*, 182.

    The public records system must have been very highly developed in the Hellenistic period, to judge by the official records that Alexander the Great insisted on keeping for the whole duration of his expedition. The story goes that most of those records, which were kept in the tent of Alexander's chief registrar, Eumenes of Cardia, were destroyed by fire, whereupon Alexander ordered new copies to be made from the copies kept by the satraps and from the military dispatches. See H. Berve, *Das Alexanderreich auf prosopographischer Grundlage*, II, Munich 1926, 156-158; on archives in Egypt in the Ptolemaic and Roman periods, see E. Posner, *Archives in the Ancient World*, Cambridge, Mass. 1972.
129. On the character of the Museum and the post of Master see p. 166.
130. See p. 241 (nn. 124-125).
131. Philo Judaeus, *Embassy to Gaius*, 151: 'For there is elsewhere no precinct like that which is called the Sebasteum, a temple to Caesar on shipboard, situated on an eminence facing the harbours famed for their excellent moorage, huge and conspicuous, fitted on a scale not found elsewhere with dedicated offerings, around it a girdle of pictures and statues in silver and gold, forming a precinct of vast breadth, embellished with porticoes, libraries, chambers, groves, gateways and wide open courts and everything which lavish expenditure could produce to beautify it – the whole a hope of safety to the voyager either going into or out of the harbour.' See also C. Wendel, *Kleine Schriften zum antiken Buch- und Bibliothekswesen*, ed. W. Krieg, Köln 1974, 149.
132. Suetonius, *Domitian* 20; *Claudius* 42. Claudius was an educated man who wrote (in Greek) histories of the Etruscans and the Carthaginians. In his honour the Museum was enlarged and public readings from his two history books were instituted, to be held on fixed dates each year in one of the Museum's lecture halls. Hadrian, a great book-lover and admirer of Greek learning, appointed his teacher L. Iulius Vestinus to be director of the Greek and Latin libraries in Rome and also Master of the Museum in Alexandria (*IG*, XIV 1085).
133. See Turner, *Ἑλληνικοί πάπυροι*, 108.
134. Two earlier instances of book-burning had been recorded in the history of the Mediterranean peoples: once in the case of Protagoras's books (see p. 88) and once under King Seleucus I (see p. 226, n. 9).
135. Pap. Faiyûm 87. On the philosophers of the Museum see Dio Cassius, LXXVII.7.3.
136. See Turner, *Ἑλληνικοί πάπυροι*, 121.
137. Pap. Oxy. 2471. After the postscript to this letter someone has added in a different hand: 'Harpocration says that Demetrius the bookseller has got them. I

have instructed Apollonides to send me some of my own books, which you will hear about in due course from Seleucus himself. If you find any, apart from those I already possess, have them copied and send them to me. Diodorus and his friends also have some that I haven't got.'

138. The first edition of the lexicon was published at Lyon in 1683, with notes by P. J. Maussaci and with Latin translation.
139. K. Ohly, 'Stichometrische Untersuchungen', *ZB*, Beiheft 61 (1928) 88-89.
140. A reference to the use of slaves for copying books exists from the Classical period (see p. 110), but that is the only time the subject is mentioned.
141. Ammianus Marcellinus, XXII.16.15.
142. E. Gibbon, *The History of the Decline and Fall of the Roman Empire*, II, London 1788, 462.
143. The earliest known official reference to books in New Rome (i.e. Constantinople) concerns the Emperor Constantine the Great, who ordered these fifty copies of the Scriptures on smooth vellum.
144. Turner, *Ἑλληνικοί πάπυροι*; Mioni, *Εἰσαγωγή...*, 45 ff. On the origins of the codex see A. Blanchard (ed.), *Les débuts du codex* [*Bibliologia* 9], Turnhout 1989, with introduction by Jean Irigoin. See also the bibliographical and critical article by J. Irigoin, 'Les manuscrits grecs 1931-1960', *Lustrum* 8 (1962) 287-302.
145. Pliny, *Natural History*, XIII.13.
146. See Turner, *Ἑλληνικοί πάπυροι*, 22-24; Mioni, *op. cit.*, 47.
147. C. H. Roberts, 'Books in the Graeco-Roman World and in the New Testament' in *The Cambridge History of the Bible*, I, Cambridge 1970, 48-66.
148. See Turner, *Ἑλληνικοί πάπυροι*, 30.
149. On the peculiarities of the script used in this document, see Turner, *Ἑλληνικοί πάπυροι*, 125, 130.
150. See W. Schubart, *Das Buch bei den Griechen und Römern*, Heidelberg 1962, 163 ff.; M. Norsa, *La scrittura letteraria greca*, Florence 1939, 23; Mioni, *op. cit.*, 51-53. The earliest known palimpsest is the fifth-century manuscript Parisinus gr. 9, where the original biblical text was rubbed out and overwritten with works by Ephraim the Syrian in the thirteenth century.
151. For further information about the owners of papyri in Alexandria see Turner, *Ἑλληνικοί πάπυροι*, 107-132, esp. 124 ff.
152. Socrates of Constantinople, *Ecclesiastical History*, VII.14.15. Cyril of Alexandria failed to have the Alexandrian philosophy school closed down. An interesting philosophical memorandum of the second half of the fifth century, on papyrus, tells us a good deal about the social pattern of general education: see Bell, *Egypt from Alexander...*, 116.
153. Eutychios, *Chronicle*, II.316 (ed. Pococke).
154. 'Abd al-Latîf (1160-1231) of Baghdad was an eminent physician and writer, and also a traveller who obtained letters of recommendation and set out to meet the most prominent contemporary men of letters and visit their workplaces. He was an exceptionally gifted man, and through his voracious reading he acquired a store of knowledge that enabled him, in his work as a practitioner and teacher of medicine, to correct Galen on certain points of anatomy. On his travels in Egypt see Abd al Latîf, *Relation de l'Égypte*, tr. Silvestre de Sacy, Paris 1810, 183.
155. See Ali ibn al-Qifṭī, *Kitab Ikhbar al-'Ulama bi-Akhbar al-Hukama*, in Ibn al-Qifṭī, *Ta'rih Al-Hukama*, ed. J. Lippert, Leipzig 1903, 1004.
156. It seems to me that the debate over whether this John Grammaticus is to be identified with John Philoponus, which if proved would undermine the credibility of Ibn al-Qifṭī's story, is not the crucial

issue, as John Philoponus certainly was a major figure on both the literary and political scene: he was a Neoplatonist and the author of numerous commentaries on Aristotle, whose philosophical system he used as the basis for his defence of Christian doctrine, and he was Bishop of Alexandria. See G. Furlani, 'Giovanni il Filopono e l'incendio della Biblioteca di Alessandria', *Bulletin de la Société Archéologique d'Alexandrie* 21 (1925) 59-68; M. Meyerhof, 'Joannes Grammatikos [Philoponos] von Alexandrien und die arabische Medizin', *Mitteilungen des deutsches Instituts für aegyptische Altertumskunde in Kairo* 2 (1932) 1-21; Canfora, *'Η Χαμένη Βιβλιοθήκη...*, 96-110; el-Abbadi, *'Η 'Αρχαία Βιβλιοθήκη...*, 192-194.

John Philoponus was born near the end of the fifth century and studied under Ammonius Hermeiou in Alexandria. He developed into one of the intellectual giants of his age, who influenced Islamic as well as Byzantine thinking and whose legacy was invaluable to natural scientists throughout the Middle Ages and right down to the time of Galileo. The date of his death is unknown, but it could not have been later than 567, over seventy years before the fall of Alexandria to the Arabs.

157. See A. Cameron, 'New Themes and Styles in Greek literature: Seventh-Eighth Centuries', in A. Cameron and L. I. Conrad (eds.), *The Byzantine and Early Islamic Near East*, Princeton 1992, 81-105.
158. Most of the secretaries in the Ummayad administration were descended from the Salihids, allies of the Byzantines who were Orthodox Christians. See I. Shahid, *Byzantium and the Arabs in the Fifth Century*, Washington, D. C. 1989, 304-306.
159. The chief spokesman for this anti-Byzantine and anti-Christian propaganda campaign, in its early stages, was al-Gāhiz, who went to live in Baghdad and spent most of his life there. See C. Pellat, *The Life and Works of Jāḥiz*, Berkeley/Los Angeles 1969, 5-9.
160. See D. Gutas, *'Η 'Αρχαία 'Ελληνική Σκέψη στόν 'Αραβικό Πολιτισμό. Τό κίνημα τῶν ἑλληνοαραβικῶν μεταφράσεων στή Βαγδάτη κατά τήν πρώιμη ἀββασίδικη περίοδο (205-405/8ος-10ος αἰώνας)*, Athens 2000, 75 ff.
161. See Gutas, *op. cit.*, 2.
162. On Aristotelian philosophy and the Arab world see M. Bouyges, *Averroès. Tafsir ma ba'd at tabi'at*, Beirut 1952; R. Arnaldez, 'L'histoire de la pensée grecque vue par les arabes', *Bulletin de la Société Française Philosophique* 72/3 (1978) 117-168; D. Gutas, *Avicenna and the Aristotelian Tradition*, Leiden/New York 1988; G. Endress, '"Der erste Lehrer". Der arabische Aristoteles und das Konzept der Philosophie im Islam', in U. Tworuschka (ed.), *Gottes ist der Orient, Gottes ist der Okzident*, Köln 1991, 151-181.
163. A variety of conflicting theories have been advanced concerning the significance and function of the House of Wisdom: see Y. Eche, *Les bibliothèques arabes publiques et semi-publiques en Mésopotamie, Syrie, Égypte au Moyen Âge*, Damascus 1967, 9-57; M. G. Balty-Guesdon, 'Le *Bayt al-hikma* de Baghdad', *Arabica* 39 (1992) 131-150; Gutas, *'Η 'Αρχαία 'Ελληνική...*, 75-85.
164. For a verdict on the credibility of this source (Theophanes Continuatus) with regard to the story about Leo, and the reasons for doubting that the episode ever took place, see P. Lemerle, *'Ο πρῶτος βυζαντινός οὑμανισμός: Σημειώσεις καί παρατηρήσεις γιά τήν ἐκπαίδευση καί τήν παιδεία στό Βυζάντιο ἀπό τίς ἀρχές ὥς τόν 10ο αἰώνα* (= *Le premier humanisme byzantin...*, tr. Maria Nystazopoulou-Pelekidou), Athens 1981, 129-153; N. G. Wil-

son, *Scholars of Byzantium*, Baltimore 1983, 79-80; D. Pingree, 'Classical and Byzantine Astrology in Sassanian Persia', *Dumbarton Oaks Papers* 43 (1989) 237.

165. 'Three days' journey from Constantinople, in the land of the Romans [i.e. Byzantines] there is an edifice with a huge door that is always locked. In the old days, when the Greeks worshipped idols and stars, this building was a far-famed temple. One day an Arab traveller with an inquiring mind came there and wanted to see inside the building. He therefore asked the Roman Emperor to open the door for him, but the Emperor refused, because it had remained closed since the time when the Romans embraced Christianity. But the traveller persisted with his request, and eventually the Emperor agreed to grant his wish. On his orders the huge door was unlocked and the traveller entered the building. Inside, among inscriptions and marble reliefs the like of which had never been seen before, was an unimaginably large collection of ancient books, some of them in an excellent state of preservation while others were worm-eaten. When the Arab traveller left, the door was firmly closed behind him.' See E. Arrigoni, 'Ecumenismo Romano-Cristiano a Bisanzio e tramonto del concetto di Ellade ed Elleni nell' impero d'Oriente prima del mille', *Nuova Rivista Storica* 55 (1971) 151.

166. Al-Hakim II, nicknamed al-Mostansir (or Montaser Billah), the ninth king of Granada and the second Ummayad caliph of Spain, was born early in the tenth century and died in 976.

167. On the size and contents of the French royal library from Charlemagne's time to 1800, see S. Balayé, *La Bibliothèque Nationale des origines à 1800*, Geneva 1988. On the library of the Monastery of St. John on Patmos, founded by St. Christodoulos, see Staikos, *The Great Libraries...*, 267-283.

168. Exactly when paper was first imported into Byzantium is not known. The new material was at first called *bagdatikos* ('from Baghdad') or, more often, *bambykios*, which probably denoted that it came from the town of Bambyce (Hierapolis), west of the Euphrates in northern Syria. See J. Irigoin, 'Les premiers manuscrits grecs écrits sur papier et le problème du bombycin', *Scriptorium* 4 (1950) 194-204; Id., 'Les débuts de l'emploi du papier à Byzance', *BZ* 46 (1953) 314-319. On the introduction of paper to the West see J. Irigoin, 'Les origines de la fabrication du papier en Italie', *Papiergeschichte* 13 (1963) 62-67; and esp. G. Piccard, 'Carta bombycina, carta papyri, pergamena graeca. Ein Beitrag zur Geschichte der Beschreibstoffe im Mittelalter', *Archivalische Zeitschrift* 61 (1965) 46-75.

IV

HELLENISTIC PERIOD

Other Libraries from Pergamum to Ai Khanoum

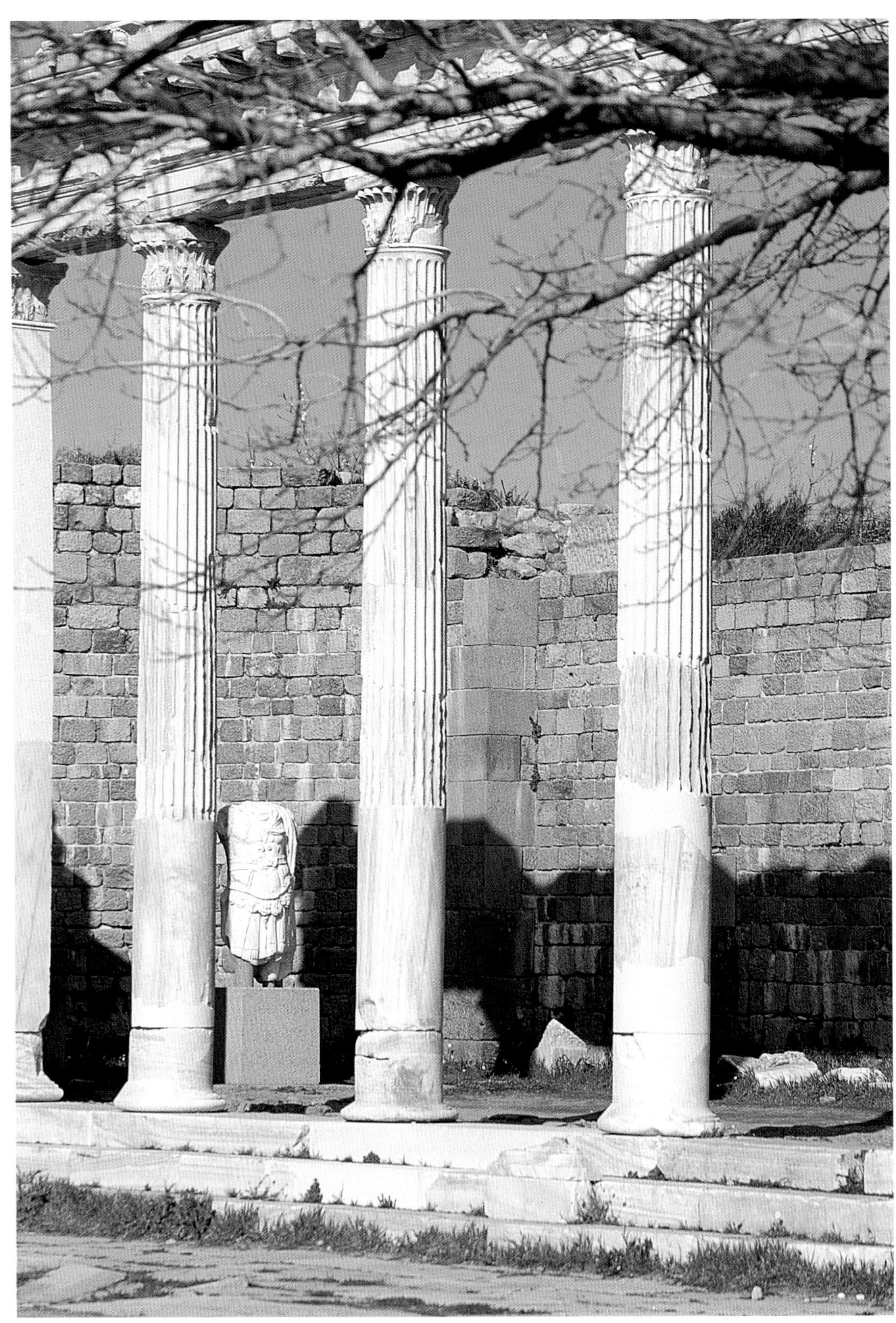

OTHER LIBRARIES IN THE HELLENISTIC PERIOD

From Pergamum to Ai Khanoum

The Great Library of Alexandria symbolized the city's intellectual supremacy in the then known world, and it was undoubtedly there that the most serious attempts were made to gather together and disseminate the works of 'every branch of learning' produced by the Greek and Near Eastern civilizations. Alexandria was also the birthplace of the discipline of literary studies and until the middle of the second century B.C. it led the way in the field of textual emendation, producing recensions of works written from the mythical era down to the end of the Classical period. However, the founding of great libraries and the growth of textual studies were characteristic features of other kingdoms also ruled by Alexander the Great's successors and of other intellectual centres with traditions going back to the Classical period,[1] many of which managed to remain administratively independent of the ambitious Macedonian kings. Two libraries are particularly worth mentioning for their importance to historians of books. One, at Pergamum, was founded by the Attalids, who tried for a long time to create a library rivalling that of the Ptolemies in Alexandria; the other, mainly archival, is significant because it was part of a Greek cultural centre at one of the most remote outposts of the Greek world, at Ai Khanoum in Bactria.

The kingdom of Pergamum. Pergamum, near the Asia Minor coast opposite Lesbos, was originally a hill fortress with the country around it. Forty years after the territorial war between Lysimachus and Seleucus in 282-281 B.C., it became the capital of a new kingdom. Pergamum belonged to Lysimachus, whose right-hand man, Philetaerus of Tieum, was responsible for the royal exchequer. When Lysimachus was killed, Philetaerus went over to Seleucus with the 9,000 talents from the exchequer and by adroit wire-pulling managed to carve out a virtually independent territory which he ruled from 281 to 263. His successor was Eumenes I (263-241), who stepped down in favour of Attalus I (241-197), the first king of Pergamum. Attalus and his eldest son and successor,

103. The restored portion of the Roman Traianeum on the acropolis of Pergamum. Photo: Dora Minaidi.

Eumenes II Soter (born 221, reigned 197-159), both enlarged their kingdom by repelling the marauding Galatians and, more importantly, winning territory from the Seleucids.[2] In fact, to secure their borders against the expansionary designs of Antiochus III, they allied themselves with the Romans; after the battle and treaty of Apamea (188 B.C.) the kingdom of Pergamum extended over the whole of Asia Minor and was, in a manner of speaking, the guardian of Rome's interests in the region. It now enjoyed the wholehearted support of Rome; but, against that, it had made itself indirectly dependent on that support. Nevertheless, despite becoming embroiled in the Macedonian Wars and having to cope with the machinations of the Romans, Eumenes II managed to retain his throne until his death in 159.

104. Head of Philetaerus, ruler of Pergamum and founder of the Attalid dynasty. Naples, Museo Archeologico Nazionale.

Eumenes was succeeded by his brother, Attalus II Philadelphus Euergetes (159-138 B.C.), who successfully kept the peace at home in spite of opposition to his pro-Roman policy. Although Attalus extended his sovereignty to the neighbouring kingdoms of Syria, Cappadocia and Bithynia, which were riven by civil wars, he turned Pergamum into a virtual Roman satellite state, thus preparing the way for its cession to Rome in 133 by Attalus III Philometor (138-133).

The foundation of the Library. The Pergamum Library was the most prestigious in the Hellenistic period after the Universal Library in Alexandria. Very little is known about its organization and its aims, but excavation has made it possible to reconstruct its architectural shell. It is the oldest library in the Greek world of which anything remains.

Attalus I, who initiated a programme of beautifying Pergamum with great works of art and monuments (such as the marble altar of Zeus Soter) and filling his court with eminent scholars and men of letters, was probably the originator of the idea of founding a library to rival that of the Ptolemies. He himself wrote a book on geography that was probably one of the sources used by

Strabo, and he would almost certainly have had a private library which may perhaps have formed the nucleus of Pergamum Royal Library. According to the sources, the founder of the Royal Library was his successor, Eumenes II, who acceded to the throne in 197 B.C. Like the Ptolemies, the Attalids tried to heighten the prestige of their library and ensure that it would function efficiently by associating it with a leading representative of Athenian academic life. Lacydes, who was head of Plato's Academy from 241/240 to 216/215, and Lycon, who inherited the Peripatetic school from Strato, both declined the invitation to Pergamum,[3] while Aristophanes of Byzantium, the Director of the Alexandrian

105. Pergamum: partial view of the terrace with the Temple of Athena and the Library. Photo: Dora Minaidi.

Library, was unable to go because Ptolemy V was determined to keep the scholars of the Museum in Alexandria, by force if necessary.[4] The only prominent scholar that Eumenes II managed to attract to take charge of the Library was the Stoic philosopher Crates of Mallus.[5]

To judge by the subsequent course of events, it would seem that the kings of Pergamum had no intention of competing with the Museum in the field of textual studies and literary research by setting up a school of poets and literary scholars to rival that of Alexandria. At Pergamum we do not find teachers being succeeded by their pupils, and it was as philosophers – predominantly orthodox Stoics – rather than as textual critics that the scholars of the Pergamum Library approached the literary tradition.

106. Head of Attalus I Soter, the first king of Pergamum. Berlin, Archaeological Museum.

The Library at its zenith. The high point in the history of the Pergamum Library, or rather the period about which we know most, is the reign of Eumenes II, its reputed founder. It would seem that Crates was the person who did most to enlarge the Library and was the prime mover in the field of textual studies at Pergamum.

Crates assists the development of parchment

Crates was born at Mallus in Cilicia and, according to *Souda*, was a contemporary of Aristarchus (second century B.C.). He studied under Diogenes of Seleucia and practised the allegorizing exegesis of poetry first advocated by the orthodox Stoics. The only one of his pupils to distinguish himself was the philosopher Panaetius. Crates's greatest achievement was to have introduced the Roman literati to the study of grammar during his prolonged stay in Rome in 168 B.C. He had gone there on a diplomatic mission from Eumenes II, but an accident immobilized him for several months and he stayed on, teaching and lecturing on poetry and grammar. Crates is said to have invented new methods

107. Reconstruction of the propylon leading in to the Temple of Athena and the Pergamum Library. Berlin, Pergamonmuseum.

ΒΑΣΙΛΕΥΣ ΕΥΜΕΝΗΣ ΑΘΗΝΑΙ ΝΙΚΗΦΟΡΩΙ

108. The statue of Athena that stood in the main room of the Pergamum Library. According to W. Hoepfner, she had an owl in her right hand and a spear in her left. Berlin, Pergamonmuseum.

of treating lambskin to produce a finer writing surface and to have advocated the promotion of exports to Rome. From that time on, skins prepared for writing on were called 'Pergamene', as John the Lydian (5th-6th centuries A.D.) informs us: 'The Romans call them "Pergamene skins".'[6] According to an ancient legend, parchment was 'invented' by the Pergamenes when Ptolemy V, Eumenes II's contemporary, prohibited the export of papyrus to Pergamum because of the jealous rivalry between the two great libraries.[7] Actually, however, animal skins had been used as writing materials well before that, first in the Near East and from the fifth century B.C. by the Greeks in Asia Minor, according to Herodotus.

Organization and textual studies. Nothing whatever is known about the organization and administration of the Pergamum Library. The only evidence we have for the existence of an official post of Director of the Library comes from Diogenes Laertius, who says (VII.34) that the position was held by a certain Athenodorus. This was Athenodorus Cordylion of Tarsus, a philosopher of the first century B.C. (when Pergamum was under Roman dominion), who lived in Rome with Cato of Utica from 70

B.C.[8] Athenodorus was caught tampering with the text of books in the Pergamum Library by deleting passages that he considered inconsonant with the teaching of the Stoics: for this he was taken to court and dismissed as Director of the Library.[9]

Artists, philosophers and grammarians at the Pergamene court

Already in Attalus I's reign (241-197) the sculptor and writer Antigonus of Carystus had come to Pergamum, where he made statues to immortalize Attalus's victories over the Galatians.[10] One of his books, *Lives of the Philosophers*, was an important work. At about the same time, towards the end of the third century B.C., the mathematician and astronomer Apollonius of Perge was teaching at Pergamum, and he dedicated seven of the eight books of his *Conics* to Attalos I.[11] Biton, a writer on engineering of the second century B.C., wrote a treatise entitled *Construction of Engines of War and Catapults*, which he dedicated to Attalus I, II or III. Polemon of Ilium, a traveller and geographer of the third and second centuries B.C., toured Greece, Sicily and Italy and wrote a book of antiquarian interest about the Athens Acropolis, the Sacred Way to Eleusis and the treasuries at Delphi, with a considerable amount of scientific detail.[12] Finally, Artemon of Cassandreia, a grammarian of the second or first century B.C., lived at Pergamum and wrote books about books: *Book Collecting* and *The Use of Books*, and perhaps some others about libraries.[13] Quite possibly his works were used by Varro in *De bibliothecis*, as Artemon was the only person we know of who wrote on such subjects.

Round about 145 B.C. – when many intellectuals including Aristarchus, the Director of the Library, had been driven out of Alexandria by Ptolemy VIII's persecution, a number of literary scholars decided to go and work with Crates at Pergamum. One of those was Apollodorus of Athens, and Menecleus of Barce may have been another.[14]

The Pinakes *of the Pergamum Library*

When the Library was being organized, a catalogue, again entitled *Pinakes*, was compiled. These anonymous *Pinakes*, now lost, are rarely mentioned by ancient writers: only once in connection with the work of a comic playwright and twice with reference to orators. Clearly they were in no way comparable to the *Pinakes* compiled by Callimachus in Alexandria.[15] Athenaeus, for example, quotes a passage from a comedy by Alexis entitled *The Teacher of Profligacy*, taken from a source that he describes as reliable, but says that he has not been able to find a single copy of the play, even though he has read and quoted from eight hundred plays of the Middle Comedy; and he adds that he has not found the play listed anywhere in the *Pinakes* of Callimachus and Aristophanes of Byzantium or in the *Pinakes* of the Pergamum Library.[16]

The problem of pseudepigraphy. The feverish haste with which the Attalids sought to obtain as many rare and valuable books as possible is first attested by Strabo, who informs us that Neleus's heirs had had to hide the original manuscripts of Aristotle and Theophrastus in a cave to keep them out of the grasping hands of the kings of Pergamum.[17] The problem of forged and spurious works is treated in some detail by Galen, who was an expert on anything to do with books.[18] He informs us, for example, that the Pergamenes bought a copy of the *Orations* of Demosthenes which appeared to be more complete than the one in Alexandria since it contained a 'new' Philippic which Demosthenes had delivered a few months before the battle of Chaeronea and, even more remarkably, a letter from Philip to the Athenians. However, this last anomaly seems not to have aroused the Pergamene scholars' suspicions,[19] and so the new Pergamene edition of the *Orations* was believed to be authentic until further examination of the books in the Alexandrian Library revealed that the 'new' Philippic was not new at all: it already existed in Book VII of the *Philippica* by Anaximenes of Lampsacus.[20]

Expansion of the Library. The only information we have about the size of the Attalids' library is a solitary reference in Plutarch's *Life of Antony*, and Plutarch himself expresses reservations about its reliability because its source, a certain Calvisius (Calvisius Sabinus?) was hostile to Mark Antony.[21] Antony is said to have given Cleopatra 200,000 volumes from the Library at Pergamum, and many scholars take the view that the gift was connected with the burning of the Universal Library when Caesar was under siege in 47 B.C. No other historian mentions the story of Calvisius – not even the great Galen, a very prolific writer who was a native of Pergamum, nor his fellow-citizen Telephus, a grammarian, as far as we know from the little that *Souda* tells us about him.[22]

The size of the Library

Ai Khanoum. The 'archival library' in the palace of Ai Khanoum, in Bactria, has a section to itself not so much because it was the farthest-flung outpost of the Greek world, in the heart of the Buddhist Orient, as because it is the oldest library in which Greek literary works have been found.

Ai Khanoum, in the north-east of Afghanistan, was one of the many kingdoms through which the Silk Road ran. French archaeologists excavated a city dating from the third century B.C. in which they discovered a gymnasium, a theatre and a sanctuary dedicated to the city's founder. There was even a stele with a large collection of Delphic sayings inscribed on its base by the Peripatetic philosopher Clearchus of Soli, proving that Ai Khanoum kept closely in touch with the traditional centres of the Greek world.

A library in Bactria

The 'archival library'[23] in the palace was founded by King Eucratides, a contemporary of the Parthian king Mithradates I (second century B.C.). The salient feature of the palace complex was a square peristyle courtyard with a door on one side leading into a smaller court: opening on to the latter were several rooms used as shops, some of them selling luxury goods, which led the French archaeologists to describe the shops collectively as 'the treasury'. Between the two courtyards there was a small oblong room used as an 'archival library': not a public library, nor yet a library for academic study and research, but a royal archive that was an integral part of the palace. There the excavators found many scattered pieces of papyrus and parchment inscribed with fragments of philosophical dialogues and one play. The most remarkable thing about this room was the method used for storing the documents, for there was no trace of bookcases of any kind attached to, or built into, the walls, but only sherds of earthenware storage jars strewn on the floor.[24] This shows that the librarians kept their papyrus rolls in jars of the kind that were used in 'archival libraries' in Egypt.[25]

109. Silver tetradrachms with effigies of Eucratides I, whom Strabo called 'king of a thousand cities' (ca. *170-145* B.C.).

Other libraries in the Hellenistic period. The most important of the other libraries, after Pergamum, was perhaps the one at Antioch, the capital of the Seleucid kingdom of Syria. It was probably founded in the reign of Antiochus I (224/3-188/7 B.C.) and appears to have been a public library.[26] The only evidence for this is the implication in *Souda* that Euphorion of Chalcis, a poet of the third century B.C., was Antiochus III's librarian: 'He came to Antiochus the Great ... and was appointed by him to be in charge of the public library there.' His period of office is dated to *circa* 220 B.C.

Euphorion, born in 275 B.C., studied first in Athens (under Lacydes at the Academy) and then in Antioch. His poetic style is very mannered, and a group of later Greek and Roman poets – Nicander of Colophon and Parthenius of Nicaea, Catullus and other members of the group of *neoterici* (New Poets) who imitated him – were derisively called *cantores Euphorionis* by Cicero. Euphorion made use of the heritage of earlier Greek poetry and, perhaps in the course of the Library's programme of literary and textual studies, prepared new recensions of numerous poetry collections, with glossaries. During his term as Director of the Library he wrote a number of learned works (of which only scanty fragments have survived), including *Historical Commentaries* and a Hippocratic lexicon.[27]

The Seleucids' library

110. Silver tetradrachm with an effigy of Seleucus I of Antioch or Alexander the Great on the obverse and Victory laying a wreath on a trophy on the reverse (ca. *300* B.C.).

Thanks to the cultivation of literature and the trade in books, Antioch appears to have established itself as a major book centre. Early Christian writers rank it with Carthage, Alexandria and Constantinople as one of the best markets,[28] and no less a person than the Byzantine Emperor Julian 'the Apostate' (361-363) chose Antioch as the home for the scattered library of his teacher George of Cappadocia,[29] which he housed in the Temple of Trajan. *Souda* states that the temple and library were burnt down by the Antiochene mob in the reign of Julian's Christian successor.

On the evidence to be gleaned from reliable sources, it would seem that libraries – literary as well as archival – were generally attached to palaces. When the Roman general Aemilius Paullus defeated King Perseus of Macedon in 168 B.C., he took the contents of Perseus's library back to Rome with him. Plutarch (*Aemilius Paullus*, XXVIII) informs us that he then gave 'the king's books' to his sons, who were devoted to learning. The young Publius Aemilius, who was adopted into the cultured family of Publius Cornelius Scipio (the son of Scipio Africanus Major) and took the name of Scipio Aemilianus, was thus brought into contact with Greek historians and philosophers living in Rome.[30] It is therefore quite likely that he not only kept the books his father had given to him but added to them, as his collection subsequently became the nucleus of Rome's first public library, founded by Pollio shortly after 39 B.C.[31] Lucullus, too, after his victorious campaign against Mithradates VI of Pontus in the first century B.C., brought the defeated king's books back with him as his spoils of war. Among them was a case full of medical textbooks, which Pompey appropriated for himself and had translated into Latin.[32]

Gymnasium libraries. Besides the great public, royal and academic libraries, there was one other important category: the libraries in gymnasia. Gymnasia existed for the purpose of educating the young: it is a well-attested fact that young men went there not only for athletic training but also for education in what we would nowadays call the humanities, namely grammar, music, rhetoric and philosophy.[33]

A model educational institution

One such educational establishment was the Pompeion, a building between the Dipylon and the Sacred Gate at the north-western edge of Athens, excavated by Wolfram Hoepfner.[34] The name of the Pompeion is derived from the word *pompe* (procession), because it was from there that the solemn procession set off for the Acropolis in the Great Panathenaea festival. It was built at a time of austerity in Athens, *circa* 400 B.C., just after the Athenians' humiliating defeat by the Spartans in the Peloponnesian War. To strengthen the city's human resources by building up a reserve of young men with good all-round schooling – not only military training but an education in academic subjects and the arts as well – the institution of *ephebeia* was introduced by Thrasybulus. The ephebes, as they were called, were men aged from eighteen to twenty: on reaching their eighteenth birthday they were entered in the official roll of citizens and started compulsory military service.

The benches along the side walls of the Pompeion served as desks for the ephebes, who often scratched their names on the stone to mark their places. The institution of *ephebeia* had the desired effect of strengthening the Athenian state, as the school turned out four hundred freshly-trained soldiers every year. On the evidence of later tradition and our knowledge of the prevalence of book-learning in early fourth-century Athens, there must have been a small library in the Pompeion for study purposes. The Pompeion is the only surviving gymnasium of the Classical period. About ten years after the Pompeion was built, Plato's Academy moved to a site nearby: its architectural design was similar in every respect to that of the Pompeion.

The Gymnasium of Ptolemy. Another gymnasium was built in Athens in the second century B.C.: according to Cicero (*De finibus*, V.1.1) and Pausanias (I.17.2), it was founded and endowed by Ptolemy VI Philometor (reigned 181-145). Its remains have not yet been identified, but it must have been somewhere north of the Acropolis.[35] The Ptolemaeum library is mentioned in several inscriptions of the second and first centuries B.C., from which we learn that under the terms of a decree its stock of books was to be enlarged by gifts from the students themselves, each of whom was required to donate a hundred papyrus rolls to the library on completing his studies. According to these inscriptions, the books included Euripides's plays and Homer's epics.[36]

Gymnasium in Piraeus(?). A fragment of an inscription listing book titles, found in Piraeus and dated to *circa* 100 B.C., may be part of a stele commemorating a gift to a gymnasium library or a public library. Among the books listed are works by Homer, tragedies, comedies (including plays by Menander and Diphilus) and works by philosophers (including Nicomachus) and rhetoricians.[37]

Gifts of books to school libraries

Gymnasia on Rhodes and Cos. Rhodes and Cos were two great intellectual and cultural centres in the Aegean where many eminent literary scholars found work and a new home after leaving Alexandria in the second century B.C. Both islands had reputable schools of philosophy and medicine and they were certainly major book centres. Evidence concerning their libraries is to be found in the ruins of the buildings themselves (see pp. 290-292) and in fragments of inscriptions listing book titles, which may have been put up to commemorate gifts to libraries. One such list, found on Rhodes and dated to the second century B.C., gives the titles of works by rhetoricians and historians. Since there was a decree on gifts to libraries stipulating that the heads of the gymnasia were responsible for taking delivery of books and cataloguing them, this list may well refer to a donation to a gymnasium library.[38]

Another inscription of the second century B.C. informs us that a certain Diocles and his son Apollodorus donated a hundred books to an unspecified library, and others would appear to have followed their example by making gifts of money and books.[39]

111. Fragment of a marble inscription (ca. *100* B.C.*) listing book titles, probably commemorating a gift. Piraeus, Archaeological Museum.*

- - - - - - - κε . . ̣ . .
[- - - - Μετεκ]βαίνο[υσαι]?
- - - - - ς Μελέαγρο[ς]
[- - - - π]ερὶ Αἰσχύ(λ)ου
[- - - Ἀλέ]ξανδρον Δὶς [ἐξ]-
[απατῶν - - - Κιθ]αριστὴς Δακτ[ύ]-
[λιος - - - Ἀ]λκμέων ἀλλο-
[- - - Ἀν]ταῖος Ἀμφιάρα-
[ος - - -] τοῦ ὀφθαλμοῦ
[- - - Εὐκλ]είδου Αἰσχίνης
[- - - - κ]ατὰ Χα(ρ)ίαν κα -
- - - - - - σα τὰ περὶ Ἀθη-
[ν - - -] Δ· τῶν μετὰ vac.
[- - - - κα]τὰ Χαρίαν καὶ Λα-
- - - - - - - α· Ἀχαιοῦ Ἐργῖ-
[νος - - -] Ἀσκληπιάδου
- - - - - - ς· Σιληνοῦ Χρυ-
[ς - - - - η]νοδώρου Φοῖνιξ
- - - - - - οι· Σοφοκλέ- vac.
[ους - - - -]φρύνης ἐκ τ-
[- - - - - - ἐ]κ τοῦ κύκλου
- - - - - - - ν Ἀμφιάραος
[- - - - Ἠλ]έκτρα Ἡρα-
[κλῆς - - -]ν vv Μυσο[ὶ]
[- - - - Μ]οῦσαι Ἀλέξ[αν]-
[δρος - - - Αἰθ]ίοπες Α - -
[- - - - Ἰφιγέν]εια Ἱππ[όνους]?

[.]μη - - - - - - - - -
ἀφοπλι - - - - - - - -
[ο]υ· Κράτητ[ος - - - -]
πνιάστρια [- - - - - - Δη]-
μοσθένου κα[τὰ - - - -]
[τ]ῶν Ἑλλανίκου[- · Διφί]-
λου Σφαττόμεν[ος Αἰρησι]-
τείχης Τήθη Ἀπ[οβάτης Ἑ]-
κάτη Στρατιῶτ[ης - - Θερα]-
πευταί(?) Συνω[ρὶς Φιλάδελ]-
φος Τελεσία⟨ια⟩[ς· Εὐριπίδου]
Σκύριοι Σθενέβ[οια Σκίρων]
[Σ]άτυρο(ι) Σίσυ[φος Συλεὺς]
Θυέστης Θησε[ὺς Δίκτυς]
Δανάη Πολύι[δος Πελιά]-
δες· v Ἅλαι· Πλ[εισθένης Πα]-
λαμήδης Π - - - - - -
Πηλεὺς Π[ειρίθους Πρω]-
τεσίλαος - - - - - - -
Φιλοκτήτη[ς Φαέθων Φοῖ]-
νιξ Φρίξος Φ[οίνισσαι]
- - - Ἀφιδν' [Ἀρχέλα]-
[ος Ἀλκ]μήνη Ἀλέ[ξανδρος]
[Ἀλόπη] Εὐρυσθ(ε)ὺς - - -
. . . ̣ . . . . στις - - -

Notes

IV
HELLENISTIC PERIOD

Other Libraries from Pergamum to Ai Khanoum

NOTES

1. Archaeological excavations in the Hellenistic kingdoms tend to confirm the rule that from the third century B.C. every major Greek city had its library. For a list of all the known libraries in the Graeco-Roman world: see J. Tøsberg, *Offentlige bibliotheker: Romerriget i det 2. arhundrede e Chr.*, Copenhagen 1976, 9-12. One such foundation on the island of Cos – one of the earliest examples of a public library endowed by private benefaction, like the Gennadius Library in Athens today – started a tradition that lasted at least until the end of the Hellenistic period.
2. See E. Hansen, *The Attalids of Pergamon*, Ithaca 1972[2]; H.J. Schalles, 'Untersuchungen zur Kulturpolitik der pergamenischen Herrscher im dritten Jahrhundert v. Chr.', *Istanbuler Forschungen* 36 (1985).
3. Diog. Laer., V.67. Lacydes was head of the Academy from 241/240 to 216/215. Lycon, a native of Ilium (Troy) who had inherited the Peripatetic school from Strato, had a high reputation and received generous support from Eumenes and Attalus.
4. See p. 182.
5. Suetonius, *De grammaticis et rhetoribus*, II: 'Crates ... was sent to the Senate by King Attalus ... at about the time when Ennius died.'
6. John the Lydian, *On the Months* I.28. The word 'parchment' and its equivalents in most other European languages are derived from the Greek *pergamene*.
7. Varro (*De bibliothecis*?). See also *RE*, suppl. 7 (1940), 1221; and cf. Pliny, *Natural History*, XIII.70: 'Soon, when King Ptolemy – on account of the rivalry between himself and King Eumenes in the matter of libraries – suppressed [the export of] paper, Varro informs us that parchment was invented.'
8. Athenodorus would appear to have been a friend of Antipater of Tyre and Diodotus the Stoic, who were members of Cicero's circle. Many Stoic philosophers are known to have taught privately in Rome, some of them living in the luxurious villas of the aristocracy. The last of this line whose name is on record was Arius Didymus, whom Augustus appointed 'court philosopher'.
9. Diogenes Laertius, in his *Life of Zeno* (VII.34), has a passage in which he mentions Athenodorus's censorship: 'All the unsatisfactory doctrines and assertions of the Stoics were cut out of their books by Athenodorus the Stoic, who was Director of the Library at Pergamum. They were subsequently reinstated, as Athenodorus was detected and found himself in a situation of great danger; and so much for those doctrines of [Zeno's] which were impugned.'
10. See U. von Wilamowitz-Moellendorf, *Antigonos von Karystos* [*Philologische Untersuchungen*, IV], Berlin 1881.
11. See P.M. Fraser, *Ptolemaic Alexandria*, 3 vols., Oxford 1972, I, 415-422.
12. Polemon was a very erudite man who specialized in antiquarianism, that is travelling for the sole purpose of writing about antiquities, and ancient monuments in particular, rather than the natural environment (geography). See also p. 198.
13. Athenaeus, *Deipnosophistae*, XII.515e, XV.694a.
14. See R. Pfeiffer, *Ἱστορία τῆς Κλασσικῆς Φιλολογίας. Ἀπό τῶν Ἀρχῶν μέχρι τοῦ τέλους τῶν Ἑλληνιστικῶν Χρόνων* (= *History of Classical Scholarship: From the beginnings to the end of the Hellenistic age*, Oxford 1968, tr. P. Xenos et al.), Athens 1972, 300 ff.; on the persecution of Alexandrian literary scholars, *ibid.*, 253.

15. See F. Schmidt, *Die Pinakes des Kallimachos*, Kiel 1924, 28; O. Regenbogen, «Πίναξ» in *RE*, 20 (1950), 1424 ff.
16. Athenaeus, *Deipnosophistae*, VIII.336d-e: 'I myself have not come across the play. Although I have read more than eight hundred plays of the so-called Middle Comedy and have made excerpts of them, I have not found *The Teacher of Profligacy*, and I do not know of anyone who thought it worth cataloguing. Certainly neither Callimachus nor Aristophanes has catalogued it, nor have even those who compiled the catalogues in Pergamum.'
17. See p. 122.
18. Others besides Galen who wrote about the problem of pseudepigraphy were Olympiodorus, John Philoponus and Elias of Alexandria: see pp. 239-240 (nn. 109, 110, 111).
19. Even before the great Berlin papyrus (inv. 9780) brought to light much of the original text of *Didymus on Demosthenes*, the titles of many of Didymus's commentaries on Attic orators, and excerpts from them, were already known. See H. Diels and W. Schubart (eds.), *Didymos, Kommentar zu Demosthenes (Papyrus 9780)* [*Berliner Klassikertexte*, 1], Berlin 1904, XXX ff. On the Pergamene edition of Demosthenes's *Orations* and the 'new' Philippic see L. Canfora, *Ἡ Χαμένη Βιβλιοθήκη τῆς Ἀλεξανδρείας* (= *La biblioteca scomparsa*, Palermo 1986, tr. F. Arvanitis), Athens 1989, 60-62, 144.
20. Anaximenes of Lampsacus, a historian and teacher of rhetoric of the fourth century B.C., taught Alexander the Great and wrote the so-called *Rhetoric to Alexander*.
21. Plutarch, *Antony*, LVIII. See also F. Münzer, 'C. Calvinius Sabinus', in *RE*, 3 (1899), 1411.
22. Telephus, who was born at Pergamum and was active in the second century A.D., was a very versatile writer who, according to *Souda*, wrote books on literature, history, biography, grammar and antiquarian subjects.
23. See C. Rapin, 'Les textes littéraires grecs de la trésorerie d'Aï Khanoum', *BCH* 111 (1987) 258-265.
24. *Ibid.*, 263. For the way in which similar containers were used by the Egyptians for keeping archives, see E. Posner, *Archives in the Ancient World*, Cambridge, Mass. 1972, 86-88; J. Černý, *Paper and Books in Ancient Egypt*, London 1952, 29.
25. The Egyptian document storage jars were just like the ones found at Ai Khanoum – oval-bodied, flat-bottomed, with or without handles – and identical to the jars used as coffers in public treasuries or for storing oil or perfumes: see C. Rapin, 'Les inscriptions économiques de la trésorerie hellénistique d'Aï Khanoum (Afghanistan)', *BCH* 107 (1983) 357-358.
26. See E. R. Bevan, *The House of Seleucus*, II, new edn. London 1966.
27. See Pfeiffer, *op. cit.*, 144, 178.
28. See T. Kleberg, 'Book Auctions in Ancient Rome?', *Libri* 22 (1973) 1 ff.; R. J. Starr, 'The Used-Book Trade in the Roman World', *Phoenix* 44 (1990) 148 ff.
29. Julian, *Letters* 106, 107 (Bidez-Cumont numbering):

JULIAN THE APOSTATE TO PORPHYRIUS

George's library was very large and complete and contained works by philosophers of every school and by many commentators: not the least, in this latter category, were numerous books of all kinds by the Galilaeans [i.e. Christians]. Therefore make a thorough search for the contents of the library in their entirety, and have them sent to Antioch, for I would have you know that you yourself will incur the severest penalty if you do not track them down with all diligence, question everybody under the slightest suspicion of having purloined any books, cross-examine the suspects thoroughly and take sworn statements from them and, in addition, torture the slaves, until you have compelled them – if you cannot persuade them – to hand them all over.

TO ECDICIUS, PREFECT OF EGYPT

Some men have a passion for horses, others for birds, others for wild beasts; but I, from childhood, have been possessed by a passionate longing to acquire books. It would therefore be absurd if I should let these be appropriated by men whose inordinate desire for wealth cannot be satisfied by gold alone, and who have no qualms about stealing these also. I therefore desire you to find all the books that belonged to George, as a personal favour to me. For there were many philosophical works in his house, and many on rhetoric, as well as many on the doctrines of the impious Galilaeans. These last I should wish to be utterly annihilated; but in case other, more useful, works are accidentally destroyed along with them, let all these also be sought with the utmost thoroughness. Let George's secretary take charge of this search for you, and if he hunts for them faithfully let him know that he will obtain his freedom as a reward, but if he should prove in any way dishonest in the business he will be put to the torture. And I know what books George had – many of them, at any rate, if not all – because he lent me some of them to copy when I was in Cappadocia, and these he received back.

30. Plutarch, *Aemilius Paullus*, VI.28.
31. See pp. 204, 241 (n. 125).
32. Suetonius, *De grammaticis*, XV; Pliny, *Nat. Hist.*, XXV.5-7. Mithradates's interest in medicine probably stemmed from practical considerations, for he wished to protect himself against enemies intent on poisoning him. Pliny evidently believed the popular story that he took daily doses of small quantities of poison and antidotes to make himself immune to all kinds of poison. See H. Funaioli, *Grammaticae romanae fragmenta*, Leipzig 1907, 403-404.
33. On gymnasium libraries see: J. Delorme, *Gymnasion. Étude sur les monuments consacrés à l'éducation en Grèce*, Paris 1960; R. Nicolai, 'Le bibliotheche dei ginnasi', *Nuovi Annali della Scuola Speciale per Archivisti e Bibliotecari* 1 (1987) 17 ff.
34. On the excavation of the Pompeion see W. Hoepfner, *Das Pompeion und seine Nachfolgerbauten*, Berlin 1976; Id. (ed.), *Antike Bibliotheken*, Mainz 2002, 53-55, 67-80. On the nature of the *Ephebeion*, its relationship to the Spartan system of training hoplites and its role as a model for similar institutions in the Greek world, see H.-I. Marrou, *Ἱστορία τῆς Ἐκπαιδεύσεως κατά τήν Ἀρχαιότητα* (= *Histoire de l'éducation dans l'antiquité*, Paris 1948, tr. Th. Fotinopoulos), Athens 1961, 163 ff.
35. With reference to the site of Ptolemy's gymnasium, see J. Travlos, *Pictorial Dictionary of Ancient Athens*, New York 1975, 236; Tøsberg, *op. cit.*, 73-77; Lora Lee Johnson, *The Hellenistic and Roman Library: Studies pertaining to their architectural form* (doctoral dissertation, Brown University), Providence, R. I., 1984, 73. It may be possible for its location to be identified by reference to the position of the Aglaurion: see G. S. Dontas, 'The True Aglaurion', *Hesperia* 52 (1983) 48-63.
36. *IG*, II², 1009, 1029, 1030, 1040-1043.
37. *IG*, II², 2363. See L. Robert, 'Notes d'épigraphie hellénistique', *BCH* 59 (1935) 421-425; K. Sp. Staikos, *Βιβλιοθῆκες. Ἀπό τήν Ἀρχαιότητα ἕως τήν Ἀναγέννηση καί Σημαντικές Οὐμανιστικές καί Μοναστηριακές Βιβλιοθῆκες (3000 π.Χ.-1600 μ.Χ.)* (exhibition catalogue), Athens 1997, 34-45.
38. See G. Ch. Papachristodoulou, «Τό ἑλληνιστικό Γυμνάσιο τῆς Ρόδου: Νέα γιά τή βιβλιοθήκη του», in *Akten des XIII. Internationalen Kongresses für klassischen Archäologie*, Mainz 1990, 500 ff.
39. Robert, *loc. cit.* By a curious coincidence, Diocles and Apollodorus are the names of two of the four grammarians mentioned in the Oxyrrhynchus papyrus listing the Directors of the Alexandrian Library (Pap. Oxy. 1241): see p. 178.

V

ARCHITECTURE

TYPOLOGY AND EQUIPMENT
OF ARCHIVAL AND ACADEMIC LIBRARIES

112. Reconstruction drawing of an 'archival library' in the palace at Knossos containing clay tablets and diptychs and papyrus documents, stored in wooden boxes, pithoi *(storage jars) and baskets. Drawn by Stavroula Lazari from an original by K.Sp. Staikos.*

ARCHITECTURE

Typology and Equipment of Archival and Academic Libraries

In the Minoan and Mycenaean worlds, written documents (whether incised on clay or written on other materials) were kept in locked rooms even before they started to be properly classified and arranged in record offices. From at least as early as the Middle Bronze Age (*ca.* 1500 B.C.) it became necessary, chiefly because of changes in social conditions and the administrative system of the royal palaces, for financial, commercial and some other records to be kept systematically, and so special rooms were set aside solely for that purpose. Because of the quantity and variety of written material needing to be stored, it was an invariable rule – from the very earliest days of primitive 'archival libraries' – that the way each document was filed depended on its shape and the material of which it was made. Given the bureaucratic organization of Minoan and Mycenaean palaces and the wide extent of their trade, chiefly with the Aegean islands and coastlands but also with other countries in the Near East, the subject is not one that ought to be dealt with in hypothetical terms; but that is the only way it can be approached owing to the complete absence of illustrations or descriptions of scribes in their working environment, perhaps because their profession was surrounded by an air of mystery.

Archival libraries in the Minoan and Mycenaean civilizations. Archaeological finds from the Minoan and Mycenaean civilizations (3000-1100 B.C.) in Crete, the Aegean islands, the Peloponnese and central Greece provide no evidence of any particular architectural approach to the rooms used as record offices, such as the Room of the Chariot Tablets at Knossos or Rooms 7 and 8 at Pylos.[1] The side walls show no sign of having had recesses to be used as 'bookcases'. Traces of wall benches have been found in the Pylos archive rooms: they were probably used either as ledges on which to stand storage jars and baskets full of tablets, or as bases for shelving to hold small boxes of tablets or other documents, or as seats for the scribes and archivists.

Developing a filing system. The 'documents' on which the Minoans and Mycenaeans recorded their commercial transactions in the Bronze Age were clay tablets for the most part,[2] sometimes diptychs or polyptychs,[3] and sometimes perhaps papyrus rolls and sheets of papyrus or parchment for more permanent records. The method used for storing these 'books' was dictated by two considerations: first, that it should be both safe and practical, taking into account the shape of the documents and the material of which they were made, and secondly that every document should be easily accessible. As already mentioned in Chapter I (pp. 42-43), the tablets were often kept in earthenware storage jars or wicker baskets with incised clay labels attached to them to identify their contents.[4] Wooden and plaster boxes with vertical partitions were the most suitable for storing tablets, and the boxes may have been arranged according to some filing system. Diptychs and polyptychs used as notebooks (where the writing could be erased and overwritten, as on a blackboard), with their wooden frames and rectangular shape, were easy to store: either lying flat, in vertical stacks, or standing vertically like books on a bookshelf. They could be identified either by clay sealings (which were tied on to the wooden frame of the tablet with a cord threaded through a hole in the sealing) or by some kind of marking on the spine. Papyrus rolls, assuming that they were in use in the pre-Homeric period, could be stored either in round or square baskets or on wooden shelves affixed to the walls, perhaps divided into triangular pigeonholes so that the rolls could be grouped together according to their subject matter. They were labelled with clay sealings tied on with string, like the wax or metal seals attached to patriarchal *sigillia* in the Orthodox Church.[5] Large or small wooden or plaster boxes were probably used for filing single sheets of papyrus or parchment or particularly valuable documents such as international trade agreements and treaties.

113. A Late Bronze Age diptych found in the sunken Mycenaean ship off Ulu Burun.

Was there a filing system for tablets?

From Homer to Aristotle. When the Minoan Pictographic and Linear A and B scripts went out of use, the Greeks adopted the Phoenician alphabetic script and modified it to form the Greek alphabet. One consequence was the gradual ascendancy of the form of book that survived until the Late Roman period: the papyrus roll.[6] Papyrus rolls were used for setting down the whole of Greek literature in writing, in permanent form, while diptychs, polyptychs and rolls or sheets of parchment[7] were used in schools and gymnasia for learning the language and learning to read and write. Polyptychs were sometimes used for letter-writing and official documents, and also for note-taking at lectures.

The papyrus roll takes over

114. Schoolroom scenes showing a teacher holding a diptych and another holding a papyrus roll. Vase-painting by Duris on a kylix of the 5th c. B.C. Berlin, Archaeological Museum.

CHAPTER V
Typology and equipment of libraries

Private libraries. The first private libraries formed by philosophers such as Philolaus, Heraclitus and Anaxagoras were too small to make any organizational or architectural demands, and the same is true of the first book collections belonging to itinerant rhapsodists and their guilds from the sixth century B.C. onwards. These libraries consisted of a limited number of papyrus rolls that were kept in portable wooden containers (*κιβώτια* or *κιβωτοί*), or else in cupboards with other objects. One such wooden container, described as having four doors, was listed among Alcibiades's personal possessions when they were put up for sale in 415 B.C.: it was probably a cupboard with a shelf across the middle and double folding doors, used for storing books and perhaps other things as well.[8]

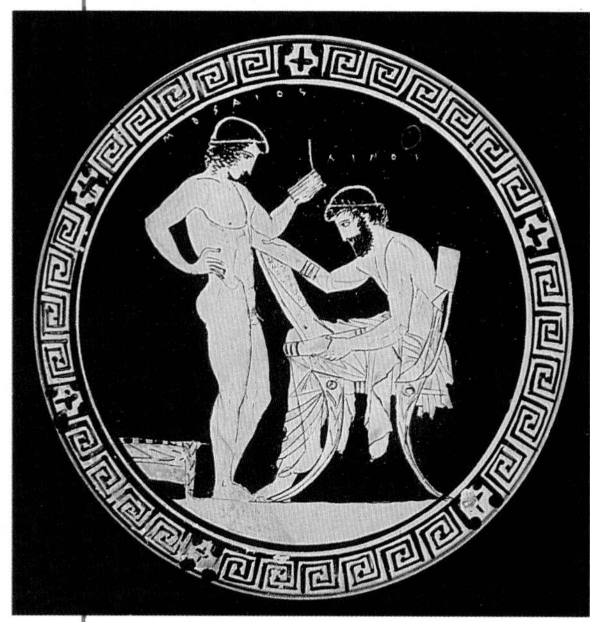

115. Vase-painting by the Eretria Painter, ca. 430 B.C. The singer Linus, giving a lesson to Musaeus, pulls open a papyrus roll.

Another type of 'bookcase' in existence from the fifth century B.C. was a small wooden chest with a lid at the top. There are numerous vase-paintings depicting such book chests: in one, on a kylix by Onesimus, the chest is on the floor in front of a young reader, with a papyrus roll lying on top of it. The roll bears the title *Chironeia* – a reference to Chiron, the centaur of Greek mythology who was the mentor of several heroes – presumably to indicate that it is an educational book. A fifth-century lecythus has a painting that shows a book chest with the lid open in front of a standing woman who is unrolling a papyrus, and a painting on a fourth-century amphora depicts a similar open chest on the floor between a female pupil and her teacher, the scene probably being a recreation room in a private house.[9]

The first bookcases: wooden chests

Book chests of this kind, large or small, may well have been the usual storage places for books in private houses, even when houses had special rooms for reading and copying books.[10] However, bigger book collections used reg-

116. Lecythus, 5th c. B.C., with a painting of a woman reading a papyrus roll that she has taken out of the open wooden chest. Paris, Musée du Louvre.

117. Crater, 4th c. B.C. A young woman is having a music lesson, with an open wooden chest on the floor in front of her. Würzburg, Martin-von-Wagner Museum.

ularly in teaching or other work – the libraries used in support of the 'fifty-drachma lectures' of Hippias, Prodicus and other sophists, for example – probably needed proper shelving. It would seem that there must have been some such system of book storage in Alexis's comedy *Linus*, where Linus, a teacher, invites his pupil Heracles to look through the titles in his library at his leisure and pick out any book he wants from among the works of Orpheus, Homer, Hesiod, Epicharmus and Choerilus. Linus was disappointed when Heracles, whom he calls 'a true philosopher', passes over the great poets and chooses a cookery book by Simus instead.[11]

As far as one can tell from by the results of archaeological excavations so far, there do not appear to have been any firm rules governing library architecture in the Classical period. Each library or book room seems to have been laid out and equipped to suit the purposes for which its owner used it, the size of his purse and his own idiosyncrasies. If we are to believe Cicero (*Epistulae ad familiares*, V.3.25-27), for example, Demosthenes, unlike most Roman scholars and men of letters, thought the ideal environment for reading, thinking and writing was a secluded room, if possible with no windows and no natural light, where there was nothing visible or audible to distract him. There, working by lamplight, usually in the quiet of the night, he found the peace of mind and inner strength he needed to write his speeches. No doubt it was in just such an impersonal room, where he copied out books (including Thucydides's *History*, as mentioned earlier), that he kept books by other writers and the copies of his own various writings.[12]

118. Vase-painting by Onesimus depicting a student reading a papyrus roll with a book chest in front of him, while his teachers look on. Berlin, Archaeological Museum.

Demosthenes's ideal library

Vitruvius, in his description of a Greek house (*De architectura*, VI.7.1-5), has the following passage (VI.7.3): 'If a peristyle has one portico higher than the rest, it is called a Rhodian peristyle. These houses have magnificent vestibules and elegant gates, and the porticos of the peristyles are decorated with stucco and plastering and inlaid ceilings. In the porticos to the north the cyziceni, triclinia, and pinacothecæ, are situated. The libraries are on the east side, the exedræ on the west, and to the south are the square oeci, of such ample dimensions that there is room therein for four triclinia and the attendants on them, as well as for the games.' However, this description does not fit the typology of the Classical Greek houses that have been excavated: Vitruvius must have been writing about villas of the Late Hellenistic period, which sometimes occupied a whole city block.[13] Such villas have been excavated on Delos, including the House of Dionysus and the House of the Pediments, in both of which the rooms identified as libraries opened on to the central courtyard with its peristyle colonnade.

Greek houses

Public libraries. Athenaeus's list of great book collectors in the pre-Christian era is headed by the names of two rulers who founded public libraries: Polycrates of Samos and Pisistratus of Athens. About Polycrates's library nothing whatever is known, apart from that solitary reference in Athenaeus, but the one started by Pisistratus is mentioned frequently by ancient writers, who tell us not only what led him to found a library but also what happened to its books.[14] To recapitulate briefly, they were taken by Xerxes as spoils of war, together with other works of art, and carried off to Persepolis, and were subsequently brought back to Athens by Seleucus I Nicator. It is also known that they were housed on the Acropolis for a time,[15] but we cannot be sure whether that original collection of books was part of an archive kept in the Metroön, nor whether it continued to exist as part of the literature collection kept in the archives[16] in the time of Lycurgus (338-326), when, at Aristotle's insistence, a decree was issued to the effect that official copies of the three great tragedians' works were to be

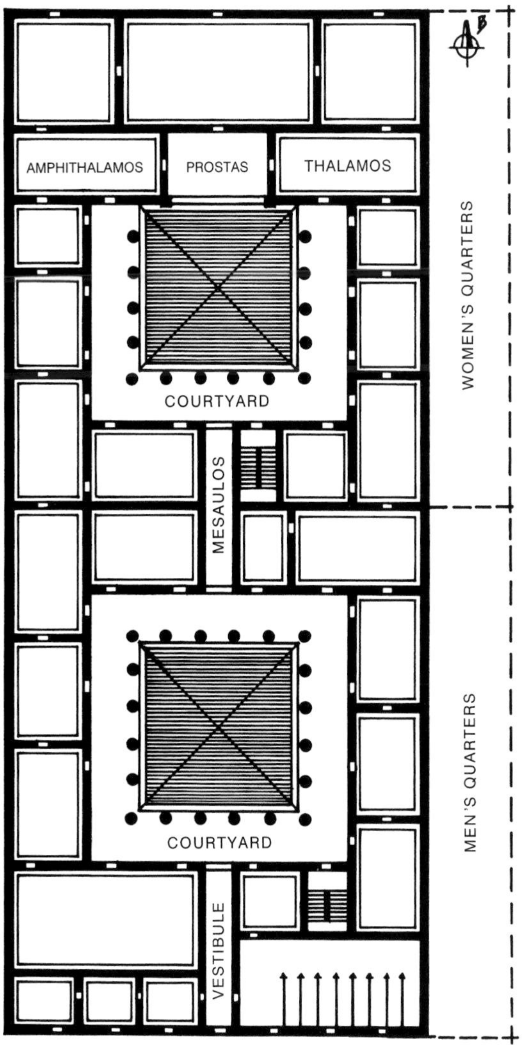

119. Plan drawn by W. A. Becker from Vitruvius's description of a Greek house. Thalamos: matrimonial bedchamber. Prostas: antechamber. Amphithalamos: women's sitting-room? Mesaulos: corridor between men's and women's quarters.

deposited in the Athenian state archives.[17] Whatever the answer may be, there is no surviving evidence of the architectural design and layout of any public library before the end of the Classical period.

Academic libraries. All four of the great philosophy schools founded in Athens from the fourth century B.C. onwards – Plato's Academy, Aristotle's Lyceum, the Garden of Epicurus and Zeno's Stoa – are known to have had large collections of books used as teaching and study aids. And, as we have seen, there is enough evidence available, including catalogues of written works, for us to be able to trace the history of these libraries.[18] The two about which the most is known are the Academy (mainly from archaeological finds) and the Lyceum (mainly from literary evidence).

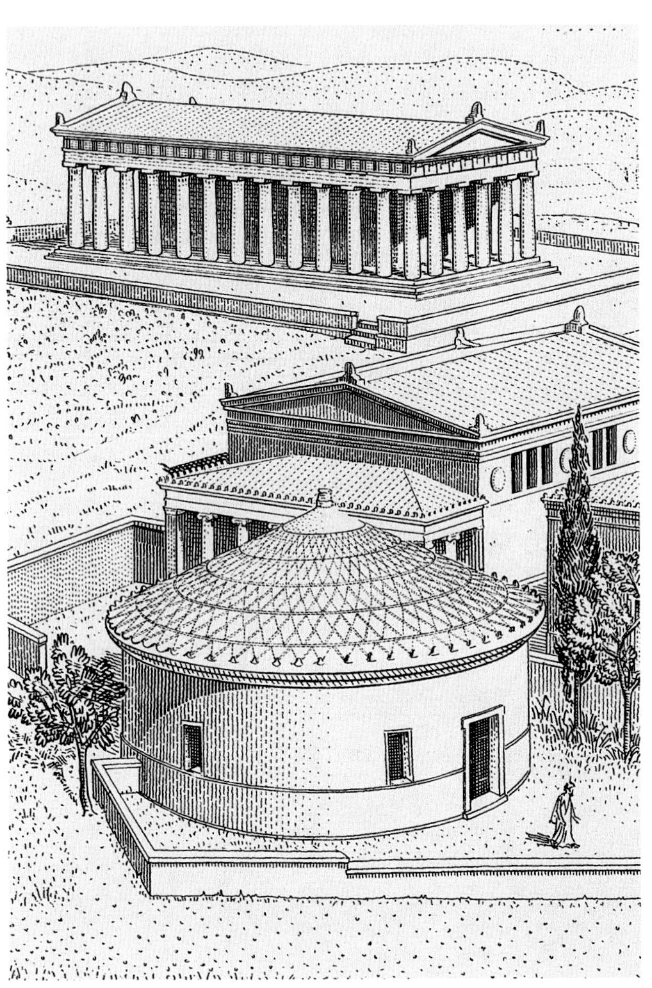

120. Reconstruction drawing of the Tholos near the New and Old Bouleuteria. The Old Bouleuterion, besides serving as a council house, was used for the storage of the official state archives. Drawn by J. Travlos.

The remains of Plato's Academy, excavated by Filippos Stavropoulos, give us a clear picture of the whole building complex, which was constructed round a large central courtyard. An entrance gate in the centre of the façade led into a rectangular courtyard surrounded on three sides by a single-storey roofed colonnade. At the far side of the courtyard, facing the gateway, was the portico leading in to a large central room and two smaller rooms on each side. In the middle of the courtyard there stood an altar. An oblong plinth in front of the portico leading in to the main room may have been a base for statues of the Muses.

Wolfram Hoepfner believes that there were reading rooms in the colonnades at the front end of the courtyard and along the two sides, and that the two square rooms (*oikoi*) flanking the portico at the far end contained couches. The central room, which was the main hall of the library and measured 6 x 11 metres, was bare of bookcases and was probably used mainly for ceremonial purposes, while the flanking rooms contained bookcases, perhaps in two tiers. There may also have been bookcases in recesses in the walls of the main hall, probably with wooden benches in front of them so that the room could be used a lecture hall in accordance with Plato's standard practice.[19]

An academic library of original design

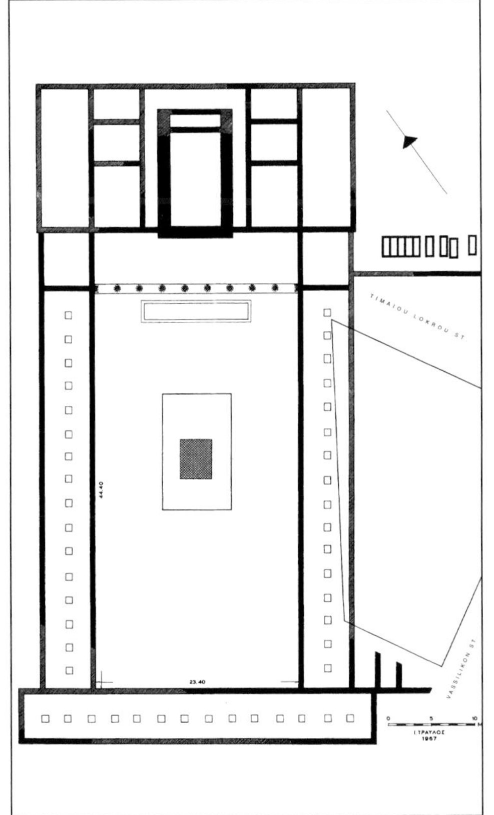

121. Plato's Academy, after archaeological excavations. Drawing by J. Travlos.

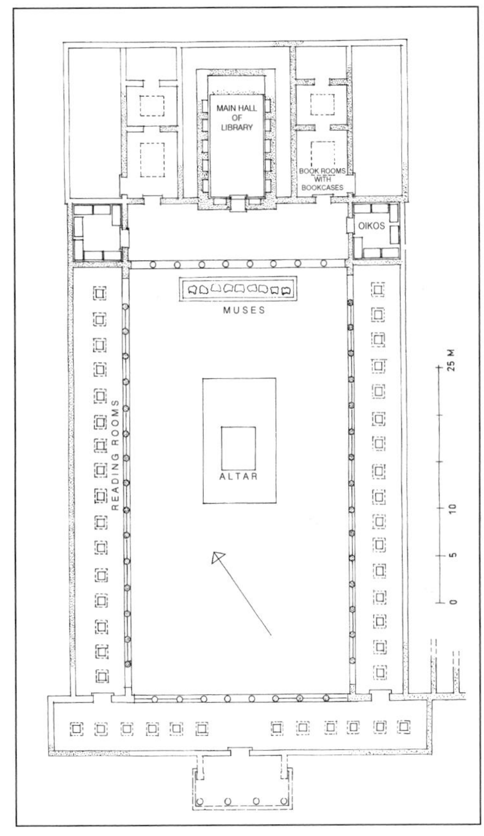

122. Plato's Academy: Hoepfner's conjectures regarding the functions of the various parts of the building.

The Lyceum. The Lyceum may have been situated in the site where excavation started some years ago for the construction of the new Museum of Modern Art.[20] So far, however, the only evidence we have for its architectural design and layout come from Theophrastus's will, written at the time when

ΦΥΣΙΚΩΝ
ΔΟΞΑΙ
ΦΥΣΙΚΑ
ΠΟΛΙΤΙΚΑ
ΗΘΙΚΑ
ΙΣΤΟΡΙΑΙ

the Lyceum came to be known as the Peripatos.[21] The will contains references to the damage done by the Macedonians when Demetrius Poliorcetes captured Athens and quelled the rebellion there. It would appear that the main hall of the Lyceum was called the Museum (*Mouseion*) and was adorned with statues of goddesses. There was also a sanctuary containing a bust of Aristotle and other votive offerings. The Museum was connected by a short stoa to the other buildings, and there was another colonnade, the Lower Stoa, with maps hanging on the walls. Theophrastus also mentions the altar, which he desired to be repaired and made 'as beautiful and elegant as possible'. Architecturally, therefore, the Lyceum was evidently not unlike Plato's Academy, but it must have been much bigger and would have had many more rooms, since the total number of students and auditors at the Peripatos in Theophrastus's time was said to have been about two thousand. We should remember, too, that Alexander the Great gave Aristotle a grant of eight hundred talents to improve the facilities at the Lyceum.[22]

Although the Lyceum certainly had a large and fine collection of books, there is no surviving documentary evidence concerning the premises where they were kept. One can only assume that the organization and running of the library must have been excellent, as the Ptolemies always wanted to have the head of the Lyceum as Director of their Universal Library: the post is said to have been offered to Aristotle himself (though that cannot be true) and it was certainly offered to his successors Theophrastus, Strato and Lycon.

The Universal Library in Alexandria

Hellenistic period. A comparison between the remains of the Pergamum Library and of Plato's Academy suggests that the architectural design of Hellenistic libraries followed the model of libraries in Classical Athens. Strabo's description of the Ptolemies' Universal Library, discussed earlier in this book, is too brief to provide a basis even for a conjectural reconstruction of the architecture of the Museum complex. The main building, the paved walk and the 'exedra' mentioned by Strabo sound like nothing more than recollections of the typical architecture of fourth-century philosophy schools (the Academy and the Lyceum). And it seems strange that the architecture of the main Museum building (which had been the original Library and now housed part of the

123. Reconstruction drawing of a reading room in Aristotle's Lyceum with papyrus rolls, diptychs and polyptychs stacked on the open-fronted bookshelves and with closed bookcases for more books. Drawn by Stavroula Lazari from an original by K.Sp. Staikos.

Library), with its paved walk, its 'exedra', its roofed colonnades, its courtyards and its grounds, should have differed from that of other large or small contemporary academic institutions of the same period. Examination of the architectural design of the main hall of the Pergamum Library reveals that such rooms were designed to hold only a token quantity of books, not the main collection. Around them were auxiliary buildings, probably characterless structures with no architectural pretensions, where the books were kept: something like the *tameia tois biblois* ('treasuries' or 'storerooms' full of books) mentioned by Aphthonius in connection with the Serapeum library.[23] The number of papyrus rolls in the Alexandrian Library was so vast – as we have seen, it is estimated that there were at least 500,000 of them[24] – that five thousand square metres of bookshelf space were required for them. As the process of collecting the books continued over a long period and followed no preordained plan (since the project seemed like a utopian dream), it is to be supposed that the bulk of this enormous collection was housed in outbuildings that sprang up like the cells of a beehive, with big and small rooms connected to each other by roofed stoas and hidden corridors. Quite possibly the contents of the rooms were organized in accordance with the classification system used in Callimachus's *Pinakes*, with a separate room or building for each genre of writing: history, medicine, philosophy, poetry, prose literature and so on.

Problems of library architecture

One other point worth making is that nowhere in ancient literature is there any mention of libraries in the form in which we know them today, having a central reading room lined with bookcases as a frame of reference for the building's character and architecture. The terms 'great library' and 'daughter library' were first used in connection with the Ptolemies' Universal Library by Plutarch (early first century A.D.) and subsequently by Aphthonius (fourth century) and Ioannes Tzetzes (twelfth century). Strabo, who mentions the Ptolemies' Library and the one at Pergamum, uses the word *bibliotheke* indiscriminately to describe both of them and Aristotle's library, meaning simply a collection of books.

The Pergamum Library. More than a century has passed since Alexander Conze and Karl Dziatzko published their conclusions based on the finds from the Library at Pergamum,[25] and the results of recent archaeological and architectural research give us a much clearer picture of what the Library was like.[26]

The Library was situated on the acropolis, just to the east of the theatre and north of a two-storey stoa bounding the terrace on which the Temple of Athena Polias stood. These buildings were laid out and built in the reign of Eumenes

II (197-159 B.C.). Opening off the upper floor of the stoa there was a row of four large rooms. The first and biggest of these was the 'Museum' or main hall of the Library, measuring 13.50x16 m. and about 6.50 m. high, which was entered through a door in the north wall of the stoa. It was illuminated by two rows of windows (one in the far wall and one in the right-hand wall) about 3.70 m. above the ground. In it there was a continuous Π-shaped plinth along the two sides and the far end, fifty centimetres in from the wall, supporting a structure three metres in height with twenty recesses containing wooden bookcases with doors. A large statue of Athena stood in front of the plinth at the far end, facing the main entrance, and there may have been busts of poets and other writers on top of the bookcases, as tablets inscribed with the names of Alcaeus, Herodotus and Timotheus of Miletus have been found nearby. There may have been a wooden bench-like structure all along the front of the Π-shaped plinth, serving both as a step up to the higher bookshelves and as seating for those attending meetings and ceremonies.

The library building

Wooden cupboard-type bookcases about 1.70x1.00 m. in size, with double folding doors and (according to Hoepfner) colonnettes at the sides,[27] must have held about 3,200 papyrus rolls or even more, by my calculations. Some idea of the reputed wealth of the Pergamum Library can be gained from the fact that Mark Antony is said by Calvisius to have given Cleopatra 200,000 rolls taken from there.[28]

Closed bookcases the norm

Closed cupboards (*armaria*) were the non-portable bookcases of the ancient world. They were usually made of wood and, in large monumental libraries, they were recessed into alcoves in interior walls (or in structures specially built for the purpose) with a space between the interior and exterior walls as a protection against damp. What was of vital importance in designing these bookcases was to guard them against humidity and to provide adequate ventilation. Although it is possible to work out the approximate size of the bookcases from the size of the alcoves found in various libraries, nothing is known about the way the bookcases were partitioned to enable the rolls to be found easily: whether they had horizontal shelves, vertical partitions or X-shaped pigeonholes.

The earliest reference to closed bookcases in monumental libraries, as far as I am aware, occurs in Vitruvius's *De architectura* in connection with the

124. Plan of the acropolis of Pergamum in the reign of Eumenes II, showing the main buildings, including the theatre, the agora, the Temple of Athena Polias and the Library. Drawn by W. Hoepfner.

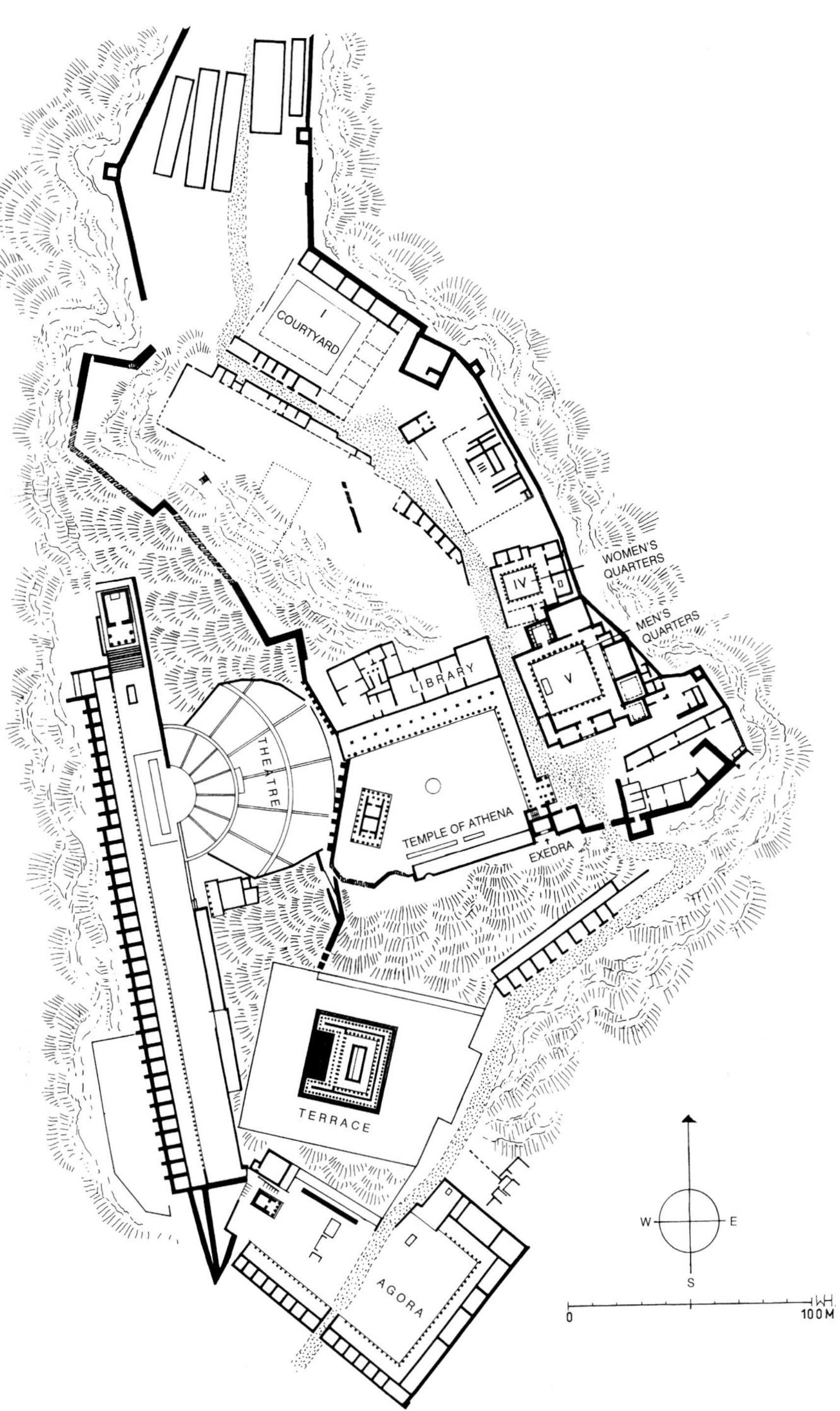
I
COURTYARD
WOMEN'S QUARTERS
IV
MEN'S QUARTERS
V
LIBRARY
THEATRE
TEMPLE OF ATHENA
EXEDRA
TERRACE
AGORA
W
E
S
0
100 M
WH.

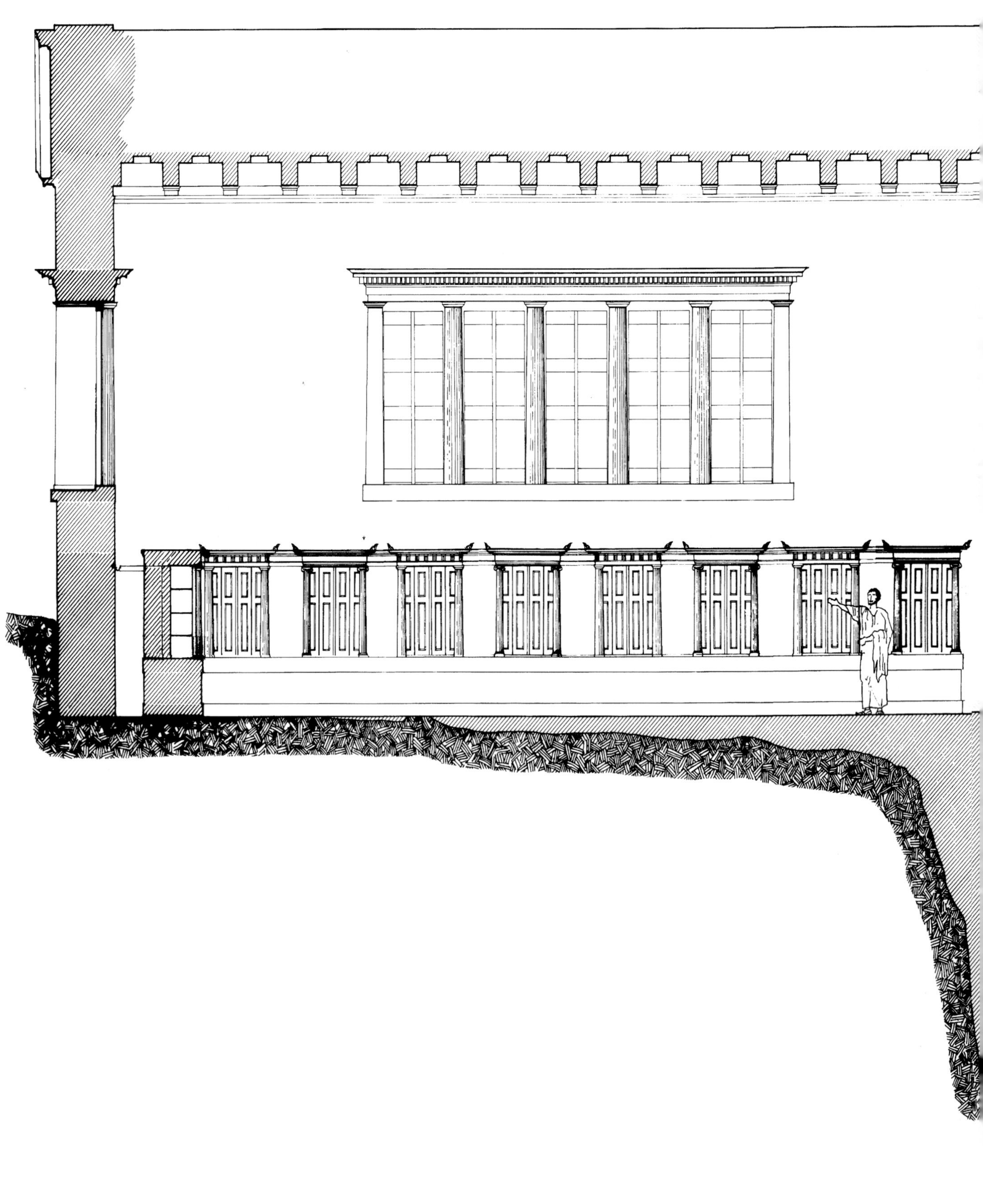

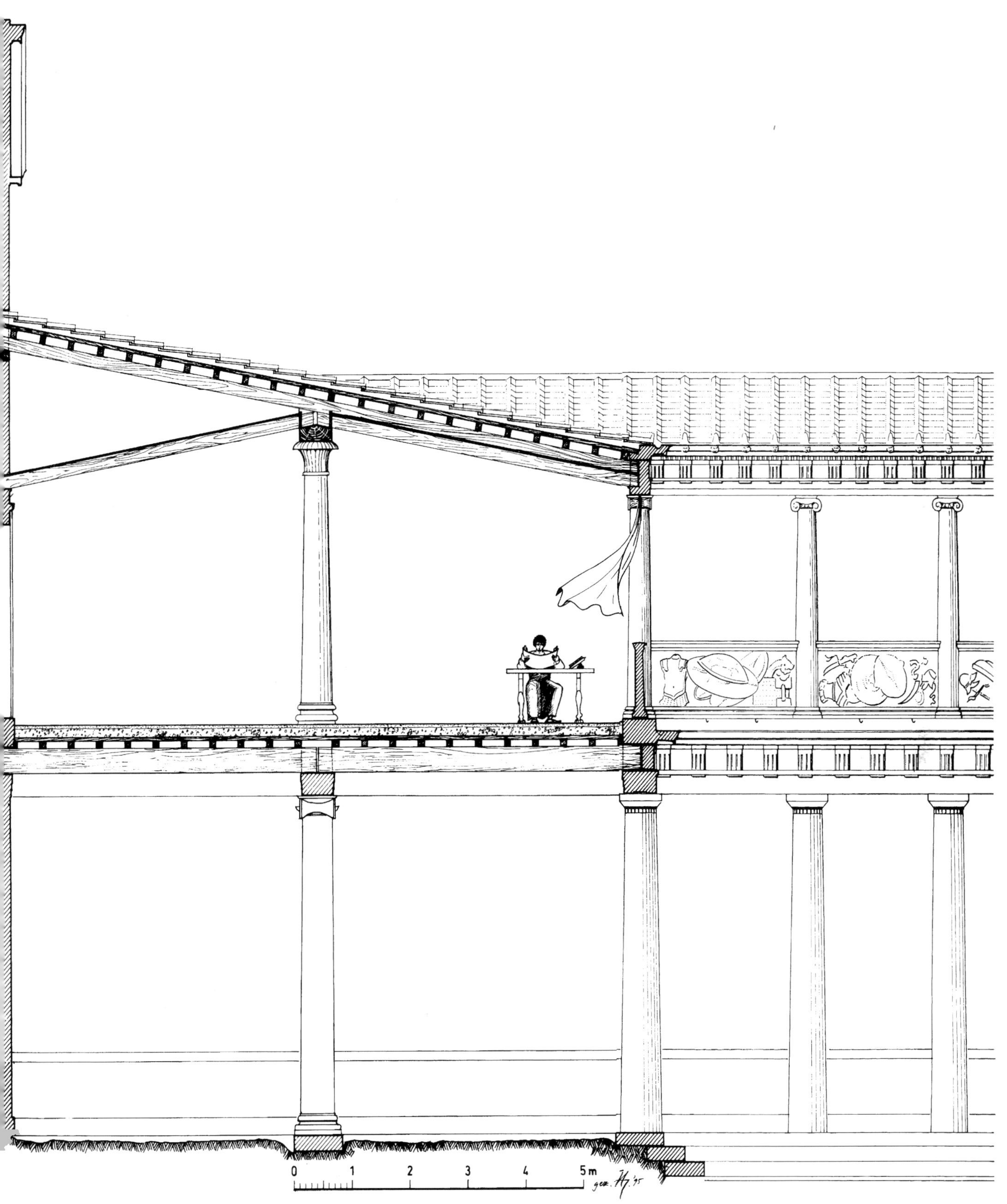

0 1 2 3 4 5m

appointment of Aristophanes of Byzantium as director of the Alexandrian Library. At a poetry competition in the Museum attended by Ptolemy V Epiphanes (reigned 204-180 B.C.), Aristophanes, who was one of the judges, took countless books out of the *armaria* (*certis armariis infinita volumina eduxit*) to prove that most of the entries had been plagiarized.[29]

Athena the patron goddess of libraries

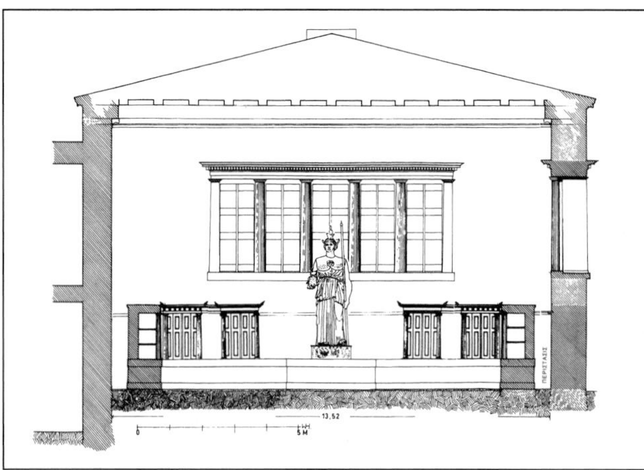

126. Reconstruction drawing of the main hall of the Pergamum Library, showing the imposing statue of Athena in the centre and closed bookcases on the plinth on either side. Drawn by W. Hoepfner.

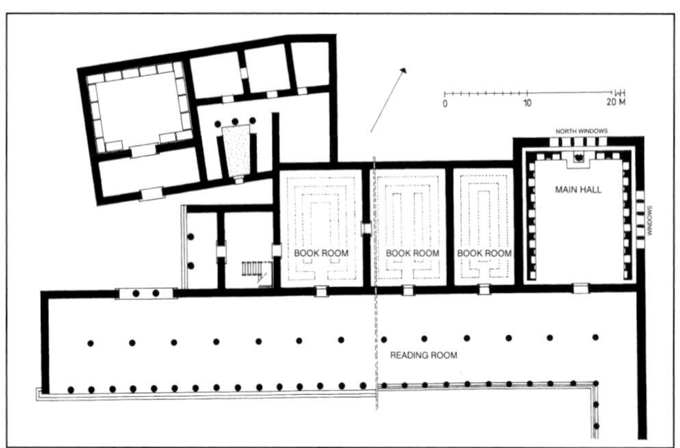

127. Plan of the Pergamum Library, showing the main hall, the auxiliary rooms and the two-storey stoa, which had a saddle roof and served as a reading room. Drawn by W. Hoepfner.

The approximate number of books contained by ancient libraries can be calculated from the number and size of the alcoves in their main halls. Since we know that the books in some libraries were numbered in tens or hundreds of thousands, it is safe to conclude that the vast majority of them were kept not in the main hall but in auxiliary rooms, which could always be added to as the need arose. In other words they were storerooms, both for classified and sorted books and for the great mass of unsorted material and unused papyrus rolls.

Gymnasia. Gymnasia were already important educational institutions in the Classical period, and by the Hellenistic period they had developed into grand building complexes of a comparable standard

☞

125. Reconstruction drawing of the main hall of the Pergamum Library, showing the two-storey stoa which served as a reading room. Drawn by I. Arvaniti.

128. Reconstruction drawing of a closed bookcase in the main hall of the Pergamum Library, showing the double folding doors and the elaborate frame resembling a portico. Drawn by W. Hoepfner.

to a top-ranking modern university, and with comparable facilities: running-tracks, wrestling-schools and other sports facilities, classrooms, concert halls, lecture halls, paved walks, banqueting rooms and book rooms. Every city had its gymnasium, while the bigger and more important cities such as Alexandria, Pergamum and Rhodes had two or more gymnasia and libraries. Under the Roman Empire, Pergamum is said to have had no less than eight libraries. Jean Delorme, in his exhaustive study of Greek gymnasia, summarizes the evidence drawn from ancient sources and the results of archaeological excavations.[30] Of the innumerable gymnasia that existed – at Delos, Smyrna (the 'gymnasium of Homer'), Pergamum and Cos, to name only a few – I shall describe the libraries attached to the great gymnasium on Rhodes and the gymnasium at Nysa ad Maeandrum.

129. Fragments of inscriptions (2nd c. B.C.*) which, though not found* in situ, *come from the library of the Pergamum gymnasium.*

Rhodes. The city of Rhodes, whose high reputation for scholarship dated back to the Classical period (owing to the philosophy school established there probably by Aristotle's favourite pupil, Eudemus) and was enhanced by its close contacts with the literary scholars of the Alexandrian Library, had more than one gymnasium. The biggest of them, opened soon after the foundation of the new city of Rhodes in 408 B.C., stood on the slopes of the acropolis below the sanctuary of Apollo and had an imposing stadium and two palaestrae, one for ephebes and one for younger boys.[31]

The library was an integral part of a complex of buildings interconnected by corridors and flights of steps. The main hall measured approximately 20.50 x 11.70 m. and was entered by a door in the east wall of a north-south corridor. In the north wall of the room (on the left as you entered) there was a row of eight recesses, each 1.95 m. wide and 0.60 m. up from the floor, that held closed wooden bookcases: the arched shape of the recesses as they are now, following their modern restoration, is conjectural. Patches of discoloration on the masonry indicate that the library has been badly damaged by fire at least once. The room may perhaps have been illuminated by a row of windows in the wall opposite the bookcases. The north wall (the wall behind the bookcases) backed on to another room of the same size, which was reached by small doorways in two of the recesses. This north room may have been used as a reading room, a scriptorium or a storeroom for books, or for some other purpose connected with the running of the library. The inscription discovered by G.Ch. Papachristodoulou mentions three decrees concerning the organization of the library and gifts of books.[32] There is also a reference to a κιβωτός (a portable wooden container), which was probably an archive of material relating to the regulations of the gymnasium and library. In the wall of the corridor directly opposite the door of the main hall there was another door leading into a rather bigger room which was probably used for banquets and ceremonies.

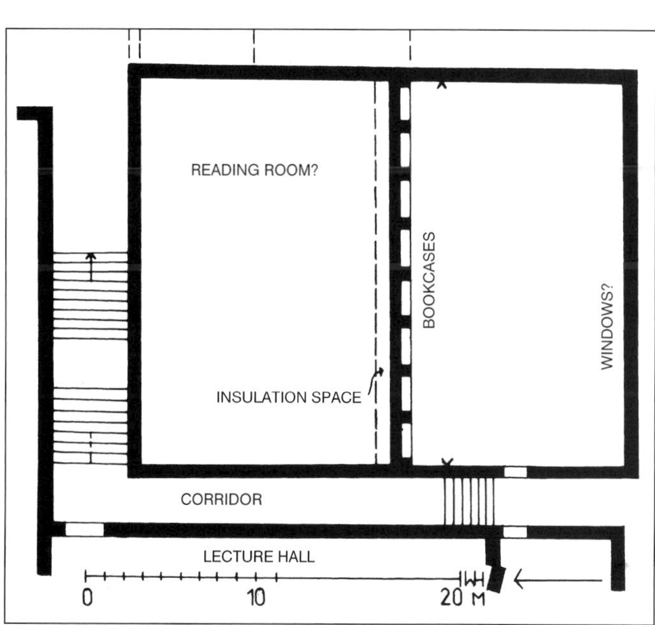

130. Reconstructed plan of the library of the great gymnasium at Rhodes, showing the alcoves for the bookcases in the main hall. Drawn by W. Hoepfner.

Nysa. Nysa ad Maeandrum, a town in Asia Minor on the right bank of the River Maeander, east of Tralles on the main road from Ephesus to Antioch, had a large gymnasium with a 192-metre stadium and two large palaestrae. Strabo attended lectures by Aristodemus of Alexandria in 40 B.C. North of the palaestrae and in line with their central axis are the ruins of a monumental library, identified as such by the archaeologist W. von Diest[33] on the strength of the characteristic alcoves, which resemble those in the Library of Celsus at Ephesus.

The library building has a columned façade that is also reminiscent of the Library of Celsus, and the architecture of its main room is a fine example of the precautions taken to guard the books against one of their deadliest enemies: moisture.[34] The central nucleus of the building is a room measuring 10 x 15 m. with an interior wall running round three sides. The interior wall has twenty-six alcoves on two levels, to hold the bookcases, and is surrounded on all three sides by a passage two storeys high, widening at intervals into vaulted chambers: this provided extra space and also served to protect the main room by insulating it. The way into this passage is through a small door to the left of the main entrance, and there were two windows to provide ventilation.

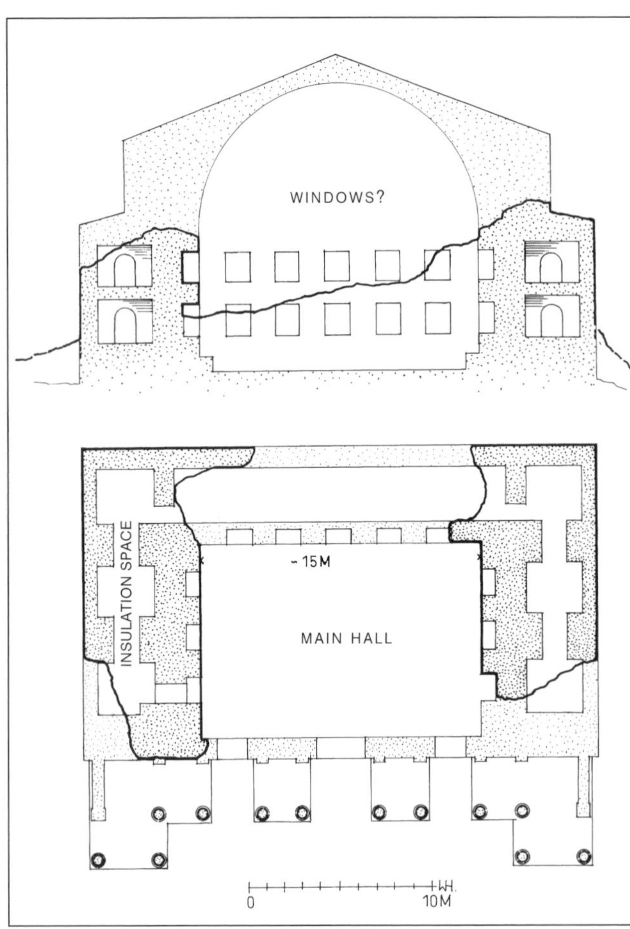

131. Reconstructed plan and section of the Nysa gymnasium library, showing the characteristic alcoves in the main hall and the walls and spaces providing insulation and ventilation on three sides. Drawn by W. Hoepfner.

In the main hall of the library, which had a vaulted ceiling, there may have been a statue of Athena, the patron goddess of literature and libraries. If so, it would probably have been in the usual place for such statues: in front of the back wall, directly opposite the entrance, in a position corresponding to that of the altar in a church. No trace has been found of any wooden or other structure showing how the upper tier of bookcases was reached.

132. The ruins of the library of the great gymnasium at Rhodes, showing the characteristic recesses for wooden bookcases.

133. Ruins of the north wall of the main hall of the gymnasium library at Nysa.

Notes

V
ARCHITECTURE
Typology and Equipment of Archival and Academic Libraries

NOTES

1. See pp. 42-44, 58 (nn. 58-59), 59 (nn. 63-64). On the Linear B archives in general see M. S. Ruipérez and J. L. Melena, *Οἱ Μυκηναῖοι Ἕλληνες* (= *Los Griegos micénicos*, Madrid 1990, tr. Melina Panayiotidou), Athens 1996, 50-70.
2. On the tablets and scripts used in the Bronze Age see pp. 7 ff. On the shapes of the tablets see p. 39-40.
3. The fact that the Mycenaeans sometimes wrote on diptychs is proved by the finds from the Ulu Burun shipwreck: see R. Payton, 'The Ulu Burun Writing-Board Set', *Anatolian Studies* 91 (1991) 99-106.

   The tablets of which diptychs were made consisted of wooden boards with a raised frame to keep the writing surface in place, and the stylus used for writing on it was a sharpened reed. The writing surface was either *maltha* (a thinly-spread mixture of wax with pitch or thick grease) or gypsum plaster. Two or more tablets bound together with cords or leather thongs threaded through holes in their frames made a notebook of a few 'pages' – a diptych or polyptych – which Euripides calls *polythyroi diaptychai* ('many-leaved tablets'). Plato's pupil Philip of Opus used similar tablets to take rough notes of the *Laws* ('on wax': Diog. Laer., III.37), from which he produced an edition of the text. See H. Blanck, *Τό βιβλίο στήν ἀρχαιότητα* (= *Das Buch in der Antike*, Munich 1992, tr. D. G. Georgovasilis and M. Pfreimter), Athens 1994, 67 ff.; G. Cavallo, 'Le tavolette come supporto della scrittura: qualche testimonianza indiretta', in Élisabeth Lalou (ed.), *Les tablettes à écrire de l'antiquité à l'époque moderne* [*Bibliologia* 12], Turnhout 1992, 97-105.
4. On sealings see pp. 44-46.
5. See pp. 40-43 ('Did books exist in the Minoan-Mycenaean era?').
6. Herodotus was the first traveller to Egypt to leave a written account which has survived to our own time. At the beginning of it he sums up his impressions of that remarkable land in a memorable sentence: Egypt, he says, is a gift of the Nile.

   Along the banks of the Nile grows the papyrus plant (*Cyperus papyrus*), first described by Theophrastus in his *Enquiry into Plants*. Papyrus, a tall, sedge-like reed that flourishes in hot, wet climates, was cultivated all along the Nile valley, but especially in the delta and the district around Arsinoe. A stylized representation of its flower-head was adopted at a very early date as the emblem of Lower Egypt. The most reliable description we have of the treatment of papyrus to make cylindrical rolls comes from Pliny the Elder (*Natural History*, XIII.11 ff.), but he does not reveal all the secrets of the process: no doubt they would have been learnt by trial and error and passed on by word of mouth from one generation of specialist craftsmen to the next.

   The process of treating the papyrus reed to make a flat sheet suitable for writing on in ink was as follows. First of all the cortex was removed from a freshly-cut length of the lower part of the triangular stem, to expose the pith. Skilled craftsmen then sliced the pith very carefully into wafer-thin vertical strips, making them as long as possible. The strips of pith were laid side by side, just touching or just overlapping, on a hard wet surface, with all the fibres lying in the same direction. The a second layer of strips of pith was laid on top of the first and at right angles to it. A few taps with a broad-headed hammer were enough to stick the two layers of pith together without the need for any adhesive. When dried and rubbed with pumice stone to make it smooth, durable and flexible, the sheet of papyrus was ready for use. The sheets were then glued together, edge to edge, to make a continuous roll.

The papyrus industry was virtually an Egyptian monopoly, although the plant did grow in some other places as well, such as Ethiopia. In Egypt papyrus had been used as a writing material from a very early date, perhaps even before the third millennium: the earliest papyrus sheet so far discovered, though not written on, dates from the First Dynasty, that is around 3000 B.C. The oldest extant papyrus with writing on it is a passage of text written in hieroglyphics dating from the reign of King Djedkare-Isesi of the Fifth Dynasty (*c.* 2400): it almost certainly came from a temple near Abusir, where some other papyrus fragments were found in excavations by the German Archaeological School.

On Pliny's description of the papyrus see D. Cirillo, *Il Papiro*, with intro. by M. Gigante, Naples 1983 (a collector's edition, printed on Carta Amatruda di Amalfi, of *Dominici Cyrilli Medicinae Doctoris ... Cyperus Papyrus*, originally printed by Bodoni at Parma in 1796). On the organization of the market in ancient Egypt, the manufacture of papyrus rolls and the different qualities available, see: J. Černý, *Paper and Books in Ancient Egypt*, London 1952; A. Lucas, *Ancient Egyptian Materials and Industries*, 4th edn. revised by J.R. Harris, London 1962. On the manufacture of papyrus from the Ptolemaic period onwards see N. Lewis, *L'industrie du papyrus dans l'Égypte gréco-romaine*, Paris 1934.

Besides describing the manufacturing process, Pliny lists the standard sizes of papyrus roll with the names by which the various sizes were known in his own time. The biggest was the *charta augusta*, or simply *augusta*, with a width of thirteen fingers (about 24 cm.), while the smallest was *emporetica*, a mere six fingers (about 10 cm.) wide. The usual number of sheets in a roll was twenty. See D. Diringer, *The Book Before Printing: Ancient, medieval and oriental*, New York 1982, 113-169.

7. Besides tablets, diptychs and papyrus rolls, there were times when the Greeks were reduced to writing on treated animal skins, which Herodotus (V.58) calls *diphtherai*.

Herodotus says that the Ionians had always used the word 'skins' to mean 'books', because in bygone times, when papyrus had been hard to obtain, they did actually use goat and sheep skins to write on, as many foreign peoples still did in his own time. His statement is more significant for what it implies about the causes of the papyrus shortage in Ionia than for the information that skins were used to take its place. The inference to be drawn from the words he uses is that at some time in the past the supply of papyrus rolls to Ionia had dried up as a result of political disturbances, and that for some time thereafter papyrus had been replaced by animal skins. The events he is alluding to should perhaps be dated to the early decades of the fifth century.

The statement of Diodorus Siculus (II.22.4) that Ctesias of Cnidus, the author of the *Persica*, had educated himself by reading Persian books written on sheep and goat skins is not relevant to the present discussion. Ctesias says that the Persians used 'royal skins' (*βασιλικαί διφθέραι*) for their historical records, and his statement has been confirmed by the discovery of the archives of the satrap Arsames (5th c. B.C.) written on treated skins: see G.R. Driver, *Aramaic Documents of the Fifth Century B.C.*, Oxford 1954; also, for more general information on this subject, R. R. Johnson, *The Role of Parchment in Greco-Roman Antiquity* (dissertation), Los Angeles/Ann Arbor 1988. Whatever the truth of the matter may be, there is no doubt that parchment books were known in Athens, and Euripides – who had a big library himself – commented on the fact, describing them as 'skins with black writing on them' (Euripides, fr. 627: see A. Nauck, *Tragicorum Graecorum Fragmenta*, Leipzig 1889).

8. See E. G. Bude, *Armarium und Κιβωτός*, Berlin 1939. A similar cupboard with 'two tiers and four doors' was published by W. Hoepfner, 'Eine Ausstellung mit nachgebauten griechischen Bibliotheksmöbeln', in W. Hoepfner (ed.), *Antike Bibliotheken*, Mainz 2002, 6.
9. On the evolution of the storage systems used for books from the earliest times, see C. Wendel, *Kleine Schriften zum antiken Buch- und Bibliothekswesen*, ed. W. Krieg, Köln 1974, 64 ff. An exhibition held in Berlin in 2000 featured modern reconstructions of cupboards and chests from ancient private and monumental libraries: see Hoepfner, 'Eine Ausstellung...', 5-8.
10. On ancient Greek house design see W. Hoepfner et al. (eds.), *Geschichte des Wohnens*, I: *5000 v. Chr. - 500 n. Chr. Vorgeschichte - Frühgeschichte - Antike*, Stuttgart 1999, 223 ff.
11. Alexis, *Linus*, 135.
12. On the copies that Demosthenes made of Thucydides's *History*, see p. 101.
13. Interior courtyards were the main feature of ancient Greek houses, and indeed of Roman houses too. Sometimes they were completely unroofed and sometimes they had roofed colonnades round the sides. See Ch. Bouras, *Παραδόσεις Ἱστορίας τῆς Ἀρχιτεκτονικῆς*, Athens 1980, 430.
14. See p. 74.
15. See p. 76.
16. The organization of ancient Greek city-states was largely based on the existence of all kinds of written material in the civic archives. There were marble and wooden stelae, potsherds, diptychs and polyptychs, metal plaquettes, papyrus sheets and rolls, inscribed with decrees and resolutions relating to the government and the workings of the constitution, there were records of international trade agreements and treaties: in fact, the archives were the 'written memoirs' of each city. In addition to the laws and regulations governing everyday life and the conduct of public affairs generally, the archives also contained various documents concerning the citizens personally, such as birth and death certificates, wills, details of their military service, court verdicts and title deeds to land. The record offices were known by different names in different places: the *demosion*, *demosia grammata*, *chreophylakion*, *grammateion*, *grammatophylakion*, *syngraphophylakion*.

    Besides the civic archives, similar records were kept of military campaigns, with particulars of persons and equipment and their movements in the field. An important example of this kind of archive was Alexander the Great's collection of campaign records, which, as already mentioned, which were kept by his chief registrar, Eumenes of Cardia. Among the documents kept in Alexander's archive were logbooks in which the happenings of each day – in the field, in Alexander's court and anywhere in the empire – were recorded under the supervision of the chief registrar.

    See R. Dareste, 'Le χρεωφυλάκιον dans les villes grecques', *BCH* 6 (1882) 242-243; E. Weiss, *Griechisches Privatrecht auf rechtsvergleichender Grundlage*, I, Vienna 1923; T. Homolle, *Les Archives de l'inten-*

dance sacrée à Délos (315-166 av. J.-C.) [*Bibliothèque des Écoles Françaises d'Athènes et de Rome* 49], Paris 1887; B. Haussoulier, *La vie municipale en Attique*, Paris 1883; R.E. Wycherley, *The Athenian Agora*, III: *Literary and Epigraphical Testimonia*, Princeton 1957; E. Posner, *Archives in the Ancient World*, Cambridge, Mass. 1972; W. Lambrinudakis and M. Wörrle, 'Ein hellenistisches Reformgesetz über das öffentliche Urkundenwesen von Paros', *Chiron* 13 (1983) 283-368; Stella Georgoudi, 'Manières d'archivage et archives de cités', in M. Detienne (ed.), *Les savoirs de l'écriture. En Grèce ancienne* [*Cahiers de philologie. Série Apparat critique* 14], Lille : Presses universitaires, 1992, 221-247.

17. See p. 118.
18. See pp. 105-110.
19. See J. Travlos, *Pictorial Dictionary of Ancient Athens*, New York 1975, 42; W. Hoepfner, 'Platons Akademie. Eine neue Interpretation der Ruiner', in Hoepfner (ed.), *Antike Bibliotheken*, 56-62.
20. The archaeological excavations now being carried out on this site are under the supervision of Evi Lygouri. See also Hoepfner, 'Platons Akademie...', 62.
21. Diog. Laer., v.51. On the Lyceum library and the heads of the Lyceum see pp. 106, 108, 115, 118-119.
22. See p. 112.
23. See p. 174.
24. See p. 188.
25. A. Conze, 'Die pergamenische Bibliothek', *Sitzungsberichte der Berliner Akademie der Wissenschaften* 53 (1884) 1257 ff.; K. Dziatzko, *Untersuchungen über ausgewählte Kapitel des antiken Buchwesens*, Leipzig 1900.
26. See H. Mielsch, 'Die Bibliotheken und die Kunstsammlungen der Könige von Pergamon', *AA* (1995) 763 ff.; V.M. Strocka, 'Noch einmal zur Bibliothek von Pergamon', *AA* (2000) 155 ff.; W. Hoepfner, 'Die Bibliothek Eumenes' II in Pergamon', in Hoepfner (ed.), *Antike Bibliotheken*, 41-52.
27. See W. Hoepfner, *Zu griechischen Bibliotheken und Bücherschränken*, Berlin/New York 1996/1997; Id., 'Die Bibliothek...', in Hoepfner (ed.), *Antike Bibliotheken*; Id., 'Eine Ausstellung...', *ibid.*, 5.
28. See p. 256.
29. Vitruvius, *De architectura*, VII.Praef.7.
30. J. Delorme, *Gymnasion. Étude sur les monuments consacrés à l'éducation en Grèce*, Paris 1960. See also R. Nicolai, 'Le biblioteche dei ginnasi', *Nuovi Annali della Scuola Speciale per Archivisti e Bibliotecari* 1 (1987) 17 ff.
31. See W. Hoepfner, 'Pergamon-Rhodos-Nysa-Athen', in Hoepfner (ed.), *Antike Bibliotheken*, 68-72.
32. On the inscription relating to a gift of books, see p. 260.
33. W. von Diest, *Nysa ad Maeandrum*, Berlin 1913.
34. See Hoepfner, 'Pergamon-Rhodos...', in Hoepfner (ed.), *Antike Bibliotheken*, 73-78.

ABBREVIATIONS – BIBLIOGRAPHY

ABBREVIATIONS

AA = *Archäologischer Anzeiger* (Berlin).

AE = *Ἀρχαιολογικὴ Ἐφημερίς* (*Archaeologike Ephemeris*) (Athens).

AGGW = *Abhandlungen der Göttinger Gesellschaft der Wissenschaften*.

AJA = *American Journal of Archaeology*.

AJP = *American Journal of Philology*.

Anthropos = *Anthropos: Internationale Zeitschrift für Völker- und Sprachenkunde* (Freiburg, Switzerland).

Archaeology = *Archaeology: A magazine dealing with the antiquity of the world* (New York).

Archives Before Writing = P. Ferioli, E. Fiandra, G. G. Fisore and M. Frangipane (eds.), *Archives Before Writing: Proceedings of the International Colloquium, Oriolo Romano, October 23-25, 1991*, Rome/Turin 1994.

BCH = *Bulletin de Correspondance Hellénique*.

BICS = *Bulletin of the Institute of Classical Studies* (London).

BSA = *Annual of the British School at Athens*.

BZ = *Byzantinische Zeitschrift*.

CAH = *Cambridge Ancient History*.

CIAG = *Commentaria in Aristotelem Graeca*, Berlin: Reimer, 1882-1909.

CJ = *Classical Journal*.

Crète mycénienne = J. Driessen and A. Farnoux (eds.), *La Crète mycénienne. Actes de la Table Ronde tenue à l'École Française d'Athènes du 26-28 mars 1991* [*BCH* Suppl. 30], Paris 1997.

FGrHist = *Die Fragmente der griechischen Historiker*, ed. F. Jacoby, Berlin/Leiden 1923- .

GAS = F. Sezgin, *Geschichte des arabischen Schrifttums*, Leiden 1967- .

JHS = *Journal of Hellenic Studies*.

Kadmos = *Kadmos: Zeitschrift für vor- und frühgriechische Epigraphik* (Berlin).

Kleine Pauly = *Der Kleine Pauly: Lexicon der Antike auf der Grundlage von Pauly's Realencyclopädie der Classischen Altertumswissenschaft*, Stuttgart: A. Druckenmüller, 1964-1975.

KRS = Kirk, G.S., J.E. Raven and M. Schofield, *Οἱ Προσωκρατικοί Φιλόσοφοι* (= *The Presocratic Philosophers*, 2nd edn., Cambridge 1983, tr. D. Kurtovik), Athens: N.B.C.F., 1988.

ΚΣ = *Κυπριακαί Σπουδαί* (*Kypriakai Spoudai*) (Nicosia).

Minoica = *Minoica: Festschrift zum 80. Geburtstag von Johannes Sundwall*, ed. E. Grumach, Berlin 1958.

Minos = *Minos: Revista de filologia egea* (Salamanca).

N.B.C.F. = National Bank of Greece Cultural Foundation.

NP = *Der neue Pauly: Enzyklopädie der Antike*, ed. H. Cancik and H. Schneider, 15 vols., Stuttgart/Weimar: J.B. Metzler, 1996-2001.

PG = J.P. Migne, *Patrologiae Cursus Completus. Series Graeco-Latina*, vols. 1-161, Paris 1857-1866.

Problems in Decipherment = Y. Duhoux, T.G. Palaima and J. Bennet (eds.), *Problems in Decipherment*, Louvain-la-Neuve: Peeters, 1989.

Pylos Comes Alive = C.W. Shelmerdine and T.G. Palaima (eds.), *Pylos Comes Alive: Industry and Administration in a Mycenaean Palace. A Symposium of the N.Y. Society of the Archaeological Institute of America and Fordham University, May 4-5, 1984*, New York 1984.

RA = *Revue d'Archéologie* (Paris).

RE = *Paulys Real-Encyclopädie der classischen Altertumswissenschaft*, ed. G. Wissowa et al., Stuttgart/Munich 1893-1978.

SIMA = *Studies in Mediterranean Archaeology*.

SMEA = *Studi Micenei ed Egeo-Anatolici*.

Studies Bennett = J.-P. Olivier and T.G. Palaima (eds.), *Texts, Tablets and Scribes: Studies in Mycenaean Epigraphy and Economy Offered to Emmett L. Bennett, Jr.* [*Minos* Suppl. 10], Salamanca 1988.

Studies Chadwick = J.T. Killen, J.L. Melena and J.-P. Olivier (eds.), *Studies in Mycenaean and Classical Greek Presented to John Chadwick* [*Minos* 20-22], Salamanca 1987.

Système palatial = E. Lévy (ed.), *Le système palatial en Orient, en Grèce et à Rome. Actes du colloque de Strasbourg 19-22 juin 1985* [*Travaux du centre de recherche sur le Proche-Orient et la Grèce antiques*], Strasbourg 1987.

TAPA = *Transactions and Proceedings of the American Philological Association*.

UF = *Ugarit-Forschungen: Internationales Jahrbuch für die Altertumskunde Syrien-Palästinas* (Kevelaer/Neukirchen-Vluyn).

ZB = *Zentralblatt für Bibliothekswesen*.

BIBLIOGRAPHY

el-Abbadi, M., *Ἡ Ἀρχαία Βιβλιοθήκη τῆς Ἀλεξανδρείας. Ἡ Ζωή καί ἡ Μοίρα της* (= *The Life and Fate of the Ancient Library of Alexandria*, Paris 1990, tr. Lena Kassimi), Athens: Smili, 1998.

Abbott, K. M., «Φιλόλογος», in *RE*, 19/2 (1938), 2510-2514.

Abd al Latîf, *Relation de l'Égypte*, tr. Silvestre de Sacy, Paris 1810.

Acts of the International Archaeological Symposium 'The Mycenaeans in the Eastern Mediterranean', Nicosia, 27th March-2nd April, 1972, Nicosia: Department of Antiquities, 1973.

Acts of the International Archaeological Symposium 'The Relations between Cyprus and Crete, ca. 2000-500 B.C.', 16th-22nd April, 1978, Nicosia: Department of Antiquities, 1979.

Alexiou, S., 'Neue hieroglyphisch Siegel aus Kreta', *Kadmos* 2 (1963) 79-83.

——, *Μινωικός πολιτισμός. Μέ ὁδηγό τῶν Ἀνακτόρων Κνωσοῦ, Φαιστοῦ, Μαλίων*, Iraklion: Sp. Alexiou's Sons [1969].

Alford, H. L., *The Seated Figure in Archaic Greek Sculpture* (dissertation, UCLA), Los Angeles 1978.

Andrewes, A., 'The Tyranny of Pisistratus', in *CAH*, III.3, Cambridge 1982², 372-374, 392-416.

Andronikos, M., "Μυκηναϊκή καί Ἑλληνική γραφή", in *Μελέτες γιά τήν Ἑλληνική γλώσσα/Studies in Greek Linguistics. Proceedings of the 8th Annual Meeting of the Department of Linguistics, Faculty of Philosophy, Aristotle University of Thessaloniki (A Festschrift for John Chadwick)*, Thessaloniki: A. Kyriakidis, 1987, 1-24.

Apthorp, M. J., *The Manuscript Evidence for Interpolation in Homer*, Heidelberg: Winter, 1980.

Aravantinos, V., 'The Mycenaean Incised Sealings from Thebes: Problems of Contents and Functions', *Aegaeum* 5 (1990) 149-164.

Aravantinos, V. L., L. Godart and Anna Sacconi, *Thèbes: Fouilles de la Cadmée*, I. *Les tablettes en linéaire B de la odos Pelopidou*, Pisa/Rome: Istituti Editoriali e Poligrafici Internazionali, 2001.

Archibald, R. C., 'The Cattle Problem of Archimedes', *American Mathematic Monthly* 25 (1918) 411-414.

Arnaldez, R., 'L'histoire de la pensée grecque vue par les arabes', *Bulletin de la Société Française Philosophique* 72/3 (1978) 117-168.

Arrigoni, E., 'Ecumenismo Romano-Cristiano a Bisanzio e tramonto del concetto di Ellade ed Elleni nell' impero d'Oriente prima del mille', *Nuova Rivista Storica* 55 (1971) 133-161.

Åström, P., and S. A. Eriksson, *Fingerprints and Archaeology* [*SIMA* 28], Göteborg 1980.

Babiniotis, G., *Συνοπτική Ἱστορία τῆς Ἑλληνικῆς Γλώσσας*, Athens 2002[5].

Balayé, S., *La Bibliothèque Nationale des origines à 1800*, Geneva: Librairie Droz, 1988.

Balty-Guesdon, M. G., 'Le *Bayt al-hikma* de Baghdad', *Arabica* 39 (1992) 131-150.

Baumstark, A., *Syrisch-arabische Biographien des Aristoteles* (dissertation), Heidelberg 1898.

Bayer, E., 'Demetrius Phalereus', *Tübinger Beiträge zur Altertumswissenschaft* 36 (1942) 105 ff.

Beazley, J. D., 'Hymn to Hermes', *AJA* 52 (1948) 336 ff.

Bekker, I., *Anecdota Graeca*, Berlin 1816.

Bell, H. I., *Egypt from Alexander the Great to the Arab Conquest*, Oxford: Clarendon Press, 1948.

—, *Cults and Creeds in Graeco-Roman Egypt*, Liverpool: University Press, 1953.

Bellamy, R., 'Bellerophon's Tablet', *CJ* 84 (1988-1989) 289-307.

Benakis, L. G., 'Philosophy in Athens (from Anaxagoras to Damascius)', in *Athens: From the Classical Period to the Present Day (5th century B.C. - A.D. 2000)*, ed. Ch. Bouras, M. B. Sakellariou, K. Sp. Staikos and Evi Touloupa, Athens: Kotinos, 2003, 109-143.

Bennet, J., 'The Structure of the Linear B Administration at Knossos', *AJA* 89 (1985) 231-249

Bennett, E. L., Jr., *The Pylos Tablets*, Princeton: Princeton University Press, 1955.

—, 'Some Minoan Texts in the Iraklion Museum', in *Minoica*, 35-49.

—, 'Anonymous Writers in Mycenaean Palaces', *Archaeology* 13 (1960) 26-32.

—, 'Michael Ventris and the Pelasgian Solution', in *Problems in Decipherment*, 9-24.

Bennett, E. L., Jr., and J.-P. Olivier, *The Pylos Tablets Transcribed*, 2 vols., Rome: Edizioni dell' Ateneo, 1973-1976.

Berve, H., *Das Alexanderreich auf prosopographischer Grundlage*, II, Munich 1926.

—, *Die Tyrannis bei den Griechen*, II, Munich 1967.

Bethe, E., *Buch und Bild im Altertum*, Amsterdam 1964.

Bevan, E. R., *The House of Seleucus*, new edn. London: Routledge & Kegan Paul, 1966.

Bickerman, E. J., *The Jews in the Greek Age*, Cambridge, Mass./London: Harvard University Press, 1988.

Bidez, J., *Un singulier naufrage littéraire dans l'antiquité*, Brussels 1943.

Bietak, M., 'Connections between Egypt and the Minoan World: New results from Tell el-Dab'a/Avaris' in W. V. Davies and E. Schofield (eds.), *Egypt, the Aegean and the Levant: Interconnections in the Second Millennium B.C.*, London: Trustees of the British Museum, 1995, 19-27.

Bietak, M., and N. Marinatos, 'Avaris (Tell el-Dab'a) and the Minoan World', in Karetsou, *Κρήτη-Αἴγυπτος...*, 40-44.

Birt, T., *Das antike Buchwesen*, Berlin 1882.

Black, J. A., and W. J. Tait, 'Archives and Libraries in the Ancient Near East', in Jack M. Sasson (ed.), *Civilizations of the Ancient Near East*, New York: Scribners, 1995, IV, 2197-2209.

Blanchard, A. (ed.), *Les débuts du codex* [*Bibliologia* 9], Turnhout: Brepols, 1989.

Blanchard, A., and A. Bataille (eds.), 'Fragments sur papyrus du *Sikyonios* de Ménandre', *Recherches de Papyrologie* 3 (1964) 103-176.

Blanck, H., *Τό βιβλίο στήν ἀρχαιότητα* (= *Das Buch in der Antike*, Munich 1992, tr. D. G. Georgovasilis and M. Pfreimter), Athens: D. M. Papadimas, 1994.

Borges, J. L., *Διερευνήσεις* (= *Otras inquisiciones*, tr. A. Kyriakidis), Athens: Ypsilon Books, 1990.

Boufidis, N. K., "Κρητομυκηναϊκαί ἐπιγραφαί ἐξ Ἀρκαλοχωρίου", *AE* (1953-54/2) 61-74.

Bouras, Ch., *Παραδόσεις Ἱστορίας τῆς Ἀρχιτεκτονικῆς*, Athens 1980.

Bouyges, M., *Averroès. Tafsir ma ba'd at tabi'at*, Beirut: Dar el-Machreq, 1952.

Boyancé, C., 'Le culte des Muses chez les philosophes grecs', *Bibliothèque des Écoles Françaises d'Athènes et de Rome* 141 (1937) 329 ff.

Boyce, Mary, 'Middle Persian Literature', in *Handbuch der Orientalistik*, 1.4: *Iranistik*, 2: *Literatur*, 1, ed. B. Spuler, Leiden: Brill, 1968, 57-59.

Brice, W. C., *Inscriptions in the Minoan Linear Script of Class A*, Oxford: University Press for the Society of Antiquaries, 1961.

Brouskari, M. S., *The Acropolis Museum: A Descriptive Catalogue*, Athens 1974.

Brown, A., *Arthur Evans and the Palace of Minos*, Oxford: Ashmolean Museum, 1986.

Buchholz, H. G., and V. Karageorghis, *Prehistoric Greece and Cyprus*, tr. F. Garvie, London: Phaidon, 1973.

Bude, E. G., *Armarium und Κιβωτός*, Berlin 1939.

Buffière, F., *Les mythes d'Homère et la pensée grecque*, Paris 1956.

Burkert, W., 'La genèse des choses et des mots: Le papyrus de Derveni entre Anaxagore et Cratyle', *Études Philosophiques* 25 (1970) 443-455.

—, 'Kynaithos, Polycrates and the Homeric Hymn to Apollo', in *Arktouros: Hellenic Studies presented to Bernard M. W. Knox*, ed. G. W. Bowersock, W. Burkert and M. C. J. Putnam, Berlin/New York 1979, 53-62.

Burzachechi, M., 'Ricerche epigrafiche sulle antiche bibliotheche del mondo greco', *Rendiconti dell' Accademia dei Lincei* 18 (1963) 75 ff. and 39 (1984) 307 ff.

Cadogan, G., *Palaces of Minoan Crete*, London 1976.

Camera, C., 'Una presunta scuola degli scrivani a Cnosso', *SMEA* 7 (1968) 116-128.

Cameron, A., 'New Themes and Styles in Greek literature: Seventh-Eighth Centuries', in A. Cameron and L. I. Conrad (eds.), *The Byzantine and Early Islamic Near East*, Princeton 1992, 81-105.

Canfora, L., *Ἡ Χαμένη Βιβλιοθήκη τῆς Ἀλεξανδρείας* (= *La biblioteca scomparsa*, Palermo 1986, tr. F. Arvanitis), Athens: Alexandria Editions, 1989.

Caskey, J. L., 'Inscriptions and Potters' Marks from Ayia Irini in Keos', *Kadmos* 9 (1970) 107-117.

Cavallo, G., 'Le tavolette come supporto della scrittura: qualche testimonianza indiretta', in Élisabeth Lalou (ed.), *Les tablettes à écrire de l'antiquité à l'époque moderne* [*Bibliologia* 12], Turnhout: Brepols, 1992, 97-105.

Černý, J., *Paper and Books in Ancient Egypt*, London: H. K. Lewis, 1952.

Chadwick, J., 'The Archive of the Room of the Chariot Tablets at Knossos', in *Minutes of the London Seminar 12.10.1966* (photocopy in the Ashmolean Library, Oxford), 329-331.

—, 'The Archive of the Room of the Chariot Tablets at Knossos', *BICS* 14 (1967) 103-104.

—, 'Linear B', in T. A. Sebeok (ed.), *Current Trends in Linguistics*, 11: *Diachronic, Areal and Typological Linguistics*, The Hague/Paris: Mouton, 1973, 537-568.

—, *The Mycenaean World*, Cambridge: Cambridge University Press, 1976.

—, 'The Minoan Origin of the Classical Cypriot Script', in *Acts of the International Archaeological Symposium 'The Relations Between Cyprus and Crete, ca. 2000-500 B.C.*', Nicosia 1979, 139-143.

—, *Linear B and Related Scripts*, London: British Museum Publications, 1987.

Chadwick, J., L. Godart, J. T. Killen, J.-P. Olivier, A. Sacconi and I. A. Sakellarakis, *Corpus of Mycenaean Inscriptions from Knossos*, I-II, Cambridge/Rome: Cambridge University Press, 1986-1990.

Chapouthier, F., *Les écritures minoënnes au Palais de Mallia* [*Études Crétoises* 2], Paris: P. Geuthner, 1930.

Cherniss, H., *The Riddle of the Early Academy*, Berkeley: University of California Press, 1945.

—, *Das Problem der frühen Akademie*, Heidelberg 1965.

Christensen, A., *L'Iran sous les Sassanides*, Copenhagen: Ejnar Munksgaard, 1944[2].

Cirillo, D., *Il Papiro*, with intro. by M. Gigante, Naples 1983 (a collector's edition of *Dominici Cyrilli Medicinae Doctoris ... Cyperus Papyrus*, originally printed by Bodoni at Parma in 1796).

Clark, J. W., *The Care of Books: An essay on the development of libraries and their fittings from the earliest times to the end of the eighteenth century*, Cambridge 1901.

Conze, A., 'Die pergamenische Bibliothek', *Sitzungsberichte der Berliner Akademie der Wissenschaften* 53 (1884) 1257 ff.

Cook, E. F., *The Odyssey in Athens: Myths of Cultural Origins*, Ithaca/London: Cornell University Press, 1995.

Crielaard, J. P., 'Homer, History and Archaeology: Some Remarks on the Date of the Homeric World', in *Homeric Questions: Essays in Philology, Ancient History and Archaeology, including the papers of a conference organized by the Netherlands Institute at Athens (15 May 1993)*, Amsterdam: Gieben, 1995, 201-288.

Daniel, J. F., 'Prolegomena to the Cypro-Minoan Script', *AJA* 45 (1941) 249-282.

Dareste, R., 'Le χρεωφυλάκιον dans les villes grecques', *BCH* 6 (1882) 242-243.

Davison, J. A., 'Peisistratus and Homer', *TAPA* 86 (1955) 1-21.

—, 'Notes on the Panathenaea', *JHS* 78 (1958) 23-42.

—, 'Addenda to Notes on the Panathenaea', *JHS* 82 (1962) 141-142.

—, 'Literature and Literacy in Ancient Greece', *Phoenix* 16 (1962) 152.

Della Seta, A., 'Il disco di Phaistos', *Rendiconti della Reale Accademia dei Lincei* 18 (1909) 297-367.

Delorme, J., *Gymnasion. Étude sur les monuments consacrés à l'éducation en Grèce*, Paris: E. de Boccard, 1960.

—, *Παγκόσμια Χρονολογική Ἱστορία* (= *Chronologie des civilisations*, tr. and ed. K. Dokou et al.), I, Athens: Pairidis, 1985.

Demakopoulou, Katie (ed.), *The Mycenaean World: Five Centuries of Early Greek Culture, 1600-1100 BC*, Athens: Ministry of Culture/ICOM, 1988.

Derenne, E., *Les procès d'impiété intentés aux philosophes au Vème et au IVème siècles*, Liège 1930.

Diels, H., *Doxographi Graeci*, Berlin 1879.

—, *Die Fragmente der Vorsokratiker*, ed. W. Kranz, Berlin 1951-1954.

Diels, H. and W. Schubart (eds.), *Didymos, Kommentar zu Demosthenes (Papyrus 9780)* [*Berliner Klassikertexte*, 1], Berlin 1904.

Diest, W. von, *Nysa ad Maeandrum*, Berlin: G. Reimer, 1913.

Dietz, K. M., *Protagoras von Abdeira: Untersuchungen zu seinem Denken* (doctoral dissertation), Bonn 1976.

Diringer, D., *The Book Before Printing: Ancient, medieval and oriental*, New York 1982.

Doblhofer, E., *Voices in Stone: The Decipherment of Ancient Scripts and Writings*, tr. M. Savill, London: Paladin, 1973.

Dontas, G. S., 'The True Aglaurion', Hesperia 52 (1983) 48-63.

Dorival, G., 'La fixation du canon de la Bible. Entre Jérusalem et Alexandrie', in Giard and Jacob, *Des Alexandries*, I, 115-134.

Dorival, G., M. Harl and O. Munnich, *La Bible grecque des Septante. Du judaïsme hellénistique au christianisme ancien*, Paris: Éditions du Cerf, 1994[2].

Dougherty, R. P., 'Writing upon Parchment and Papyrus among the Babylonians and Assyrians', *Journal of the American Oriental Society* 42 (1928) 109-135.

Drachmann, A. B. (ed.), *Scholia vetera in Pindari carmina*, III, Leipzig: Teubner, 1927.

Driessen, J., 'The Scribes of the "Room of the Chariot Tablets"', in *Studies Bennett*, 123-165.

—, *An Early Destruction in the Mycenaean Palace at Knossos: A New Interpretation of the Excavation Field-Notes of the South-East Area of the West Wing* [*Acta Archaeologica Lovaniensia, Monographiae* 2], Leuven 1990.

—, *The Scribes of the Room of the Chariot Tablets at Knossos. Interdisciplinary Approach to the Study of a Linear B Deposit* [*Minos* Suppl. 15], Salamanca 2000, 230-232.

Driessen, J., and C. F. Macdonald, *The Troubled Island: Minoan Crete before and after the Santorini Eruption* [*Aegaeum* 17], Liège/Austin 1997.

Driver, G. R., *Aramaic Documents of the Fifth Century B.C.*, Oxford 1954.

Droysen, J. G., *Ἱστορία τῶν Διαδόχων τοῦ Μεγάλου Ἀλεξάνδρου* (= *Geschichte des Hellenismus: Geschichte der Epigonen*, Gotha, 1843, tr. and annotated by R. I. Apostolidis), new edn., 2 vols., Athens: Credit Bank, 1992.

Duhoux, Y., 'Le linéaire A: problèmes de déchiffrement', in *Problems in Decipherment*, 59-120.

Düring, I., 'Ariston or Hermippus?', *Classica et Mediaevalia* 17 (1956) 11-12.

—, *Aristotle in the Ancient Biographical Tradition* [*Studia Graeca et Latina Gothoburgensia* 5], Göteborg 1957.

—, *Ὁ Ἀριστοτέλης. Παρουσίαση καί Ἑρμηνεία τῆς Σκέψης του* (= *Aristoteles. Darstellung und Interpretation seines Denkens*, tr. P. Kotzia-Panteli), I-II, Athens: N.B.C.F., 1991-1994.

Durrbach, F. (ed.), *Choix d'inscriptions de Délos*, I, Paris: Ernest Leroux, 1921.

Dziatzko, K., *Untersuchungen über ausgewählte Kapitel des antiken Buchwesens*, Leipzig: Teubner, 1900.

Easterling, P. E., and B. M. W. Knox, *Ἱστορία τῆς ἀρχαίας Ἑλληνικῆς Λογοτεχνίας*

(= *The Cambridge History of Classical Literature*, I: *Greek Literature*, tr. N. Konomis et al.), Athens: D. M. Papadimas, 1994.

Eche, Y., *Les bibliothèques arabes publiques et semi-publiques en Mésopotamie, Syrie, Égypte au Moyen Âge*, Damascus: Institut Français de Damas, 1967.

Edgar, C. C., and A. J. Evans, *Excavations at Phylacopi in Melos* [*Hellenic Society suppl. paper* 4], London 1904, 177-185.

Edmonds, J. M., *Greek Elegy and Iambus*, I, Cambridge, Mass.: Loeb, 1968.

Edwards, M. W., *Homer, Poet of the Iliad*, Baltimore/London 1987.

—, (ed.), *The Iliad: A Commentary* (General Editor G. S. Kirk), V, Cambridge: Cambridge University Press, 1991.

Eichgrün, E., *Kallimachos und Apollonios Rhodios* (doctoral dissertation), Berlin 1961.

Endress, G., '"Der erste Lehrer". Der arabische Aristoteles und das Konzept der Philosophie im Islam', in U. Tworuschka (ed.), *Gottes ist der Orient, Gottes ist der Okzident*, Köln 1991, 151-181.

Ephron, H. D., 'Mycenaean Greek: A Lesson in Cryptanalysis', *Minos* 7 (1961) 63-100.

Erman, A., *Die Literatur des Aegypter*, Leipzig 1923 (Eng. trans. by A. M. Blackman, London 1927).

Evans, A. J., 'Knossos: Summary Report of the Excavations in 1900', *BSA* 6 (1899-1900) 24.

—, *Scripta Minoa* I, Oxford 1909.

—, *The Palace of Minos at Knossos*, I-IV, London: Macmillan, 1921-1935.

Finley, M. I., *Early Greece: The Bronze and Archaic Ages*, London: Chatto & Windus, 1970.

Flacelière, R., *Ὁ Δημόσιος καί Ἰδιωτικός Βίος τῶν Ἀρχαίων Ἑλλήνων* (= *La vie quotidienne en Grèce au siècle de Périclès*, Paris 1959, tr. G. D. Vandoros), Athens: D. M. Papadimas, 1990.

Flach, H. L. M., *Hesychii Milesii Onomatologi qua supersunt*, Leipzig 1883.

Ford, A., *Homer, The Poetry of the Past*, Ithaca/London: Cornell University Press, 1992.

Forsdyke, E. J., 'The Mavro Spelio Cemetery at Knossos', *BSA* 28 (1926-1927) 243-296.

Fougeas, Methodios G. (Bishop of Pisidia), *Ἡ Ἑλληνιστική Ἰουδαϊκή Παράδοση*, Athens: Nea Synora/A. A. Livanis, 1995.

Fraenkel, E., 'Vermutungen zum Aetna-Festspiel des Aeschylus', *Eranos* 52 (1954) 61-75.

Fraser, P. M., 'Two Studies on the Cult of Sarapis in the Hellenistic World', in *Opuscula Atheniensia*, III [*Skrifter utgivna av Svenska Institutet i Athen*, 4°, VII], Lund 1960, 1-54.

—, *Ptolemaic Alexandria*, 3 vols., Oxford: Clarendon Press, 1972.

Freudenthal, J., *Hellenistische Studien*, II: *Alexander Polyhistor und die von ihm erhaltenen Reste jüdäischer und samaritanischer Geschichtwerke II*, Breslau 1875.

Fritz, K. von, 'Die Bedeutung des Aristoteles für die Geschichtsschreibung', *Entretiens Fondation Hardt* 4 (1958) 86-128.

Fritz, K. von, and E. Kapp, *Aristotle's Constitution of Athens and Related Texts*, New York 1950.

Funaioli, H., *Grammaticae romanae fragmenta*, Leipzig 1907.

Furlani, G., 'Giovanni il Filopono e l'incendio della Biblioteca di Alessandria', *Bulletin de la Société Archéologique d'Alexandrie* 21 (1925) 59-68.

Gaiser, K., *Platons ungeschriebene Lehre*, Stuttgart 1963.

Galanopoulos, A. G., and E. Bacon, *Atlantis: The Truth behind the Legend*, London: Thomas Nelson and Sons, 1969.

Gardiner, A. H., *Late Egyptian Stories* [*Bibliotheca Aegyptiaca* 1], Brussels 1932.

Georgoudi, Stella, 'Manières d'archivage et archives de cités', in M. Detienne (ed.), *Les savoirs de l'écriture. En Grèce ancienne* [*Cahiers de philologie. Série Apparat critique* 14], Lille : Presses universitaires, 1992, 221-247.

Giard, L., and C. Jacob (eds.), *Des Alexandries*, I: *Du livre au texte*, Paris: Bibliothèque Nationale de France, 2001.

Gibbon, E., *The History of the Decline and Fall of the Roman Empire*, II, London 1788.

Ginsberg, H. L., *The Legend of King Keret: A Canaanite epic of the Bronze Age*, [*BASOR Supplementary Studies* 2-3], New Haven, Conn.: American Schools of Oriental Research, 1946.

Godart, L., 'La scrittura Lineare A', *La parola del passato* 31 (1976) 30-47.

—, *Ὁ Δίσκος τῆς Φαιστοῦ. Τό αἴνιγμα μιᾶς γραφῆς τοῦ Αἰγαίου*, Athens: Itanos, 1995.

Godart, L., and J.-P. Olivier, *Receuil des inscriptions en linéaire A* [*Études Crétoises* 21], vols. I-V, Paris: Librairie Orientaliste Paul Geuthner, 1976-1985.

Gordon, C. H., *Ugaritic Literature*, Rome: Pontificum Institutum Biblicum, 1940.

—, *Homer and Bible: The origin and character of East Mediterranean literature*, Ventnor, N. J.: Ventnor Publishers, 1967.

Graham, A. J., 'The *Odyssey*, History and Women', in Beth Cohen (ed.), *The Distaff Side: Representing the Female in Homer's Odyssey*, Oxford/New York 1995, 3-17.

Graindor, P., *La guerre d'Alexandrie. Receuil de travaux publiés par la' Faculté des Lettres (septième fascicule)*, Cairo: Imprimerie Misr, 1931.

Grayeff, F., *Aristotle and his School: An Inquiry into the History of the Peripatos with a Commentary on Metaphysics Z, H, Λ and Θ*, London: Duckworth, 1974.

Grote, G., *A History of Greece; From the Earliest Period to the Close of the Generation Contemporary with Alexander the Great*, II, London: John Murray, 1872[4].

Grumach, E., 'Die Korrecturen des Diskus von Phaistos', *Kadmos* 1 (1962) 16-26.

—, 'Neue Bügelkannen aus Tiruns', *Kadmos* 1 (1962) 85-86.

Grumach, E., and J. Sakellarakis, 'Die neuen Hieroglyphensiegel vom Phourni, Archanes I', *Kadmos* 5 (1966) 109-114.

Guarducci, M., *Epigrafia Greca*, 3 vols., Rome 1967, 1969, 1974.

Gutas, D., *Avicenna and the Aristotelian Tradition*, Leiden/New York: E. J. Brill, 1988.

—, *Ἡ Ἀρχαία Ἑλληνική Σκέψη στόν Ἀραβικό Πολιτισμό. Τό κίνημα τῶν ἑλληνοαραβικῶν μεταφράσεων στή Βαγδάτη κατά τήν πρώιμη ἀββασίδικη περίοδο (205-405/8ος-10ος αἰώνας)*, Athens: Periplous, 2000.

Guthrie, W. K. C., *The Greeks and Their Gods*, London: Methuen, 1950.

—, *A History of Greek Philosophy*, 6 vols., Cambridge 1962-1981.

—, *Οἱ Σοφιστές* (= *The Sophists*, Cambridge 1971, tr. D. Tsekourakis), Athens: N.B.C.F., 1991.

Hadot, I., 'Elias [2]', in *NP*, 3 (1997), 991.

Hägg, R., and N. Marinatos (eds.), *The Minoan Thalassocracy: Myth and Reality. Proceedings of the Third International Symposium of the Swedish Institute in Athens, 31 May – 5 June 1981*, Stockholm 1984.

Hainsworth, J. B. (ed.), *The Iliad: A Commentary* (General Editor G. S. Kirk), III, Cambridge: Cambridge University Press, 1993.

Hansen, E., *The Attalids of Pergamon*, Ithaca 1972[2].

Harris, E. C., *Principles of Archaeological Stratigraphy*, London: Academic Press, 1979.

Haussoulier, B., *La vie municipale en Attique. Essai sur l'organisation des dèmes au quatrième siècle*, Paris 1883.

Havelock, E. A., *Preface to Plato*, Cambridge, Mass., 1963.

Heibges, J. S., 'Hermippos [6]', in *RE*, 8/1 (1912), 845-852.

Heitz, E. (ed.), *Aristotelis Fragmenta* [= *Aristotelis opera omnia*, IV.2], Paris: Didot, 1869.

Hengel, M., 'The Ideology of the Letter of Aristeas', *Harvard Theological Review* 51 (1958) 59-85.

Hengel, M., *Judaism and Hellenism: Studies in their encounter in Palestine during the Early Hellenistic period*, London 1974.

Heubeck, A., 'L'origine della Lineare B', *SMEA* 23 (1982) 195-207.

Hintenlang, H., *Untersuchungen zu den Homer-Aporien des Aristoteles* (dissertation), Heidelberg 1961.

Hoepfner, W., *Das Pompeion und seine Nachfolgerbauten*, Berlin 1976.

—, *Zu griechischen Bibliotheken und Bücherschränken*, Berlin/New York 1996/1997.

—, et al. (eds.), *Geschichte des Wohnens*, I: *5000 v. Chr. - 500 n. Chr. Vorgeschichte - Frühgeschichte - Antike*, Stuttgart: Deutsche Verlags-Anstalt, 1999.

—, 'Eine Ausstellung mit nachgebauten griechischen Bibliotheksmöbeln', in W. Hoepfner (ed.), *Antike Bibliotheken*, Mainz: Philipp von Zabern, 2002, 5-8.

—, 'Die Bibliothek Eumenes' II in Pergamon', in Hoepfner (ed.), *Antike Bibliotheken*, 41-52.

—, 'Platons Akademie. Eine neue Interpretation der Ruiner', in Hoepfner (ed.), *Antike Bibliotheken*, 56-62.

—, 'Pergamon-Rhodos-Nysa-Athen', in Hoepfner (ed.), *Antike Bibliotheken*, 67-80.

Homolle, T., *Les Archives de l'intendance sacrée à Délos (315-166 av. J.-C.)* [*Bibliothèque des Écoles Françaises d'Athènes et de Rome* 49], Paris 1887.

Hood, M. S. F., *The Minoans: Crete in the Bronze Age*, London: Thames & Hudson, 1971.

Hooker, J. T., *Mycenaean Greece*, London 1977.

—, *The Origin of the Linear B Script* [*Minos* Suppl. 8], Salamanca 1979*.

—, *Linear B: An Introduction*, Bristol 1980.

—, (ed.), *Reading the Past: Ancient Writing from Cuneiform to the Alphabet*, London 1993.

Horwitz, W. J., 'The Ugaritic Scribe', *UF* 11 (1979) 389-394.

Hourmouziadis, N., *Ἕνας Ἀθηναῖος θεατής στά ἐν ἄστει Διονύσια*, Athens: Society for the Study of Neohellenic Culture and General Education, 1988.

Hunger, H., *Βυζαντινή Λογοτεχνία. Ἡ λόγια κοσμική γραμματεία τῶν Βυζαντινῶν* (= *Die höchsprachliche profane Literatur der Byzantiner*, Munich 1978, tr. G. Ch. Makris et al.), II, Athens: N.B.C.F., 1992.

Hutchinson, R. W., *Prehistoric Crete*, Harmondsworth 1962.

Ibn al Qifti, Ali, *Kitab Ikhbar al-'Ulama bi-Akhbar al-Hukama*, in Ibn al Qifti, *Ta'rih Al-Hukama*, ed. J. Lippert, Leipzig 1903.

Irigoin, J., 'Les premiers manuscrits grecs écrits sur papier et le problème du bombycin', *Scriptorium* 4 (1950) 194-204.

—, 'Les débuts de l'emploi du papier à Byzance', *BZ* 46 (1953) 314-319.

—, 'Les deux plus anciens livres grecs', *Revue des études grecques* 75 (1962) XXIV-XXV.

—, 'Les manuscrits grecs 1931-1960', *Lustrum* 8 (1962) 287-302.

—, 'Les origines de la fabrication du papier en Italie', *Papiergeschichte* 13 (1963) 62-67.

—, *Le livre grec des origines à la Renaissance*, Paris: Bibliothèque Nationale de France, 2001.

Jaeger, W., *Παιδεία: Ἡ μόρφωσις τοῦ Ἕλληνος ἀνθρώπου* (= *Paideia. Die Formung des griechischen Menschen*, tr. G. P. Verrios), III, Athens 1974.

Jan, C. von (ed.), *Musici Scriptores Graeci*, Leipzig: Teubner, 1895.

Janko, R., *Homer, Hesiod and the Hymns: Diachronic Development in Epic Diction*, Cambridge 1982.

—, (ed.), *The Iliad: A Commentary* (General Editor G. S. Kirk), IV, Cambridge: Cambridge University Press, 1992.

Jeffery, L. H., *The Local Scripts of Archaic Greece: A study of the origin of the Greek alphabet and its development from the eighth to the fifth centuries B.C.* (expanded by A. W. Johnston), Oxford: Clarendon Press, 1990².

Johnson, Lora Lee, *The Hellenistic and Roman Library: Studies pertaining to their architectural form* (doctoral dissertation, Brown University), Providence, R. I., 1984.

Johnson, R. R., *The Role of Parchment in Greco-Roman Antiquity* (dissertation), Los Angeles/Ann Arbor 1988.

Jones, W. H. S., *The Medical Writings of Anonymus Londiniensis*, Cambridge 1947.

Kaibel, G., 'Die Prolegomena Περί Κωμῳδίας', *Abhandlungen der Göttinger Gesellschaft der Wissenschaften*, N.F., II 4 (1898) 4 ff.

—, (ed.), *Comicorum Graecorum Fragmenta*, Berlin 1899.

Kakridis, I. Th., *Ἑλληνική Μυθολογία. Τρωικός Πόλεμος*, V, Athens: Ekdotike Athenon, 1986.

Karageorghis, Jacqueline V., 'Quelques observations sur l'origine du syllabaire chypro-minoen', *RA* 2 (1958) 1-19.

—, Jacqueline V., 'Histoire de l'écriture chypriote', *ΚΣ* 25 (1961) 43-60.

Karageorghis, Jacqueline, and O. Masson (eds.), *The History of the Greek Language in Cyprus: Proceedings of an International Symposium sponsored by the Pierides Foundation, Larnaca, 8-13 September 1986*, Nicosia 1988.

Karageorghis, V., "Οἱ ἀρχαῖοι Ἕλληνες στήν Κύπρο" in Demakopoulou, *The Mycenaean World*, 64-65.

—, *Οἱ πρῶτοι Ἕλληνες στήν Κύπρο. Ἀρχαιολογικές μαρτυρίες*, tr. D. Kyriakou and K. Touloumis, Athens: D. M. Papadimas, 1991.

Karetsou, Alexandra (ed.), *Κρήτη-Αἴγυπτος. Πολιτισμικοί δεσμοί τριῶν χιλιετιῶν*, Athens 2000.

Kelesidou-Galanou, A., *Ἡ κάθαρση τῆς θεότητας στή φιλοσοφία τοῦ Ξενοφάνη* (dissertation), Athens 1969.

Kenyon, F. G., *Books and Readers in Ancient Greece and Rome*, Oxford: Clarendon Press, 1951.

Kirk, G. S. (ed.), *The Iliad: A Commentary*, Cambridge 1985-1993 (vols. I-II by G. S. Kirk, 1985-1990, vol. III by J. B. Hainsworth, 1993, vol. IV by R. Janko, 1992, vol. V by M. W. Edwards, 1991).

Kleberg, T., 'Book Auctions in Ancient Rome?', *Libri* 22 (1973) 1 ff.

—, 'La Grecia a l'epoca ellenistica', in G. Cavallo (ed.), *Libri editori e pubblico nel mondo antico*, Rome/Bari 1989, 27-39.

Kober, Alice E., 'Evidence of Inflection in the "Chariot Tablets" from Knossos', *AJA* 49 (1945) 141-151, 50 (1946) 268-276, 52 (1948) 91-99.

—, 'The Minoan Scripts: Fact and Theory', *AJA* 52 (1948) 82-103.

Koch, Th. (ed.), *Comicorum Graecorum Fragmenta*, I, Leipzig 1881.

Kontoleon, N. M., «Ἀρχίλοχος καί Πάρος», *Ἐπετηρίς τῆς Ἑταιρείας Κυκλαδικῶν Μελετῶν* 5 (1965) 53-103.

—, 'Zwei Beschriftete Scherben aus Naxos', *Kadmos* 4 (1965) 84-85.

Koster, W. J. W. (ed.), *Scholia in Aristophanem*, IV/I, Groningen 1960.

—, 'Scholium Plautinum plene editum', *Mnemosyne*, 4th ser., 14 (1961) 23 ff.

Krecher, J., 'Schreiberschulung in Ugarit: Die Tradition von Listen und sumerischen Texten', *UF* 1 (1969) 131-158.

Κρήτη-Αἴγυπτος. Πολιτισμικοί δεσμοί τριῶν χιλιετιῶν, ed. Alexandra Karetsou and Maria Andreadaki-Vlazaki with N. Papadakis, Iraklion 2000.

Kroh, P., *Λεξικό Ἀρχαίων συγγραφέων Ἑλλήνων καί Λατίνων*, tr. and ed. by D. Lypourlis and L. Tromaras, Thessaloniki: University Studio Press, 1996.

Kuch, H., *Φιλόλογος. Untersuchung eines Wortes von seinem ersten Auftreten in der Tradition bis zur ersten überlieferten lexikalischen Festlegung* [*Schriften der Sektion für Altertumswissenschaft* 48], Berlin: Deutsche Akademie der Wissenschaften zu Berlin, 1965.

Lambrinudakis, W., and M. Wörrle, 'Ein hellenistisches Reformgesetz über das öffentliche Urkundenwesen von Paros', *Chiron* 13 (1983) 283-368.

La Roche, J., *Die homerische Textkritik im Alterthum*, Leipzig 1866.

Latte, K., 'Glossographika', *Philologus* 80 (1925) 125 ff.

Launey, M., 'Recherches sur les armées hellénistiques', *Bibliothèque des Écoles Françaises d'Athènes et de Rome* 169 (1949/50) 273, 1163.

Lefebvre, G., *Romans et contes égyptiens de l'époque pharaonique*, Paris: Maisonneuve, 1988.

Lembessi, A., J.-P. Olivier and L. Godart, "Πινακίδες Γραμμικῆς Α ἐξ Ἀρχανῶν", *AE* (1974) 113-167.

Lemerle, P., *Ὁ πρῶτος βυζαντινός οὐμανισμός: Σημειώσεις καί παρατηρήσεις γιά τήν ἐκπαίδευση καί τήν παιδεία στό Βυζάντιο ἀπό τίς ἀρχές ὥς τόν 10ο αἰώνα* (= *Le premier humanisme byzantin...*, tr. Maria Nystazopoulou-Pelekidou), Athens: N.B.C.F., 1981.

Lesky, A., *Ἱστορία τῆς ἀρχαίας Ἑλληνικῆς Λογοτεχνίας* (= *Geschichte der griechischen Literatur*, Bern 1957/58, tr. A. G. Tsopanakis), Thessaloniki: Kyriakidis Bros., 1983.

Lewis, N., *L'industrie du papyrus dans l'Égypte gréco-romaine*, Paris: L. Rodstein, 1934.

——, 'The Non-Scholar Members of the Alexandrian Museum', *Mnemosyne*, 4th ser., 16 (1963) 257-261.

Lewy, H., 'Aristotle and the Jewish Sage according to Clearchos of Soli', *Harvard Theological Review* 31 (1938) 217.

Linforth, I. M., *The Arts of Orpheus*, Berkeley 1941.

Littig, F., *Andronikos von Rhodos* (doctoral dissertation), Munich 1890.

Long, A. A., *Hellenistic Philosophy: Stoics, Epicureans, Sceptics*, London: Duckworth, 1974.

Lord, A. B., *The Singers of Tales* [*Harvard Studies in Comparative Literature* 24], Cambridge, Mass.: Harvard University Press, 1960.

Lord, C., 'On the Early History of the Aristotelian Corpus', *AJP* 107 (1986) 137-161.

Lucas, A., *Ancient Egyptian Materials and Industries*, 4th edn. revised by J. R. Harris, London: Edward Arnold, 1962.

Luce, J. V., *The End of Atlantis*, London: Thames & Hudson, 1969.

Lynch, J. P., *Aristotle's School: A Study of a Greek Educational Institution*, Berkeley: University of California Press, 1972.

MacLeod, R. M. (ed.), *The Library of Alexandria: Centre of Learning in the Ancient World*, London/New York: I. B. Tauris, 2001[2].

Macler, F., 'Extraits de la Chronique de Maribas Kaldoyo (Mar Abas Katina[?])', *Journal Asiatique* (May-June 1903) 491 ff.

Mahaffy, J. P., *A History of Egypt under the Ptolemaic Dynasty*, London 1898.

Manacorda, M. A., 'Scuola e insegnanti', in M. Vegetti (ed.), *Oralità, scrittura, spettácolo*, Turin: Boringhieri, 1983.

Maravelias, Ch. E., *Τά Ἐρωτικά Ποιήματα τῆς Ἀρχαίας Αἰγύπτου*, Athens: Armos, 1996.

Marinatos, S., 'Ausgrabungen und Funde auf Kreta 1934-1935', *AA* (1935) 252-254.

——, 'Zur Entzifferung der mykenischen Schrift', *Minos* 4 (1956) 13-16.

——, *Excavations at Thera*, IV, Athens: Library of the Athens Archaeological Society, 1971.

Marinatos, S., and M. Hirmer, *Crete and Mycenae*, London 1960.

Marrou, H.-I., *Ἱστορία τῆς Ἐκπαιδεύσεως κατά τήν Ἀρχαιότητα* (= *Histoire de l'éducation dans l'antiquité*, Paris 1948, tr. Th. Fotinopoulos), Athens 1961.

Martini, E., 'Demetrios von Phaleron', in *RE*, 4 (1901), 2817-2841.

Maspero, G., *Les contes populaires de l'Égypte ancienne*, Paris 1882 (reissued Paris: Maisonneuve & Larose, 1988).

Masson, O., *Les inscriptions chypriotes syllabiques*, Paris: E. de Bocard, 1983.

Μέγα Ἐτυμολογικόν, ed. Fredericus Sylburgius, Heidelberg: Hieronymus Commelinus, 1594.

Meyerhof, M., 'Joannes Grammatikos [Philoponos] von Alexandrien und die arabische Medizin', *Mitteilungen des deutsches Instituts für aegyptische Altertumskunde in Kairo* 2 (1932) 1-21.

Mielsch, H., 'Die Bibliotheken und die Kunstsammlungen der Könige von Pergamon', *AA* (1995) 763-779.

Mioni, E., *Εἰσαγωγή στήν Ἑλληνική Παλαιογραφία* (= *Introduzione alla Paleografia Greca*, Padua 1973, tr. N. M. Panayotakis), Athens: N.B.C.F., 1977.

Mitford, T. B., 'The Hellenistic Inscriptions of Old Paphos', *BSA* 56 (1961) 1-41.

Mitford, T. B., and O. Masson, 'The Cypriot Syllabary', in *CAH*, III.3, Cambridge 1982^2, 71-82.

Montanari, F., 'Hermippos aus Smyrna', in *NP*, 5 (1998), 439-440.

Moraux, P., *Les listes anciennes des ouvrages d'Aristote*, Louvain: Éditions Universitaires de Louvain, 1951.

—, *Der Aristotelismus bei den Griechen von Andronikos bis Alexander von Aphrodisias*, I, Berlin 1973.

Müller, C. (ed.), *Oratores Attici*, 2 vols., Paris 1847-1848.

Müller, C. W., 'Protagoras über die Götter', *Hermes* 95 (1967) 140-159.

Müller-Graupa, E., «Mouseion», in *RE*, 16 (1933), 797-821.

Münzer, F., 'C. Calvinius Sabinus', in *RE*, 3 (1899), 1411.

Mylonas, G. E., 'Priam's Troy and the Date of its Fall', *Hesperia* 33 (1964) 352-380.

—, *Mycenae and the Mycenaean Age*, Princeton: Princeton University Press, 1966.

Mylonas-Shear, Ione, *Tales of Heroes: The Origins of the Homeric Texts*, New Rochelle/Athens: Aristide D. Caratzas, 2000.

Nagy, G., *Poetry as Performance: Homer and Beyond*, Cambridge/New York: Cambridge University Press, 1996.

Nauck, A., *Tragicorum Graecorum Fragmenta*, Leipzig 1889.

Neils, J., *Goddess and Polis: The Panathenaic Festival in Ancient Athens* (with contributions by E. J. W. Barber, D. G. Kyle, B. S. Ridgway and H. A. Shapiro), Princeton 1991.

Nelson, H. H., et al., *Medinet Habu I* and *II* [= *Medinet Habu I: Earlier Historical Records of Ramses III; Medinet Habu II: Later Historical Records of Ramses III*] [*Oriental Institute Publications* 8-9], Chicago: University of Chicago, 1930-1932.

Nicolai, R., 'Le bibliotheche dei ginnasi', *Nuovi Annali della Scuola Speciale per Archivisti e Bibliotecari* 1 (1987) 17 ff.

Norsa, M., *La scrittura letteraria greca*, Florence 1939.

Ohly, K., 'Stichometrische Untersuchungen', *ZB*, Beiheft 61 (1928) 88-89.

Oliver, R. P., 'The First Medicean MS of Tacitus and the Titulature of Ancient Books', *TAPA* 82 (1951) 232 ff.

Olivier, J.-P., *Les Scribes de Cnossos. Essai de classement des archives d'un palais mycénien*, Rome: Edizioni dell' Ateneo, 1967.

—, 'Encore des corrections du disque de Phaistos', in *Antichità Cretesi: Studi in onore di Doro Levi*, ed. G. P. Carratelli and G. Rizza, I, Catania 1973, 182-185.

—, 'Le disque de Phaistos', édition photographique, *BCH* 99 (1975) 5-34.

—, 'La scrittura geroglifica cretese', *La parola del passato* 31 (1976) 17-23.

—, 'La bague en or de Mauro Spelio et inscription en linéaire A', in Lydie Hadermann-Misguich et al. (eds.), *Rayonnement grec: Hommages à C. Delvoye*, Brussels: Éditions de l'Université, 1982.

—, 'Administrations at Knossos and Pylos. What Differences?' in *Pylos Comes Alive*, 15.

—, 'Structure des archives palatiales en Linéaire A et en Linéaire B', in *Système palatial*, 227-235.

—, 'Des extraits de contrats de vente d'esclaves dans les tablettes de Knossos', in *Studies Chadwick*, 497-498.

—, 'The Possible Methods in Deciphering the Pictographic Cretan Script', in *Problems in Decipherment*, 39-58.

Olivier, J.-P., and L. Godart, *Corpus hieroglyphicarum inscriptionum Cretae* [*Études Crétoises* 31], Paris 1996.

Ong, W. J., *Προφορικότητα καί Ἐγγραμματοσύνη* (= *Orality and Literacy*, tr. Kostas Hadjikyriakou, ed. Theodoros Paradellis), Iraklion: University of Crete Publications, 1997.

Otto, W., *Priester und Tempel im hellenistischen Ägypten*, I, Rome: Bardi, 1971.

Packard, D. W., *Minoan Linear A*, Berkeley/Los Angeles/London: University of California Press, 1974.

Page, D. L., *The Santorini Volcano and the Destruction of Minoan Crete*, London: Society for the Promotion of Hellenic Studies, 1970.

Palaima, T. G., 'Evidence for the Identification of a Master Scribe at Pylos', *AJA* 84 (1980) 226.

—, *The Scribes of Pylos*, Rome: Edizioni dell' Ateneo, 1988.

——, 'Cypro-Minoan Scripts: Problems of Historical Context', in *Problems in Decipherment*, 121-187.

——, 'Seal-Users and Script-Users/Nodules and Tablets at LM IB Hagia Triada' in *Archives Before Writing*, 307-337.

Palaima, T. G., and J. C. Wright, 'Ins and Outs of the Archives at Pylos: Form and Function in a Mycenaean Palace', *AJA* 89 (1985) 251-262.

Palmer, L. R., *Descriptive and Comparative Linguistics*, London: Faber, 1978.

Panayiotopoulos, D., "Ἡ γένεση δύο κωδίκων ἐπικοινωνίας στό παράδειγμα τῆς ἀρχαίας Αἰγύπτου", *Περίαπτο* 1 (1998) 14-28.

——, "Ἡ ἀφήγηση τοῦ Μίν. Τό χρονικό μιᾶς αἰγυπτιακῆς ἀποστολῆς στή Μινωική Κρήτη" in A. Haniotis (ed.), *Ἔργα καί Ἡμέρες στήν Κρήτη. Ἀπό τήν Προϊστορία στό Μεσοπόλεμο*, Iraklion 2000, [1]-53.

Papachristodoulou, G. Ch., «Τό ἑλληνιστικό Γυμνάσιο τῆς Ρόδου: Νέα γιά τή βιβλιοθήκη του», in *Akten des XIII. Internationalen Kongresses für klassischen Archäologie*, Mainz 1990, 500 ff.

Parry, M., *The Making of Homeric Verse: The Collected Papers of Milman Parry*, ed. Adam Parry, Oxford: Clarendon Press, 1971.

Parsons, E. A., *The Alexandrian Library, Glory of the Hellenic World: Its Rise, Antiquities, and Destructions*, New York: American Elsevier Publishing Co., 1967[3].

Parthey, G., *Das alexandrische Museum*, Berlin 1838.

Pasquali, G., 'Biblioteca', in *Enciclopedia Italiana*.

Payne, H., *Archaic Marble Sculpture from the Acropolis*, London: Cresset Press, 1936.

Payton, R., 'The Ulu Burun Writing-Board Set', *Anatolian Studies* 91 (1991) 99-106.

Pedersén, O., *Archives and Libraries in the Near East 1500-300 B.C.*, Bethesda, Md.: CDL Press, 1998.

Pellat, C., *The Life and Works of Jāḥiẓ*, Berkeley/Los Angeles 1969.

Pelletier, A., *Lettre d'Aristée à Philocrate* [*Sources Chrétiennes* 89], Paris: Éditions du Cerf, 1962.

Pendlebury, J. D. S., *The Archaeology of Crete*, London 1939.

Pernier, L., 'Il disco di Phaestos con caratteri pittografici', *Ausonia* 3 (1908) 255-302.

——, 'Un singolare monumento della scrittura pittografica cretese', *Rendiconti della Reale Accademia dei Lincei, Classe di Scienze Morali, Storiche e Filologiche* 5 (1908) No. 17, 642-651.

Pfeiffer, R., *Callimachus*, 2 vols., Oxford: Clarendon Press, 1949-1953

——, *Ἱστορία τῆς Κλασικῆς Φιλολογίας. Ἀπό τῶν Ἀρχῶν μέχρι τοῦ τέλους τῶν Ἑλληνιστικῶν Χρόνων* (= *History of Classical Scholarship: From the Beginnings to the End of the Hellenistic Age*, Oxford 1968, tr. P. Xenos et al.), Athens: Academy of Athens, 1972.

——, 'Die Sophisten, ihre Zeitgenossen und Schüler im fünften und vierten Jahrhundert', in C. J. Classen (ed.), *Sophistik*, Darmstadt: Wissenschaftliche Buchgesellschaft, 1976, 170-219.

Piccard, G., 'Carta bombycina, carta papyri, pergamena graeca. Ein Beitrag zur Geschichte der Beschreibstoffe im Mittelalter', *Archivalische Zeitschrift* 61 (1965) 46-75.

Pickard-Cambridge, A., *The Dramatic Festivals of Athens*, 2nd edn. revised by J. Gould and D. M. Lewis, Oxford 1968.

Pingree, D., 'Classical and Byzantine Astrology in Sassanian Persia', *Dumbarton Oaks Papers* 43 (1989) 227-239.

Pinner, H. L., *The World of Books in Classical Antiquity*, Leiden: A. W. Sijthoff, 1948.

Piteros, Ch., J.-P. Olivier and J. L. Melena, 'Les inscriptions en linéaire B des nodules de Thèbes (1982): la fouille, les documents, les possibilités d'interprétation', *BCH* 114/1 (1990) 103-184.

Platthy, J., *Sources on the Earliest Greek Libraries with the Testimonia*, Amsterdam: Adolf M. Hakkert, 1968.

Pöhlmann, E., *Griechische Musikfragmente. Ein Weg zur altgriechischen Musik*, Nürnberg 1960.

Pope, M. W. M., *Aegean Writing and Linear A* [*SIMA* 8], Lund 1964.

——, 'Ventris Decipherment: First Causes', in *Problems in Decipherment*, 25-38.

Posner, E., *Archives in the Ancient World*, Cambridge, Mass.: Harvard University Press, 1972.

Potts, D. T., 'Before Alexandria: Libraries in the Ancient Near East', in MacLeod, *The Library of Alexandria*, 19-33.

Rainey, A. F., 'The Scribe in Ugarit', *Proceedings of the Israel Academy of Sciences and Humanities* 11 (1969) 136-146.

Raison, J., and M. W. M. Pope, *Index transnuméré du linéaire A*, Louvain 1977.

Rapin, C., 'Les inscriptions économiques de la trésorerie hellénistique d'Aï Khanoum (Afghanistan)', *BCH* 107 (1983) 315-372.

——, 'Les textes littéraires grecs de la trésorerie d'Aï Khanoum', *BCH* 111 (1987) 225-266.

Reden, Sibylle von, *Ugarit und seine Welt*, Bergische Gladbach: Lübbe Verlag, 1992.

Regenbogen, O., 'Theophrastos', in *RE*, suppl. 7 (1940), 1535 ff.

——, «Πίναξ», in *RE*, 20 (1950), 1409-1482, esp. 1423-1438.

Renfrew, A. C., and W. C. Brice, 'A Linear A Tablet Fragment from Phylacopi in Melos', *Kadmos* 16 (1977) 111-119.

Reynolds, L. D., and N. G. Wilson, *Ἀντιγραφεῖς καί Φιλόλογοι: Τό ἱστορικό τῆς παράδοσης τῶν κλασικῶν κειμένων* (= *Scribes and Scholars: A guide to the transmission of Greek and Latin literature*, 2nd edn., London 1975, tr. N. M. Panayotakis), Athens: N.B.C.F., 1981.

Richardson, N. J., 'Aristotle and Hellenistic Scholarship', in O. Reverdin and B. Grange (eds.), *La philologie grecque à l'époque hellénistique et romaine* [*Entretiens sur l'antiquité classique* 40], Vandoeuvres/Geneva: Fondation Hardt, 1993, 7-38.

Rist, J. H., *Stoic Philosophy*, Cambridge 1969.

Robert, L., 'Notes d'épigraphie hellénistique', *BCH* 59 (1935) 421-437.

Roberts, C. H., 'Books in the Graeco-Roman World and in the New Testament' in *The Cambridge History of the Bible*, I, Cambridge 1970, 48-66.

Robinson, A., *The Man Who Deciphered Linear B: The Story of Michael Ventris*, London: Thames & Hudson, 2002.

Romilly, Jacqueline de, *Οἱ Μεγάλοι Σοφιστές στήν Ἀθήνα τοῦ Περικλῆ* (= *Les grands sophistes dans l'Athènes de Périclès*, Paris 1988, tr. F. I. Kakridis), Athens: Institute of the Book/M. Kardamitsas, 1994.

—, *Ἀλκιβιάδης* (= *Alcibiadès*, tr. Athina-Babi Athanasiou and Katerina Miliaressi), Athens: Asty, 1995.

Ross, W. D., *Plato's Theory of Ideas*, Oxford: Clarendon Press, 1951.

—, *Ἀριστοτέλης* (= *Aristotle*, tr. Marilisa Mitsou), Athens: N.B.C.F., 1993².

Rostagni, A., 'I Bibliotecari Alessandrini', in his *Scritti minori*, I and II.1, Turin: Bottega d'Erasmo, 1955-1956.

Rostovtzeff, M., *The Social and Economic History of the Hellenistic World*, 3 vols., Oxford: Clarendon Press, 1941.

Rowe, A., *The Discovery of the Famous Temple and Enclosure of Sarapis at Alexandria* [*Annales du Service des Antiquités de l'Égypte*, Suppl. 12], Cairo 1946.

Ruipérez, M. S., and J. L. Melena, *Οἱ Μυκηναῖοι Ἕλληνες* (= *Los Griegos micénicos*, Madrid 1990, tr. Melina Panayiotidou), Athens: Institute of the Book/M. Kardamitsas, 1996.

Sakellarakis, J. and E., *Ἀρχάνες, μιά νέα ματιά στή Μινωική Κρήτη*, 2 vols., Athens: Ammos, 1997.

Schachermeyr, F., *Die minoische Kultur des alten Kreta*, Stuttgart 1964.

—, *Ägäis und Orient. Die überseeischen Kulturbeziehungen von Kreta und Mykenai mit Ägypten, der Levante und Kleinasien unter besonderer Berücksichtigung des 2. Jahrtausends v. Chr.*, Vienna: Österreichische Akademie der Wissenschaften, 1967.

Schaeffer, C. F. A., *The Cuneiform Text of Ras Schamra – Ugarit*, London 1939.

Schaller, B., 'Hekataios von Abdera über die Juden. Zur Frage der Echtheit und der Datierung', *Zeitschrift für die neutestamentliche Wissenschaft und die Kunde der älteren Kirche* 54 (1963) 15-31.

Schalles, H. J., 'Untersuchungen zur Kulturpolitik der pergamenischen Herrscher im dritten Jahrhundert v. Chr.', *Istanbuler Forschungen* 36 (1985).

Schmekel, A., *Die Philosophie der mittleren Stoa in ihrem geschichtlichen Zusammenhange*, Berlin 1892.

Schmidt, F., *Die Pinakes des Kallimachos*, Kiel 1924.

Schneidewin, F. W., *De Laso Hermionensi*, Göttingen 1842-1843.

Schofield, M., *Ἡ στωική ἰδέα τῆς πόλης* (= *The Stoic Idea of the City*, Cambridge 1991, tr. Chloe Balla), Athens: N.B.C.F., 1997.

Schott, S., *Les chants d'amour de l'Égypte ancienne* (trans. from the German by P. Krieger) [*L'Orient Ancien Illustré* 9], Paris 1956.

Schubart, W., *Das Buch bei den Griechen und Römern*, Heidelberg 1962.

Schürer, E., *The History of the Jewish People in the Age of Jesus Christ (175 B.C. - A.D. 135)*, new English version revised and edited by Geza Vermes et al., I-III, Edinburgh 1987-1995.

Shahid, I., *Byzantium and the Arabs in the Fifth Century*, Washington, D.C.: Dumbarton Oaks, 1989.

Shaki, M., 'The Denkard Account of the Zoroastrian Scriptures', *Archív Orientální* 49 (1981) 114-125.

Sigalas, A., *Ἱστορία τῆς ἑλληνικῆς γραφῆς*, Thessaloniki: Centre for Byzantine Studies, 1974[2].

Simon, E., *Festivals of Attica: An archaeological commentary*, Madison/London: University of Wisconsin Press, 1983.

Sittig, E., 'Methodologisches zur Entzifferung der kretischen Silbenschrift Linear B', *Minos* 3 (1954) 10-19.

Sjöquist, K-E., and P. Åström, *Pylos: Palmprints and Palmleaves*, Göteborg: Åströms, 1985.

—, *Knossos: Keepers and Kneaders* [*SIMA Pocketbook* 82], Göteborg 1991.

Skouteropoulos, N. M., *Ἡ Ἀρχαία Σοφιστική: Τά σωζόμενα ἀποσπάσματα* (fragments edited, translated into Modern Greek and annotated by —), Athens: Gnosi, 1991.

Snodgrass, A. M., *The Dark Age of Greece*, Edinburgh: Edinburgh University Press, 1971.

Solmsen, F., 'The Tablets of Zeus', *Classical Quarterly* 38 (1944) 27-30.

Sperling, A., *Apellikon der Grammatiker und sein Verhältnis zum Judentum*, Dresden 1886.

Spyropoulos, Th., and J. Chadwick, *The Thebes Tablets* II [*Minos* Suppl. 4], Salamanca 1975.

Stahr, A., *Aristotelia*, I-II, Halle 1832.

Staikos, K. Sp., *Βιβλιοθήκη. Ἀπό τήν Ἀρχαιότητα ἕως τήν Ἀναγέννηση καί σημαντικές Οὐμανιστικές καί Μοναστηριακές Βιβλιοθῆκες (3000 π.Χ. – 1600 μ.Χ.)* (exhibition catalogue), Athens 1997, 34-45.

—, *The Great Libraries from Antiquity to the Renaissance (3000 B.C. to A.D. 1600)* (= *Βιβλιοθῆκες. Ἀπό τήν Ἀρχαιότητα ἕως τήν Ἀναγέννηση καί Σημαντικές Οὐμανιστικές καί Μοναστηριακές Βιβλιοθῆκες (3000 π.Χ.-1600 μ.Χ.)*, tr. T. Cullen), New Castle, Del.: Oak Knoll Press/London: The British Library, 2000.

Starr, R. J., 'The Used-Book Trade in the Roman World', *Phoenix* 44 (1990) 148 ff.

Stavrianopoulou, Eftychia, "Μία ἀσυνήθιστη μέρα τοῦ ἀνακτορικοῦ γραφέα Κεραμέα" in A. Haniotis (ed.), *Ἔργα καί Ἡμέρες στήν Κρήτη. Ἀπό τήν Προϊστορία στό Μεσοπόλεμο*, Iraklion 2000, 73-119.

Stein, J. K., 'Deposits for Archaeologists', *Advances in Archaeological Method and Theory* 11 (1987) 337-395.

Strasburger, H., *Ptolemaios und Alexander*, Leipzig 1934.

Strocka, V. M., 'Noch einmal zur Bibliothek von Pergamon', *AA* (2000) 155-165.

Stubbings, F. H., *Mycenaean Pottery from the Levant*, Cambridge: University Press, 1951.

Symington, D., 'Late Bronze Age Writing Boards and Their Uses: Textual Evidence from Anatolia and Syria', *Anatolian Studies* 91 (1991) 111-123.

Taplin, O., *Homeric Soundings: The Shaping of the Iliad*, Oxford: Clarendon Press, 1992.

Tatakis, B. N., *Panétius de Rhodes, le fondateur du moyen Stoïcisme. Sa vie et son oeuvre*, Paris 1931.

Taylour, W. D., *Mycenaean Pottery in Italy and Adjacent Areas*, Cambridge 1958.

—, *The Mycenaeans* (revised and enlarged edition), London: Thames & Hudson, 1983.

Tcherikover, V., *Hellenistic Civilization and the Jews*, Philadelphia: Jewish Publication Society of America, 1959.

Thompson, H. A., 'The Libraries of Ancient Athens', in N. C. Wilkie and W. D. E. Coulson (eds.), *Contributions to Aegean Archaeology: Studies in Honor of William A. McDonald*, Minneapolis: Center for Ancient Studies, 1985, 295-297.

Thompson, H. A., and R. E. Wycherley, *The Athenian Agora: Results of Excavations conducted by the American School of Classical Studies at Athens*, XIV: *The Agora of Athens: The History, Shape and Uses of an Ancient City Center*, Princeton 1972.

Thompson, J. W., *Ancient Libraries*, Berkeley: University of California Press, 1940.

Tøsberg, J., *Offentlige bibliotheker: Romerriget i det 2. arhundrede e Chr.*, Copenhagen 1976.

Travlos, J., *Bildlexikon zur Topographie des antiken Athen*, Tübingen 1971

Travlos, J., *Pictorial Dictionary of Ancient Athens*, New York 1975.

Treuil, R., P. Darcque, J.-C. Poursat and G. Touchais, *Les civilisations égéennes du néolithique et de l'âge du bronze*, Paris 1989.

Treweek, A. P., 'An Examination of the Validity of the Ventris Decipherment', *BICS* 4 (1957) 10-26.

Triandi, Ismene, "Παρατηρήσεις σέ δύο ὁμάδες γλυπτῶν τοῦ τέλους τοῦ 6ου αἰώνα ἀπό τήν Ἀκρόπολη" in *The Archaeology of Athens and Attica under the Democracy: Proceedings of an International Conference celebrating 2500 years since the birth of Democracy in Greece, held in the American School of Classical Studies at Athens, December 4-6, 1992*, ed. W. D. E. Coulson, O. Palagia, T. L. Shear, Jr., H. A. Shapiro and F. J. Frost [*Oxbow Monograph* 37], Oxford 1994, 83-86.

—, *Τό Μουσεῖο τῆς Ἀκροπόλεως*, Athens 1998.

Troia – Traum und Wirklichkeit, exhibition catalogue, ed. B. Theune-Grosskopf et al., Stuttgart: Theiss, 2001.

Tsinikopoulos, D., *Φῶς ἐξ Ἀνατολῆς (Ex Oriente Lux). Λογοτεχνικά κείμενα τῆς ἀρχαίας Ἐγγύς Ἀνατολῆς*, Athens: Ellinika Grammata, 1996.

Tsouli, Maria P., 'Pre-Alphabetic Scripts in Greece' (with parallel German translation), in *The Greek Script*, Athens: Ministry of Culture, 2001, 17-39.

Turner, E. G., *Athenian Books in the Fifth and Fourth Centuries B.C.*, London 1952.

—, *Ἑλληνικοί πάπυροι: εἰσαγωγή στή μελέτη καί τή χρήση τῶν παπύρινων κειμένων* (= *Greek Papyri: An Introduction*, Oxford 1968, tr. G. M. Parasoglou), Athens: N.B.C.F., 1981.

Untersteiner, S. M., *Senofane*, Florence 1956.

Vandenabeele, F., 'La chronologie des documents en Linéaire A', *BCH* 109 (1985) 3-20.

Van Soldt, W. H., 'Labels from Ugarit', *UF* 21 (1989) 375-388.

Veenhof, Klaas R. (ed.), *Cuneiform Archives and Libraries: Papers read at the 30th Rencontre Assyriologique Internationale, Leiden 1983* [*Uitgaven van het Nederlands Historisch-Archaeologisch Instituut te Istanbul* 57], Leiden 1986.

Ventris, M., *Work Notes on Minoan Language Research and Other Unedited Papers*, ed. Anna Sacconi, Rome: Edizioni dell' Ateneo, 1988.

Ventris, M., and J. Chadwick, 'Evidence for Greek Dialect in the Mycenaean Archives', *JHS* 73 (1953) 84-103.

Vermeule, E. T., *Greece in the Bronze Age*, Chicago: University of Chicago Press, 1972[2].

Waerden, B. L. van der, *Science Awakening*, Groningen: Noordhoff, 1954.

Walker, C. B. F., 'Le cunéiforme', in Larissa Bonfante et al., *La naissance des écritures: Du cunéiforme à l'alphabet* (= *Reading the Past: Ancient Writing from Cuneiform to the Alphabet*, London 1990, tr. Christiane Zivie-Coche), Paris: Éditions du Seuil, 1994, 27-29.

Walter, N., 'Jewish-Greek Literature of the Greek Period', in the *Cambridge History of Judaism*, II: *The Hellenistic Age*, ed. W. D. Davies and L. Finkelstein, Cambridge 1990, 385-408.

Warren, P. , *The Aegean Civilizations*, London: Elsevier-Phaidon, 1975.

Wehrli, F., *Die Schule des Aristoteles*, 10 vols., Basel: Benno Schwabe & Co., 1944-1959: I, *Dikaiarchos*, 1944; II, *Aristoxenos*, 1945; III, *Klearchos*, 1948; IV, *Demetrios von Phaleron*, 1949; V, *Straton von Lampsakos*, 1950; VI, *Lykon und Ariston von Keos*, 1952; VII, *Herakleides Pontikos*, 1953; VIII, *Eudemos von Rhodos*, 1955; IX, *Phainias von Eresos, etc.*, 1957; X, *Hieronymos von Rhodos, etc.* (with index), 1959.

—, 'Demetrios von Phaleron', in *RE*, suppl. 11 (1968), 514-522.

Weingarten, J., 'The Sealing Bureaucracy of Mycenaean Knossos: The identification of some officials and their seals', in *Crète mycénienne*, 517-535.

Weiss, E., *Griechisches Privatrecht auf rechtsvergleichender Grundlage*, I, Vienna 1923.

Weitemeyer, M., 'Archive and Library Technique in Ancient Mesopotamia', *Libri* 6 (1956) 217-238.

Welles, C. B., 'The Reliability of Ptolemy as an Historian', in *Miscellanea di studi alessandrini in memoria di Augusto Rostagni*, Turin 1963, 101-106.

Wendel, C., 'Tzetzes', in *RE*, 7A_2 (1948), 1973 ff.

—, 'Das griechisch-römische Altertum' (completed by W. Göber), in F. Milkau and G. Leyh (eds.), *Handbuch der Bibliothekswissenschaft*, III.1, Wiesbaden 1955, 51 ff.

—, *Kleine Schriften zum antiken Buch- und Bibliothekswesen*, ed. W. Krieg, Köln: Greven, 1974.

Wendland, P., *Aristeae ad Philocratem epistula*, Leipzig 1900.

West, M. L. (ed.), *Hesiod: Theogony*, Oxford: Oxford University Press, 1966.

—, *Hesiod: Works and Days*, Oxford: Clarendon Press, 1978.

Westermann, A., *Vitarum Scriptores Graeci*, Braunschweig 1845.

Whitman, C. H., *Homer and the Heroic Tradition*, Cambridge, Mass./London: Harvard University Press, 1958.

Wilamowitz-Moellendorf, U. von, *Antigonos von Karystos [Philologische Untersuchungen*, IV], Berlin 1881.

Wilhelm, A., *Urkunden dramatischer Aufführungen in Athen* [*Sonderschriften des Österr. Archäolog. Instituts in Wien* VI], Vienna 1906.

Wilker, Julia, 'Frühe Büchersammlungen der Griechen' and 'Irrwege einer antiken Büchersammlung' in W. Hoepfner (ed.), *Antike Bibliotheken*, Mainz: Philipp von Zabern, 2002, 19-23, 24-29.

Wilson, N. G., *Scholars of Byzantium*, Baltimore 1983.

Winter, F., 'Schulunterricht auf griechischen Vasenbildern', *Bonner Jahrbücher* 123 (1916) 275-285.

Wiseman, D. J., 'Assyrian Writing-Boards', *Iraq* 17 (1955) 3-13.

Wood, M., *In Search of the Trojan War*, New York/Oxford 1985.

Woodard, R. D., *Greek Writing from Knossos to Homer. A Linguistic Interpretation of the Origin of the Greek Alphabet and the Continuity of Ancient Greek Literacy*, Oxford/New York: Oxford University Press, 1997.

Wormell, D. E. W., 'The Literary Tradition Concerning Hermias of Atarneus', *Yale Classical Studies* 5 (1928).

Wycherley, R. E., *The Athenian Agora*, III: *Literary and Epigraphical Testimonia*, Princeton: American School of Classical Studies at Athens, 1957.

Yule, P., *Early Cretan Seals: A Study of Chronology* [*Marburger Studien zur Vor- und Frühgeschichte* 4], Mainz: Philipp von Zabern, 1980.

Zaehner, R. C., *The Dawn and Twilight of Zoroastrianism*, New York: Weidenfeld and Nicolson, 1961.

Ziegler, K., 'Plagiat', in *RE*, 20/2 (1950), 1956-1997.

Zuntz, G., *The Text of the Epistles: A disquisition upon the Corpus Paulinum* (The Schweich Lectures of the British Academy, 1946), London: British Academy, 1953.

INDEX

INDEX

of persons, places and subjects*

Any book containing Greek proper names presents problems of transliteration. The general principles I have tried to follow are as follows:-

(1) Where a name is commonly known in a Latinized or anglicized form (e.g. Plato, Athens, Rhodes), that form is used.

(2) Greek names in antiquity and up to the end of the Heraclian dynasty of East Roman emperors (A.D. 711) are Latinized in the traditional way (e.g. Pisistratus, Thucydides, not Peisistratos, Thoukydides).

(3) From c. 711 until the emergence of the Greek independence movement (late eighteenth century) they are transliterated in accordance with the following system: α=a, β=b, γ=g, δ=d, ε=e, ζ=z, η=e, θ=th, ι=i, κ=k, λ=l, μ=m, ν=n, ξ=x, ο=o, π=p, ρ=r, σ=s, τ=t, υ=y (but αυ, ευ, ου = au, eu, ou), φ=ph, χ=ch, ψ=ps, ω=o.

(4) In the modern era they are transliterated phonetically (αυ=av or af, β=v, γι=y or yi, ευ=ev or ef, η=i, μπ=b or mb, ντ=d or nd, φ=f, χ=ch or h). So too, in general, are Modern Greek authors' names in the footnotes and Bibliography, unless their works have been published in English with their names given in a different form.

Some inconsistencies and discrepancies are almost inevitable. For these we offer our apologies.

A

* With a few exceptions, the names of modern scholars, archaeologists and architects are not listed in the Index: they are to be found in the notes to the relevant chapters.

D

E

F

G

H

I

M

R

S

T

U

THE HISTORY OF LIBRARIES IN THE WESTERN WORLD BY KONSTANTINOS SP. STAIKOS. TYPESETTING BY MARIA PERRAKI IN G.F.S. DIDOT AND G.F.S. PORSON FONTS. COMPUTER-AIDED PAGINATION BY MARY KARAVA. PREPARATION OF ILLUSTRATIONS, COLOUR SEPARATIONS, COMPUTER-AIDED STRIPPING AND FILMS BY DIAGRAMMA - CH. KOUTROUDITSOS. PROOF-READING BY ANNA HADJIANTONIOU. FIRST EDITION PRINTED FOR KOTINOS S.A. UNDER THE SUPERVISION OF PETROS BALIDIS IN 5,000 COPIES ON GARDA MATT 135 GSM PAPER IN JANUARY 2004. BOOKBINDING BY VASSILIS KYPRAIOS.